INSIDE LAWYERS'
ETHICS

Second Edition

Inside Lawyers' Ethics is a lively and practical values-based analysis of the moral dilemmas that lawyers face. It gives lawyers the confidence to understand and actively improve their ethical priorities and behaviour when confronted with major ethical challenges. It identifies the applicable law and conduct rules and analyses them in the context of four different types of ethical lawyering: zealous advocacy, responsible lawyering, moral activism and the ethics of care.

This new edition is fully updated, with a new chapter on confidentiality and new case studies and review questions from real-life legal practice in Australia based on the authors' own research. All chapters have been updated and reflect the changes to conduct rules contained in the *Australian Solicitors' Conduct Rules* (*ASCR*). This edition also contains a self-assessment instrument designed to allow readers to recognise the type of lawyering that most appeals to them. Knowledge of a preferred type will make it easier, when necessary, for new lawyers to take courageous stances in ethically challenging environments.

Online resources, including chapter outlines, case studies and weblinks, are available at www.cambridge.edu.au/academic/lawyersethics.

Inside Lawyers' Ethics promotes self-awareness and offers a positive and enriching approach to problem solving, rather than one based on the 'don't get caught' principle. It is essential reading for students of law and newly qualified legal practitioners.

Christine Parker is Professor in the Faculty of Law at Monash University.

Adrian Evans is Professor in the Faculty of Law at Monash University.

INSIDE LAWYERS' ETHICS

Second Edition

Christine Parker

and

Adrian Evans

CAMBRIDGE
UNIVERSITY PRESS

CAMBRIDGE
UNIVERSITY PRESS

477 Williamstown Road, Port Melbourne, VIC 3207, Australia

Published in the United States of America by Cambridge University Press, New York

Cambridge University Press is part of the University of Cambridge.

It furthers the University's mission by disseminating knowledge in the pursuit of education, learning and research at the highest international levels of excellence.

www.cambridge.org
Information on this title: www.cambridge.org/9781107641730

First published 2007
Reprinted 2007, 2010, 2011
Second edition 2014

Cover designed by Sardine Design
Typeset by Aptara Corp.
Printed in Australia by Ligare Pty Ltd

A catalogue record for this publication is available from the British Library

A Cataloguing-in-Publication entry is available from the catalogue of the National Library of Australia at www.nla.gov.au

ISBN 978-1-107-64173-0 Paperback

Additional resources for this publication at www.cambridge.edu.au/academic/lawyersethics

Cambridge University Press has no responsibility for the persistence or accuracy of URLs for external or third-party internet websites referred to in this publication and does not guarantee that any content on such websites is, or will remain, accurate or appropriate.

To Zachary Restall and Maria Bohan

CONTENTS

FIGURES

TABLES

ILLUSTRATIONS

CASE STUDIES

TABLE OF STATUTES

TABLE OF CASES

PREFACE TO THE SECOND EDITION

It is both pleasing and encouraging to be publishing a second edition of this book in response to the feedback (and faith) of the publishers, teachers and students who have explored our first edition. This new edition includes a new chapter on confidentiality, substantially revised chapters, and new case studies, all based on our own research and our own 'four approaches' process for legal ethical decision-making which we introduced in the first edition.

At the time of writing, the national legal profession project is stalled in a political quagmire and may or may not lead to further great changes in the regulatory and ethical environment for lawyering in Australia. We await the resolution (or whimpering end) to this experiment with interest and some trepidation.

Meantime we remain convinced that the best hope for ethical behaviour among legal professionals is for law students to learn early about the appropriate and essential connection between their humanity and their engagement in passionate and reasoned lawyering. Ethics is the bridge between the two, not just another technical legal skill to be learned at law school. Continual ethical engagement on both a personal and professional level by individual lawyers, law firms and the profession as a whole is crucial to the wellbeing of law students and lawyers, the organisations in which they study and work, our justice systems, and democratic and public policy decision-making more generally. We hope this new edition again contributes in some small way to equipping and provoking your moral engagement with the Rule of Law.

Christine Parker and Adrian Evans
Melbourne, May 2013

ACKNOWLEDGMENTS

An earlier version of Chapters 1 and 2 was published as Christine Parker, 'A Critical Morality for Australian Lawyers and Law Students' (2004) 30 *Monash University Law Review* 49–74.

Material from the *Australian Lawyers' Values Study* used in this book has been previously published in Adrian Evans and Josephine Palermo, 'Australian Law Students' Perceptions of Their Values: Interim Results in the First Year – 2001 – of a Three-Year Empirical Assessment' (2002) 5 *Legal Ethics* 103–29; Adrian Evans and Josephine Palermo, 'Zero Impact: Are Law Students' Values Affected by Law School?' (2005) 8 *Legal Ethics* 240; Josephine Palermo and Adrian Evans, 'Preparing Future Australian Lawyers: An Exposition of Changing Values over Time in the Context of Teaching about Ethical Dilemmas' (2006) 11(1) *Deakin Law Review* 104–30.

Some of the material in Chapter 3 is based on work previously published in Christine Parker, 'Competing Images of the Legal Profession: Competing Regulatory Strategies' (1997) 25(4) *International Journal of the Sociology of Law* 385–409 and in Christine Parker, *Just Lawyers: Regulation and Access to Justice* (Oxford University Press, Oxford, 1997).

The self-assessment tool discussed in Chapter 11 and published in the Appendix to this book has been previously published and is fully discussed in Adrian Evans and Helen Forgasz, 'Framing Lawyers' Choices: Factor Analysis of a Psychological Scale to Self-Assess Lawyers' Ethical Preferences' (2013) 16(1) *Legal Ethics* (forthcoming).

The authors wish to thank the following people for their kind permission to reproduce cartoons: Michael Leunig (p. 155), John Spooner (p. 174) and Jenny Coopes (p. 324).

INTRODUCTION: VALUES IN PRACTICE

Introduction: Ethics and Lawyering

CASE STUDY 1.1 THE CASE OF THE PHILANTHROPIST QC AND THE TOBACCO COMPANY

In 2012 a leading commercial and constitutional law barrister and supporter of the arts, higher education, civil liberties and medical research was appointed to the board of the fundraising arm of Australia's highest profile cancer hospital. The relevant barrister is a prominent Queens Counsel (QC) who had previously acted in many important and high profile cases for a great variety of private clients, both for and against government agencies and in royal commissions. He is also a highly successful businessman in his own right who is now among Australia's wealthiest individuals. He has used his prominence and wealth for many philanthropic purposes focused particularly on supporting higher education, including through scholarships, promoting well-informed public policy debate, and medical research. He has donated generously to public art galleries and served on the boards of the most prominent art galleries in Australia and of various other non-profit organisations.

His appointment to the board of the cancer foundation was, however, criticised because he had previously represented a prominent tobacco company in its constitutional challenge to the Australian government's plain packaging legislation for cigarettes. The plain packaging law requires that cigarettes be sold without any branding (that is, no images, colours, logos or trademarks) and with only the name of the brand (in plain lettering and standardised size) and mandated health warnings and other information on a dull brown packet. Plain packaging was recommended by the International Framework Convention on Tobacco Control (to which Australia is a signatory) to reduce tobacco consumption, especially the uptake of smoking by young people, and therefore reduce the negative health impacts of smoking. Australia is the first country in the world to introduce plain packaging laws, and the three major international tobacco companies (Philip Morris, British American Tobacco and Imperial Tobacco) joined together to challenge the legislation in the High Court of Australia, arguing that it was an unconstitutional usurping of their property rights in their brands and trademarked logos without just compensation. British American Tobacco, unlike the other companies, accepted for the purposes of the case that smoking causes serious health consequences but argued that the plain packaging laws were nonetheless an unjust appropriation of their property.[1] The High Court challenge was unsuccessful and plain packaging became law.[2]

In the previous year, the QC had acted for British American Tobacco in the High Court case and also appeared and spoke on behalf of British American Tobacco executives in hearings before a Parliamentary Committee inquiring into views as to whether the legislation should go ahead. The QC had also previously acted for British American Tobacco in its successful appeal against the Supreme Court of Victoria decision in favour of Rolah McCabe. McCabe died from lung cancer in 2002, just before that appeal was decided. She had earlier been successful in arguing that the tobacco companies had destroyed evidence relevant to determining whether her lung cancer had been caused by smoking cigarettes sold by British American Tobacco. (The *McCabe* case is further discussed below.)

The important question in 2012 was whether it was proper for the QC to sit on the board of the fundraising arm of the cancer hospital while also actively supporting the interests of tobacco manufacturers. The Chief Executive of the cancer hospital argued that the QC had a 'strong anti-tobacco stance', and that the High Court challenge 'wasn't about smoking, it was about whether aspects of the Tobacco Plain Packaging Act were inconsistent with the Constitution … It was about intellectual property, appropriation of trademark and potential compensation.' He went on to comment that 'The key clinical staff involved in our anti-smoking areas were consulted and were respectful of [the QC's] right to advocate on behalf of his client. They felt it absolutely did not undermine our collective work, which is very strong on tobacco.'[3]

A Professor of Public Health at the University of Melbourne, on the other hand, argued that 'advocating for the tobacco industry was indefensible':

> I can't think of why people would want to work for an organization whose products kill off the people who use them, particularly if you have alternative forms of employment. It certainly does seem odd that you would have someone so intimately involved in doing good for a hospital which is trying to cure people from tobacco-related disease, working for the industry that directly causes so many people to be in that hospital.[4]

1 Lenore Taylor, 'Health Issue Irrelevant, Tobacco Firms Tell Court', *The Sydney Morning Herald*, 13 March 2012, 4.
2 *JT International SA v Commonwealth of Australia* [2012] HCA 43 (5 October 2012); *British American Tobacco Australasia Limited v Commonwealth of Australia* [2012] HCA 43 (5 October 2012). See Matthew Rimmer, 'The High Court and the Marlboro Man: The Plain Packaging Decision', *The Conversation*, 18 October 2012, available at https://theconversation.com/the-high-court-and-the-marlboro-man-the-plain-packaging-decision-10014.
3 Quote from Jill Stark, 'Peter Mac Denies Tobacco Conflict', *The Sunday Age* (Melbourne), 2 September 2012, 8.
4 Ibid.

In other cases in recent years, a top criminal law barrister who is the son of Holocaust survivors and a prominent member of Melbourne's Jewish community, received newspaper coverage when he was asked to represent an alleged Nazi war criminal facing extradition proceedings.[5] Another successful QC was labelled anti-Semitic for having taken on the representation of the same accused, and was heavily criticised for having represented a coal company in a workplace death case when he stood for election as the Greens party candidate for Melbourne.[6] Further afield, in late 2012, a 23-year-old Indian student was raped and bashed by six men on a Delhi bus, before being thrown off and left to die. When she did die in a Singapore hospital some days later and the six alleged murderers were charged with her rape and murder, members of the Saket Bar Association refused en masse to represent the defendants and heatedly berated another lawyer in the court for offering to do so.[7]

These situations raise a range of questions about the proper role and conduct of lawyers. To what extent is it our role as lawyers to act as zealous advocates for any client that comes along? Should we advocate for clients and causes that we personally believe to be morally repugnant or socially irresponsible? Can we trust the legal system to sort out issues of truth and justice and to determine important questions of public policy? To what extent should we consider our duties to society, our relationships with our own families and communities, and our personal, social and political commitments outside of our legal practice in deciding what clients to take on, or how to advise and represent them? Is it appropriate for others to criticise us for the clients and causes we have advocated for?

Many of the questions raised by these scenarios are ethical questions. They raise issues like: Is it possible to be a good person and a good lawyer? What interests should we spend our life serving as a lawyer? How should we relate to clients? To what extent should we consider non-legal, particularly moral, relational and spiritual factors in attempting to solve clients' problems? What obligations do we, as lawyers, owe to others beyond our clients, for example, opposing parties, colleagues, the public interest, the courts, our families, and the communities (of social interest, faith, ethnic identity, sexuality etc) that we are a part of?

We might find answers to these questions in various ways that do not invoke ethics – our own financial interests, what others expect of us, what we find most convenient or fulfilling, and so on. Ethics is concerned with deciding what is the

---

5 D Farrant, 'Leading QC May Defend Kalejs', *The Age* (Melbourne), 23 January 2001, 1; Richard C Paddock, 'Case Tests Australian Protection of Nazi War Criminal', *The Washington Post* (Washington DC, USA), 21 January 2001, A21.

6 Peter Faris, 'Top QC Lashes Green Lawyer and Melbourne Candidate Bryan Walters', *Sunday Herald Sun* (Melbourne), 7 November 2010; Royce Millar and David Rood, 'Labor's First-Day Distraction', *The Age* (Melbourne), 2 November 2010.

7 Ben Doherty, 'Secret Trial for Delhi Accused', *The Age* (Melbourne), 8 January 2013, 6.

good or right thing to do – the right or wrong action; and with the moral evaluation of our own and others' character and actions – what does it mean to be a good person? In deciding what to do and how to be, ethics requires that we look for coherent reasons for our actions and character – reasons that explain why it is right or wrong to act according to our financial interests, or to do what others expect in certain situations, et cetera. It asks us to examine the competing interests and principles at stake in each situation and have reasons as to why one should triumph over the other, or how they can be reconciled.

In Case Study 1.1, it is not enough to say that the QC should not represent tobacco companies because he finds it distasteful to do so, or because he might anger his friends and those with whom he wishes to work on philanthropic purposes or might suffer reputational loss in the wider community. The anger of friends and associates or personal distaste are not independent ethical reasons for refusing to do something. We need to look more deeply to determine whether they indicate that some ethical principle is at stake. For example, when does the 'cab rank' rule – the rule that barristers should be available to any client who asks[8] – apply? What about the related principle that obligates a lawyer to represent someone charged with a serious criminal offence if there is no one else available to represent them? Even if there is no possibility whatsoever that the tobacco company will be unrepresented, should the QC say 'no'? Are the possibility of disloyalty to the QC's philanthropic commitments and the undermining of important public health goals more or less important in this situation, for this QC, than the values that might be furthered by representing the client, such as ensuring that important public policy questions and constitutional issues are fully argued before the High Court so that an authoritative public decision can be made? Similarly, we cannot simply say that the QC needs to earn a living and therefore should take every paying customer.

We need to consider whether there is any justification for a socially conscious lawyer, or indeed any lawyer, to earn money to feed himself and his family by working for a firm whose products have killed millions of people and may be more likely to kill more people if the lawyer's arguments succeed. Does the need to earn money override the commitment to finding a 'cure' for cancer in the broadest sense? Can a lawyerly commitment to assisting the High Court decide important cases be more important than a personal commitment as a philanthropist and humanist? What about a personal commitment to earning money or arguing challenging cases? Are these good reasons for choosing certain cases over others? Is it appropriate to take on cases such as these that might pit lawyerly identity against personal identity, and do so in a way that influences the client or the court towards what the lawyer personally believes to be a better way of doing things?

---

8 Australian Bar Association, *Model Rules*, r 21.

We can also ethically evaluate social rules, practices or attitudes to determine whether they promote right action and good character. Most of us have our own ideas about the right thing to do or what good character is. Our personal ideas about ethics are likely to have come from our family upbringing, our friends and colleagues, and any political or faith commitments we might have – our *personal ethics*. There are also more public or shared expectations that go along with our various roles. For example, the community has ideas about what it means to be a good friend, a good parent, a good citizen or a good doctor. Some of these public ideas about ethics go formally unstated. Other ethical norms are codified in legal rules and regulations. Sometimes our personal ideas about ethics (for example, on issues like euthanasia or recreational drug use) can come into conflict with community ethical norms and/or legal rules. Good ethical reasoning demands that none of these assumptions about the right thing to do or the right way to be should go unexamined.

For lawyers, apart from our own personal ethics, there are two potential sources of ethical expectations that might affect the way we do, or *should*, behave – professional conduct principles and social ethics.

Professional Conduct

Professional conduct is the law of lawyering – the published rules and regulations that apply to lawyers and the legal profession. In Australia these rules and regulations can be found in the legal practice or legal profession statutes in each State, in the various professional associations' self-regulatory professional conduct and practice rules and in the way the general law (particularly contract, tort and equity) applies to lawyers and their relationships with clients. In this book when it is necessary to refer to the statutory or self-regulatory rules governing Australian lawyers, we will generally refer to the *National Legal Practice Model Bill* (the '*Model Laws*') (2nd edn, 2006) and the Law Council of Australia's *Australian Solicitors' Conduct Rules* (2012) (the *ASCR*).[9]

Much teaching and practical discussion of lawyers' 'ethics' in the legal profession is dominated by legalism. Legalism treats legal ethics as a branch of

---

9 The *Model Laws* have been agreed between the Attorneys-General of the Australian Commonwealth and each of the States and Territories with significant input also from the Law Council of Australia (the umbrella organisation for Australian lawyers and legal professional associations). As a result the provisions of the legislation governing the legal professions of the various states and territories are increasingly becoming consistent, although the ordering of provisions and section numbers will vary from jurisdiction to jurisdiction. Similarly, the *Model Rules* have been promulgated by the Law Council of Australia, and as a result the professional conduct rules of the various states and territories now increasingly copy this model. Further nationalisation has been attempted but at the time of writing has been unsuccessful. This is further discussed in Chapter 3.

law – 'professional responsibility' or 'professional conduct' law. The professional conduct approach may cater to the need for certainty, predictability and enforceability in a context where people often consider ethics to be subjective and relative. By definition it abandons ethical judgement for rules. The law of lawyering is significant as one way in which lawyers' ethics are institutionally enforced or regulated, and can certainly be helpful in guiding behaviour. We refer in this book to the rules of conduct as being one of the sources of information that lawyers can and should use to make ethical judgements about what is the right thing to do in different situations, but these rules do not provide a basis for considering what values should motivate a lawyer's behaviour and choices about what kind of lawyer to be.

This is not to say that it is not important for society to have and enforce a law of lawyering. However, lawyers must also have an ethical perspective on being a lawyer in order to judge what rules should be made (on a professional level) and also to decide (on a personal level) what the rules mean, how to obey them, what to do when there are gaps or conflicts in the rules and whether, in some circumstances, it may even be necessary to disobey a particular rule for ethical reasons. This book, therefore, will not provide a comprehensive coverage of the law of lawyering,[10] but will provide a basis for the ethical critique of professional conduct principles.

Social Ethics

The second source of ethics for lawyers (apart from their own personal ethics) is general philosophical theories of *social ethics*. Social ethics come from general moral theory or ethical theory – philosophical work devoted to understanding what it means for something to be good or right or a duty.[11] Particularly relevant for lawyers are philosophical ideas about justice, social and environmental responsibility, minimising harm and respecting others.

Some commentators on lawyers' ethics go to the opposite extreme from legalism, and propose that general and abstract moral theories or methodologies should be applied, without elaboration or modification, to the practice of law. These fundamental moral theories generally divide into 'deontological' or rule-based theories, on the one hand, and 'teleological' or consequentialist theories, on the other. Deontological ethics and utilitarian ethics are used, respectively, as the main examples of each approach.

---

10 Other books already provide adequate coverage of the law of lawyering, particularly G E Dal Pont, *Lawyers' Professional Responsibility* (Lawbook Co, Pyrmont, NSW, 5th edn, 2013).
11 For a good overview, see Noel Preston, *Understanding Ethics* (Federation Press, Leichhardt, NSW, 3rd edn, 2007); Russ Shafer-Landau, *The Fundamentals of Morals* (Oxford University Press, New York, 2nd edn, 2011).

The most famous philosophical formulation of deontological ethics is Kant's 'categorical imperative': 'Act only according to that maxim whereby you can, at the same time, will that it should become a universal law.'[12] This is similar to the Golden Rule in the Judaeo-Christian tradition and other religious traditions, which requires people to always treat others as they would want to be treated themselves.[13] Religious formulations of ethics based on divine command are generally deontological because they set absolute rules that tend to emphasise the idea of *fairness* as important to deciding individuals' rights and entitlements. According to Kant, 'right' actions or policies are those that primarily respect individual autonomy by promoting fairness. Kantian methods refute the notion that 'the end justifies the means'. Hence it is a 'categorical imperative' – an absolute and unconditional requirement – that people never be treated merely as means to an end, but always as ends in themselves. Kantian theory argues that the means, since they often involve what happens to individuals, are at least as ethically significant as outcomes. Thus, for example, feminists have used Kantianism to argue that prostitution and pornography should be forbidden as they are dehumanising.

In a teleological approach, by contrast, right actions or policies are those that maximise good consequences and minimise bad consequences. On a teleological approach the (good) ends of an action can justify the means used to obtain those ends, even if they involve otherwise unfair treatment of individuals or organisations. Kantian ethics were a response to utilitarian ethics – a type of consequentialism, developed first by Jeremy Bentham and John Stuart Mill. Utilitarianism proposes that ethical actions are those that produce the greatest good for the greatest number of those affected by a situation.[14] Jeremy Bentham and John Stuart Mill particularly developed utilitarianism as a way for legislators and public policy makers to decide what laws to make. A famous contemporary utilitarian ethicist, Peter Singer, argues that animals should be included in the calculation of the greatest good for the greatest number as they can suffer, and argues that, to the extent young babies or people who are profoundly intellectually disabled cannot feel pleasure or pain, then they can be disregarded if someone else's happiness is at stake, as for example with abortion or the infanticide of a severely disabled child.[15]

Standard deontological and teleological moral theories can be contrasted with both virtue ethics and the ethics of care.

---

12 Immanuel Kant, *Grounding for the Metaphysics of Morals* (James W Ellington trans, Hackett, 3rd edn, 1993) 30 [1785].

13 For example Matthew 7:12.

14 Jeremy Bentham, *Political Thought*, Bhikhu Parekh (ed) (Barnes and Noble, New York, [1748–1832] 1935); John Stuart Mill, *Collected Works of John Stuart Mill*, J M Robson (ed) (Toronto, University of Toronto Press, 1963ff): *On Liberty* (1859), *CW*, v 18, 213–310 and *Utilitarianism* (1861a), *CW*, v 10, 203–59.

15 Peter Singer, *Animal Liberation* (Avon Books, New York, revised edn, 1990).

The ethics of care focuses attention on people's responsibilities to maintain relationships and communities, and to show caring responsiveness to others in specific situations. It was developed by feminists, and particularly Carol Gilligan, in the second half of the twentieth century as a correction to the traditional emphasis in deontological and utilitarian ethical theories on individual rights and duties and formal, abstract, universalist reasoning.[16] It has now been developed by theorists well beyond feminism who emphasise the interdependence of humans and the importance of sensitivity and emotional response in ethical action. Deontological and consequential ethics tend to assume that each person decides on their actions individually, in isolation from others, and that the choices they make then impact on others. The ethics of care, however, points out that most of the time our actions are so intertwined with our relationships with other people and our emotional responses to them, that the most important ethical questions are about how we relate with and respond to others, rather than how our actions impact on them. The ethics of care recognises the importance of modern psychology in understanding the intricacies of human relationships, and would stress that interpersonal skill and sensitivity are crucial tools for ethical decision-making.

Virtue ethics shifts the focus of ethical attention from particular conduct and its impact onto the inherent quality or character of the actor. Virtue ethics approaches derive from ancient philosophy and especially Aristotle's emphasis on right character as a personal virtue. A virtue ethics approach is not necessarily inconsistent with deontological, consequentialist and ethics of care approaches, but rather asks a different question. Virtue asks: What kind of person should I be in order to be a good person? The other theories by contrast ask: What is a good action? A central virtue for Aristotle was therefore 'phronesis' – practical wisdom; the ability to choose wisely. It sits alongside 'sophia' – theoretical wisdom – and other virtues such as courage, generosity, gentleness, honesty about oneself, justice and fairness, magnanimity and fortitude. Thomas Aquinas, the medieval Catholic philosopher, summarised the virtues as prudence, temperance, justice and fortitude in relation to other people, and faith, hope and virtue in relation to God. Like the ethics of care, virtue ethics sees how one relates to others as being central to ethics, but looks beyond this and asks us to consider our identity, character and motivations at a profoundly personal level.[17]

Virtue ethicists assert that intentional, ethically defensible behaviour is more likely to emerge from the ongoing process of genuine personal reflection about our

---

16 Carol Gilligan, *In a Different Voice* (Harvard University Press, Cambridge MA, 1982).

17 See Justin Oakley and Dean Cocking, *Virtue Ethics and Professional Roles* (Cambridge University Press, Cambridge, 2001). See also Robert Eli Rosen, 'Ethical Soap: LA Law and the Privileging of Character' (1989) 43 *University of Miami Law Review* 1229.

virtues (and our lack of some of them) than if we attempt to act without regard to our inner virtues (values).

Moral theories are so abstract that it can be difficult to apply them to concrete situations. Applying general moral theories to legal practice also begs one of the main questions debated in lawyers' ethics, which is: To what extent should lawyers' ethics be determined by the idea that lawyers should play a special and unique role in society? Or to what extent should lawyers be held to the same general ethical standards as anyone else? In Case Study 1.2, for example, it may be all very well for a non-lawyer to state that their highest loyalty is to their sibling.

CASE STUDY 1.2 UNDERSTANDING DIFFERENT ETHICAL APPROACHES IN PRACTICE

You are very close to your older sister, Lee, who is also a University student. You have always felt able to discuss your secrets with each other without other friends or family members finding out.

For the last few years Lee has been indulging regularly in alcohol binges and certain illegal drugs. It does not appear to be seriously affecting her study or part-time work yet, but she has exhibited increasingly erratic behaviour in the last few months. Last week Lee was found lying in the middle of the road after a party and there have been a number of times in recent months when friends had to make sure she got home safely before doing something that might harm herself or others.

Lee tells you that she is probably indulging 'a bit too much', but is planning to 'pull back' and has the situation 'under control'. Lee says she does not need your concern or help, and demands that whatever happens you do not let other members of your family know anything about the situation until she is 'out the other side'. You feel that Lee may need professional help to find her way 'out the other side'.

DISCUSSION QUESTIONS

1. Role-play (or imagine) how a conversation between yourself and Lee, after the lying in the middle of the road incident, might play out. What approach might you take to trying to get help for Lee? Should you talk to other friends or family members if you feel that Lee is not going to be able to get through to 'the other side' on her own? How would Lee view the different approaches you might take?

2. What arguments might each of you use to support or explain your preferred approach? Can you identify how the different potential

approaches draw on deontological, utilitarian, ethics of care or virtue based ethical arguments?

Now imagine that rather than Lee being your older sibling, you are a criminal defence lawyer and Lee is not a friend or relation but another lawyer who is your client. Lee has been charged in relation to the incident where she lay down in the middle of the road, but you believe you can probably persuade the police to drop the charges. Lee insists that you do everything you can to get the police to drop the charges and completely hush up the whole situation. As before, Lee insists that she has her substance use under control and needs no help or intervention.

3. Once again, role-play the conversation between yourself and Lee. Does your role as lawyer for Lee make you think differently about your ethical obligations in this situation? How do the arguments and considerations change when you are Lee's lawyer rather than sibling? What about the fact that Lee is a lawyer? Does this make things different? How?

4. What if, rather than being Lee's lawyer or sibling, you were Lee's general practitioner, rabbi, pastor, priest, imam or meditation teacher, or a friend who also happens to be a psychologist specialising in drug-abuse problems? Do these different roles that you play in society change your conception of your ethical obligations in the situation?

An Applied Ethics Approach

In this book we take a practical and applied approach to examining lawyers' ethics. Our approach accepts that lawyers must first know where they fit in relation to the social theories of ethics discussed above but asserts that more is needed, because lawyers must operate as everyday 'judges' inside fairly well-defined roles, as a part of the justice system.

We will be best able to utilise our preferences for social or personal ethical frameworks if we focus them into a number of categories that are more easily recognisable to us as lawyers. Our aim is to enable lawyers and law students to critique and evaluate professional conduct and lawyers' behaviour in practice by combining their own personal ethics with professional conduct rules and social considerations. Our focus will be on using real-life case studies to help practise an ethical evaluation process that involves awareness of the ethical issues likely to arise for lawyers in practice, the standards and values available to resolve those issues, and consideration of how we might implement our ethical decision-making in practice.

In this chapter and the next we introduce four main ethical approaches, derived from the theories mentioned above, which can help lawyers when making ethical decisions:

- Adversarial advocacy;
- Responsible lawyering;
- Moral activism; and
- Ethics of care.

In the following chapters we will examine a number of substantial topics in lawyers' ethics through case studies, and analyse the professional conduct principles and ethical approaches that might apply in each area. In each chapter we will introduce some of the major ethical issues facing lawyers in relation to the chapter's topic, and set out the conventional ('current') values that are commonly applied to resolving those issues. We will then compare current approaches with alternatives derived from our four ethical approaches ('alternative values'). Finally, we will give readers a chance to work through the current and alternative values that might apply to the topic by means of specific case studies (usually based on real cases) and questions designed to clarify and challenge the reader's own stance on each area. Our aim is to make explicit the sort of values awareness and decision-making processes we go through (or ought to go through) in order to make decisions about what is the right thing to do or the right sort of person to be in legal practice.

In real life, ethical issues usually arise in complex and ambiguous circumstances. They cannot be resolved by a rote application of a mechanical process applying abstract principles. They must be a matter of skill and character, of practical wisdom, or 'virtue', that is consciously developed over time.

Process of Ethical Reflection and Decision-Making

In order for ethical considerations to make a real difference to lawyers' behaviour, we need to think about what ethical decision-making steps we must go through in applying ethical considerations to real-life situations. It has been suggested that in any practical endeavour, ethically responsible decision-making requires at least three different steps. We must:

(1)   Be aware of the ethical issues that arise in practice, and of our own values and predispositions;

(2)   Make a choice between the range of standards and values that are available to help resolve those ethical issues; and

(3)   Implement that resolution in practice.[18]

---

18 Based on Kenneth E Goodpaster, 'The Concept of Corporate Responsibility' (1983) 2 *Journal of Business Ethics* 1, 7–9.

It is very well for philosophical theorists to propose certain theories or principles of ethics that people ought to act on (the second step). But in practice ethical decision-making also requires us to be aware that an ethical dilemma or choice even exists in the first place (the first step), and to have the creativity, skills and will to put our ethical principles into practice (the third step).

The substantive content of this book (as reflected in the chapter template outlined above) critically examines the second step – the standards and values that should apply to different ethical issues that arise in practice. But learning to reason ethically also involves practising the identification of ethical issues in the first place and creating practical resolutions to ethical dilemmas that respect ethical values. That is one of the reasons that we have included a number of scenarios throughout this book. These case studies are designed to help us learn to become aware of ethical issues, to reflect and decide on what ethical standards and values should apply to those issues, and to consider how we might put those resolutions into practice. We will often learn more about these aspects of ethical reasoning if we can discuss case studies with other people with different knowledge, values and experiences from our own. For that reason the case studies include questions that can be used as a basis for discussion in a classroom or when they arise in a law firm.

These three steps in ethical reasoning are explained in further detail below, and illustrated with a case study scenario and questions typical of those provided throughout the book. In the remaining chapters the focus will generally be on the second step. But the case studies and questions in each chapter are also designed to improve readers' ethical awareness and their ability to plan and implement practical resolutions to ethical problems.

CASE STUDY 1.3 THE LAWYER WHO DRAFTED CORRUPT CONTRACTS WITH IRAQ

The Australian Wheat Board was established by the Australian Government in 1939 to buy all wheat from Australian farmers in order to collectively market and sell it domestically (for a fixed price) and internationally (at global market prices). In 1989 the Wheat Board was reformed, lost its statutory monopoly on selling wheat within Australia, and had to compete for Australian wheat sales; however, it retained the exclusive right to market and sell Australian wheat internationally. In 1997 and 1998 the Wheat Board was reformed again to become a private company, AWB Limited, with the right to manage and market the export of Australian wheat, and to veto the possibility of competition from others. Wheat growers became shareholders and the company listed on the stock exchange.[19]

The majority of Australian wheat is exported. Indeed, by 2006, AWB was one of the largest exporters of wheat in the world, averaging AUD$4 billion annually – about 16% of world wheat trade and 3% of Australia's total exports. Among the fifty or so countries to which Australian wheat had been exported was Iraq. But trading was suspended in 1990 when the United Nations Security Council imposed trade sanctions on Iraq in response to its invasion of Kuwait. Food trade was allowed in 'humanitarian' circumstances, but Iraq had no hard currency to buy wheat even for humanitarian purposes. In 1995 the United Nations set up the Oil-for-Food Programme to soften the impact of the sanctions. It allowed Iraq to sell its oil, keep the income in a United Nations escrow account and use that income to buy humanitarian goods, including wheat, to alleviate famine and hunger caused by the trading sanctions. Only contracts favourably reviewed by the UN could be paid for from the escrow account. By 1999 about 10% of Australia's annual wheat export was going to Iraq, and this represented about 90% of all wheat sales to Iraq. AWB was the largest single exporter of any humanitarian item to Iraq.[20]

In 1999 Iraq introduced a requirement that AWB pay a fee for the transportation of the wheat from the Iraqi port to the inland silos. These fees were factored into the wheat price in the official contract documentation that was given to the United Nations for approval of payments from the escrow accounts. The price to be paid for the wheat coming out of the account was inflated by the amount of the transportation fees. The Cole Royal Commission later found that these amounts were paid back to the Iraqi government in hard currency through 'trucking fees' and 'port charges', particularly to a Jordanian trucking company, and that AWB executives knew this.

Between November 1999 and March 2003, the Iraqi government, headed by Saddam Hussein, obtained US$224 million in fees by this means. Although these payments breached UN resolutions and the provisions of the

---

19 Information in this paragraph is based on Geoff Cockfield and Linda Botterill, 'Deregulating Australia's Wheat Trade: From the Australian Wheat Board to AWB Limited' (2007) 2 *Public Policy* 44. See also Caroline Overington, *Kickback: Inside the Australian Wheat Board Scandal* (Allen & Unwin, Crows Nest, 2007).

20 Information in this paragraph and the following paragraphs is based on Kath Hall and Vivien Holmes, 'The Power of Rationalisation to Influence Lawyers' Decisions to Act Unethically' (2008) 11 *Legal Ethics* 137–53, and Linda Botterill and Anne McNaughton, 'Laying the Foundations for the Wheat Scandal: UN Sanctions, Private Actors and the Cole Inquiry' (2008) 43 *Australian Journal of Political Science* 583.

Oil-for-Food Programme, they did not directly amount to a breach of Australian law. The UN resolutions applied to the Australian state, not to private companies, and the Australian government had not legislated to make it an offence for private companies and individuals to act in breach of the UN trading sanctions on Iraq.

Nevertheless, as the Cole Royal Commission later found, these payments were essentially corrupt payment (or 'kickbacks') to ensure Iraq maintained its contract with AWB for Australian wheat under pressure from the Hussein regime. They were also akin to money laundering because they allowed the Iraqi regime to access some of the income it had obtained from selling oil under the Oil-for-Food Programme to use for its own purposes, rather than only for humanitarian purposes approved by the UN.

Around the same time, Australia, together with the US and UK, was accusing Iraq of possessing weapons of mass destruction and preparing to invade in March 2003. Weapons of mass destruction were never found and the US, UK and Australian governments were heavily criticised for their stance on Iraq, and even for breaching international law conventions and UN Security Council resolutions by invading Iraq.

In mid-2000, after an inquiry by the UN into AWB's payment of trucking fees, the Australian Wheat Board commissioned accounting and auditing firm Arthur Andersen to investigate the existence of any unethical or illegal conduct in AWB. Arthur Andersen's 2001 report pointed out that the culture of AWB required review as far as ethical dealing was concerned, and that the payment of trucking fees in Iraq was of concern. The UN did not follow up on its inquiry about the trucking fees until 2005.

AWB employed several in-house lawyers. These lawyers did not settle the contracts that included the surcharges and so it is unclear when they found out about the surcharges. But one of the lawyers did meet regularly with the executives responsible for the contracts to sort out any legal issues that arose, and one was present at the meeting that discussed the Arthur Andersen report.

Imagine that you are that lawyer. In mid-2002, AWB executives approach you with an urgent problem. A few weeks ago the Iraqi Minister for Trade halved the amount of wheat Iraq planned to buy from Australia because of their concern that Australia was supporting the United States' pro-invasion stance on Iraq. Now Iraq has alleged that a shipment of wheat from AWB is contaminated with iron filings and is seeking US$2 million in compensation. An AWB delegation in Iraq has already agreed to pay the compensation rather than lose the remaining contracts, and Iraq has now responded to the offer by reinstating its original order.

The problem, however, is how to structure the reinstated contract so as to conceal from the UN Oil-for-Food Programme the payment of the compensation, since this payment would breach the rules of the Oil-for-Food scheme. You are well aware that AWB, your client, is under tremendous pressure to maintain its sales of wheat to Iraq, as the sale of wheat to Iraq has been portrayed in the media by the government as a huge success story for Australian wheat growers and the Australian economy. Indeed the Prime Minister himself congratulated the AWB on its success in exporting wheat to Iraq. The success of the privatisation of AWB has been largely supported by their success in regaining wheat contracts with Iraq under the Oil-for-Food Programme. You are also aware of the trucking fees and the fact that they too are essential to maintaining AWB's exports to Iraq. The executives of AWB tell you that it is your job to write a contract for them that enables the contracts they have already entered into to go ahead.

Step One: Awareness of Ethical Issues

What ethical issues have arisen or might arise in the future in this situation?

- Who are the stakeholders, ie whose interests are affected?
- What interests or values are at stake in this situation from the perspective of each of these stakeholders?
- Are there any other principles or values at stake in this scenario?
- Are there any conflicts between the interests or values of the different stakeholders?
- What are your own interests and values (as the lawyer) in this scenario?
- What are the different options as to what you (the lawyer) should do, or should have done, in this scenario?

In this first stage we are simply 'auditing' the ethical issues that have or might have arisen, and what interests and values they raise – not trying to resolve them. The aim is to become aware of what interests and values (including our own personal ones) could apply to a scenario. In order to identify these, it is often helpful to start by thinking about all the different people who might have an interest in the outcome of the scenario (the 'stakeholders') and what values and interests each of them represents. Usually there will be a range of conflicting and complementary values and interests at stake in any situation, suggesting a variety of alternative and contradictory courses of action – that is what turns a situation into an ethical dilemma.

In practice the problem is that often we (and some theorists) forget that there are genuine ethical perspectives, other than those held by us or the people we spend most time with, on what to do in certain situations. Sometimes there are very major differences between our own values and those of others. In the 1960s Stanley Milgram conducted a series of famous (and highly unethical, but effective) experiments on volunteers who were asked to administer electric shocks to another person. The experiments showed that people are quite willing and able to inflict progressively more pain on another human being, up to very dangerous levels, in circumstances where the initial level of pain is insignificant, each increase in pain is small, and it is accompanied by reassurance from someone in authority that it should be done.[21] Uncontrolled police and military interrogations are another example of situations in which unethical behaviour such as torture and violence can be seen as normal in the context of police or military sub-cultures. At a more mundane level, lawyers can have their ethical awareness and imagination dulled by working in firms or being with people who see ethically questionable behaviour as 'the way lawyers do things' or 'the way we do things around here'. Ethics education can help improve ethical behaviour by making us more aware of our own value structures and alternative value structures that we might apply to our everyday lives.

DISCUSSION QUESTIONS

Think of the situation in Case Study 1.3 above. In hindsight it is easy to see that AWB engaged in corrupt behaviour in order to maintain its wheat sales to Iraq, and that their lawyers assisted them to do so. Often when ethical issues arise in real life, however, it is more difficult to discern the key ethical issues at stake. This is why Step One of any ethical decision-making process is to make yourself aware of ethical issues by auditing the interests and values at stake. It can also be helpful to closely examine case studies of ethical misconduct, such as the AWB scenario, to understand how people could have got it so wrong – which values and interests overwhelmed their thinking and which they ignored.

As well as applying the general questions set out in the description of Step One to your analysis of the ethical issues at stake in Case Study 1.3, also consider the following more specific questions:

1. Imagine that you are a senior executive at AWB. You are due to meet with your in-house lawyer to tell them about the trucking fees and

---

21 The experiment was actually a hoax – the person receiving the electric shocks was an actor who pretended to suffer the pain of each shock. However, the volunteer subjects of the experiment did not know this. For a description of the experiments and their applicability to lawyers' ethics, see David Luban, 'The Ethics of Wrongful Obedience' in D Rhode (ed), *Ethics in Practice: Lawyers' Roles, Responsibilities, and Regulation* (Oxford University Press, Oxford, 2000) 94, 96–7.

compensation payment and to ask them to write a contract. What values and interests are you and your company trying to protect in going ahead with this contract? Who do you feel loyalty to? What are the competing values and interests at stake? List all the people and organisations who might have a stake in what AWB does in this situation, and consider what interests and values they might have in the situation.

2. Are there any other options available to AWB other than going ahead with the contracts as demanded by the Iraqi regime? How would you convince yourself that it was OK to go ahead with the contracts, acceding to Iraq's demands? Can you think of anyone who could convince you not to do that?

3. Now imagine that you are the in-house lawyer who is being instructed to draft the contracts. What is your personal opinion about whether this is the right response for AWB to take to Iraq's demands? What do you value most in deciding what to do in this situation? Who do you feel loyal to in deciding what to do? What interests of your own are at stake in this situation? What might happen to you if you do draft the contracts? And if you refuse to do so?

Step Two: Application of Ethical Standards or Principles

What ethical principles should be used to resolve the issues in this scenario?

•   What professional conduct principles (the law of lawyering) might apply to this situation, including any relevant professional code of ethics?

•   What general ethical principles might apply to this scenario (eg justice and the public interest, conflicts of interest, respect for the spirit of the law, non-harm and respect for others, social and environmental responsibility)?

•   Are there any particular responsibilities that a lawyer should have in this scenario because of their role as a lawyer?

•   If there are conflicts between these various ethical standards and principles that could apply to the situation, how should they be resolved?

Ethical standards and principles provide a basis for deciding what values and interests should prevail in different circumstances. For lawyers, thinking about the ethical standards and principles that should apply to practice generally raises four main questions:

1. To what extent should lawyers' ethics be determined by a special and particular social role that lawyers should play?

Should our conduct be prescribed solely by the role of zealous (and often adversarial) advocate for clients' interests in a complex and adversarial legal system? Or is there some alternative role that prescribes how we should behave as lawyers – perhaps as an officer of the court or as a trustee of the legal system with a special responsibility for ensuring compliance? Or should we, in our professional lives, be held to the same general ethics as anyone else? For example, should we argue for positions in which we do not believe, for the sake of clients, or should this be considered lying? Further, should we always make sure we are directly advancing justice as much as possible, or do we have enough faith in the justice of the system to simply argue our clients' cases and leave it to the system to determine where justice lies?

2. How should lawyers and clients relate to one another in relation to ethical issues?

Should we consider the justice or morality of our clients' causes in choosing whether and how to represent them? Should ethical considerations – such as our assessment of the public interest, our personal moral, social or religious beliefs (or those of our clients), and the impact of various options on our clients' relationships or psyches or on the opponent – be explicitly discussed in legal advice and counselling? Should either ours or our clients' views of morality prevail over the other in deciding what to do? When there is disagreement over ethical issues, when can or should we act, refuse to act or cease to act?

3. What are lawyers' obligations towards law and justice?

Is it justifiable to help our clients test the limits of the law, provided we can argue that we, and they, are not breaching the letter of the law? Or should we preserve the spirit and integrity of the law against client interests? Should we work to reform the law and legal institutions to improve their substantive social justice; for example, by actively seeking out test cases or lobbying politically for legislative reform? How much should we need to find out about a client's honesty, guilt or innocence, before advocating for them? In what circumstances should we be considered blameworthy for helping a client to break or evade the law, or escape liability? Are there any circumstances in which we could be considered ethically justified in resisting or breaking the law or helping our clients to do so?

4. To what extent should lawyers in their daily work make sure they care for people and relationships, including themselves?

Is not the care of one human for another and for themselves the central ethical imperative? Should we pursue the moral goodness and/or best interests of our clients in the context of their relationships despite what the law says, perhaps despite even the broader dictates of social justice? How should we determine what is in the best interests of clients – is it material and financial, is it power and prestige, or is it psychological, relational, spiritual? What about our own selves? Should we work long hours in the law even if it means neglecting ourselves, our family and our relationships? Will we wish on our deathbeds that we had spent more time at the office? Or are their alternative ways of practising law and preserving our own psyche?

This chapter and the next chapter provide an overview of four different approaches to legal ethics that answer these questions in different ways, and with quite different priorities. The first and predominant one, the adversarial advocate approach (introduced in this chapter), sees lawyers' ethics as determined solely by lawyers' role as advocates of their clients' interests in a complex and adversarial system constrained only by the letter of law. No ethical considerations other than the letter of the law and the lawyer's duty of advocacy in the client's interest are relevant to ethical decision-making. This makes it very easy to go through the process of ethical decision-making. But as we shall see in the next chapter, there are both a number of criticisms of this approach and some alternatives to it.

DISCUSSION QUESTION

1. Think again about Case Study 1.3: The Lawyer Who Drafted Corrupt Contracts with Iraq. Apply the four questions above, discussing the sort of questions this raises for the in-house lawyer who is asked to draft the contracts that conceal the trucking fees and compensation payment.

How would a lawyer who wanted to go ahead and draft the contracts without protest answer those four questions? In hindsight, how would you answer those four questions in this scenario? Are there any other options available to you other than simply obeying the instructions of your client to draft the contract or refusing to do so? How might you convince yourself that it is ethically OK to go ahead and draft the contract without protest? Can you think of anyone who would disagree with you if you said: It is my job as a lawyer to draft these contracts, not to argue with my client? What should a lawyer do in this situation?

Step Three: Moral Imagination and Practical Implementation

How can the ethical thing to do actually be put into action in the current situation? What does it mean in this situation?

- What can I imagine as the possible moral alternatives? What is feasible in the current situation? What practical alternatives are available to me? What are likely to be the consequences of different alternatives?
- What personal and systemic or organisational resources would I need to access in order to do the right thing (eg legal restraint, clout, independence, collegial support, an ethics policy, character, will)?
- What skills would I need to put it into practice (eg negotiation and communication skills, moral courage)?
- [If appropriate] How can I/we prevent this sort of issue occurring again?

Finally, it is of limited use deciding on principled grounds what is the right thing to do if you lack the imagination, courage, will, skills or capacity to put it into practice. In some situations, ethical integrity might even require the sacrifice of giving up your job (because you will be sacked for behaving ethically, or because you should resign).

In others, it requires diplomacy, communication, negotiation and persuasion skills. It is always useful to consider how one might prevent ethical difficulties arising in the future; for example, by making sure your law firm's system for checking for potential conflicts of interest (in the broadest sense) when a client first makes an appointment actually works properly, or refusing to take on a client with an ethically questionable case in the first place.

DISCUSSION QUESTION

1. Consider your conclusion about how a lawyer should approach the situation in Case Study 1.3, as discussed at Step Two above. How would you put your ethical resolution into action? What will you say to the AWB executives? What will you say to any government or UN agencies who inquire about the contracts? And to the media? How will you react if you are criticised for your decision? Would some resolutions to the scenario be more difficult to implement in practice than others? In the short term? In the long term? Do you think that your assumptions about how difficult or easy certain ethical decisions are to implement influenced your choice of resolution in the first place?

Adversarial Advocacy: The Traditional Conception of Legal Ethics

Adversarial advocacy is the predominant conception of what lawyers' role and ethics ought to be in most common law countries including Australia. It is also the simplest, most absolute and, generally, the most comfortable of the four approaches. It gives a reasonably clear answer as to what to do in most situations; that is, a lawyer should advance their client's partisan interests with the maximum zeal permitted by law. This approach to legal ethics is often termed an 'amoral' one because it sees general moral theory as being irrelevant to lawyers' ethics.[22] In fact, adversarial advocacy sees the suppression of one's own individual moral opinions and consideration of general ethical concerns as a moral act in itself. The lawyer must 'turn off' these other ethical considerations in order to fulfil their proper moral role as advocate for their client. The basis for lawyers' ethics within adversarial advocacy is found in the social role that lawyers are supposed to play in the adversarial legal system.

Adversarial advocacy combines the 'principle of partisanship' and the 'principle of non-accountability'.[23] The principle of partisanship means that the lawyer should do all for the client that the client would do for themselves, if the client had the knowledge of the lawyer. This is because the adversarial system is based on party control of the proceedings, with each party ensuring that all legitimate arguments in their own favour are put forward. The principle of non-accountability follows on from this and says that the lawyer is not morally responsible for either the means or the ends of representation, provided both are lawful. If the lawyer were morally responsible, it is said, the lawyer may not be willing to act zealously to represent the client's interests.

This approach is most clearly justified in the case of trial lawyers, especially criminal defence advocates who must vigorously assert the rights of the accused against the superior power and resources of the state. By corollary, the adversarial advocate approach is least justifiable if applied to a criminal prosecutor who represents the state against the accused. It is well accepted that prosecutors should

---

22 Gerald Postema, 'Moral Responsibility in Professional Ethics' (1980) 55 *New York University Law Review* 63; Richard Wasserstrom, 'Lawyers as Professionals: Some Moral Issues' (1975) 5 *Human Rights* 1.
23 David Luban, *Lawyers and Justice: An Ethical Study* (Princeton University Press, Princeton, 1988) 7.

act as 'ministers of justice', pay elaborate attention to fairness and candour and only present to the court those facts and arguments that they believe to be well grounded (see Chapter 5). Historically, the adversarial advocate approach was essentially liberal, motivating lawyers to pursue client interests primarily against the power of the state. It was dependent on a conception of the Rule of Law which puts the courts between citizens and governments, and requires lawyers independent of the state and available to help those who want to use the law to challenge or defend themselves against the government. However, the adversarial advocate approach has extended beyond representing client interests against state interests to representing client interests against other private interests and in any situation where a lawyer is necessary. Since ours is a complex legal system, lawyers must be readily available to empower those who need to use the law to organise their affairs, settle a dispute, defend themselves against the powers of the state or establish a right against some private interest, without pre-judging their clients or being held accountable for what the client chooses to do (provided it is within the bounds of law).

Lord Brougham's 1820 defence of Queen Caroline before the House of Lords is a favourite example of the ideal in action. King George IV was trying to rid himself of Caroline by alleging that she had committed adultery, but it was well known that the King himself had been unfaithful. Lord Brougham implied that although he did not yet need to defend the Queen by attacking her husband, if such a defence did become necessary neither he nor

> even the youngest member in the profession, would hesitate to resort to such a course and fearlessly perform his duty … [A]n advocate, in the discharge of his duty, knows but one person in all the world, and that person is his client. To save that client by all means and expedients, and at all hazards and costs to other persons, and, amongst them, to himself, is his first and only duty; and in performing this duty he must not regard the alarm, the torments, the destruction which he may bring upon others. Separating the duty of a patriot from that of an advocate, he must go on reckless of consequences, though it should be his unhappy fate to involve his country in confusion.[24]

These words were controversial at the time they were stated, but the same philosophy can still be found today. In the case of *McCabe v British American Tobacco Australia Services Ltd*[25] (BAT), at first instance the Victorian Supreme Court found that Clayton Utz, the solicitors for the defendant BAT, had advised the company on a 'document retention policy' that intentionally resulted in the

---

24 Quoted in David Mellinkoff, *The Conscience of a Lawyer* (West Publishing Co, St Paul, Minnesota, 1973) 188–9.
25 [2002] VSC 73 (Eames J, 22 March 2002).

destruction of thousands of documents. These documents would have been relevant and favourable to McCabe's negligence case against the company for her mortal cancer. The court also found that the defendant and its legal advisers had misled the plaintiff and the court about the fact and the extent of BAT's document destruction. The judge struck out the defendant's defence and ordered judgment for the plaintiff, without a trial, on the basis that the destruction of documents had unfairly prejudiced the plaintiff's chances of success. This decision was later overturned on appeal.[26] But in the meantime, the lawyers for BAT were severely criticised in the media (see Chapter 10). The following comments in defence of their position illustrate the traditional, adversarial conception of the responsibility and role of the lawyer well:

> Moral judgments have no place in the advice a lawyer gives to a client, according to the chief executive partner of Clayton Utz … Asked what role a lawyer should play if a client was proposing to do something legal, but immoral, he said: 'I'm struggling to see where there would be a case where that would actually arise'. He said: 'The clients are entitled obviously to avail themselves of the full protection of the law and the lawyers are there to advance their clients' interests subject to the constraints of their professional duties and, in particular, their duties to the court. But if they operate within those constraints then they are acting appropriately'. He said a lawyer might advise on the 'appropriateness' of different strategies, but it was wrong for a lawyer to make moral judgments. 'We don't take a moral stance and it's not up to us, as advocates for a client, to take a moral stance. Ultimately that comes to a decision by the client, not the lawyer.' [The chief executive partner] said: 'We operate for a range of clients and make decisions based on a business assessment. What we aspire to ensures that we act with integrity at all times, but I don't think that involves bringing moral judgment to who we act for and who we don't act for'.[27]

In the case of barristers, the adversarial advocate approach is taken as far as the 'cab rank' rule, which requires that a barrister take on and vigorously defend a brief in any area in which he or she practises, if he or she is available and the client can pay. While solicitors have not had such an onerous duty to take on clients, once

---

26 *British American Tobacco Australia Services Ltd v Cowell* (2002) 7 VR 524. For an account of the first instance judgment, including discussion of some of the ethical issues involved, see Camille Cameron, 'Hired Guns and Smoking Guns: *McCabe v British American Tobacco Australia Ltd*' (2002) 25 *University of New South Wales Law Journal* 768.

27 From Margaret Simons, 'Lawyers Not Moral Judges: Clayton Utz Chief', *The Sunday Age* (Melbourne), 4 August 2002, 3.

they do have a client they, like barristers, owe duties of loyalty to pursue their client's case vigorously, to keep them fully informed, and to take instructions from the client. Indeed most of the rules of law and ethics governing lawyers taught in legal ethics and professional responsibility courses relate to the lawyer's duty of advocacy including the duties of confidentiality, diligence and fidelity or loyalty. These duties to clients are limited only by the general requirements of the law: A lawyer must represent his or her client to the full extent of the law. For some lawyers the adversarial advocate approach can also motivate actively choosing to work for clients who might otherwise miss out on representation because other lawyers find them or their cause distasteful or because they lack resources to pay for a lawyer.

Hence in Case Study 1.1: The Case of the Philanthropist QC and the Tobacco Company, at the beginning of this chapter, the adversarial advocate approach may require the barrister to take on cases for tobacco companies when asked, and to pursue all arguable claims, if he was available. According to the adversarial advocate approach, this should not be seen as reflecting his personal opinions and tarnishing his personal and philanthropic reputation in any way, since he would simply be acting as a representative for whichever client came along. On an adversarial advocate approach, the barrister's personal anti-smoking stance and support for medical research to prevent and cure cancer would be seen as a matter of personal loyalties and values that were irrelevant to his role as a lawyer in advocating without discrimination for any client. It would be his ethical duty to his client to not allow those loyalties to affect the quality of his representation, and there should be no implication that his lawyerly activities representing tobacco companies would affect his anti-cancer activities.

Limitations of Adversarial Advocacy

Although proponents of the adversarial advocate approach generally state that client advocacy should extend only as far as the law allows, the lawyer's duty to the law is usually left vaguely defined. Indeed, taken to its logical extreme, the adversarial advocate approach requires lawyers to resolve ambiguity in the law and their own ethical duties in favour of the client. One criticism of the adversarial advocate approach is that it prescribes only the barest obligations to the legal framework and is therefore a recipe for sabotage. While the legal system works on the basis that people will generally internalise norms and comply voluntarily, under the adversarial advocate approach

> [lawyers] are expected and even encouraged to exploit every loophole in
> the rules, take advantage of every one of their opponents' tactical mistakes
> or oversights, and stretch every legal or factual interpretation to favour their
> clients. The guiding premise of the entire system is that maintaining the
> integrity of rights-guarding procedures is more important than obtaining
> convictions or enforcing the substantive law against its violators.[28]

There is little room, within the relationship between an adversarial advocate and
their client, for the idea that the law might make legitimate claims on a client,
that people might have responsibilities as well as rights under the law, that a
democratic state might 'have a role as guarantor of freedom where liberty is most at
peril from the actions of individuals or private institutions'.[29] Individual lawyers and
their clients do not have to concern themselves directly with justice or the public
interest. This is ethically justified because as long as all the lawyers for all the parties
in any action or deal act adversarially in the narrow interests of their own client, it
is said that the legal system will make sure that the right outcome ensues. Indeed,
the adversarial advocate believes that it would be a presumptuous denial of justice
to anyone who wants to use the legal system for lawyers to act otherwise – that is,
to judge potential clients before they have had their 'day in court'. However, the
fact that the advocacy ideal prescribes devoted service to clients' ends, whatever
they may be, is problematic where the market functions so that the rich can buy up
most legal services. While our criminal defence system is supported by legal aid,
many of the best criminal lawyers will not work consistently for the fees offered by
legal aid. The advocacy ideal is also problematic when it creates a culture in which
good advocacy means a culture of excessive adversarialism that raises the costs and
length of litigation, making it more and more unaffordable (see Chapter 6).

In recent years a number of legal ethics scholars have defended the adversarial
advocate idea as a basis for lawyers' ethics against these criticisms by modifying
it to some extent. Thus Tim Dare argues that the standard conception of lawyers'
ethics as requiring adversarial advocacy has been mischaracterised (and perhaps
misapplied) as requiring 'hyper-zeal': an all-out approach to exterminate the
opposition, no matter what. An obligation of 'mere-zeal', rather than hyper-zeal, can
be morally justified on his view.[30] Daniel Markovits has provocatively proposed that
legal ethics scholarship to date has been asking the wrong question. He suggests
that rather than asking how lawyers should behave, legal ethics scholars should
concern themselves with more philosophically interesting questions such as: What
kind of a practice is lawyering? What are lawyering's immanent (or inherent) norms

---

28 Robert Gordon, 'The Independence of Lawyers' (1988) 68 *Boston University Law Review* 1, 10.
29 David Weisbrot, *Australian Lawyers* (Longman Cheshire, Melbourne, 1990) 44–5.
30 Tim Dare, *The Counsel of Rogues?: A Defence of the Standard Conception of the Lawyer's Role*
    (Ashgate, Farnham, England, 2009).

and how are these related to other moral ideals? How does lawyering fit into modern ethical life more generally?

Markovits' own response to these questions proposes that professional conduct law is 'not so much a moral as a *political* construction', and thus 'the law governing lawyers is not so much concerned with the nature or content of an individual life well-lived as with how to sustain solidarity in the face of entrenched and intractable disagreement about the good life'.[31] This then becomes the basis for his new argument for a reformulated adversarial advocate approach. Markovits asserts that in contemporary society much of the institutional structure supporting the role of lawyer as advocate has broken down, such as the self-regulating bar and the self-contained role morality it supported. Nevertheless, he argues that society still needs a legitimate adjudicatory mechanism to hold itself together and therefore still needs lawyers to act with integrity through fidelity to their clients – that is, acting as much as possible as mouthpiece for their clients' stories in criminal and civil trials.[32]

Markovits' reconceptualisation of adversarial advocacy leaves lawyers with a very reduced ethical conception of their role.[33] Alternative approaches to lawyers' ethics seek to more fully recognise the breadth and plurality of ethically significant factors that lawyers must take into account as both lawyers and people in order to exercise professional, personal and moral judgement and show integrity in their work.

There are two main alternative ways of thinking about lawyers' ethics in contrast to the adversarial ideal. The first is to accept that lawyers' ethics should be defined by their particular role in the adversarial legal system and in society, but to define that role differently from the traditional adversarial advocate approach, and the second is to abandon role morality for lawyers and argue instead that general ethics should apply to lawyers.[34]

Chapter 2 considers, firstly, a different role morality approach for lawyers – *responsible lawyering*. *Responsible lawyering*, like *adversarial advocacy*, is based on the lawyer's role in the adversary system, but sees the lawyer as having more of a mediating role between the law and clients than in adversarial advocacy, which sees the lawyer as acting primarily in the client's interests. We then consider two approaches that apply more general ethics to the legal profession – the *moral*

---

31 Daniel Markovits, 'Not Morality at All, and Certainly Not Morality as Regulative Ideal' in Christine Parker (ed) 'Forum: Philosophical Legal Ethics, Ethics, Morals and Jurisprudence' (2010) 13 *Legal Ethics* 165, 207.

32 Daniel Markovits, *A Modern Legal Ethics: Adversarial Advocacy in a Democratic Age* (Princeton University Press, Princeton, 2008).

33 See William Simon, 'Role Differentiation and Lawyers' Ethics: A Critique of Some Academic Perspectives' (2010) 23 *Georgetown Journal of Legal Ethics* 987.

34 See Justin Oakley and Dean Cocking, *Virtue Ethics and Professional Roles* (Cambridge University Press, New York, 2001) 121–36.

activist and *ethics of care* approaches. *Moral activism* sees social ethics, and particularly social justice, as the final arbiter of what lawyers' ethics should be since the legal system should be concerned with advancing justice, while the *ethics of care* approach sees relational ethics and the minimisation of harm as the most important principles that should govern lawyers' behaviour. *Responsible lawyering* suggests alternatives to and limits on excessive adversarialism within the terms of the adversary system itself, by proposing that lawyers behave as officers of the court as well as client advocates. Existing professional-conduct regulation attempts (at least half-heartedly) to put this into practice, as we shall see in the chapters that follow. *Moral activism* and the *ethics of care*, by contrast, provide external critiques to adversarialism. They propose alternatives to the partisanship and non-accountability of adversarial advocacy and even the appropriateness of the adversarial legal system itself as a method of resolving disputes and doing justice.

In Chapter 3 we go on to consider the way that the profession as a whole, and the way it is regulated, sets the ethical climate for individual lawyers' practices.

Chapters 4 through 10 look at a number of aspects of legal practice – confidentiality, criminal trial practice, civil litigation, negotiation and alternative dispute resolution, handling conflicting loyalties, lawyers' fees and costs, and acting for corporate clients. Each chapter examines in more detail what the four ethical approaches might mean, and which values would be appropriate to apply, in each of these different contexts.[35] In doing so we will critique the extent to which the rules and regulations as they currently stand do a good job of demonstrating appropriate values, and how these rules and regulations influence individual lawyers' capacity to put different values into action in practice. We will also critically analyse current standard practices in the profession and the culture of the legal profession in those areas, to see what values are reflected, whether they are appropriate, and what changes in regulation and ethical behaviour might be desirable in order to promote better values in practice. In each chapter we make extensive use of case studies to illustrate our points and also to provide an opportunity for students (and other readers) to develop their own values-based judgements on the topics covered. The concluding chapter, Chapter 11, returns to the connection between personal values and professional practice in the context of admission to the profession and large law firm employment, and finishes with further discussion of how case studies and ethics assessment can be used to build lawyers' and law students' values awareness and strengthen their ethical resolve.

---

35 Throughout chapters 4–10 we italicise the names of each of the four approaches every time we mention them, to make it easier for readers to see where we apply and discuss each one.

The invitation of this tour inside lawyers' ethics is the opportunity to look systematically behind the rules and the case law. Behind both are deeply held personal differences of approach, the knowledge of which will enrich legal practice and help to make it both more satisfying and less vulnerable to public criticism.

RECOMMENDED FURTHER READING

Ross Cranston, 'Legal Ethics and Professional Responsibility' in Ross Cranston (ed) *Legal Ethics and Professional Responsibility* (Clarendon Press, Oxford, 1995) 1.

Adrian Evans and Josephine Palermo, 'Australian Law Students' Perceptions of Their Values: Interim Results in the First Year – 2001 – of a Three-Year Empirical Assessment' (2002) 5 *Legal Ethics* 103.

Monroe Freedman, *Lawyers' Ethics in an Adversary System* (Bobbs-Merrill, Indianapolis, 1975).

Charles Freid, 'The Lawyer as Friend: The Moral Foundations of the Lawyer-Client Relation' (1976) 85 *Yale Law Journal* 1060.

David Luban, 'The Adversary System Excuse' in David Luban (ed), *The Good Lawyer: Lawyers' Roles and Lawyers' Ethics* (Rowman & Allenheld, Totowa, New Jersey, 1983) 83; reprinted in Richard Abel (ed), *Lawyers: A Critical Reader* (New Press, New York, 1997).

—— *Lawyers and Justice: An Ethical Study* (Princeton University Press, Princeton, 1988) 'Part I. Problems of Conscience: Trade Idioms and Moral Idioms'.

Daniel Markovits, 'Legal Ethics from the Lawyer's Point of View' (2003) 15 *Yale Journal of Law and the Humanities* 209.

—— *A Modern Legal Ethics: Adversarial Advocacy in a Democratic Age* (Princeton University Press, Princeton, 2008).

Donald Nicolson and Julian Webb, *Professional Legal Ethics: Critical Interrogations* (Oxford University Press, Oxford, 1999) 'Ch 7: Justifying Neutral Partisanship'.

Justin Oakley and Dean Cocking, *Virtue Ethics and Professional Roles* (Cambridge University Press, New York, 2001) 121–36.

Noel Preston, *Understanding Ethics* (The Federation Press, Leichhardt, NSW, 2nd edn, 2001).

William Simon, "'Thinking Like a Lawyer" About Ethical Questions' (1998) 27 *Hofstra Law Review* 1.

—— 'Role Differentiation and Lawyers' Ethics: A Critique of Some Academic Perspectives' (2010) 23 *Georgetown Journal of Legal Ethics* 987.

2

ALTERNATIVES TO ADVERSARIAL ADVOCACY

Different Approaches to Lawyers' Ethics

There are four main strands of ethical reasoning or considerations available for lawyers in the context of Australian legal institutions: adversarial advocacy (discussed in the previous chapter); responsible lawyering; moral activism; and ethics of care.[1] (Table 2.1 sets out a summary of the four approaches.) These four approaches are reflected in applied ethics scholarship and in the commonsense 'folk practices' of lawyers. Each emphasises a different value (or bundle of values) that lawyers could or should serve in legal practice. These four approaches are set out in this book as 'ideal types' that emphasise what is distinctive about each approach.

It would be over-simplistic to seek to brand most individual lawyers or applied legal ethics scholars as following one approach or another. In general the four different approaches tend to complement one another and build on an understanding of social ethical frameworks explored in Chapter 1. In order to develop ethical judgement, it is good to consider a scenario or issue from all points of view, and the four approaches are helpful in doing that. In many situations all four approaches will lead to agreement on the right thing to do. In some situations, the considerations mandated by another approach might temper and improve the way in which we might have approached a situation had we applied only one approach. In other situations, careful analysis will show that some ethical considerations should carry more weight than others because of the surrounding circumstances. One objective of this chapter and the previous one is to set out the justifications for the four different types of ethical considerations so that it is clear what assumptions each makes about the circumstances in which it should apply.

Ultimately, however, each of us will have to make hard choices about values and ethical considerations in difficult situations (like the case studies in this book). It is these choices that give each of us our distinctive ethical character, and it is in knowing and consistently following through on our ethical character that we develop virtue. For most lawyers, the ethical choices we make (or want to be able to make) in those 'hard' cases will tend to fall into one or other of the four approaches set out here (or perhaps some combination of them). In practice, the first and second – the adversarial advocacy and responsible lawyering approaches – are the

---

1 For a similar typology of three possible underlying values that legal practice should serve, see Charles Sampford with Christine Parker, 'Legal Regulation, Ethical Standard-Setting, and Institutional Design' in Stephen Parker and Charles Sampford (eds), *Legal Ethics and Legal Practice: Contemporary Issues* (Clarendon Press, Oxford, 1995) 11, 21–4.

Table 2.1: Four Approaches to Legal Ethics

Legal Ethical Type	Social Role of Lawyers	Relationship to Client and Law
Adversarial Advocate (The traditional conception)	Lawyers' ethics are governed by role as advocate in adversarial legal process and complex legal system: Partisanship, loyalty and non-accountability.	Lawyers' duty is to advocate client's interests as zealously as possible within the bounds of the law (barest obligation to legality) – let the chips fall where they may. Extends beyond adversary role to ensuring client autonomy in a complex legal system as required by the rule of law.
Responsible Lawyer (Officer of the court and trustee of the legal system)	Lawyers' ethics governed by role of facilitating the public administration of justice according to law in the public interest.	Duties of advocacy are tempered by duty to ensure integrity of and compliance with the spirit of the law; to ensure that issues are not decided on purely procedural or formal grounds but substantive merits. Lawyer is responsible to make law work as fairly and justly as possible. May need to act as gatekeeper of law and advocate of legal system against client.
Moral Activist (Agent for justice through law reform, public interest lawyering and client counselling)	General ethics, particularly social and political conceptions of justice, moral philosophy and promotion of substantive justice define lawyers' responsibilities.	Lawyers should take advantage of their position to improve justice in two ways: (1) Public interest lawyering and law reform activities to improve access to justice and change the law and legal institutions to make the law more substantively just (in the public interest); (2) Client counselling to seek to persuade clients of the moral thing to do or withdraw if client wants something else.
Ethics of Care (Relational lawyering)	Social role of lawyers is irrelevant. Responsibilities to people, communities and relationships should guide lawyers (and clients) as everybody else.	Preserving relationships and avoiding harm are more important than impersonal justice. The value of law, legal institutions and institutional roles of lawyers and others are derivative on relationships. People and relationships are more important than institutions such as law. The goal of the lawyer-client relationship (like all relationships) should be the moral worth and goodness of both lawyer and client, or at least the nurturing of relationships and community.

most dominant ethical approaches cited in public statements about lawyers' ethics. Many lawyers probably unthinkingly follow the dictates of these two approaches to ethical lawyering, without ever clarifying their own ethical beliefs, or the values that lie beneath them. To practise law successfully over the long term, we believe it is necessary to understand our own values and ethical beliefs. Look at Table 2.1: Can you identify an approach (or approaches) that tends to appeal to you most consistently?

There are attractions in all four approaches. The considerations of adversarial advocacy and responsible lawyering will tend to be the starting point for ethical practice in most ordinary situations. The authors of this book prefer the moral activist approach as the ultimate criterion for ethical choices in tough cases in the life of lawyering. We believe that ultimately as lawyers we are responsible for improving the way justice is done between individuals and the world at large. We are also persuaded by the ethics of care approach which says that ultimately people, our relationships, our psyches and our spiritual connectedness to each other and the world are more important than the law or any other social institution. Therefore ours is a sense of lawyering as adversarial advocate and responsible lawyer, guided by justice and moral activism and tempered by the importance of the relational and spiritual dimensions of life in community.

Our aim in this book is not, however, to persuade readers of our personal and particular views of ethics (although we would be delighted if our example and our other writing had that effect). Rather our aim is to help improve the clarity and integrity of ethical reasoning in lawyering. We recognise that each reader will find a different approach (or way of combining the approaches) attractive and convincing as a way to organise their own career and practices. We suggest, however, that all lawyers can use the four ideal types set out here (see Table 2.1 below) as a self-diagnostic aid in clarifying and critically examining their own ethical preferences as a lawyer, and also in making sure they have explored all the facts of any situation they might face as a lawyer, considered all the relevant ethical considerations, and responded appropriately.[2] Chapter 11 contains a self-assessment tool or scale to allow individual lawyers to determine the relative importance of each ethical type for their own decision-making.

The remainder of this chapter describes each of the three alternatives to adversarial advocacy. At the end of this chapter we set out another hypothetical case study with a series of questions that could form the basis for application of the four ethical approaches, and reflection and discussion with others.

---

2 As per Preston's 'ethics of response' following H Richard Niebuhr: Noel Preston, *Understanding Ethics* (Federation Press, Leichhardt, NSW, 2nd edn, 2001) Ch 4.

Responsible Lawyering: Officer of the Court and Trustee of the Legal System

The adversarial advocate is only one social role that could govern the ethics of lawyers. Another possibility is the responsible lawyer approach. The adversarial advocate approach focuses on the lawyer's role as representative of the client in the legal system. The responsible lawyer approach, by contrast, focuses on the lawyer's role as an officer of the court and guardian of the legal system. The responsible lawyer is still an advocate for the client, but he or she has an overriding duty to maintain the justice and integrity of the legal system, even against client interests, in the public interest. According to this approach to lawyers' ethics:

> ... the wellspring of a lawyer's duties to clients and to the public flows from the legal profession's unique role in society as the trustee for the forms of social order. The forms of social order include not only legislative, judicial and administrative forums, but also the process of private ordering through contract, and the negotiation and drafting of the constitutions of private organisations. Thus what the lawyer does in the privacy of the office may be seen as part of the *public* administration of justice because law is made and applied through lawyer counselling and planning, and often this 'private' law has public impacts as great as any ruling of a high court in a litigation matter. To keep *all* the forms of social order working fairly and with integrity is the obligation of the profession, and each lawyer must place that obligation above any particular client interest contrary to it. Loyalty to the fair process of law is primary and constrains lawyer behaviour on behalf of clients.[3]

Unlike the adversarial advocate, the responsible lawyer focuses on maintaining the institutions of law and justice in their best possible form. Some would argue that obedience to the rules of the legal system is important in itself. But the underlying justification for responsible lawyering, as with adversarial advocacy, is preserving the social goods that the legal system attempts to serve.

It is generally beyond contention that lawyers should obey the letter of the law and should not assist clients in breaking it. The rules of professional responsibility also include rules designed to ensure that lawyers do not abuse the court process on behalf of their clients. But in legal practice there are also many 'grey' areas

---

3 Alvin Esau, 'What Should We Teach? Three Approaches to Professional Responsibility' in Donald Buckingham et al (eds), *Legal Ethics in Canada: Theory and Practice* (Harcourt Brace, Toronto, 1996) 178, 178–9.

where lawyers and their clients have choices about how to interpret the law, the rules of professional responsibility, and whether to act in accordance with the purpose of the law or solely in the interests of the client. In choosing how to navigate those grey areas, the responsible lawyer will act in such a way as to contribute to the effectiveness and enforcement of the substantive law. He or she will not unhesitatingly use loopholes, procedural rules or barely arguable points to frustrate the substance and spirit of the law. Responsible lawyers see the practice of law as a 'public profession' in which lawyers have a mediating function between the client and the law.[4] They certainly advocate for clients' interests, but they also represent the law to their clients, and help clients comply with the law. Responsible lawyering is often to be found among those lawyers who help plan business strategies for clients in such a way that the clients' affairs are in tune with the overall regulatory environment of the business. These lawyers act as 'go-betweens' and help to keep clients and the state in greater harmony than a purely adversarial lawyer might achieve.

Thus, according to the responsible lawyer approach, not only is it desirable for lawyers to be independent of the state, but also to show some autonomy from clients and powerful private interests. Lawyers should not be too dependent on, or too close to, clients. As one legal ethicist has argued:

> ...as people professionally skilled in casuistry, finding loopholes in rules, exploiting any ambiguity and uncertainty, and playing strategic games, lawyers...can completely sabotage the framework. Clients who can afford to pay for such skills can rapidly exhaust adversaries who cannot, and thus turn the legal system into a device for evading the very rules it is designed to enforce, or worse, into a medium for extortion and oppression of the weak by the strong.[5]

As another ethicist argues, 'If lawyers do not moderate their clients' tendency to extract the maximum advantage from the legal system, we can expect legal outcomes to become increasingly skewed in favour of resourceful parties, thus undermining the legitimacy of legal institutions'.[6] Since the market will always be such that some people will be able to buy more than others, there must be some limits to what they can buy. Responsible lawyers will say no to those who are prepared to use their economic power to compromise the integrity of the justice system. Because the legal system depends on shared ideas about justice, lawyers who exercise ethical judgements that go beyond 'pure' legal advice in order to

4 See, eg, Robert Gordon, 'Corporate Law Practice as a Public Calling' (1990) 49 *Maryland Law Review* 255.

5 Ibid 259.

6 Robert Nelson, *Partners with Power: The Social Transformation of the Large Law Firm* (University of California Press, Berkeley, 1988) 234.

interpret and apply the law might also provide more prescient and strategic advice about how the law is likely to be enforced and interpreted than lawyers who do not consider the ethical perspective.

For the responsible lawyer, like the adversarial advocate, personal moral beliefs are generally irrelevant. Instead the responsible lawyer will look to the ethics inherent in their role as officer of the court and in the law itself. This approach does not see lawyers as responsible for positively pursuing substantive justice according to some external standard (unlike the moral activist approach, below). The responsible lawyer generally looks for justice within the framework of the existing legal system. It does require that lawyers take those actions that seem likely to promote 'legal justice', that is, the basic values of the legal system. It sees the lawyer's role as helping clients to pursue justice according to law, no more and no less.[7]

For example, Brad Wendel argues that the ethical significance of lawyering revolves around law's political authority as a way of coordinating compliance with the demands of morality in complex communities. This requires lawyers to maintain 'fidelity to law' as a moral enterprise in and of itself. This ethical approach puts the morality of law at the centre, as opposed to both traditional formulations of the standard conception that put client autonomy and access to law at the centre of the lawyer's role, and traditional critiques of the standard conception that argue for general accounts of justice and morality to trump the lawyer's role as partisan.[8]

Thus in Case Study 1.1, the case of the philanthropist QC and the tobacco company in Chapter 1, the responsible lawyer would have no trouble with representing tobacco companies in putting any fair arguments to the court that might protect their interests. However, the responsible lawyer might pull back from running fanciful arguments all the way to the highest court in Australia if they have little or no prospects of success. The responsible lawyer might also prefer to avoid the appearance of bias from regularly acting for tobacco companies over many years on the one hand, while also taking on a public role on the board of an anti-cancer organisation that is clearly anti-smoking on the other hand.

Responsible lawyering need not require lawyers to self-righteously force rigid interpretations of the law on unwilling clients. It does mean lawyers who creatively combine technical skill, a sense of social and legal responsibility and the vigorous pursuit of clients' interests; lawyers who do not demand 'dumb, literal obedience to every rule but creative forms of compliance that, although aiming to minimise cost and disruption to the company, effectively still realise the regulation's basic purposes'.[9] Over the last 10 to 20 years many corporate lawyers, especially

---

7 See William Simon, *The Practice of Justice: A Theory of Lawyers' Ethics* (Harvard University Press, Cambridge, MA, 1998) 9–11, 138–69 for an excellent account of this type of approach.

8 W Bradley Wendel, *Lawyers and Fidelity to Law* (Princeton University Press, Princeton, 2011).

9 Gordon, 'Corporate Law Practice', 277.

in-house counsel, in Australia and elsewhere have recognised that this type of stance for advising corporate clients is not only more personally satisfying, but also more helpful to their corporate clients than a purely adversarial approach to lawyering. Lawyers of this type do not confine themselves to being 'the ministry for stopping [suspect] business'.[10] They also engage in the creative task of designing systems for ensuring legal compliance and public legitimacy that add value to corporate products and services, improve business efficiency and enhance corporate image. Consider the way that the in-house counsel at the Australian headquarters of a multinational waste management firm considered his role. Following some issues concerning price-fixing and market-sharing conduct in the waste management industry in the US, one of his major areas of responsibility became compliance with competition and consumer protection law. This covered issues such as making sure the company's sales people and operatives were not dividing up the market with other firms and not misleading potential customers about their services. He described his role in a way consonant with the responsible lawyer approach:

> You need a fair and just outlook in how a business should be operated ... There must be an underlying sense of fairness in your character ... that you shouldn't be overly opportunistic, smart and technical. It needs to be in your character to go looking for fair solutions to problems rather than just technical legal ones. A lot of lawyers love to be wise guys and to hit people over the head with the technical stuff. But in this work it is not a question of whether something is right or wrong in the [technical] legal sense but of whether it could be perceived right or wrong [in the spirit of the law]. In a competitive industry it is to our detriment in the long run if we are seen as a bunch of wise guys.[11]

The responsible lawyering approach clearly addresses the problem of lawyers helping clients to escape, manipulate or abuse the legal system. Yet it also puts lawyers in danger of not adequately serving clients' goals and interests. As Katherine Kruse observes, 'over-zealous partisanship occurs too infrequently among lawyers whose clients are unable to pay handsomely for hourly work; and it is received

---

10 This phrase was used by compliance counsel for an insurance company in an interview with one of the authors (Sydney, 7 January 1997). See generally Christine Parker, *The Open Corporation: Effective Self-Regulation and Democracy* (Cambridge University Press, Cambridge, 2002).

11 Lawyer quoted in C Parker, *The Open Corporation*, 172. On preventive lawyering by in-house corporate lawyers see also Robert Gordon and William Simon, 'The Redemption of Professionalism?' in Robert Nelson, David Trubek and Robert Solomon (eds), *Lawyers' Ideals /Lawyers' Practices: Transformations in the American Legal Profession* (Cornell University Press, Ithaca, New York, 1992) 230, 252–3; Robert Rosen, 'The Inside Counsel Movement, Professional Judgment and Organizational Representation' (1989) 64 *Indiana Law Journal* 479.

with too much suspicion by even well-heeled clients when they get their billing statements'.[12] Probably for this reason there is no strong tradition in Australian or other common law legal systems which emphasises the responsible lawyering ideal of duty to the justice of law without also emphasising the advocacy ideal of duty to client. The responsible lawyering and adversarial advocacy approaches are often held in tension with one another in professional conduct rules and widely accepted ideas of legal ethics. This is reflected in the way that debates about ethical issues for lawyers are frequently framed as a question of how to balance the lawyer's duty to the client with the lawyer's duty to the court or, more broadly, to the integrity of the law. Yet they are also recognised as complementing one another. Both approaches derive a role for the lawyer from the system for administration of justice, and in a sense, both roles are required by our system of administration of justice. Radically adversarial, 'loophole' lawyering, untempered by the duty to the law and the court, cannot ultimately be justified by the legal system because it is destructive of the legal system.

Yet neither the adversarial advocacy approach, with its focus on individual client rights, nor the responsible lawyer approach, with its emphasis on preserving the justice of the law as it stands, leaves much scope for critique of the law in accordance with standards of social justice external to the law. The responsible lawyer approach, in particular, allows little possibility for testing the limits of the law, showing up its absurdity or pursuing a corrupt administration on a 'no holds barred' basis. In that sense it is an essentially conservative ethical approach. Moral activism, by contrast, majors on social critique and promoting reform of the law in the public interest.

Moral Activism: Agents for Justice with Clients and the Law

The second alternative approach to adversarial advocacy is to argue that it is not appropriate for lawyers to have a special ethics defined by role at all. Rather they should abide by ordinary ethics, although the application of those ethics to their practice as lawyers may have particular features. Two approaches to lawyers' ethics that propose different ways in which general ethics should apply to legal practice

12 Katherine Kruse, 'Client-Centered Answers to Legal Ethics Problems' in Christine Parker (ed) 'Forum: Philosophical Legal Ethics, Ethics, Morals and Jurisprudence' 13 (2010) *Legal Ethics* 165, 187.

are the 'moral activist' and 'ethics of care' approaches. The ethics of care is discussed in the following section. Moral activism requires that mainstream consequentialist and, to a lesser extent, deontological theories of ethics, and of justice in particular, should be applied to legal practice.

Moral activism argues that lawyers should do good according to general theories of ethics – whichever theory the individual lawyer finds attractive. Of course this need not be a formal philosophical theory – it may simply be the lawyer's personal ethics and philosophy of life. In particular, because the legal system is intended to do justice, lawyers should be particularly concerned with doing justice. Thus moral activism encourages lawyers to have their own convictions about what it means to do justice in different circumstances and to seek out ways to act out those convictions as lawyers. They cannot escape moral accountability for their actions by playing the role of adversarial advocate or even responsible lawyer. American legal ethicist David Luban, who coined the term 'moral activism', describes what it is likely to mean in practice in the following way:

> Moral activism...involves law reform – explicitly putting one's *phronesis*, one's savvy, to work for the common weal – and client counselling...And client counselling in turn means discussing with the client the rightness or wrongness of her projects, and the possible impact of those projects on 'the people,' in the same matter-of-fact and (one hopes) un-moralistic manner that one discusses the financial aspects of a representation. It may involve considerable negotiation about what will and won't be done in the course of a representation; it may eventuate in a lawyer's accepting a case only on condition that it takes a certain shape, or threatening to withdraw from a case if a client insists on pursuing a project that the lawyer finds unworthy. Crucially, moral activism envisions the possibility that it is the lawyer rather than the client who will eventually modify her moral stance...But, ultimately, the encounter may result in a parting of ways or even a betrayal by the lawyer of a client's projects, if the lawyer persists in the conviction that they are immoral or unjust.[13]

Unlike the responsible lawyer approach, moral activism is not confined by the idea of justice set out in the legal system – instead it contemplates that the legal system may need to be changed to become more just, and that lawyers may have a responsibility to do so. Moral activists argue that lawyers should use legal practice to change people, institutions and the law to make them conform more to general ideals of social and political justice. It is a tradition of active citizenship by lawyers to actively improve justice in ways that simply doing their duty by paying clients

13 David Luban, *Lawyers and Justice: An Ethical Study* (Princeton University Press, Princeton, 1988) 173–4.

and the legal system, as per the adversarial advocate and responsible lawyer approaches, leaves untouched. To the extent that the law and legal processes as they stand coincide with the lawyer's ideals of justice, then the moral activist lawyer will behave similarly to the responsible lawyer. But the moral activist lawyer does not see themselves as necessarily confined by a duty to the law where the law is unjust. They see themselves as responsible for doing justice even if that involves changing or challenging the law and, from time to time, its practitioners. Similarly where a moral activist lawyer believes in the justice of a particular client's cause, then they will behave like an adversarial advocate to the extent even of exploiting loopholes and testing the limits of the law to establish their client's cause. But a moral activist will not advocate zealously for clients where they believe their cause is not just.

Many of the obvious examples of moral activist lawyers are often those from the social democratic left (eg those lawyers who worked for little or for free to represent Indigenous clients in ground-breaking native title claims or stolen generation cases). However, a lawyer could equally be a moral activist for other causes and political beliefs. For example, in the case of the philanthropist QC and the tobacco company, a moral activist lawyer might have a strong belief that it would be wrong to act for a company that makes money out of selling a product that is addictive and fatal to a large proportion of its customers, to help them defeat public health oriented government policies such as plain packaging laws, and refuse to act. Another moral activist lawyer might take a different view and see the liberty of businesses to advertise and sell whatever products people want to buy, and the liberty of individuals to choose to use drugs that might harm themselves – and themselves only, as of the essence of a liberal democracy even though the lawyer him or herself does not do so for health reasons. A lawyer taking this view might see this as an important test case for the Constitution about whether a government can completely prohibit a certain product or not. In such a case, a moral activist approach would suggest that a lawyer should make a choice about which justice principles are most compelling and most important to pursue in the particular circumstances.

As is evident in the quotation from David Luban above, a moral activist approach to legal practice can manifest itself in several ways. First, a moral activist lawyer may try to represent only those clients who represent 'worthy causes' or those who are often the subject of injustice. Lawyers who choose to do legal aid work for a reduced fee, to pursue a career in the legal aid or community legal centre sector, or to volunteer their time for poor clients are common examples of moral activism.

Moral activism can also lead lawyers to become involved in more politicised law reform activities and representation of people and causes to create legal and social change. In this type of 'public interest' lawyering, the lawyer is as likely to seek out the client to fit the cause as the client is to seek out the lawyer. In extreme cases, the participation of individual clients is almost subordinated to the bigger cause such as a class action (against a corporation in a product liability case) or constitutional challenge (to government actions). Consider the litigation concerning the Australian government's actions in preventing 433 asylum seekers on board the Norwegian vessel, MV *Tampa*, from disembarking on Australian soil. The Victorian Public Interest Law Clearing House (PILCH) organised a team of private lawyers (a commercial law firm and senior and junior barristers) to act for free in seeking the release and delivery onto Australian soil of the asylum seekers. Because it was impossible to contact the asylum seekers on board the ship, the Victorian Council for Civil Liberties (Liberty Victoria, itself acting through public interest lawyers) became the client. In effect the public interest lawyers themselves defined the cause and the shape of the litigation in the absence of instructions from the asylum seeker clients. The Directors of PILCH comment about the case:

> Striking were the roles of the lawyers, and how they were perceived both within the legal profession and more broadly. 'How much money do you make out of defending these worthless scum?' senior counsel was asked by a member of the public. On another occasion it was '[w]hy don't you and all of your tree-hugging, libertarian, do-gooder, wanker buddies go to Afghanistan and practise your law?' In contrast, his Honour Justice French (one of the judges in the majority in the Full Court [who denied the application]) characterised the lawyers as 'acting according to the highest ideals of the law' and of '[serving] the rule of law and so the whole community'... The actions of the lawyers were bold. Amongst other things, these were proceedings against the highest echelons of government. They involved a challenge to executive power to ensure the lawful exercise of discretion and concerned conspicuous and controversial government policy. The issues were highly politicised, as the events unfolded in the weeks leading up to a federal election campaign. There is a hunger [amongst lawyers] for public interest work that is interesting, challenging, even confronting and political, and involves direct contact with 'real' people. There is also a desire to see an outcome or a challenge to the status quo, not just on a micro level for individual clients, but also on a larger scale.[14]

Not every lawyer always has the time and opportunity to get involved in public interest cases for justice causes that they really believe in. A second way in which moral activism can manifest itself is in the way that lawyers represent and advise their clients, even those clients who have not necessarily been chosen because they have a just cause. As proposed in the quotation from David Luban above, moral

---

14 Samantha Burchell and Emma Hunt, 'From Conservatism to Activism: The Evolution of the Public Interest Law Clearing House in Victoria' (2003) 28 *Alternative Law Journal* 8, 11.

activist lawyers seek to argue with and persuade clients to do what the lawyer considers the just thing, always bearing in mind the possibility that the client might also persuade the lawyer about what justice involves. Luban illustrates this style of law practice by invoking a famous instance of Abraham Lincoln's advice to one of his law practice clients:

> Yes, we can doubtless gain your case for you; we can set a whole neighbourhood at loggerheads; we can distress a widowed mother and her six fatherless children and thereby get you six hundred dollars to which you seem to have a legal claim, but which rightfully belongs, it appears to me, as much to the woman and her children as it does to you. You must remember that some things legally right are not morally right. We shall not take your case, but will give you a little advice for which we will charge you nothing. You seem to be a sprightly energetic man; we would advise you to try your hand at making six hundred dollars in some other way.[15]

Contrast this quotation with Lord Brougham's defence of Queen Caroline, quoted in Chapter 1.

As its label suggests, moral activism gives lawyers a much more proactive role in ensuring justice than either responsible lawyering or adversarial advocacy give. Indeed the justice of our current legal system is at least partially dependent on the fact that there are lawyers (motivated by moral activism) who are willing to work for reduced fees or voluntarily, for clients and causes who cannot afford any other lawyer; lawyers who seek out and are committed to public interest causes; lawyers who will fight battles no one else will fight; and lawyers who seek to reform the law, the legal system and their own profession in the interests of justice. Yet moral activism as a total approach to legal practice can also be criticised for neglecting the wisdom of adversarial advocacy – that anyone should be entitled to legal representation and the chance to argue their case in court without first having to persuade a lawyer that their case is worthwhile. Furthermore, moral activism runs the risk of encouraging lawyers to act without regard to law and procedural fairness when they do find a client they believe in. Unlike responsible lawyering, moral activism prescribes no particular duty to the law and the legal system where a lawyer believes their cause is just. Finally, as an ethical approach to lawyering, moral activism has a tendency to place the lawyer's commitment to an ideal of justice above the client. Indeed, moral activist lawyering in practice is sometimes criticised as a demonstration of a lawyer's ego that undermines their commitment to justice. The final approach – the ethics of care – puts the focus back on the lawyer's responsibilities to the client and their relationships.

---

15 Luban, *Lawyers and Justice*, 174.

Ethics of Care: Relational Lawyering

The ethics of care, like moral activism, emphasises the integration of personal ethics with legal practice. While moral activism proposes that lawyers should act in a way calculated to best promote social and political justice, the ethics of care, by contrast, is more concerned with personal and relational ethics. The ethics of care focuses on lawyers' responsibilities to people, communities and relationships. Often this approach is linked to the work of Carol Gilligan, which proposed that traditional rights-oriented theories of the development of moral reasoning privileged typically male forms of ethical reasoning and ignored the care-based ethics that many women tend to use:[16]

> Whereas the ethic of justice is founded on the idea that everyone should be treated equally, the ethic of care requires that no one should be hurt. Whereas men tend to stand on principle and act according to people's rights irrespective of the consequences, women are more pragmatic, being more concerned to uphold relationships and protect their loved ones from harm. Whereas the ethic of justice assumes that one can resolve moral dilemmas by abstract and universalistic moral reasoning, the ethic of care requires due attention to context and the specific circumstances of each moral dilemma. And in resolving such dilemmas, men tend to rank ethical principles, whereas women attempt to address the concrete needs of all and to ensure that if anyone is going to be harmed it should be those who can best bear the harm.[17]

The empirical claim made by Gilligan as to whether an ethics of care is a typically female ethics has been controversial for obvious reasons. But the general contours

---

16 Carol Gilligan, *In a Different Voice: Psychological Theory and Women's Development* (Harvard University Press, Cambridge, Massachusetts, 1982). For influential applications of Gilligan's work to lawyers' ethics, see Rand Jack and Dana Crowley Jack, *Moral Vision and Professional Decisions: The Changing Values of Women and Men Lawyers* (Cambridge University Press, Cambridge, 1989); Carrie Menkel-Meadow, 'Portia in a Different Voice: Speculations on a Women's Lawyering Process' (1985) *Berkeley Women's Law Journal* 1. For further discussion, see Carrie Menkel-Meadow, 'Portia Redux: Another Look at Gender Feminism and Legal Ethics' in S Parker and C Sampford (eds) *Legal Ethics and Legal Practice* 25. For evidence that there is a difference between the values orientation of male and female law students in Australia on some issues, see Adrian Evans and Josephine Palermo, 'Australian Law Students' Perceptions of their Values: Interim Results in the First Year – 2001 – of a Three-Year Empirical Assessment' (2002) 5 *Legal Ethics* 103.

17 Caroline Maughan and Julian Webb, *Lawyering Skills and the Legal Process* (Butterworths, London, 1995) 36.

of an ethics of care have developed a life beyond the gender debate. The ethics of care has been generally accepted as an alternative approach to ethical reasoning in general, and to the application of ethics in legal practice in particular.

Legal ethicist Thomas Shaffer also developed the language of an 'ethics of care' to describe his deeply humanist, relationship and faith-based application of ethics to legal practice.[18] Because it is a contextual style of ethical reasoning, the ethics of care can be difficult to grasp. One teacher of legal ethics has explained Shaffer's rich descriptions of what it involves in the following way:

> The ethics of care is risky. Shaffer attempts to convey its meaning through a series of contrasting terms and through a cast of contrasting characters. The ethics of care is not representation but ministry; it rests not on loyalty but on fidelity, not on contract but on covenant…Ministry focuses on the relationship between lawyer and client; it makes relationships central. Shaffer's view of relationships is teleological; they are goal directed, 'going somewhere'. He argues their proper goal is conversion, conversion to truth and goodness. Achieving a conversion requires movement, change. Inducing change requires an ability to persuade. Those who wish to persuade must be open to persuasion. These ideas diverge radically from traditional ideas of law practice. It is not the standard view that lawyer-client relationships are in their essence commitments by a person toward another's growth toward goodness and toward his own growth. It is not the standard view that one's effectiveness as a lawyer might be measured by the strength of that commitment rather than by the number of cases he wins. If growth through relationships is central, morals and moral growth often will be the subjects of relationships…[19]

In both Gilligan's and Shaffer's conceptions, the ethics of care for lawyers focuses on trying to serve the best interests of both clients and others in a holistic way that incorporates moral, emotional and relational dimensions of a problem into the legal solution. It is particularly concerned with preserving or restoring (even reconciling) relationships and avoiding harm. It sees relationships, including both the client's network of relationships and the lawyer's own relationships with colleagues, family and community, as more important than the institutions of the law or systemic and

---

18 Thomas L Shaffer, *On Being a Christian and a Lawyer: Law for the Innocent* (Brigham Young University Press, Provo, Utah, 1981); Thomas L Shaffer and Robert F Cochran, *Lawyers, Clients and Moral Responsibility* (West Publishing Co, St Paul, Minnesota, 1994). See also Reid Mortensen, 'The Lawyer as Parent: Sympathy, Care and Character in Lawyers' Ethics' (2009) 12 *Legal Ethics* 1.

19 Mark Weisberg, 'Integrating Personal and Professional Lives: An Essay on Thomas Shaffer's *On Being a Christian and a Lawyer*' (1984) 9 *Queen's Law Journal* 367, 375.

social ideas of justice and ethics. An ethics of care will discard fundamental rules of professional conduct if circumstances seem to demand it. Consider for example the following case study:

> You are acting for a mother of three small children in a divorce and intervention order matter. Your client has previously shown you some old photographs of bruises and marks on the children which she claims were inflicted not by their father, but by her new boyfriend. One of the children now has blurred vision. Your client now instructs you to stop all legal proceedings as she intends to return to the children's father with her children. You believe the children will be at risk if this happens but you know 'mandatory reporting' does not apply to lawyers in your state. Would you break client confidentiality and inform the relevant welfare department of your fears?[20]

In their survey of 700 recent Australian law students in the *Australian Lawyers' Values Study*, Evans and Palermo found that most (59.3%) reported that they would breach client confidentiality in this scenario.[21] (A set of questions and guide for discussing this scenario are provided in Chapter 11.)

While few lawyers might label their approach an 'ethics of care', the concerns that motivate academic discussion of the ethics of care have also been tremendously influential in legal practice in recent times in incremental, if not revolutionary ways. There are at least three practical ways in which 'ethics of care' concerns have influenced legal practice in recent times.[22]

First, the ethics of care encourages lawyers to take a more *holistic* view of clients and their problems. Thus lawyers following the ethics of care are likely to spend more time listening to and discussing the broader concerns of clients and the way that legal issues are likely to impact on other aspects of their lives and relationships. At the very least, the ethics of care encourages lawyers and clients to consider the non-legal and non-financial consequences (eg reputational, relational and psychological) of different legal options. Some lawyers even refer clients for advice or counselling for the non-legal aspects of their legal problems or incorporate relational and psychological wellbeing more explicitly into legal representation (eg through movements such as therapeutic jurisprudence).[23] Holistic lawyering is also a feature of many clinical approaches to legal education. More particularly, the ethics of care encourages lawyers and clients to see ethics and the moral goodness

---

20 Evans and Palermo, 'Australian Law Students' Perceptions of their Values', 114.
21 Ibid 115.
22 The three ways are based on Maughan and Webb, *Lawyering Skills*, 118–20.
23 See M King, 'Applying Therapeutic Jurisprudence from the Bench' (2003) 28 *Alternative Law Journal* 172.

of the client and lawyer as an explicit part of the lawyer-client relationship. It assumes that lawyers and clients will want to discuss the ethical implications of different courses of action, as well as the social, psychological, financial and other consequences. But it does not presume that the lawyer's initial view of the ethics of a client's situation is automatically correct. Rather it emphasises dialogue about ethics and respect for each other's positions.

Thus, secondly, the ethics of care emphasises dialogue between lawyer and client and *participatory* approaches to lawyering. The lawyer-client relationship is built on mutual trust and shared knowledge. At the most mundane level, this means that lawyers have a responsibility to make sure that clients understand the consequences, costs and uncertainties associated with the various alternative courses of action available to them so that the client can choose which option to pursue in an informed way. More ambitiously, the ethics of care puts a premium on the lawyer spending time listening to the broader concerns of the client so that the legal solution they offer fits in with the other aspects of the client's life. For example, the ethics of care is supported by the legislated costs disclosure process (see Chapter 9). It also requires the lawyer and client to agree as to any course of action that is taken. Neither can decide for the other – the (fully informed, authentic) consent of both to any course of action is considered necessary, as the lawyer-client relationship is seen as a partnership in which both parties are equally responsible. Therefore legal advice is likely to be offered in dialogue with the client, rather than the client being told what to do. But at the same time, the lawyer will not take actions in representing a client that the lawyer does not feel ethically (and generally) comfortable with for him or herself.

Thirdly, because the ethics of care asks lawyers (and clients) to see themselves within a network of relationships and to understand the feelings and experiences of others within those relationships, they are likely to look for *non-adversarial ways to resolve disputes* and preserve relationships, if possible. Therefore lawyers will recommend dialogic, non-litigious means to resolve disputes such as negotiation, mediation and other forms of alternative dispute resolution. There will be less emphasis on positional bargaining and more on creative, 'win-win' resolutions. It has been suggested that following an ethics of care, cases that do go to court 'would be conducted on the basis of "good faith" principles. These would suggest a need for: (a) more dialogue and fuller disclosure between parties; (b) respect for the interests of other parties, resulting in avoidance of trial and pre-trial adversarial tactics; and (c) less intimidating advocacy when in court'.[24] Outside of the dispute resolution context, the ethics of care lawyer is also likely to take a collaborative, preventive, problem-solving approach to deals and transactions.

24 Maughan and Webb, *Lawyering Skills*, 119.

Each of these three aspects of legal practice – holism, lawyer-client participation, and a preventive, problem-solving approach – are now regularly advised in books, seminars and, to an extent, conduct rules on legal interviewing, advising and 'client care'. Many lawyers have chosen to devote themselves to advocating and promoting alternative dispute resolution precisely because they (and their clients) are disenchanted with adversarialism as a way of resolving disputes and prefer to be part of a problem-solving, relationship-preserving way of practising law, whether the concern is with business or family relationships. Similarly, the profession as a whole has also recognised that 'client care' – effective communication with clients and participation by clients in decision-making – is necessary for delivering legal services effectively, and preventing client complaints and public disenchantment with the profession. These are everyday ways in which the ethics of care have influenced legal practice.

Consider also the following description of a lawyer-client relationship as an example of a more unusual way in which an ethics of care might be demonstrated:

> My first legal client in St Kilda, in March 1985, was a sex worker named Julie. She arrived at St Kilda Baptist Church, which surprising as it might sound, houses a legal office, five minutes before her case was due to start at the St Kilda Court … I hurriedly threw on my coat and we started walking to the old St Kilda Court … I could not help noticing that she was sporting an ugly black eye, with bruising extending down over the cheek bone and towards her chin. I thought she had been callously bashed. I was wrong. I asked her cautiously and sympathetically how she had received the bruising. Julie told me bluntly that her nerves had got to her the previous night when she realised that she might go to prison because of her many prior convictions for theft and prostitution, and so she had attempted to shoot up in her arm. After a number of failed attempts to locate a vein, she had got angry, and in desperation had injected heroin into a vein in her cheek. I inwardly freaked, but tried to look unshocked … My plea in mitigation of the offence convinced the magistrate to give her one more chance before prison and he imposed yet another fine. Julie was ecstatic and told me indelicately how many clients it would take to pay out the fine … She planted a big kiss on my cheek and graciously invited me out for lunch. I must confess to some deep-seated, middle-class ambivalence, and I hesitated before accepting … She replied with delight that she knew a soup kitchen down the road that provided a great free lunch … My judgements of Julie dissolved when she told me how she had been raped at fifteen by one of many different men who had passed through her mother's life and home. She felt so 'dirty' that she decided she would never let any man do that to her again. She would at least make them pay! I understand how in a tragically coherent way she was taking back power over her life. Who was I to judge? [We arrived] at the meal program.

> Unannounced, she commanded silence by telling everyone, including those serving, to shut up because she wanted to introduce her lawyer, who was the best legal eagle in town. I politely waved to the many street people gathering for lunch and lined up and got my dinner.[25]

The narrator is a lawyer, who also happens to be a minister of religion. His care for his client's legal rights, but also the rest of her life, is obvious from his description of his encounter with her, and the way in which he is willing to enter into her life. But the care and respect that this lawyer shows his client is met by an equal care and respect shown by the client towards the lawyer in telling him her story and taking him to lunch to meet her community. Consistent with the ethics of care, the human, relational aspects of the lawyer-client interaction are here considered central by both lawyer and client.

In the case of the philanthropist QC and the tobacco company – Case Study 1.1 in Chapter 1 – an ethics of care approach would require the barrister to consider not only what was in the best interests (including for the moral worthiness) of his potential client, but also the ramifications of taking on this client for his own relationships within his family and community. In relation to the client, the ethics of care is concerned with humans and human feelings, not artificial, legal persons such as companies. So an ethics of care approach would not concern itself with the economic rights of a company to keep marketing a product, regardless of whether the product is seen as helpful or harmful to society. The ethics of care would expect the lawyer to look for the individual human and relational dimensions of the work to try to make sure that humans and good relationships are put first. Thus a lawyer taking an ethics of care approach might seek to engage the tobacco company executives as individuals to find out how they see their own responsibilities to and care for the health and authority of those who buy their products. An ethics of care lawyer will aim to make sure that their own practice as a lawyer enriches or at least does not detract from the moral worth and care of those he or she deals with. Such a lawyer might be concerned to find alternative ways to meet public health goals that do not involve contracted litigation or excessive legislation. They might be particularly concerned in this case that the prospects of success in the High Court are very low and in the meantime relationships and the reputation of caring for smokers will be further damaged. Once one starts to apply the ethics of care to a situation like this, it becomes obvious that a lawyer prioritising this approach would probably tend not to specialise in higher court litigation in the first place, but rather in the practice of preventive law and dispute resolution.

25 Tim Costello, *Streets of Hope: Finding God in St Kilda* (Allen & Unwin, St Leonards, NSW, 1998), 1–3.

The ethics of care also requires a potential lawyer to ask what impact the representation would have on their own personal relationships and community. In this case, the QC does indeed do a lot of caring in his personal life through involvement with various charitable purposes to which he gives substantially and encourages others to give. In deciding whether to act for tobacco companies, from an ethics of care perspective such a lawyer might consider whether that representation would be a betrayal of those charitable causes and the people he has worked with and helped as part of that. For example, he might want to consider how his relationships with the fundraising board of the cancer hospital would function if on the one hand he continues to represent tobacco companies and on the other hand he happens to be sitting on the board alongside a representative of the hospital's patients who had lung cancer caused by smoking and is a passionate anti-smoking activist.

The ethics of care, in line with a virtue ethics approach, suggests that a lawyer's fundamental moral character carries through from his or her work as a lawyer to his or her relationships and activities outside of work. An ethics of care lawyer would not want to do legal work (or to do it in such a way) that they could not explain and feel comfortable with explaining to their friends or children, or associates in a charitable, political or religious community to whom they feel loyalty. The QC in Case Study 1.1 would therefore need to think through whether it was possible to continue acting for tobacco companies in a way that he could 'own' and explain without embarrassment to people at the cancer hospital, or whether this would be, practically speaking, impossible.

The ethics of care approach is more focused on the client's best interests than the moral activist or responsible lawyer approaches. However, unlike the adversarial advocate approach, it sees the client's best interests in the context of the client's network of relationships. The moral activist sees the individual client as more dispensable in the cause of justice and social change. The ethics of care approach is more interested in personal change than social change. The caring lawyer wants the client to become the best person they can be and intends to be active in that relationship. In that sense the ethics of care is as concerned with the ethics of the client as with the ethics of the lawyer, and it sees them as being inter-dependent. However, the ethics of care approach can have quite a conservative impact. Because the emphasis is on the goodness and worth of the individual client and preserving relationships, caring does not necessarily focus on the systemic injustices in a situation; and because a caring lawyer can tend to avoid conflict, they might downplay the importance of activism and adversarialism to achieve larger scale legal and political change. Yet in the final analysis, lawyers who address larger scale and systemic injustices are necessary to create the conditions in which caring relationships can flourish between autonomous people who can choose their own goals and values.

Conclusion

Most lawyers are unlikely to talk in terms of 'adversarial advocacy', 'responsible lawyering', 'moral activism' or the 'ethics of care'. Unless this conceptual language is explored in law school, they are even less likely to talk about character and virtue. But who we happen to be in a character sense and who we are trying to be are nevertheless live issues as we struggle to reconcile, for example, why we might help a tobacco company to sell its toxic product while advocating for better lung cancer care through sitting on the board of a cancer hospital.

Knowing what makes your life worth living and, for example, whether a particular virtue is most important to you are powerful tools in the self-understanding required to practice law in a fulfilling and therefore successful manner. We all implicitly act on intuitions and personal philosophies of life and lawyering. The challenge is to turn our implicit understandings into explicit self-knowledge by one means or another. The logic in one or more of these four approaches provides one such avenue. Because they are based on applied legal ethics theory as well as underlying social ethical frameworks, these four ethical approaches have some theoretical coherence and are capable of providing us with a principled set of considerations that we ought to respond to in deciding what to do in any particular situation.

These four approaches can be seen as options on an a la carte menu – each of us could choose which approach we prefer for the purpose of guiding our own lives as lawyers and for assessing others. Or they could be seen as the tools and ingredients available for creating our own individual dishes – there are a range of arguments and considerations available which can be combined and used in a variety of ways, each unique to each of us in the circumstances of our own lives. But each approach requires a conscious response from us – a decision about whether to use it in each situation and if not, why not; or if so, how? Some of the most thoughtful commentators on legal ethics and the skill of teaching legal ethics argue that the key to understanding and learning legal ethics is a process of judgement: '[M]oral decision making involves identifying which principle is most important given the particularities of the situation ... reducing judgement to rules or formulas lands us in an infinite regress of rules'.[26]

Moral judgement that goes beyond rules and formulas is likely to be messy. The approaches set out here provide a series of questions and considerations that can help us structure the mess. But it is up to each of us to decide what to 'cook' with them. What combination of ethical approaches resonates most strongly with you in the following case study?

---

26 David Luban and Michael Milleman, 'Good Judgment: Ethics Teaching in Dark Times' (1995) 9 *Georgetown Journal of Legal Ethics* 31, 39.

CASE STUDY 2.1   A LAW FIRM'S ETHICS POLICY

You are a relatively new partner at a successful general practice law firm based in the capital city in your state. Your firm has grown a lot in the last few years but, rather than making everyone in the firm happy about its success, the growth and change has caused an identity crisis. The firm started as a small boutique commercial practice with a small number of regular clients in the technology and entertainment businesses that the lawyers knew and worked with from start-up to success. In recent years the firm has rapidly added a substantial general commercial and litigation practice that is now dominating the firm. Many of the lawyers who originally joined the firm because they wanted to work for a small, progressive, creative firm with interesting clients are unhappy about this direction.

The partners want their firm to maintain a distinct identity. However, they also want to grow to become one of the largest and most successful firms. In order to do this, they want to make sure they attract and retain the brightest, most ambitious and creative young lawyers and law graduates to come and work for the firm and commit themselves to building up the firm's practice.

The partners have realised that in order to address their firm's identity crisis and retain the young lawyers they want to keep in the firm, one important and wholly original strategy will be to develop and publicise an ethics policy for the whole firm that clearly defines which clients the firm will and will not act for, and what they will do for them. Their concern about their firm's identity is genuine, but capital city lawyering is very competitive and they know they must find a way to distinguish themselves responsibly from everyone else. There is not a large firm in existence that uses its website to stand out ethically, but the partners are persuaded that they can attract the right sort of clients (who want expertise and loyalty, but not spin or dishonesty – and who will pay their account in time) if their website emphasises ethical propriety. Thus they are convinced that they can make a virtue out of necessity by creating a clear ethical 'brand' identity for the purposes of attracting both clients and lawyers.

You have only been a partner for a year or so and already have a reputation for being good at listening to the concerns of the junior lawyers and communicating these to the partnership. You have therefore been given the task of listening to the lawyers' various concerns about the way the firm is currently operating, and making the first draft of the suggested ethics policy for the firm. That draft ethics policy will then be debated and finessed by the whole firm.

You have already started talking to junior lawyers about their concerns. Among the ethical concerns you have heard about are:

Robert did not want to represent a company that manufactures gambling machines because he has seen in his own family how damaging a gambling addiction can be. He was in a section of the firm where he was assigned to a file representing a gambling machine manufacturer, and did manage to arrange to move to another section. He says: 'It took me about eight months to work my way out of this assignment. The way I did it was by playing squash with this one partner and telling him I was interested in (his area of practice).'[27]

Jasmine says that she was surprised by the everyday realities of practice in a successful commercial law firm. She says she had no idea as a graduate starting work at a law firm of 'the amount of commitment that I was expected to give my clients' including the ones she had ethical doubts about, such as large industrial cases where she was acting for defendant industrial companies, like tobacco cases. She says she questions 'the meaningfulness of all this'.[28]

Sam says: 'We represented a client in a plant closing case that was opposed by the community. That one made me think a lot because I grew up in (a poor community) which used to have a heavy manufacturing base and everyone worked in the mills. I watched the plants close and watched the parents of friends get laid off and watched the community go down hill from there. I recognise that was very possible in this case. While I'm representing the company, I recognise the community's interests also. Intellectually, though, it's easy to see that the basis for the community's lawsuit has no merit … I guess what I ended up doing was concentrating on the legal issues because that was really all that I had control over.'[29]

Roger says: 'We had a case where a company wanted to develop a hazardous waste incinerator in a poor area. What we did was perfectly legal. We bought the land from owners. We told them we were developing an industrial park, which was semi-true. But, this case went against my general convictions about environmental issues, particularly putting something like this in a poor area where people can't or won't resist. But I convinced myself that there's always another side. By the time I was done, I thought our client was closer to the right side of things than the townspeople. The stuff has to go somewhere. I tended to accept what the client was saying about all the precautions they would take.'[30]

27 Robert Granfield and Thomas Koenig, '"It's Hard to Be a Human Being and a Lawyer": Young Attorneys and the Confrontation with Ethical Ambiguity in Legal Practice' (2003) 105 *West Virginia Law Review* 495, 509.
28 Ibid.
29 Ibid 514.
30 Ibid 518.

Gloria resigned recently because she felt uncomfortable about a situation she found herself in during a settlement conference. The firm was acting for the manufacturer of a laundry machine that was arguing that the machine was safe and that it was the workers' fault when their hands were caught in the machine and permanently disabled. One of the plaintiffs was a poorly educated, elderly Vietnamese woman who worked a cuff and collar press that heats up to 175 degrees centigrade. The operator puts a wet shirt in the machine, presses a button and the top of the machine lowers and presses it. Gloria says: 'When (the disabled woman) walked into the room, she and I were the only women in the room. All the other lawyers and experts were male. She just immediately felt that she and I were on the same side because we were both women. Well, (because she didn't understand the situation) she just spilled her guts. She told me that she and her employer had co-operated together to disconnect the safety features. You could not make your quota with the safety system in place. The outcome of the case was that the woman didn't get anything. The whole thing made me sick. I felt – and this is not the attitude of a lawyer but the attitude of a human being – that we should have just given her the money (that the company paid the law firm) and told her to go home. It's hard to be a human being and a lawyer!'[31]

DISCUSSION QUESTIONS

1. Use the stories above as starting off points. How would each of the four ethical approaches to lawyering apply to each of the situations that the young lawyers found themselves in?

2. Your task is to draft an ethics policy for your firm that will identify what clients the firm will act for and how it will represent them. The policy should help prevent ethical issues arising, help lawyers in the firm understand what the role of the firm is and how their work is meaningful in the legal system, and set out what should happen when ethical issues of these kinds do arise for lawyers in the firm. What would each of the four ethical approaches say about what should be included in this ethics policy? Where would they conflict with each other?

3. Try drafting a policy and discussing it with your peers. Now consider how you would persuade others in your firm that yours is both a good

---

31 Ibid 496.

and a practical policy? What objections might there be? This exercise could be role-played with a mock meeting of the firm, with different participants representing different approaches to lawyering and different practice areas.

4. After the exercise is finished, discuss and consider with your peers how your views have developed during the discussion. Can you identify which ethical type is more attractive to you and why, as a result of drafting the ethics policy? Can you justify that preference verbally to your peers? What might this mean for where you would choose to work?

RECOMMENDED FURTHER READING

Joseph Allegretti, 'Rights, Roles, Relationships: The Wisdom of Solomon and the Ethics of Lawyers' (1992) 25 *Creighton Law Review* 1119.

David Luban, *Lawyers and Justice: An Ethical Study* (Princeton University Press, Princeton, 1988).

Reid Mortensen, 'The Lawyer as Parent: Sympathy, Care and Character in Lawyers' Ethics' (2009) 12 *Legal Ethics* 1.

Justin Oakley and Dean Cocking, *Virtue Ethics and Professional Roles* (Cambridge University Press, New York, 2001).

Christine Parker (ed) 'Forum: Philosophical Legal Ethics, Ethics, Morals and Jurisprudence' 13 (2010) *Legal Ethics* 165.

Stephen Pepper, 'The Lawyer's Amoral Ethical Role: A Defense, A Problem and Some Possibilities' (1986) *American Bar Foundation Research Journal* 613.

Charles Sampford and Sophie Blencowe, 'Educating Lawyers to be Ethical Advisers' in Kim Economides (ed), *Ethical Challenges to Legal Education and Conduct* (Hart Publishing, Oxford, 1998) 315; summarised in Charles Sampford, 'Educating Lawyers to be Ethical Advisers' (1999) 19 *Proctor* 19.

Thomas L Shaffer and Robert F Cochran, *Lawyers, Clients and Moral Responsibility* (West Publishing Co, St Paul, Minnesota, 1994).

William H Simon, *The Practice of Justice: A Theory of Lawyers' Ethics* (Harvard University Press, Cambridge, Massachusetts, 1998).

Stan Van Hooft, *Understanding Virtue Ethics* (Acumen, Chesham, UK, 2006).

W Bradley Wendel, 'Professionalism as Interpretation' (2005) 99 *Northwestern University Law Review* 1167.

—— *Lawyers and Fidelity to Law* (Princeton University Press, Princeton, 2011).

THE RESPONSIBILITY CLIMATE: PROFESSIONALISM AND THE REGULATION OF LAWYERS' ETHICS

3

Introduction

This chapter considers how the structure and processes of the regulatory systems that govern the legal profession are relevant to lawyers' ethics and behaviour – that is, the significance of 'institutions' for lawyers' ethics. Traditionally, as we shall see, the legal profession self-regulated on the basis of blind confidence that any misbehaviour by lawyers was an *individual* anomaly, while the culture and practices of the profession as a *whole* were ethical.[1] Most lawyers probably spend more time thinking about their personal ethics than the way the legal profession as a whole is structured and regulated. But the ethical character of lawyers' practices does not depend on personal factors alone. In practice, personal ethical decisions will either be supported or undermined by the surrounding 'institutional' ethical culture and processes in which they are embedded. Personal ethics will be influenced by institutional constraints such as who sets and enforces the rules that govern the legal profession; what ethical and conduct issues the rules address; what values are represented in what the rules say; and whose interests are promoted, and whose are ignored, in those rules – the interests of lawyers, clients, the community or the profession?

In this chapter we consider two principal ways in which the ethics demonstrated by the legal profession as a whole are likely to impact on lawyers' individual and personal ethics: First, we consider the ethical dimensions of different models of regulation of the legal profession – self-regulation, co-regulation and independent regulation. Secondly, we focus on a particular issue where institutional and personal ethics interact with one another – the use of interest on clients' trust account balances.

The previous two chapters introduced four different ways of thinking about which values should characterise legal practice – and therefore any regulatory system for lawyers. In the following chapters we will look at a number of specific topics or areas and examine in more detail what these approaches might mean, and which values would be appropriate to apply in these different contexts. In doing so we will critique the extent to which the rules and regulations as they currently stand do a good job of demonstrating the right values, and how these rules and regulations influence individual lawyers' capacity to put different values into action in practice. We shall highlight a number of examples where current regulation fails to give lawyers adequate guidance as to how to put values into action (such as the lack of guidance on the public interest exceptions to confidentiality obligations to facilitate whistleblowing – Chapter 4), or where lack of enforcement (such as prosecutors' duties – Chapter 5; excessive adversarialism – Chapter 6; and ethics in negotiation and alternative dispute resolution – Chapter 7) or the wording of the rules themselves (such as allowing clients with potentially conflicting interests to be simultaneously represented – Chapter 8) seem to undermine appropriate

---

1 Christine Parker, 'Regulation of the Ethics of Australian Legal Practice: Autonomy and Responsiveness' (2002) 25 *University of New South Wales Law Journal* 676.

values. We will also see a number of examples where 'cultural', taken-for-granted assumptions and practices of the legal profession probably promote unethical conduct by individual lawyers that has not been addressed by rules and regulation (such as widespread lack of effective communication and dialogue with clients about billing – Chapter 9; and the rationalisation of unethical conduct on behalf of clients in commercial lawyering – Chapter 10).

Like any other occupation or business, a wide range of laws and regulations apply to legal practice.[2] The most important of these are the duty of care owed by lawyers to clients in negligence and contract at common law, and the fiduciary duties and other obligations, such as confidentiality, owed by lawyers to their clients in equity. All sorts of other areas of law, such as anti-discrimination, corporate, environmental, and trade practices regulation, also apply to legal practice just as they apply to other businesses, and are enforced against lawyers and law firms by regulatory agencies.

In this chapter, however, we focus on the rules and regulatory regimes that have been created to apply specifically to lawyers under the legislation and case law governing the legal professions of each of the States and Territories. In particular, we focus firstly on the still largely self-regulatory and character-based system for admission to the profession and for the issue and renewal of practising certificates, and then the co-regulatory complaints handling and disciplinary systems for lawyers, before turning to the funding of the whole regulatory system.

Self-Regulation: Professional Community and Social Trustee Professionalism

Barristers and the History of Professional Moral Community

The regulatory structures for the legal profession in the various States and Territories in Australia are still heavily influenced by the fact that historically the

---

2 See David Wilkins, 'Who Should Regulate Lawyers?' (1992) 105 *Harvard Law Review* 799; David Wilkins, 'Afterword: How Should We Determine Who Should Regulate Lawyers? – Managing Conflict and Context in Professional Regulation' (1996) 65 *Fordham Law Review* 465. See also C Parker, ibid. David Wilkins divides enforcement/regulatory controls for the legal profession into four categories: (1) disciplinary controls (traditional self-regulation); (2) liability controls (negligence etc); (3) institutional controls (enforced by courts and state administrative agencies on lawyers who practise before them); (4) legislative controls (enforced by a special independent regulator or commission or even by the government).

legal profession regulated itself.[3] This tradition derives from the practice of English barristers who, from at least the end of the 15th century, were self-regulated by the strict hierarchies of Inns of Court where students, barristers and benchers lived together. The idea of self-regulation is still justified to some extent by the ideal of the legal profession as a coherent moral community that socialises its members into appropriate and ethical behaviour as it teaches and maintains the craft of lawyering.[4] That is, self-regulation rests on the notion of the legal profession as a community that is responsible for ensuring that lawyers play their important twin roles as adversarial advocates and responsible lawyers with the important social function of establishing and maintaining the rule of law.

This conception of lawyers and the legal profession distinguishes lawyers and their regulation from both the apparent chaos and self-interest of businesses competing in the market and the bureaucracy of government organisations.[5] Professional self-regulation of ethics is said to be necessary because we can trust neither market forces nor state regulation to inculcate ethics. Rather, ethics must be the concern of sufficiently cohered self-regulating occupations which teach each member to look away from their self-interest and towards the whole professional community and the role it is supposed to serve for the legal system and thus for society. The more protection given to these groups the better their ethics will be.[6] In juxtaposing professionalism to markets and bureaucracies, these foundational accounts of professionalism in social theory conceptualise professionalism as an institution that cultivates ethical responsibility, and autonomy, in a way that capitalist, commercial, bureaucratic, and hierarchical business modes of organising work cannot do.[7]

The Social Bargain: Social Trustee Professionalism

Solicitors organised themselves into professional associations in the 18th century in a direct attempt to emulate the success of the Inns of Court in acquiring political

3   For accounts of how this model developed historically see Julian Disney et al, *Lawyers* (Lawbook Co, North Ryde, NSW, 2nd edn, 1986) 6; William S Holdsworth, *A History of English Law* (Sweet & Maxwell, London, 1937) vol 6, 443. This brief summary is based on material previously published by the first author in Christine Parker, 'Competing Images of the Legal Profession: Competing Regulatory Strategies' (1997) 25(4) *International Journal of the Sociology of Law* 385–409.

4   Emile Durkheim, *Professional Ethics and Civic Morals* (Routledge, Oxford, [1957] 1992). This is also true of the other traditional professions.

5   See Talcott Parsons, 'The Professions and Social Structure' in Talcott Parsons (ed), *Essays in Sociological Theory* (The Free Press, Glencoe, Illinois, 1954) 34–49; Eliot Freidson, *Professionalism Reborn: Theory, Prophecy and Policy* (Polity, Cambridge, 1994).

6   See Emile Durkheim, *Professional Ethics and Civic Morals* (Routledge, London, 1992) 12–13, 23–4.

7   Julia Evetts, 'The Sociological Analysis of Professionalism: Occupational Change in the Modern World' (2003) 18 *International Sociology* 395, 404.

influence and in inculcating common standards of professional conduct and ethics through a self-regulatory community.[8] In 1828 the Supreme Court was granted powers of admission and regulation over the NSW legal profession.[9] The members of the Sydney Law Library Society, established in 1842, decided in 1843 to form the NSW Law Society, and similar societies formed in 1862 and 1872 with the purpose of pursuing ethical self-regulation. In 1884 the Incorporated Law Institute of NSW was established and later became known as the Law Society of NSW. It first acquired statutory powers of regulation in 1935, as a result of amendments to the *Legal Practitioners Act 1898* (NSW), and gained substantial powers comparable to those of the English Law Society by 1941.[10] The situation in each of the other States was similar except for South Australia and Western Australia, where Conduct Boards dominated by the legal profession – but independent of the legal professional associations – were set up to control admission, and complaints handling and discipline of admitted members of the profession.

At the pinnacle of self-regulation, the professional associations promulgated and enforced standards of professional conduct, investigated and prosecuted complaints, and provided the disciplinary tribunals to hear charges. They also decided on qualifications for admission, issued practising certificates, policed compliance with trust account rules, and administered fidelity funds and insurance schemes. They also protected lawyers' monopolies on legal work, set standard fees, and prohibited most forms of competition between lawyers, including any form of advertising or price competition.

The rationale for this degree of self-regulation built on the historical ideal of the legal profession as a self-regulating moral community (mentioned above), by seeing the self-regulating profession as entering into a bargain with the state and community who allow it to self-regulate because of its obscure but expert knowledge and its superior institutions of socialisation and social control. On this view, lawyers (and members of the other traditional professions such as medicine, the clergy and the military) are seen as different from members of other occupations or markets because they are 'trained in and integrated with, a distinctive part of our cultural tradition, having a fiduciary responsibility for its maintenance, development and implementation'.[11] That is, the profession is a social trustee for the Rule of Law.[12]

8 See Alan Paterson, 'Professionalism and the Legal Services Market' (1996) 3 *International Journal of the Legal Profession* 137; B Abel-Smith and R Stevens, *Lawyers and the Courts: A Sociological Study of the English Legal System 1750–1965*, (Heinemann, London, 1967) 23, 187–92.

9 David Weisbrot, *Australian Lawyers* (Longman Cheshire, Melbourne, 1990) 166.

10 New South Wales Law Reform Commission, *The Legal Profession: Discussion Paper No. 1 – General Regulation* (New South Wales Law Reform Commission, Sydney, 1979) 43.

11 Parsons, 'The Professions and Social Structure', 381.

12 Terence Halliday and Lucien Karpik (eds), *Fates of Political Freedom: The Legal Complex in the British Post-Colony* (Cambridge University Press, Cambridge, 2011); Terence Halliday,

The regulation of the profession could thus be seen as a social bargain characterised by trust: The legal professional community takes on the burden of specially regulating itself since it alone is competent to do so. In return, it is suggested, society at large and clients trust them and protect them from interference, supervision and competition, as well as giving them higher remuneration and social status. But these privileges can hypothetically be withdrawn if the profession fails to regulate itself in the public interest:

> [T]he larger society has obtained an *indirect* social control by yielding *direct* social control to the professional community, which thus can make judgments according to its own norms...Thus it is that the social control of the professional community over its members may be seen as a response to the threat of the larger lay society to control it. Failure to discipline would mean both a loss of prestige in the society, and a loss of community autonomy.[13]

Of itself, this social bargain may not be sufficient to make every individual professional altruistic, but it means that the profession as a whole will be motivated to organise, regulate and socialise individual lawyers to serve and not exploit clients.[14] The state and broader community might enter into dialogue with the profession to make adjustments to the social bargain from time to time, but overall the value of professional community must be recognised for its role in advocating for and sustaining the integrity of the legal process and the Rule of Law.[15]

Lucien Karpik and Malcolm Feeley (eds), *Fighting for Political Freedom: Comparative Studies of the Legal Complex and Political Change* (Hart Publishing, Portland, 2007); Terence Halliday and Lucien Karpik (eds) *Lawyers and the Rise of Western Political Liberalism: Europe and North America from the Eighteenth to Twentieth Centuries* (Oxford University Press, Oxford, 1997); Cf Ronen Shamir, *Managing Legal Uncertainty: Elite Lawyers in the New Deal* (Duke University Press, Durham, 1995); Yves Dezalay and Bryant Garth, *Dealing in Virtue: International Commercial Arbitration and the Construction of a Transnational Legal Order* (The University of Chicago Press, Chicago, 1996).

13 William Goode, 'Community within a Community: The Professions' (1957) 22 *American Sociological Review* 198.

14 This theory of a social bargain between the profession and both the community and the state has also received contemporary support from Bernard Barber, *The Logic and Limits of Trust* (Rutgers University Press, New Brunswick, 1983), and Terence Halliday, *Beyond Monopoly: Lawyers, State Crises and Professional Empowerment* (University of Chicago Press, Chicago, 1987).

15 See generally Halliday, *Beyond Monopoly*; Andrew Boon, 'Professionalism Under the Legal Services Act 2007' (2010) 17 *International Journal of the Legal Profession* 195; Alan Paterson, 'Self-Regulation and the Future of the Profession' in David Hayton (ed), *Law's Future(s): British Legal Developments in the 21st Century* (Hart Publishing, Oxford, 2000) 29–52. See Christine Parker, *Just Lawyers: Regulation and Access to Justice* (Oxford University Press, Oxford, 1999) 140–73 (assessing this literature and suggesting a revision to the approach it takes, in order to better make the legal profession accountable to broader access to justice concerns).

There are three main justifications for a continuing self-regulatory bargain proposed by the social trustee view of professionalism, and each of them draws on the twin roles of lawyers as *adversarial advocates* and *responsible lawyers*:[16]

- *First*, it is assumed that only lawyers are knowledgeable enough about the law to set standards for their own practice. Clients and the general public lack the expertise to participate in setting and enforcing the ethics and standards of the legal profession. The whole point of law being a profession was that clients needed to trust lawyers to serve their interests in the legal system (as *adversarial advocates*) because they did not know how to do so themselves. The public likewise needed to trust lawyers to act honourably and 'professionally' as *responsible lawyers* by advocating vigorously for clients without breaching their duties to the court and the law. Only lawyers and courts had the experience and expertise to understand how that delicate balance should be maintained, thus self-regulation is necessary.

It followed that since professions are responsible for, and learned in, bodies of knowledge and practice of great value to society, they must be specially regulated to ensure they are suitably trained and certified to interpret, develop, improve and practically apply this tradition for the benefit of others.[17] This also justified unusually restrictive rules (such as the fiduciary duties to avoid conflicts of interest and protect confidentiality, discussed in Chapters 4 and 8) to protect individual clients from being dominated by professionals who would usually know so much more than them:

> The problems brought to the professional are usually those the client cannot solve, and only the professional can solve. The client does not usually choose his professional by a measurable criterion of competence, and after the work is done, the client is not usually competent to judge if it was properly done.[18]

Economists have also shown that failure occurs in the market for professional services because of 'informational asymmetry, in which the seller knows the quality of his service or product, but the buyer does not.'[19] Intervention in the market to ensure minimum quality standards is thus necessary.[20] The functionalists argued

---

16 See Harry Arthurs, 'The Dead Parrot: Does Professional Self-Regulation Exhibit Vital Signs?' (1995) 33 *Alberta Law Review 800*; Parker, *Just Lawyers*, 112–14.

17 Parsons, 'The Professions and Social Structure', 372.

18 Goode, 'Community within a Community: The Professions' 196.

19 Hayne Leland, 'Quacks, Lemons and Licensing: A Theory of Minimum Quality Standards' (1979) 87 *Journal of Political Economy* 1329.

20 George Akerlof, 'The Market for "Lemons": Quality Uncertainty and the Market Mechanism' (1970) 84 *Quarterly Journal of Economics* 488–500; Kenneth Arrow, 'Uncertainty and the Welfare Economics of Medical Care' (1963) 53(3) *American Economic Review* 941–73; Leland, 'Quacks, Lemons and Licensing'.

that since unqualified persons are not competent to meddle in professional affairs, professionals must be trusted to do this special regulation themselves: 'Professionals *profess*. They profess to know better than others the nature of certain matters, and to know better than their clients what ails them or their affairs ... Since the professional does profess, he asks that he be trusted.'[21]

- *Second*, the profession argued, the state should not be involved in regulating lawyers. This was because it was necessary that lawyers remain completely independent of government, so that they could defend individuals and society against the state where necessary (as *adversarial advocates*) without bias or fear of reprisal. Separation was also important because lawyers need to be able to defend the Rule of Law and use their expertise to maintain and gradually reform the legal system from a disinterested, rather than a party political, perspective as *responsible lawyers*.

- *Third*, just as the state should not directly regulate lawyers because this might corrupt the Rule of Law with partisan interests, nor should the profession be thrown open to the competitive forces of the market because this might corrupt the Rule of Law with self-interest. It should be in the nature of all the professions to be trusted to self-regulate because the members of professions were motivated by higher goals beyond self-interest in a competitive market-place. If they failed to self-regulate for the benefit of the public, so the argument went, their monopoly on legal practice and/or the right to self-regulate could always be removed by government. This threat of loss of privileges is supposed to be a sufficient incentive to make sure the legal profession (and also other professions) regulated themselves properly.[22]

Traditional Self-Regulation

Traditional self-regulation focused on setting strict entry, or 'admission', requirements to the profession in the attempt to ensure that only well qualified people of good character entered the profession – lawyers that clients could trust. Lawyers were admitted into practice on the basis of academic legal qualifications, practical training and 'good fame and character'.[23]

---

21 Everett Hughes, 'Professions' (1963) 92 *Daedalus* 656.
22 See Paterson, 'Professionalism and the Legal Services Market' 137.
23 See *Re Davis* (1947) 75 CLR 409; *Ex parte Lenehan* (1948) 77 CLR 403; *ReB* [1981] 2 NSWLR 372. See also G E Dal Pont, *Lawyers' Professional Responsibility* (Lawbook Co, Pyrmont, NSW, 5th edn, 2013) Ch 2: Admission to Practice; Reid Mortensen, 'Lawyers' Character, Moral Insight and Ethical Blindness' (2002) 22 *Queensland Lawyer* 166.

Once entry to the profession had been attained, under the traditional model, lawyers were assumed to be sufficiently expert, competent and capable of serving clients well. The ongoing regulation of lawyers' practice focused on maintaining standards of character, not competence.[24] Thus traditional self-regulation focused on discovering and sanctioning failures of character such as dishonesty (especially knowingly or deliberately misleading a court or tribunal, or falsifying a document), breach of trust account rules (including lawyer misappropriation of client funds) and other fiduciary duties (particularly conflicts of interests – see Chapter 8). Traditional self-regulation did little to make sure that lawyers maintained an appropriate standard of competence or client service. It was assumed that competence would take care of itself through individual lawyers' steadily increasing experience. Only in the case of 'gross negligence' could a lawyer be sanctioned for lack of care and competence.[25] This was despite the fact that the vast majority of complaints clients make about lawyers concern poor service – delay, incompetence, over-charging and discourtesy or failure to communicate. These complaints were not even seriously investigated by disciplinary authorities until relatively recently. Overcharging was generally only disciplined where it was blatant and dishonest. Indeed price-fixing (which generally inflates prices) was entrenched by self-regulatory rules (see Chapter 9), and competition of any kind (that might lower fees) was discouraged. Self-regulatory authorities were also unlikely to act against lawyers for conduct that was against the public interest but in the interests of clients, such as abuse of the court process by frivolous or vexatious claims or claims for an ulterior purpose, or for excessive adversarialism that wastes the resources of the court and/or the parties (see Chapter 6).

The main sanctions available as the outcome of disciplinary action were (and still are) expulsion of the lawyer from the profession, or suspension from practice, and monetary fines. A series of lesser sanctions including reprimands, restrictions on practising certificates, and the requirement to attend continuing legal education are also common outcomes. The courts were (and indeed remain) clear that the purpose of these sanctions is to protect the public from professionals that are not worthy of their trust, and to protect the reputation and privileges of the whole profession by ridding the profession of unethical individuals: 'A disbarring order is

---

24 See Parker, *Just Lawyers*, 13–17. See also William Felstiner, 'Professional Inattention: Origins and Consequences' in Keith Hawkins (ed), *The Human Face of Law: Essays in Honour of Donald Harris* (Clarendon, Oxford, 1997) 121; Parker, 'Regulation of the Ethics of Australian Legal Practice', 689–93.

25 See *Re Moseley* (1925) 25 SR (NSW) 174. Mere incompetence or deficiency in professional service is still not sufficient to amount to professional misconduct: See *Pillai v Messiter (No 2)* (1989) 16 NSWLR 197.

in no sense punitive in character. When such an order is made, it is made, from the public point of view, for the protection of those who require protection and, from the professional point of view, in order that abuse of privilege may not lead to loss of privilege'[26] (ie, of the profession as a whole).

The assumption in this system is that unethical conduct is the result of dishonest behaviour by individual lawyers of bad character, who must be cast out or have their character reformed. Sanctions against individual lawyers are seen as sufficient to maintain the standards of the profession, since the only threat to those standards is the individual 'bad egg'. Indeed the courts suggest that the appropriate response to serious misconduct should generally be disbarment or suspension from practice because of the view that it is better to cast someone out of the profession than punish them, even very severely, while allowing them to remain in the profession.

On the other hand, the courts also say that a practitioner who is completely candid with the profession and the court about their past misbehaviour, acknowledges that it was wrong and shows remorse, contrition and a demonstrated change of behaviour can be given a much lesser sanction than might have been expected given their misconduct, as they have shown that they have redeemed their character. Lawyers who have already been disbarred can also be granted re-admission to the profession on this basis.[27] The High Court of Australia decided the case of *A Solicitor*[28] on this basis. In that case disciplinary action had been taken against a solicitor who had been convicted of criminal offences relating to the sexual abuse of his step-daughters. The High Court decided that the incidents of sex abuse occurred as an isolated episode when the practitioner was under a lot of pressure, and that in the meantime the practitioner had shown contrition and rehabilitated himself (through seeking psychological counselling). However, the High Court's finding that the practitioner had shown contrition, had rehabilitated himself and was free to practise as a lawyer is odd in light of the fact that he had also hidden from the Law Society (that is, the regulator) the fact he had been convicted (but later acquitted on appeal) of further sexual offences against the step-daughters during those five years that it took for his disciplinary case to be investigated, prepared, heard and appealed. The High Court accepted that this amounted to a serious disciplinary offence, but found that the fact that the practitioner had been effectively suspended from practice for five years while the

---

26 *Clyne v New South Wales Bar Association* (1960) 104 CLR 186, 201–2. See also Linda Haller, 'Disciplinary Fines: Deterrence or Retribution?' (2002) 5 *Legal Ethics* 152; and Linda Haller, 'Smoke and Mirrors: Public Health or Hazard?' (2005) 8 *Legal Ethics* 70.

27 Dal Pont, *Lawyers' Professional Responsibility*, [2.130], [2.140], [23.130], [24.20]; Mortensen, 'Lawyers' Character'.

28 *A Solicitor v Council of the Law Society of New South Wales* (2004) 216 CLR 253. See also Haller, 'Smoke and Mirrors'; Suzanne Le Mire, 'Striking Off: Criminal Lawyers and Disclosure of their Convictions' (2005) 79 *Australian Law Journal* 641.

case progressed was sanction enough. The courts in previous cases have generally insisted on complete candour towards regulatory authorities as a condition for admission or re-admission after a history of unacceptable behaviour.[29]

The Character of a Member of a Self-Regulating Profession: Suitability for Admission and Renewal of Practising Certificates

Today, the regulation of the legal profession still reflects the historical self-regulatory ideal of the profession as a moral community that socialises its members into the appropriate role and character. Admission to the profession is still largely controlled by the Supreme Courts of the various States and Territories, and these courts also retain their inherent jurisdiction to 'strike off' practitioners who fail to live up to the standards of a fit and proper person. Some law societies (eg Western Australia and Victoria) have lost formal control of the ability to issue and renew (or refuse to issue and renew) practising certificates, but the organised profession is still very much in control of the administrative licensing process in most jurisdictions. Even in Victoria, the Legal Services Board has delegated the licensing process back to the profession and is likely to leave that delegation intact for the foreseeable future. Linda Haller argues that the power to control practising certificates may be even more important for regulatory authority than disciplinary control, because administrative withdrawal of a right of practice may be less expensive for regulators than the commencement of contested disciplinary proceedings.[30]

Only those who have the required knowledge (the law degree[31]), have completed a practical legal training requirement, have proficiency in English, and are 'fit and proper'[32] to be admitted can be admitted to, and remain in, the

29 Compare the decision in the same case in the New South Wales Supreme Court: *Council of the Law Society of New South Wales v A Solicitor* [2002] NSWCA 62 (Unreported, Mason P, Sheller and Giles JJA, 12 March 2002).
30 Linda Haller, 'Discipline vs Regulation: Lessons from the Collapse of Tasmania's Legal Profession Reform Bill' (2005) 12(1&2) *E Law – Murdoch University Electronic Journal of Law* [1] <www.murdoch.edu.au/elaw/issues/v12n1_2/Haller12_1.html> at 12 July 2006.
31 Strictly the requirement is to complete the required 'Priestley 11' subjects: Law Council of Australia, Law Admissions Consultative Committee, Prescribed Academic Areas of Knowledge, (2009) available at <www.lawcouncil.asn.au/lacc/documents/admission_policies.cfm> at 4 May 2013. The areas are: criminal law and procedure, torts, contracts, property, equity (including trusts), company law, administrative law, constitutional law, civil procedure, evidence, and ethics and professional responsibility.
32 Francesca Bartlett and Linda Haller, 'Disclosing Lawyers: Questioning Law and Process in the Admission of Australian Lawyers' (2013) 41 *Federal Law Review* forthcoming; Mortensen, 'Lawyers' Character'; Alice Woolley, 'Tending the Bar: The Good Character Requirement for Law Society Admission' (2007) 30 *Dalhousie Law Journal* 27.

legal profession (*Model Laws* cl 307, 308 and *Legal Profession National Law* 2.2.3). Usually, it is only the last of these requirements that ever causes any difficulty or contention. To be 'fit and proper' a candidate for admission must show they are of 'good fame and character'. Being 'fit and proper' and of 'good fame and character' could mean almost anything: For potential lawyers, it is generally demonstrated by the absence of anything that would cast doubt on the suitability of the person for admission to the profession, such as a prior criminal history or any other indication of dishonesty, continuing mental illness that makes the candidate unfit to practise law and, on rare occasions, continued disregard for the political and social norms of the era (including perhaps the membership of suspect political organisations).[33]

This suggests that one of the implicit intentions of the admission requirements is to ensure that only those who are not only trustworthy but also conservative in their political allegiance, and unlikely to ridicule or cause embarrassment to the rest of the legal profession, are able to enter the profession. It is easy to agree that a history of criminal deceit should raise questions about whether someone should be excluded from practice, especially if they conceal that history from the admission authorities.[34] But occasionally there has been a case where someone has been refused admission to the profession because of the way they have expressed their more personal moral opinions and political convictions by ridiculing the establishment, especially the judicial establishment. Case Study 3.1 below, the *Wendy Bacon* case, is such a case. It raises questions about the extent to which dissent from dominant political and personal values will be tolerated within the legal profession.

Although the *Bacon* case was decided twenty-five years ago, in contemporary times there continue to be pressures on the free expression by citizens, and even by lawyers, of political and moral dissent which is arguably one of the hallmarks of democracy. In particular, anti-terrorism legislation in Australia now allows government to insist that only certain 'extra-reliable' lawyers, cleared for security, be allowed to represent those charged with terrorist offences.[35] Sedition legislation introduced into Australia could, over time, swing the balance against the admission of lawyers who, for example, call for the downfall of the government or even, perhaps, argue for non-violent civil disobedience. The Public Interest Advocacy Centre (PIAC) observed to a Senate Committee hearing inquiring into new

33 See Dal Pont, *Lawyers' Professional Responsibility*, [2.42] – [2.105] for a general summary of the requirements. See also *Re Davis* (1947) 75 CLR 409; *Ex parte Lenehan* (1948) 77 CLR 403; *Re B* [1981] 2 NSWLR 372; *Victorian Lawyers RPA Ltd v X* (2001) 3 VR 601; *Re Legal Practitioners Act 1970* [2003] ACTSC 11 (Unreported, Higgins CJ, Crispin and Connolly JJ, 13 March 2003); *XY v Board of Examiners* [2005] VSC 250 (Unreported, Habersberger J, 15 July 2005).

34 See Mortensen, 'Lawyers' Character', 166.

35 *National Security Information (Criminal and Civil Proceedings) Act 2004* (Cth) s 39.

anti-terrorism legislation in 2005 that a 'Bring Johnny [former Prime Minister, John Howard] Down' poster or public rallying call could be interpreted as an incitement to violence and therefore grounds for a prosecution for sedition under the proposed legislation. Other developments such as employee psychological testing, media concentration in the hands of large businesses, increasing international wealth imbalance, even the possibility of genetically engineered 'designer babies', may also promote a climate of conformity in which all kinds of people are afraid to express modestly dissenting opinions.

It is easy to assume that free speech is reasonably safe, particularly for lawyers, but *Wendy Bacon* shows that complacency about lawyers' rights to dissent is unwise. Potential new lawyers who are politically critical of established priorities may find it hard to get through the admission gate in the future.

CASE STUDY 3.1   THE WENDY BACON CASE

Wendy Bacon, a journalist and political activist, sought, but was denied, admission to legal practice in the early 1980s.[36] Her case is probably the best-known Australian example of a refusal to admit someone to practice because of conflict between a practitioner's own personal morality and the political and cultural mores of a generation.

Between 1970, when she was 24, and 1981, when she was aged 35, Wendy Bacon participated in a string of activist causes on issues including calling for the repeal of existing pornography laws; maintenance of the residential amenity in the Rocks area of Sydney Harbour; the dismissal of the Whitlam Labor government by the Governor-General in 1975; the export of uranium; the treatment of prisoners – especially female prisoners; New South Wales police corruption; and the then fairly restrictive censorship laws. Over this period, Ms Bacon was arrested numerous times and received 10 convictions for offences associated with her protest activities such as daubing political slogans on buildings (including the slogan 'justice is just arse'), impersonating a nun and displaying an obscene publication outside a court (as part of a protest on obscenity laws), indecent language, failure to leave premises when required to leave, and disobeying the police.

When she later applied for admission to practice, Ms Bacon was very candid about all this activity, and much else that had not resulted in any prosecution. But

36 *Re B* [1981] 2 NSWLR 372. See also Wendy Bacon, 'I Fought the Law ...', *The Sydney Morning Herald*, 22 November 2003, 6.

she was still denied admission, even though there were no convictions against her for dishonesty or violence, and despite her candour with the admitting authorities and the court. But the members of the NSW Court of Appeal relied, they said, upon a separate allegation that she had been dishonest.

The Court said that crucial to the question of Wendy Bacon's fitness for practice was an incident in 1979 (only a couple of years before her application for admission) when she provided bail for a criminal defendant on charges that she was helping him defend. Ms Bacon told the Court that she had borrowed the money for the bail from a mutual friend and had not provided the money herself.[37] But the New South Wales Court of Appeal, in deciding her admission application, did not believe her and found her deceit fatal to her admission application:

> That a person can be trusted to tell the truth and, regardless of the ends, not participate in a breach of the law is fundamental to being a barrister... The bail matter and her evidence in respect of it establish she is not fit to be a barrister.[38]

The Court went to some pains to assert that, of itself, being a political radical, or holding extremist views on sex, religion or philosophy was no bar to admission.[39] The judges also agreed that matters from the past that could be characterised as 'youthful indiscretions' might be set to one side.[40] But, having concluded that she had lied about the bail matter, they were scathing of her claim that her previous attitudes had changed. The Court considered that Ms Bacon was unfit to practise because her claim that her previous attitudes had changed was in essence only partly true, and she remained prepared to break the law if she thought the cause was worthy enough. According to the Court, it was a question of 'whether a person who aspires to serve the law can be said to be fit to do so when it is demonstrated that in the zealous pursuit of political goals she will break the law if she regards it as impeding the success of her cause'. The court pointed out that she had done so in the past and her dishonesty about the bail matter meant she remained prepared to do so again.[41]

---

37 This is generally considered unethical: See, eg, Victorian Bar Council, *Practice Rules* (The Victorian Bar Inc, Melbourne, 2005), Rule 160, which says that a barrister must not promote or be a party to any arrangement whereby the bail provided by a surety is obtained by using the accused's money, or by which the surety is given an indemnity by the accused, or a third party acting on behalf of the accused. Nor should a practitioner become surety for their own client's bail.

38 *Re B* [1981] 2 NSWLR 372, 395 (Moffitt P).

39 Ibid 380 (Moffitt P).

40 Ibid 381 (Moffitt P).

41 Ibid 402 (Reynolds JA); see also 395 (Moffitt P).

DISCUSSION QUESTIONS

1. Bacon appears to have been undone by what the court determined to be a lie[42] over something that she no doubt considered important at the time – the release from custody of a friend in need – yet that lie apparently cost her her application for admission. Should the attitude of preparedness to break the law in the cause of caring for a friend, if bona fide, be a barrier to practice?

2. Over 400 years ago, the English Lord Chancellor, Sir Thomas More, determined that a law of Henry VIII, which he considered unjust, had to be passively opposed, and lost his life for his opposition.[43] No one expects a death sentence for disregarding any law in Australia today, but does the *Wendy Bacon* case suggest that we can only have lawyers who will obey the law regardless of all other considerations? Is a person who asks whether a law is just or not in the circumstances, before deciding whether to obey it, the sort of person who should, or should not, be admitted into the legal profession?

3. When you face a conflict between your values and 'the law', which will be your priority?

In 2003 Wendy Bacon wrote an article for the *Sydney Morning Herald* reflecting on her experience 22 years earlier. After she had been refused admission to the profession by the Admissions Board, her only option for 'appeal' was to apply to the Supreme Court for a declaration that she was of good fame and character. She comments that:

> In practice this meant placing my extremely unconventional life before a group of male, middle-aged and mostly conservative judges... In hindsight, I can say that I regret asking the Supreme Court to pass judgment on my character. It was a demeaning process. Cross-examination, as Porter [counsel on the other side in her case] admits, is not always an effective way to reach the truth. In his book, he observes that while I did not weaken under cross-examination, I did myself a disservice by playing more to the public gallery than the judges. While I do not agree, I experienced a tension between being true to my beliefs and giving brief opinions that would not damage me too much with the

---

42 Note that Ms Bacon herself continued to maintain at her admission that she did not lie and she did not know about the circumstances that indicated that the bail money had probably come from the accused himself.

43 Peter Ackroyd, *The Life of Thomas More* (Chatto & Windus, London, 1998); Randy Lee, 'Robert Bolt's *A Man For All Seasons* and the Art of Discerning Integrity' (2000) 9 *Widener Journal of Public Law* 305.

judges. In fact, I would have done a greater service to both myself and the law if I had expressed more fully my continuing view that most of the freedoms we have today would not exist if people, often supported by progressive lawyers, had not confronted authority and broken unjust laws.[44]

4. What do you think? In hindsight, was it better that Wendy Bacon was not admitted to the profession, or should she have been admitted? Given her current views expressed above, should she be admitted now, if she sought admission?

Co-Regulation and Independent Regulation of the Legal Profession Today: Complaints Handling and Discipline

The Legal Profession as a Conspiracy Against the Laity

In contrast to the traditional image of the legal profession as a self-regulating moral community, since the early 1980s government policy in Australia (and also in Britain, Canada and New Zealand) has been to see the profession as a business that must be regulated in a way that ensures competition and a consumer service orientation. The Trade Practices Commission (now the Australian Competition and Consumer Commission) decided in 1989 to review the legal profession and determine the extent to which it complied with antitrust principles, and its final report was handed down in 1994. In 1993, the *Hilmer Report* into gaps in implementation of competition policy reform in Australia identified the legal profession as a problem area.[45] The thrust of the Trade Practices Commission's criticisms is illustrated in the following passage from its final report in 1994:

---

44 Bacon, 'I Fought the Law...'.
45 F Hilmer, M Rayner and G Taperell, *National Competition Policy (The Hilmer Report)* (Australian Government Publishing Service, Canberra, 1993). For a fuller account of this process and its consequences, see Parker, *Just Lawyers* 121–39.

The Australian legal profession is heavily over-regulated and in urgent need of comprehensive reform. It is highly regulated compared to other sectors of the economy and those regulations combine to impose substantial restrictions on the commercial conduct of lawyers and on the extent to which lawyers are free to compete with each other for business. As a result, the current regulatory regime has adverse effects on the cost and efficiency of legal services and their prices to business and final consumers ... Reform of the extensive system of regulation applied to the legal profession is an important part of the agenda for micro-economic reform and the development of a national approach to competition policy ... [46]

Competition reformers see the legal profession as no different from any other industry which must be subject to micro-economic reform. Their image of the legal profession is of a cartel which managed in the 20th century to achieve monopoly rents and privileges by exploiting self-regulation. At its most extreme, the picture of the legal profession as cartel is justified by the neo-classical economics of Milton Friedman. In his theory, special regulation always becomes 'a tool in the hands of a special producer group to obtain a monopoly position at the expense of the rest of the public'.[47] Social critiques of the professions in the 1980s and 1990s were also dominated by a perspective that complements this economic critique. Sociologists have seen professions as occupational groups organised to maximise their power by claiming the status of 'profession' and the privileges that go with it. Magali Sarfatti Larson described the 'professional project' as to the use of claims to special knowledge and skills to strive both for market control (economic power) through monopolisation, and social status (social power) through a collective mobility project.[48] The most important strategy in this struggle is to control professional education so that the profession holds a collective monopoly on knowledge or expertise itself, as well as on the supply of producers:

> In a perfect market situation, the sovereignty resides, theoretically, in the consumer. The professions ultimately depend on the public's willingness to accept and legitimize the superiority of their knowledge and skills. The singular characteristic of professional power is, however, that the profession has the exclusive privilege of defining *both* the content of its knowledge and the legitimate conditions of access to it, while the unequal distribution of knowledge protects and enhances this power [emphasis in the original].[49]

46 Trade Practices Commission, *Study of the Professions: Legal – Final Report* (Trade Practices Commission, Canberra, 1994) 3–4; See also Hilmer et al, *National Competition Policy*, 133–7.

47 Milton Friedman, 'Chapter IX: Occupational Licensure' in *Capitalism and Freedom* (University of Chicago Press, Chicago, 1962) 148.

48 Magali Larson, *The Rise of Professionalism* (University of California Press, Berkeley and Los Angeles, 1977) xvi.

49 Ibid 48.

This theory sees traditional self-regulation and its justifications as nothing more than support for the self-interested professional project. It is suggested that traditional professional claims of disinterested public service and of a social bargain mandating self-regulation form part of an ideology which justifies and obscures the social structural inequalities caused by professionalism, and inspires individual professionals in their efforts. Furthermore, self-regulation is actually aimed at ensuring that competition between members is minimised and the profession acts in solidarity to advance the collective goals of monopoly and status. The profession provides a clear path for individual members to achieve power and prestige within this tightly regulated structure so that they remain committed to a unified profession and contribute, deliberately or not, to its collective project.[50] On this view, the legal profession is an autonomous collective organisation aimed and organised to secure its economic and social self-interest through the control of entry, competition and internal regulation. It is a 'conspiracy against the laity', inherently unworthy of trust.

Regulation of the Legal Profession as a Business

It is ironic 'that much of the criticism of professionalism by radicals seems to advance the implicit alternative of the individualistic free market that underlies capitalism'.[51] But the policy consequence of accepting the market control theory of the profession is to 'reform' lawyers by breaking down professional organisation and self-regulation, forcing more competition and treating law more like a business. As mentioned above, one of the profession's arguments for self-regulation was that law is a profession with ethical values beyond those of the market. Some scholars of the legal profession, however, have pointed out that if we examine the nature of the way law is actually practised these days, it is subject to such strong market pressure that it is hard to see how the case can be made that it is a profession with different values to general business. Richard Abel, who has studied the legal professions in the UK and US for many years, is one who takes this view:

---

50 Ibid 70–74. A number of studies published in the 1980s and 1990s supported the application of Larson's theory to the legal profession: Abel shows how this theory explains the history and behaviour of the legal profession in the United Kingdom in Richard Abel, *The Legal Profession in England and Wales* (Basil Blackwell, Oxford, 1988), and the United States, in Richard Abel, *American Lawyers* (Oxford University Press, New York, 1989). Weisbrot, *Australian Lawyers* and Pat O'Malley, *Law, Capitalism and Democracy* (Allen & Unwin, Sydney, 1983) have attempted to do the same for Australia.

51 Eliot Freidson, 'Professionalism as Model and Ideology' in Robert L Nelson, David Trubek and Rayman L Solomon (eds), *Lawyers' Ideals/Lawyers' Practices: Transformations in the American Legal Profession* (Cornell University Press, New York, 1992) 219.

The lawyer today (and even more tomorrow) is an entrepreneur selling his services to an increasingly competitive market, an employee whose labor is exploited, an employer exploiting subordinates – all increasingly dependent on state or capital for business and therefore increasingly subject to their control. Although the ideal of professionalism undoubtedly will linger on as an ever more anachronistic warrant of legitimacy, as an economic, social, and political institution the profession is moribund.[52]

Even if we are not as cynical as Abel, the profession's arguments in favour of self-regulation are not convincing. Harry Arthurs, another scholar of the legal profession, has shown convincingly how the three classic arguments for self-regulation (as described above in the subsection headed, 'The Social Bargain: Social Trustee Professionalism') fail:[53]

- *First*, self-regulation is not necessary to defend individuals and society from the power of the state – other countries like Sweden manage well without it. Anyway, just because the profession does not self-regulate does not mean it must be controlled by the state – it can be independently regulated.

- *Second*, although lawyers claim to be the only ones who know how to regulate themselves, the legal profession has declined to regulate itself properly. Individual lawyers with appropriate expertise can be used in the regulatory process without having to totally hand over regulation to self-regulatory professional associations.

- *Finally*, the argument that professions have always been self-governing is circular. Just because it has been so in the past does not mean it must be so in the future. Indeed the argument for self-regulation belies the reality that occupational groups have been trying for nearly 200 years to claim 'professional' status for themselves as a means of controlling the market for their services.[54] The self-regulating 'professions' are really just those occupations that have succeeded in establishing a monopoly that they control.

It is also possible that the burden of self-regulation may be more onerous than any of its supposed advantages. The need for the profession to constantly defend professional independence in complaints handling, investigation and prosecution against charges of bias is demoralising and distracting. The reality that any professional association will find it hard to represent the interests of all members politically, while at the same time choosing to prosecute some of those members,

52 Richard Abel, 'Toward a Political Economy of Lawyers' (1981) *Wisconsin Law Review* 1117, 1186–7.
53 Arthurs, 'The Dead Parrot'.
54 Richard Abel, 'Why Does the ABA Promulgate Ethical Rules?' (1981) 59 *Texas Law Review* 639; Larson, *The Rise of Professionalism*; Parker, *Just Lawyers*, 109–12, 112–21 (for critique of this approach).

must at some level eventually operate to confuse the priorities and concentration of the leadership. Sometimes, the prosecution of peers by peers can be subverted for internal political purposes. At the least, the trust of the membership in the leadership is undermined by the threat of such prosecutions, and personal ethics too are likely to be undermined by institutionally suspect practices.

Harry Arthurs concludes his indictment of self-regulation by invoking Monty Python's famous dead parrot sketch: '...this parrot of self-regulation is definitely deceased; it is pushing up the daisies; it has joined the choir invisible; it is bereft of life; it has met its maker; it is no more; it is bleeding demised'.[55]

Where then might we find a better geography for lawyers' responsibility? Charles Sampford argues that individual development of a 'positive morality' is *the* important part of the answer to the diverse range of values that lawyers encounter in practice.[56] The view that a personal morality is essential to deal with the numerous (morally) significant situations that are encountered in legal practice seems obvious. The conduct rules will not be enough. Below we will examine the way self-regulation has been altered in each of the States and Territories by incorporating co-dependent and independent regulators into the system for governing the legal profession. But the point in critiquing rules and their enforcers in this way is not necessarily to argue about *who* should be regulating the profession, but *what* values should be represented in the regulation of the profession (whoever does it), and how well that regulation connects with everyday practices to help lawyers to be ethical. This is not to say, of course, that we do not need anyone watching over us, but rather that watchdogs tend to make us cringe and act furtively rather than more transparently and in a public-spirited manner.

Self-regulation has been ineffective at promoting the right values and critiquing the structure and culture of actual practice. But it is not necessarily the case that just because there is independent regulation or regulation via the market that this will be any better. Consider, for example, the fact that competition policy is probably the external regulatory force that has had most impact on the regulation of the legal profession in Australia.[57] Federal and State governments and an independent regulator, the Australian Competition and Consumer Commission, have all imposed

---

55 Arthurs, 'The Dead Parrot', 809. In the Monty Python sketch the pet shop owner tries to convince a customer that a clearly dead parrot is alive.

56 Charles Sampford with Christine Parker, 'Legal Regulation, Ethical Standard-Setting, and Institutional Design' in Stephen Parker and Charles Sampford (eds), *Legal Ethics and Legal Practice: Contemporary Issues* (Clarendon Press, Oxford, 1995) 11.

57 Christine Parker, 'Converting the Lawyers: The Dynamics of Competition and Accountability Reform' (1997) 33 *The Australian and New Zealand Journal of Sociology* 39; Ed Shinnick, Fred Bruinsma and Christine Parker, 'Aspects of Regulatory Reform in the Legal Profession: Australia, Ireland and the Netherlands' (2003) 10 *International Journal of the Legal Profession* 237, 242–7.

regulation (and deregulation) promoting competition on the profession. But this has not necessarily been helpful in promoting ethical practice. For example, Jim Spigelman, Chief Justice of New South Wales, has argued that essential public protections that are bound up in the current concerns of legal regulation may be abandoned to the market in competition regulation:[58]

> The role of the profession in the administration of justice cannot be characterised simply as the provision of services to consumers. There are structural and institutional issues here of great significance. Competition regulators tend not to understand, or if they understand tend not to value, rival institutional traditions to that of the market. A market does not value history and tradition. As I said at my swearing-in, a market wakes up every morning with a completely blank mind, like Noddy.[59]

If Spigelman is correct, limited rationalist economics provides little help for us in deciding whether or not and how to implement ethical regulatory structures. In the end, the moral stance of those structures is important.

It has been suggested that the profession and the community might be able to re-negotiate legal professionalism so that the profession still maintains a role in its own regulation and is also more responsive to other values – that is, some sort of co-regulation.[60] It may be that a wise government will even encourage some self-regulation, particularly within specialisations, if for no other reason than to harness natural interest in self-improvement as a consolidating force in professional formation.[61] At the most basic level, this is already achieved by regulators' employment of practising lawyers as investigators. But whoever the regulator, the important things are the extent to which any regulatory system seeks to institutionalise the right values and virtues (not just that of prohibiting obvious dishonesty), and that it does so in a way that critiques current practices and cultures, not just individual misconduct.

---

58 Chief Justice J J Spigelman, 'The 2002 Lawyers' Lecture: Are Lawyers Lemons? – Competition Principles and Professional Regulation' (speech delivered at the St James Ethics Centre Lawyers' Lecture Series, Sydney, 29 October 2002) <www.lawlink.nsw.gov.au/lawlink/ supreme court/11 sc.nsf/pages/SCO_speech_spigelman_291002> at 12 July 2006.

59 Ibid.

60 Parker, *Just Lawyers*, 'Ch 7: Renegotiating the Regulation of the Legal Profession'; Paterson, 'Professionalism and the Legal Services Market'; William Hurlburt, *The Self-Regulation of the Legal Profession in Canada, and in England and Wales* (Law Society of Alberta and Alberta Law Reform Institute, Edmonton, Canada, 2000) 140.

61 Parker, 'Regulation of the Ethics of Australian Legal Practice', 702: '... if we wish to make legal practice more responsive to ethical concerns and community values, then a fruitful strategy might be to bypass the traditional professional associations and look to more specific groups of lawyers to elaborate their own standards of ethical responsiveness'.

National Regulation?

Traditionally the regulation of lawyers was controlled by the States and Territories. But a nationally agreed regulatory structure for the legal profession is gradually evolving. First the States and Territories agreed on a model law framework for regulation of the legal profession consisting of:

- A set of model provisions for State and Territory legislation governing the legal profession – the *Legal Profession – Model Laws Project Model Provisions* ('*Model Laws*').[62] The *Model Laws* were a co-operative effort of the Standing Committee of Attorneys-General (SCAG) (all the Attorneys-General of the States and Territories and the Commonwealth) together with the Law Council of Australia (the national umbrella association for State and Territory legal professional associations); and

- A national set of ethical rules – the Law Council of Australia's *Model Rules of Professional Conduct and Practice* ('*Model Rules*').[63]

It was left up to the governments and professional associations in each State and Territory to decide to what extent they wish to adopt the *Model Laws* and/or the *Model Rules*. There are no regulatory or enforcement bodies for the legal profession at a national level.

The *Model Laws* reflect the fact that the Attorneys-General and the Law Council were prepared to agree on a uniform national structure for all regulatory arrangements for the legal profession except discipline and complaint investigation (examined in detail below) and rules of conduct, which they agreed were the business of the legal profession associations in each State and Territory. The *Model Laws* contain no prescription about whether elements of self-regulation should be retained or not. It is left completely up to each State and Territory to decide what body or bodies in that State or Territory will be responsible for receiving, investigating and prosecuting complaints (*Model Laws*, Part 11). It may well be that the Law Council considered that the *Model Laws* were only likely to succeed if local professional associations, in alliance with their Attorneys-General, were free to retain the control of the structures for complaints handling and discipline – an example of the parochial tail of the federal system wagging the national dog.

---

62 Australian Government – Attorney-General's Department (2004) <www.ag.gov.au/ Consultations/Pages/NationalLegalProfessionalReform.aspx> at 12 July 2006. See Daryl Williams, Attorney-General for Australia, on behalf of the Standing Committee of Attorneys-General, 'Communique: Historic Agreement on National Legal Profession' (Press Release, 7 August 2003) announcing agreement to proceed with the SCAG *Legal Profession – Model Laws Project*.

63 Law Council of Australia, *Model Rules of Professional Conduct and Practice* (2002) <www. lawcouncil.asn.au/policy/1957352449.html> at 12 July 2006. The *Model Rules* were first promulgated in February 1997.

Nor do the *Model Laws* make any attempt to set out what substantive values should animate legal practice, or be reflected in the codes of professional conduct promulgated for the profession.[64] It is as if the Attorneys-General and the Law Council of Australia consider that the regulation of the legal profession is a purely technical, neutral matter in which no particular values are at all significant.

The *Model Laws* thus have the appearance of an ethically neutral framework for individual jurisdictions to manage their local profession. The *Model Rules* contain only brief statements of principle at the beginning of each section, and no commentary on the principles underlying the rules or guidance as to how to apply them in practice. In reality, the *Model Laws* lack a 'positive morality' (in the sense advocated by Sampford), and the value structure they promote offers little more than apathy towards the moral challenges facing the profession. The guiding principles of legal practice that were contained in some earlier legislation[65] are nowhere to be found in the *National Law*. The *Model Rules* were, however, better drafted, clearer and more comprehensive than the very patchy professional conduct and practice rules that previously existed in the various States and Territories. The law societies and bar associations that make up the institutional membership of the Law Council of Australia have been encouraged to adopt them with or without local modification. They have been substantially adopted in New South Wales, South Australia and Victoria, and other jurisdictions are likely to follow suit.[66]

More recently, the Council of Australian Governments has attempted to establish a National Legal Profession Reform in which co-operative legislation would be enacted in each of the States and Territories and a national regulatory body for the legal profession established. State and Territory professional associations and regulators would still exist but under the coordination of the co-operative legislative scheme and national regulatory body. This scheme would consist of:

- The *Legal Profession National Law*, drafted by the National Legal Profession Reform Taskforce, which would be legislated by whichever States and Territories chose to opt into the scheme; and

- The *Australian Solicitors Conduct Rules* (*ASCR*), drafted by the Law Council of Australia. These are based on the earlier *Model Rules*, but with significant changes in two important areas of legal ethics: confidentiality (see Chapter 4) and conflicts of interest (see Chapter 8). In both these areas, the impact of an effective and continuing self-regulation of the profession is evident. In respect

---

64 See *Model Laws* pt 16 on power to make legal profession rules, which says nothing of any substance. The now repealed *Legal Practice Act 1996* (Vic) s 64 set out several guiding principles for legal practice that were to be reflected in any code of practice promulgated by the legal profession associations. But these were omitted from the *Legal Profession Act 2004* (Vic) which replaced it.

65 See n 66 reference to *Legal Practice Act 1996* (Vic) s 64.

66 See Dal Pont, *Lawyers' Professional Responsibility*, [1.105].

of conflicts of interest in particular, the capacity of the Law Council of Australia through its Large Law Firms Group to legitimate and license conflicts of interest for large firms is a striking development, taking the *ASCR* well beyond the *Model Rules*. The degree of moral ambivalence now contained in the *ASCR* conflicts rules[67] can be readily appreciated by reference to the *Draft Commentary* which the Law Council of Australia has proposed as an addendum to these rules in order to explain and justify their changes.[68]

The *National Law* is very much a work in progress. Only Victoria, New South Wales and the Northern Territory are definitely committed to its implementation and are likely to implement it during 2013–14. New South Wales will locate the national regulator in Sydney while Victoria will 'host' the uniform legislation, with other jurisdictions then enacting mirror provisions locally. However, it is plausible that other jurisdictions will join over time, particularly if national law firms apply consistent pressure and if the costs of practice within a national model start to decline relative to compliance with differing State-based regimes.

In later chapters of this book, we refer to the *Australian Solicitors Conduct Rules* as the national standard for professional conduct and practice rules, rather than any of the local versions of the *Model Rules* made by State and Territory professional associations and regulators in particular jurisdictions. However, we will critique the details of many specific provisions of the *Rules* and point out gaps and lack of specification in their coverage.

Co-Regulation and Independent Regulation: Complaints Handling and Disciplinary Investigations and Prosecutions

The purposes and powers of the professional regulators' complaints handling functions have also been expanded to include resolving consumer complaints about poor service by lawyers, lawyers' bills and fees, and incompetence. Independent legal services commissioners have also been introduced in New South Wales, Queensland and Victoria to receive and resolve consumer complaints about lawyers, and to investigate conduct complaints about lawyers and prosecute disciplinary action where there is sufficient evidence. But, as we shall see in the case studies below, the legal profession in each of these jurisdictions has still managed to maintain involvement, to a greater or lesser extent, in investigating or resolving complaints and prosecuting disciplinary action. Each of these three States

---

67 *Australian Solicitors' Conduct Rules* 10 and 11. See <www.lawcouncil.asn.au/programs/national_profession/conduct-rules.cfm> accessed 10 May 2013.

68 Law Council of Australia, Draft Commentary to ASCR. See <www.lawcouncil.asn.au/programs/national_profession/conduct-rules.cfm> accessed 10 May 2013.

has a regulatory structure for the legal profession with elements of both independent regulation and self-regulation, known as *co-regulation*. The legal professions in the Australian Capital Territory, Northern Territory and Tasmania still *self-regulate*, with some layperson representation in their processes, while the legal professions in South Australia and Western Australia are *independently regulated*.

Table 3.1 summarises the different approaches taken to complaints handling and the prosecution of disciplinary action in each of the Australian States and Territories, according to whether the profession functionally controls its own complaints and prosecutions (*self-regulation*), shares control with some external body (*co-regulation*) or is *independently regulated*.[69] In all cases other than Tasmania and the two Territories – where self-regulation continues – the governance of the external regulator is also described in Table 3.1, in order to indicate the often considerable cultural influence exerted by the profession inside that regulator.

Disciplinary offences are prosecuted in specialist tribunals dominated by practising lawyers in the Australian Capital Territory, Northern Territory, South Australia and Tasmania. In New South Wales, Victoria and Western Australia they are decided in the general administrative tribunals for those States. In Queensland they are prosecuted in a specialist tribunal constituted by a current Supreme Court judge. Courts of superior jurisdiction in Australia also have an inherent jurisdiction to discipline lawyers and to hear appeals on disciplinary decisions from the lower tribunals.

Despite all these reforms, there are still few cases of disciplinary action being taken against lawyers for breach of their duty to the court or the law (as we shall see in Chapters 6, 7 and 10). Nor have there yet been many cases of discipline for failures of customer service and poor billing practices, or in respect of conflicts of interest inside the largest law firms. It is hard to believe that there really are so few cases in each of these categories where disciplinary action might be warranted. The overall focus of the regulatory system is still on the bad character of individual lawyers, rather than systemic change to address public concerns about consumer service quality and the administration of justice, although the New South Wales and Queensland Legal Services Commissioners in particular have attempted more proactive and educative initiatives to improve the regulatory systems and standards of consumer service in the legal profession.[70]

---

69 For more detail see Dal Pont, *Lawyers' Professional Responsibility*, 'Ch 24: Disciplinary Procedures' 531–57.

70 See John Briton, 'Regulating for Risk', paper presented to the Conference of Regulatory Officers, 2011, Sydney available at <www.lsc.qld.gov.au/publications/speeches-and-papers> at 5 May 2013; John Briton and Scott McLean, 'Incorporated Legal Practices: Dragging the Regulation of the Legal Profession into the Modern Era' (2008) 11 *Legal Ethics* 241; Steve Mark, 'Assuring Competence in a Changing Legal Services Market – The New Regulatory Context' Legal Education and Training Review (LETR) Symposium, Manchester, UK, 10–11 July 2012, available at <www.olsc.nsw.gov.au/lawlink/olsc/ll_olsc.nsf/pages/OLSC_speeches> at 5 May 2013.

Table 3.1: Different Regulatory Arrangements for Complaints Handling and Prosecuting Disciplinary Action in Australia – June 2006

Jurisdiction	Regulatory Approach	Regulating Bodies	Composition of External Prosecutor/Regulator and Limits to Independence
New South Wales	Co-regulation	Law Society of New South Wales/NSW Bar Association/Legal Services Commissioner	A single Legal Services Commissioner (former lawyer), but the LSC refers some investigations to the profession
Queensland	Co-regulation	Law Society of Queensland/Bar Association of Queensland/Legal Services Commissioner	A single Legal Services Commissioner
Tasmania	Self-regulation	Law Society of Tasmania	None
Victoria	Co-regulation	Legal Services Board/ Legal Services Commissioner/Law Institute of Victoria/ Victorian Bar Council	Legal Services Board: 1 Chair (originally a lawyer), 3 elected lawyers, and 3 non-lawyers nominated by the Attorney-General. A single Legal Services Commissioner (originally a lawyer), who is also the Chief Executive of the Legal Services Board
South Australia	Independent regulation	Legal Practitioners Conduct Board	Presiding Member and 3 ordinary members (all nominated by SA Law Society), plus 3 other members nominated by the Attorney-General[71]
Western Australia	Independent regulation	Legal Practice Board/Legal Profession Complaints Committee	Legal Profession Complaints Committee: 1 Chair and 6 members of the Legal Practice Board, plus 2 community representatives appointed by the Attorney-General
Northern Territory	Self-regulation	Law Society of the NT	None
ACT	Self-regulation	Law Society of the ACT/ACT Bar Association/ Complaints Investigating Committee	None

71 The structure of South Australian lawyers' regulation is under review following the *McGee* case (see Chapter 11).

For the remainder of this chapter we will first look at the ways in which self-regulation has been challenged and changed in various States and Territories and, second, critically examine the institutional context of the way interest on clients' trust account funds is used.

DISCUSSION QUESTIONS

In the following subsections we describe the pressures on self-regulation that have led to reforms to the way the legal profession is regulated in New South Wales, Queensland, Tasmania and Victoria. (See Table 3.1 above for a schematic summary of the situation in each of the States and Territories.)
As you read these descriptions, consider the following questions:

1. What are the weaknesses of self-regulation as demonstrated by what has occurred in each of these jurisdictions? What were, or are, its strengths?

2. What do these case studies indicate about which stakeholder interests and ethical values were recognised, and which were ignored in the traditional self-regulatory arrangements for the legal profession? Which stakeholder interests and ethical values are reflected in the various reforms to the regulation of the legal professions in each jurisdiction, as far as you can tell from the facts given here?

3. Do you think that each of the various co-regulatory arrangements that were introduced in New South Wales, Victoria and, to a lesser extent, Queensland represent an appropriate balance between independence and professional expertise and involvement in lawyer regulation? Which do you prefer and why? How would a new independent regulator at the national level change the balance?

4. What difference do you think it would make to the way you would think about your own behaviour and ethics as a lawyer whether legal profession regulation is self-regulation, co-regulation or independent regulation? For example, are you likely to pay more attention to rules developed by other lawyers than to those developed by an independent regulator? Or are you likely to prefer a more general moral sense to lawyers' rules? Are lawyers more likely to feel that if they do anything wrong they will be dealt with kindly if the regulator is their own professional association, rather than an independent commissioner?

New South Wales

In New South Wales, the most populous state, the Legal Services Commissioner (LSC), an independent regulator, receives all complaints made about lawyers. But the system is one of co-regulation, not independent regulation. The LSC investigates and concludes all consumer complaints – that is, those that raise consumer disputes about bills, delay and lack of communication – and these are about two thirds of all complaints. However, the LSC refers the vast majority of the one third of complaints that involve allegations about professional conduct back to the two professional organisations – the Law Society (solicitors) and the Bar Association (barristers) – to investigate and prosecute any disciplinary action. Control by the LSC is emphasised by his or her capacity, although seldom exercised, to recall a complaint investigation from the profession. The LSC can also review complaints that the professional associations have dismissed without taking any action. Former LSC, Steve Mark, has indicated that he did not refer complaints for investigation to the Law Society if they concerned someone who might be connected to the Council of the Society. He explained his approach as follows:

> In relation to complaints and discipline, the powers to investigate and prosecute conduct complaints is [sic] shared equally between my Office and the professional associations. While I have the overall responsibility of overseeing the process, the professional associations play an active and vital role within it ... [A] strong relationship has developed between my Office and the professional associations for the purpose of improving the profession and ensuring that their high ethical standards are met. This co-regulatory regime is, in my view, the best existing model for regulation of the legal profession as it encourages the profession to continue on its path of self-regulation and improvement, albeit with direction from my Office. It also seems to me that it would be counter-productive if the role of the professional associations were limited to defending its members against charges of misconduct as this would create an adversarial relationship between them and my Office and also be of concern to the ethical members of the profession that their association was acting as an advocate for the worst of its members ... My thesis is that it is imperative that the legal profession play a much more active and pro-active role in the regulation of the profession both through traditional modes of self-regulation and through creative submissions and suggestions to Government for achieving outcomes to benefit the community directly rather than feasting now with the reality of starvation in the future when Government inevitably intervenes.[72]

---

72 Steve Mark, 'Is State Regulation of the Legal Profession Inevitable?' (paper presented at the Pacific Rim Conference, Heron Island, October 2003) <www.lawlink.nsw.gov.au/lawlink/ olsc/ll olsc.nsf/ pages/OLSC heron> at 12 July 2006.

Opinions differ as to as to whether the balance between independent regulation and self-regulation in this model is appropriate. On the one hand, the LSC appears to be trusted by government and the profession. There have been no specific allegations of any improper decision-making by either the profession or the LSC in the performance of their roles. In fact, when the New South Wales Bar was perceived to be seriously deficient in its willingness to remove from practice those senior barristers who had failed to pay income tax for many years, and who had then declared themselves bankrupt in order to further escape payment, the LSC was reportedly active in his insistence that the NSW Bar Association proceed in an open disciplinary process against the recalcitrant lawyers.[73] The Bar Association had initially reacted defensively to the scandal, saying that it had not done anything about the barristers' conduct because no complaint had ever been made to it.

But there is also another view that the profession may still be too dominant in the power-sharing arrangements. For example, in relation to the bankrupt barristers, the bar did eventually take disciplinary action against a number of lawyers who had failed to pay their tax and possibly used bankruptcy to avoid their tax debts. But the bar did little to do anything pro-active to try to ensure that such a scandal did not occur again, until they were pushed to do so. Consistent with the traditional approach of self-regulation, their focus was on reactive discipline of the barristers identified as problems. In the meantime the Attorney-General had to act to change the rules to put in place a more sustainable system for identifying potential misconduct in the future and for investigating all misconduct from the past. This occurred only after the Commonwealth requested the States to produce a uniform approach to ensure that barristers who became bankrupt were required to report this to their professional association, which would then be required to apply a 'fit and proper' person test to determine if the barrister could continue in practice.[74]

Overall, the New South Wales regulatory system seems to have proved adept at resolving such conflict issues as may have occurred without obvious deficit to the public interest. To that extent, it might be said that co-regulation on the New South Wales model is 'workable'. It might also be that the current Commissioner's personal skills and powers of persuasion are, in practice, sufficient to discretely manage what could be described as a continuing conflict of interest in the involvement of the profession in its own disciplinary processes. Such a system may not be sustainable with different personalities in key positions. In Victoria

73 Chris Merritt, 'Hearsay', *The Australian Financial Review* (Sydney), 23 March 2001, 35. See, for example, *New South Wales Bar Association v Cummins* (2001) 52 NSWLR 279.
74 Richard Ackland, 'Time to Stop Fudging about Bankrupts at the Bar', *The Sydney Morning Herald*, 2 March 2001, 12; Paul Barry, 'Rich Lawyers Dodging Income Tax', *The Sydney Morning Herald*, 26 February 2001, 1; Ruth McColl, 'Disclosure Will Give Barristers' Watchdog a Real Bite', *The Sydney Morning Herald*, 2 March 2001, 12.

(see below) the previous co-regulatory system was widely viewed as unworkable because of tensions between the independent regulators and self-regulators. As we see in the discussion of the situation in Queensland below, it can also be argued that any involvement of legal professional associations in the regulation of lawyers is a conflict of interest.

Queensland

In Queensland, self-regulation by the two professional associations for solicitors and barristers ended in 2004 as the result of major criticisms of the way the Queensland Law Society (QLS) carried out its regulatory responsibilities by the State Attorney-General, the Legal Ombudsman and the press. The event that sparked the furore was allegations that Brisbane law firm Baker Johnson had been guilty of a whole range of unprofessional, unethical and fraudulent conduct in relation to its 'no-win, no-fee' clients. Most dramatically, in one instance Baker Johnson had won a case for a client but then effectively diverted to itself the entire compensation payout for the payment of fees, and gone on to sue the client for additional fees under a 'no-win, no-fee' arrangement.[75] Complaints about Baker Johnson's conduct had been made to the QLS, but the local newspaper and the Attorney-General criticised the QLS for failing to either investigate or prosecute Baker Johnson, and for having inadequate complaints-handling procedures in general, leading to numerous unresolved complaints.[76]

The Attorney-General publicly questioned the value of lawyers' self-regulation and asked the then Queensland Legal Ombudsman, Jack Nimmo, to investigate. In his report, Mr Nimmo concluded that the QLS's complaints handling service was '...nothing but a post office box'. He found that complainants were unhappy with the fact that QLS's practice was to merely refer a copy of their complaint to the solicitor for response, and then send that back to the complainant. He commented that '...for the complainant to be forwarded a copy of the solicitor's response, the contents of which have already been disputed, stating that "on the face of it the response appears to answer your complaint" is inadequate'.[77]

Nimmo set out options for reforming the QLS's self-regulatory complaints-handling functions, but made it quite plain that he preferred the option in which complaints handling, investigation and prosecution of disciplinary action were taken

75 *Baker Johnson v Jorgensen* [2002] QDC 205 (Unreported, McGill DCJ, 26 July 2002). This case and the ethical issues raised by 'no-win, no-fee' agreements are discussed further in Chapter 8.

76 Jack Nimmo, *The Queensland Law Society and Baker Johnson Lawyers* (Legal Ombudsman, Brisbane, 2002) 2–3 <www.justice.qld.gov.au/dept/pdfs/baker.pdf> at 15 June 2006. See also Haller, 'Discipline vs Regulation'.

77 Nimmo, *The Queensland Law Society and Baker Johnson Lawyers*, 6–7.

away from the QLS and Barristers Board and given to an independent regulator, assisted by lawyers.[78] When the Attorney-General subsequently announced that he was stripping the QLS of its powers and handing them to a new Legal Services Commissioner,[79] no one was surprised, although the QLS has managed to 'claw-back' some investigations, on a similar basis to that existing in New South Wales (as described above).[80]

The New South Wales Legal Services Commissioner's view on the value of legal professional associations staying involved in professional regulation (set out in the previous subsection) can be contrasted with that of Jack Nimmo, the former Queensland Legal Ombudsman. Mr Nimmo agreed that lawyers' expertise is needed when a regulator is investigating complaints against lawyers, but disagreed that the profession as an institution should have any role to play in its own regulation:

> From the outset, I emphasise that I fully support the regulation of the profession and investigation of complaints against the legal profession by like professionals. In making this statement, it is also my recommendation that any professionals conducting 'the regulatory role' should be completely independent of the QLS and their associated functions. It is my opinion that QLS has a conflict of interest in maintaining a regulatory role as well as maintaining their role as a society to benefit the profession. This conflict has appeared to have marred its image in their handling of complaints against [Baker Johnson] lawyers. The reported quotes of 'Caesar judging Caesar' and the like appear justified.[81]

This history illustrates clearly the need to align personal and institutional ethics, if lawyers are to be able to practise ethically. The inactivity and delay in the QLS's investigation and prosecution of Baker Johnson and other legal practitioners – described by Mr Nimmo as the consequence of an unacceptable conflict of interest between the QLS's role as a union and its complaints handling role – allowed those lawyers to remain in practice, and continue to avoid scrutiny for acts which were subsequently criticised severely in both civil and disciplinary proceedings.[82] The growing publicity about QLS's investigatory inactivity may even have encouraged other recalcitrant lawyers in the belief that self-regulation worked to their advantage.

Reflecting this whole experience, the new Queensland regime is perhaps the most 'independent' of the co-regulation jurisdictions. While investigations can

---

78 Ibid 10–12.
79 Sam Strutt, 'Watchdog Set to End Self-Regulation', *The Australian Financial Review* (Sydney), 16 May 2003, 57.
80 Chris Griffith, 'Law Society Hits Reform Process', *The Courier-Mail* (Brisbane), 7 May 2003, 5; the *Legal Profession Act 2004* (Qld) s 182(2) allows the Commissioner to refer investigations back to the QLS or the Bar.
81 Nimmo, *The Queensland Law Society and Baker Johnson Lawyers*, 9.
82 Ibid 3.

still be delegated to the professional associations, all power to decide on and institute disciplinary action against lawyers is now in the hands of the single Legal Services Commissioner.[83] One of the Commissioner's first successful disciplinary actions was the removal of one of the founders of Baker Johnson from the roll of practitioners.[84]

Tasmania

In a manner similar to the Queensland about-face on self-regulation, the Tasmanian government also became determined to shake up the Tasmanian Law Society (TLS) after the collapse of a number of solicitors' mortgage schemes that ultimately led to criminal proceedings against some lawyers. One firm apparently lost up to $20 million of clients' funds.[85] The government was convinced that the TLS had mismanaged the regulatory framework for solicitors' mortgage practices so that the losses went undiscovered until it was too late.[86] The government intended to divest the Tasmanian profession of self-regulatory functions by establishing a new Legal Profession Board, consisting of two non-lawyers and four legal practitioners (to be appointed by the Attorney-General from a list of nominations from the profession). The TLS president was initially reported to be in support of the government's agenda.[87] Later, however, the TLS announced that while it supported the idea that the Board should take over the power to investigate and prosecute complaints against lawyers, it opposed the Board taking over the TLS's other regulatory powers, particularly the power to issue practising certificates, because the new bureaucracy would be too costly compared with the existing system. The government responded that the TLS was prepared to dispense with prosecutions '… because that's been trouble for them', but wanted to keep control over the issue of practising certificates because there was money to be made there (lawyers pay a large fee for their practising certificates each year).[88] Regulatory reform is now on hold in Tasmania after the Upper House insisted on an amendment giving control of practising certificates back to the Law Society. This provoked the Attorney-General to adjourn further debate on her legislation indefinitely, despite her initial

---

83 See the *Legal Profession Act 2004* (Qld) s 182(2); Linda Haller, 'Imperfect Practice under the Legal Profession Act 2004 (Qld)' (2004) 23 *University of Queensland Law Journal* 411, 420.

84 *Baker v Legal Services Commissioner* [2006] QCA 145 (Unreported, McPherson, Jerrard JJA and Douglas J, 5 May 2006).

85 'Lawyers Could Lose Power to Investigate Complaints', *The Advocate* (Burnie), 22 June 2000, 4; Anne Barbeliuk, 'Move to Shake Up Law Society', *The Mercury* (Hobart), 21 May 2000, 3; Haller, 'Discipline vs Regulation'.

86 Martine Haley, 'New Watchdog to Regulate Lawyers', *The Mercury* (Hobart), 18 April 2003, 5.

87 Ibid.

88 Ellen Whinnett, 'Legal Battle', *The Mercury* (Hobart), 4 September 2003, 1.

determination that ethical change was necessary after the behaviour mentioned above became known.

Victoria

After over a hundred years of self-regulation, Victoria's regulatory system began a decade of major change in 1993 when its Solicitors' Guarantee (fidelity) Fund entered a state of technical deficit following major defalcations of clients' funds, contributed to in turn by the economic downturn of 1989–92.[89] The reaction of the then Kennett conservative government was to instigate a major inquiry into the regulatory system, which recommended the introduction of a new co-regulatory system. In 1997 the *Legal Practice Act 1996* came into force. The Act removed control of the fidelity compensation process from the Law Institute of Victoria (LIV) (the solicitors' association) and introduced a tri-level structure that added both complexity and a measure of external accountability to the system. A non-lawyer Legal Ombudsman (LOV) acquired the ability to investigate complaints against lawyers, alongside the LIV and the Victorian Bar, and when necessary to review the exercise by the professional associations of their regulatory functions.

The two women who filled the Legal Ombudsman position at different times exercised their powers with vigour. Both also attracted sustained criticism from the legal professional associations for securing some successful prosecutions of prominent solicitors, while openly challenging the competency of the LIV and Bar as regulators.[90] In fact, the LOV was a determined if sometimes provocative complaints handler, and arguably played a critical role in addressing a number of ethical shortcomings of the professions' approach to complaint investigation and prosecution. It was ironic and unfortunate that, despite the cogency of their criticisms, the style of both Legal Ombudsmen – activist women with little tolerance for what they perceived as sexism within the profession – contributed to the demise of the office. Both incumbents believed they had little option but to challenge the existing system. Both felt it important to put their concerns on the record, in writing, rather than resolve a matter by a telephone call to the CEO of the LIV or Bar. This style could easily be misinterpreted as a lack of respect rather than, as the two women believed, the maintenance of an appropriate arms'-length relationship between independent regulator and self-regulators in complaint investigation.

---

89 Adrian Evans, 'A Concise History of the Solicitors' Guarantee Fund (Vic): A Marriage of Principle and Pragmatism' (2000) 26 *Monash University Law Review* 74, 139.
90 See, eg, Legal Ombudsman, *Annual Report 2002/03* (Legal Ombudsman, Melbourne, 2003) 'Unlawful Acts by Law Institute and Victorian Bar' 8–9.

The Victorian Attorney-General was known to be concerned by the complexity of the system and the perceived cost of duplicating regulatory arrangements. But his announcement of a review of those arrangements in June 2000[91] was preceded in February of that year by the fining of a former Victorian Law Institute president for misconduct arising from a conflict of interest. This prosecution had been commenced by the Ombudsman and justified with a determined statement about '... investigat[ing] a complaint without fear or favour'.[92]

As a result of the review,[93] the Attorney-General eventually put in place a new system that came into operation at the beginning of 2006.[94] The completely independent Legal Ombudsman and the existing peak regulator, the Legal Practice Board, were replaced by a new seven-member Legal Services Board and Legal Services Commissioner (LSC). The LSC receives all complaints about lawyers (where previously complaints could be made to the LOV, the LIV or the Bar) and may handle all investigations itself; but as in New South Wales, the LSC routinely refers many investigations and power to make recommendations about prosecutions back to the professional organisations. The Legal Services Board issues practising certificates, administers and manages the trust accounting system and the fidelity fund, and can make and approve legal profession rules. The LSC is also CEO of the Legal Services Board. This function will necessarily involve taking direction from the new Board, the composition of which includes at least three lawyers elected by the profession. However in the LSC's other role as complaints handler, investigator and prosecutor, they are to operate 'independently' of the Legal Services Board.

The Attorney-General was quite annoyed by suggestions that the interrelationship between the new Board and Commissioner would entrench a conflict of interest, and later defended the arrangements vigorously:

> This Commissioner will be absolutely independent in terms of his or her complaint-handling function. The Commissioner will not be subject to the Board's direction and will retain ultimate oversight of these matters ... Significantly, the majority of [the Legal Services Board] will not be elected by the legal profession. The importance of this attribute of the new system should not be understated. It is inaccurate at best, and downright

---

91 Office of the Attorney-General, Victoria, 'Another Step in Modernising the Legal Profession' (Press Release, 9 June 2000) <www.dpc.vic.gov.au/pressrel> at 12 July 2006.

92 Darrin Farrant, 'Rape Case Conflict Proves Costly for Lawyer', *The Age* (Melbourne), 28 February 2000, 6. See also Darrin Farrant, 'Lawyer Slated on Client Conflict', *The Age* (Melbourne), 10 February 2000, 5.

93 Peter Sallmann and Richard Wright, *Regulation of the Victorian Legal Profession: Report of the Review of the Legal Practice Act 1996* (Victorian Department of Justice, Melbourne, 2001).

94 *Legal Profession Act 2004* (Vic); Fergus Shiel, 'New System for Legal Complaints', *The Age* (Melbourne), 25 July 2003, 5.

misleading at worst, to suggest that the new commissioner will be at the 'financial and personal mercy of the Board'. This discounts the myriad of checks and balances that have been carefully crafted into the legislation.[95]

While the present LSC is perceived to be subtle, perceptive and discrete in his approach, the present Victorian version of co-regulation nevertheless raises questions about the capacity of self-regulatory and independent regulatory institutions to coexist in a way that promotes lawyers' ethics.[96] Figure 3.1 sets out the nature of the relationship between the Legal Services Commissioner, the Legal Services Board and professional associations. There is no question about the integrity of the current LSC, but the major problem with this structure, as a structure, is the lack of arms'-length relationships between those responsible for key functions of the Act. A key ethical function of the Act is to ensure that complaints are not, in practice, dealt with by the profession itself. But although it is not possible for the LSC to *delegate* their power to receive and investigate a complaint to a professional organisation, *referral* of the power to investigate a complaint is possible, and occurs in the normal course of events.

South Australia and Western Australia

South Australia and Western Australia, in contrast to all of the other States, have removed the principal regulatory roles from the organised profession.[97] There have been no significant assertions in either State that the structure of regulation interferes with the personal ethics of practitioners or their ability to act independently of government.

Northern Territory and the ACT

Both Territories have always maintained entirely self-regulatory mechanisms for complaints handling and disciplinary procedures.[98] Their practitioners have maintained that the small size of these jurisdictions compels a cost-sensitive (self-regulatory) approach,[99] and this view has dominated despite the implicit pressure

---

95 Rob Hulls, 'Streamlined Path to Legal Complaints Fair and Just', *The Australian Financial Review* (Sydney), 21 January 2005, 62.
96 For stronger statements of the authors' views, see Catherine Bragg et al, 'Hulls' Legal Reforms Will Help Only "Bad" Lawyers', *The Age* (Melbourne), 29 August 2003, 13; Adrian Evans and Christine Parker, 'Too Close for Comfort', *The Australian Financial Review* (Sydney), 10 December 2004, 47.
97 *Legal Practitioners Act 1893* (WA) ss 25(1)(b), 27(1)(c); *Legal Practitioners Act 1981* (SA) ss 74(1)(a), 76.
98 *Legal Practitioners Act 1974* (NT) s 47; *Legal Profession Act 2006* (ACT) ch 4 and s 577.
99 Josh Massoud, 'Profession Trades Blows as Regulation Debate Hits ACT', *Lawyers Weekly* (Sydney), 15 August 2003, 4.

Figure 3.1 Key Relationships of the *Legal Profession Act 2004* (Vic) Affecting Independence in the Relationship Between the Legal Services Board and the Legal Services Commissioner in the Investigation of Complaints

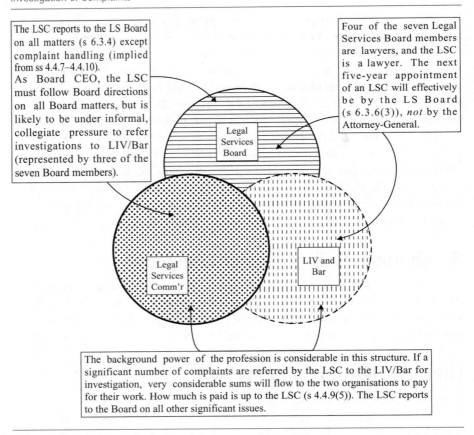

The LSC reports to the LS Board on all matters (s 6.3.4) except complaint handling (implied from ss 4.4.7–4.4.10).
As Board CEO, the LSC must follow Board directions on all Board matters, but is likely to be under informal, collegiate pressure to refer investigations to LIV/Bar (represented by three of the seven Board members).

Four of the seven Legal Services Board members are lawyers, and the LSC is a lawyer. The next five-year appointment of an LSC will effectively be by the LS Board (s 6.3.6(3)), *not* by the Attorney-General.

Legal Services Board

Legal Services Comm'r

LIV and Bar

The background power of the profession is considerable in this structure. If a significant number of complaints are referred by the LSC to the LIV/Bar for investigation, very considerable sums will flow to the two organisations to pay for their work. How much is paid is up to the LSC (s 4.4.9(5)). The LSC reports to the Board on all other significant issues.

of the national Legal Profession Project Model Laws for nationally consistent complaints-handling structures.[100]

The Ethics of Fidelity and Appropriation: Funding the Regulation of the Profession

A second major area where there is a tension between institutional and personal ethics arises from the phenomenon of practitioners' trust accounts, where clients' funds are held on trust for them until needed. Lawyers typically hold such

---

100 Williams, 'Communique' (Press release, 7 Aug 2003).

money for short periods when their clients are about to purchase real estate, or are winding up a deceased estate. These funds earn interest amounting annually to many millions of dollars, but much of that interest goes to the law societies, legal aid and legal education, rather than to the clients who own the deposits. This strange appropriation, which generally occurs without clients' knowledge or consent, raises an ethical problem.[101]

When lawyers steal trust funds from one of their firm's clients, compensation is ordinarily payable by each one of a number of State-based 'fidelity funds'. These are administered by a mixture of law societies or independent regulators, depending on whether the profession has retained a degree of self-regulation or not in each jurisdiction (see *National Law*, Part 4.5). The regulator can try to recover the money from the thieving lawyer and, if they still have any, this recovery will be used to offset what the fund has to repay the former client.

Originally, fidelity funds were financed just by levies on lawyers. Then, in the early 1960s, someone in Victoria worked out that the existing Victorian fund – which was then close to deficit because of a string of thefts – could be topped up by the interest that banks were not paying to anyone, in respect of the trust balances maintained in practitioners' trust accounts.[102] So much money became available from this source[103] that most governments quickly decided to use the excess cash for a variety of other purposes, principally legal aid, but also for the cost of lawyer regulation, practical legal training and other good causes related to the legal profession.

The legally sanctioned diversion of interest from clients' accounts began as a means of financing fidelity compensation – an ethical imperative if the profession was to retain the trust of clients. But after the 1960s, fidelity compensation became a secondary purpose. Nowadays the appropriation mainly occurs because clients, as a rule, do not know they can receive this interest if they ask for it, and if it is economical to calculate and pay it. Indeed, the diversion process benefits from the fact that solicitors commonly do *not* advise their clients that they could be receiving at least some of the interest themselves. The situation is so endemic that there is now an implicit institutional ethic of statutory diversion of clients' trust account interest to professional and public purposes, in practical opposition to the personal ethic of the fiduciary, which at common law requires the lawyer to conserve the interest in the hands of the client. When a depositor puts money in the bank, they usually also receive some interest, even if they do not ask for it.[104]

---

101 See Adrian Evans, 'A Concise History of the Solicitors' Guarantee Fund (Vic)'; Reid Mortensen, 'Interest on Lawyers' Trust Accounts' (2005) 27 *Sydney Law Review* 289.
102 Evans, 'A Concise History of the Solicitors' Guarantee Fund (Vic)', 92–5.
103 Estimated at over $100 million annually, across Australia: see Mortensen, 'Interest on Lawyers' Trust Accounts', 321.
104 Ibid 312–16.

- Do you realise that you may be disregarding a fiduciary responsibility by not informing your clients of their right to receive the interest?

- Why do you think the law societies will not acknowledge that there is a latent conflict of interest behind their silence on the issue?

- Why is it that there is no conduct rule requiring you to advise your clients about their funds' interest-earning potential?

This is a story of inter-dependence rather than independence, of organisations and governments so tied to each other in financial terms that an effective silence prevails as to the morality of the source and means of funding.

Law societies are at least vaguely aware of the fact that the interest on clients' individual trust balances can now be easily and inexpensively calculated and paid to clients.[105] Where manual accounting systems have been the norm, the 'donation' process has been, on the whole, reasonable because the technical task and cost of accurately calculating interest on a sub-account with a tiny balance has, historically at least, often been higher than the interest itself. The Law Society of England and Wales has since the mid-1960s[106] attempted a rough calculation and paid interest to clients in situations where the amount on deposit with the practitioner was sufficiently large, but even that initiative is now effectively redundant. Digital computing has changed everything, and in Scotland it is now recognised that it is possible to economically calculate and pay interest to clients on all trust balances.[107] With mobile banking growing quickly, clients are becoming more comfortable with transferring funds only when actually needed and their willingness to leave money sitting in a trust account pending a settlement will steadily recede. The question that never really arose in the past – that is, what do the ethics of the situation require? – is now of international concern.

Whenever the profession is asked why there is no move to make a rule requiring practitioners to discuss an interest-earning trust deposit with their clients, it is said sincerely that the expropriation of interest is quite legal, that the expropriation is no different in principle to taxation, and that the funds are used for good purposes. No one argues that the funds are not used for good purposes – legal aid, for example, has received over $100 million in Victoria alone from this source. However, the argument that the appropriation is legal misses the point. It is not the transfer *per se* that is questionable, but the decision to permit the transfer in the first place.

---

105 For example, Westpac has a 'Deskbank' program that can pay interest to client accounts for individual practitioners, allowing them to offer lower net fees to clients by crediting their own interest entitlement against the cost of legal services.

106 Adrian Evans, *The Development and Control of the Solicitors' Guarantee Fund (Victoria) and its Ethical Implications for the Legal Profession* (LLM Thesis, Monash University, 1997) 161, 243–5.

107 Ibid 197.

The legislation is merely permissive. Why do some lawyers choose to deposit large client balances in separate interest-bearing accounts – known as 'controlled' accounts – on behalf of some but not all clients?

Secondly, taxation is theoretically compulsory. The payment of *clients'* interest to all these purposes, noble as they are, is, however, essentially optional: the diversion occurs because, so far, lawyers are not asked to turn their minds to the fiduciary duty to consider whether, given the capacity of modern technology, the capital held for clients could earn interest for them.

Thirdly, there is no contest with the assertion that much of the interest is used for socially important purposes, particularly legal aid, as mentioned above. That may be good if the utilitarian approach – the greatest good for the greatest number – is applied. But if the alternative Kantian approach, that 'means are as important as ends', is regarded as crucial, especially to law and lawyers, then the appropriation of interest on client funds without client consent is a problem. If the virtuous lawyer is someone who values their integrity and fidelity, will they not wish first to stay faithful to their clients and tell them about their right to their own interest?

The current approach is, however, entrenched at the level of government and law societies. Perhaps it will take a class action by a group of disgruntled clients or an entrepreneurial approach by the banks – using mobile banking technology – to reaffirm the central (ethical) proposition that 'interest follows principal'.[108]

Internationally, whether there is too little money to adequately finance fidelity compensation, as in many United States jurisdictions, or an excess of funds, as in Australia and South Africa, the source of funds is a continuing dilemma. In the United States, the levies which local bar associations are prepared to impose on their membership are in general far too low to support more than basic compensation mechanisms, with payment caps that seem meagre by international comparison.[109] In sharp contrast, the use of interest on clients' trust balances is readily applied to pay for fidelity compensation in most Australian States and South Africa.[110] The levels of compensation are generous and there is little or no public pressure to examine these systems because, on the one hand, the compensation schemes have

---

108 The issue came before the US Supreme Court in *Phillips v Washington Legal Foundation*, 524 US 156 (1998) in the context of a challenge to the use of Interest on Lawyers Trust Accounts (IOLTA) funds. The Court affirmed the (unremarkable) general principle that the owner of a capital sum is also the owner of the interest on that sum. Note also the earlier *Brown v Inland Revenue Commissioners* [1965] AC 244, where the House of Lords established the primacy of clients' ownership of trust account interest under the fiduciary principles of English law. The case led to rules first gazetted in 1965 that provided – pre low-cost computing – for the payment of minimum amounts of interest to clients according to a table specifying a threshold capital amount held by practitioners in trust: see *Solicitors Accounts Rules 1991* (UK) r 21(1).

109 Evans, *The Development and Control of the Solicitors' Guarantee Fund (Victoria)*, 163–8.

110 Ibid 173.

very good reputations for efficiency and fairness, while on the other, the clients who support the mechanism are in the main unaware of their 'donations' to those other clients who lose out to thefts by their practitioners.

DISCUSSION QUESTIONS

1. What are the arguments, if any, *in favour* of using interest on lawyers' trust accounts for public purposes from the perspective of each of the four ethical approaches set out in Chapters 1 and 2 – *adversarial advocacy, responsible lawyering, moral activism* and the *ethics of care?*

2. What are the arguments *against* using interest on lawyers' trust accounts for public purposes from each of the four approaches?

3. The choice between competing views about interest on lawyers' trust accounts is the choice facing all ethical conundrums: which value is more important? With legal aid crying out for funds and daily injustice occurring to those who are unrepresented, does it really matter if clients do not know what happens to the interest on their money if it can be used for a good purpose? Or is it always wrong to breach the fiduciary duty to the client by appropriating their money without their consent, regardless of the fact that legislation endorses the appropriation?

Conclusion

Ongoing reform to the regulation of lawyers is important because ethical behaviour is a function of individual values as well as the social and market context of lawyers' practices. Legal regulation and ethical standard setting are part of the moral economy of the whole profession that supports or detracts from the right values being demonstrated in these three areas. But regulation is just one aspect of the whole story.

In 1986, the American Bar Association Commission on Professionalism urged lawyers to adopt higher standards than those required by disciplinary rules, and named a devotion to public service as the *dominant* feature of professionalism.[111] The objective of this chapter has been to critique current legal regulatory structures

---

111 American Bar Association Commission on Professionalism, *In the Spirit of Public Service: A Blueprint for the Rekindling of Lawyer Professionalism* (American Bar Association, Chicago, 1986) 10, 50.

from an ethical perspective – that is, with professionalism in mind. We have provided examples of those structures which affect a lawyer's personal ethics.

It is possible to conclude that the institutional structures of the profession are fair – that significant self-regulation is fundamental to lawyers' self-respect and hence to their *willingness* to 'behave'; and that appropriation of clients' interest for good public service purposes far outweighs any minor losses of interest to some clients. It is also possible to take contrary views. At bottom, attitudes to these contrasting positions ought to be guided by the question: Which viewpoint will best assist me to practise ethically? In answering this question, lawyers will be acting in their local environment but must also consider what is happening internationally. It is now a cliché to describe legal practice as global. Lawyers are entitled to practise in an economically efficient manner in order to compete, yet clients and the consumer movement will also not be denied lawyers of virtue and transparent, international ethical standards in lawyering.

RECOMMENDED FURTHER READING

G E Dal Pont, *Lawyers' Professional Responsibility* (Lawbook Co, Pyrmont, NSW, 5th edn, 2013) 'Ch 1: The Concept of Professional Responsibility' and 'Ch 24: Disciplinary Procedures'.

Linda Haller, 'Professional Discipline for Incompetent Lawyers?: Developments in the UK and Australia' (2010) 17 *International Journal of the Legal Profession* 83.

Reid Mortensen, 'Interest on Lawyers' Trust Accounts' (2005) 27 *Sydney Law Review* 289.

Donald Nicolson and Julian Webb, *Professional Legal Ethics: Critical Interrogations* (Oxford University, Oxford, 1999) 'Ch 4: The Regulatory Context – Ethics and Professional Self-Regulation'.

Christine Parker, *Just Lawyers: Regulation and Access to Justice* (Oxford University Press, Oxford, 1999) 'Ch 6: Competing Images of the Legal Profession – Competing Regulatory Strategies' and 'Ch 7: Renegotiating the Regulation of the Legal Profession'.

Deborah Rhode, *In the Interests of Justice: Reforming the Legal Profession* (Oxford University Press, New York, 2000) especially 'Ch 6: Regulation of the Profession'.

David Wilkins, 'Who Should Regulate Lawyers?' (1992) 105 *Harvard Law Review* 799.

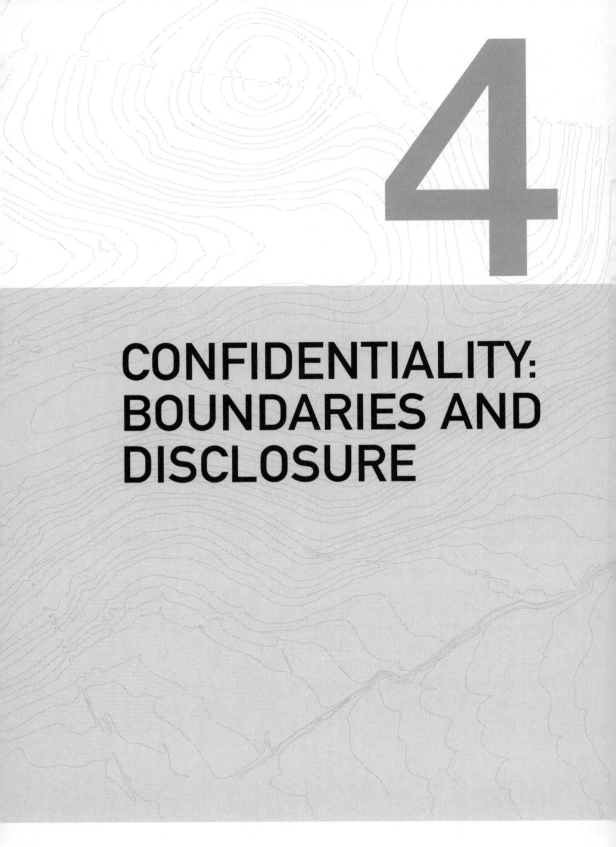

4

CONFIDENTIALITY: BOUNDARIES AND DISCLOSURE

Introduction

The profession has traditionally seen it as a cornerstone of professional responsibility that lawyers serve each client's interest loyally, carefully and confidentially. The most strict and onerous rules in the law of lawyering relate to this trilogy of duties of loyalty, confidentiality and care. Although there is much case law and commentary on the detail of each obligation, their main contours are quite clear.[1]

First, clients need to be able to trust their lawyers to provide advice and represent them in the legal system completely uninfluenced by any concern other than the client's interests. We examine lawyers' obligations to avoid situations involving a *conflict of interest* between a lawyer's personal interest and their duty to a client, or a *conflict of duties* owed to two or more clients, in Chapter 8.

Second, lawyers also owe a general duty of *care* to their clients. Many of the most common client complaints against lawyers to independent regulators relate to everyday breaches of the duty of care, such as failures of lawyers to communicate with their clients in a clear and timely manner. Gross breaches of care can be subject to disciplinary action, and clients can also sue lawyers for negligence or breach of contract if they do not take reasonable care to protect and advance their clients' interests, and to perform their legal work competently. We discuss the complaints and discipline system in Chapter 3.

The topic for this chapter is the third duty, confidentiality. Lawyers' obligation of confidentiality is based on the assumption that clients must be able to fully inform their lawyer of all relevant facts, 'confident' that the information will not be passed on to anyone else for any other purpose. Lawyers therefore have strict obligations to maintain the *confidentiality* of information relating to the representation of each client, and generally must not disclose or otherwise use that information for other purposes. This duty of confidentiality continues forever – after the client's matter has been finalised, and even after the client is dead. This means that lawyers (and their law firms) cannot act against a former client in relation to any matter in which they have received relevant confidential information from that client. Lawyers who breach their confidentiality obligations to clients can be sued by those clients in general law, and also disciplined for misconduct. In fact the law considers lawyers' obligations of confidentiality so important that much that is communicated between lawyer and client is also protected from disclosure to courts, police and regulatory authorities (all of whom can normally compel disclosure of information) by client legal privilege.

---

1 For a thorough account see G E Dal Pont, *Lawyers' Professional Responsibility* (Lawbook Co, Pyrmont, NSW, 5th edn, 2013) 'Part II: Lawyers' Duty to the Client'.

Limits to Confidentiality

In practice, however, the obligation of confidentiality is not as simple and straightforward as it might appear. Lawyers may still be very concerned with maintaining confidentiality, but social media like *Instagram, Linked-In* and *YouTube* and traditional broadcast media thrive on completely trivial breaches of confidence, sometimes with tragic consequences. Less obvious but perhaps more relevant to confidentiality and privacy are the increasingly pervasive CCTV cameras, mobile phone tracking, failed passwords, *Google* maps and many other avenues of electronic surveillance. Once information has been uploaded to the internet, it is potentially recoverable forever. 'Cloud' servers, where much of our data is now stored, may be as 'secure' as is the atmosphere from global warming. What we think is confidential is increasingly vulnerable to the prying eyes of those who want to put the time or money into finding it out.

If global disclosure, legal or otherwise, is an inevitable and unstoppable trend, is it misleading for lawyers to say to their new clients 'Everything you tell me is confidential'? In reality, a lot of client information is already known by others and, increasingly, lawyers are under pressure to give up the secrets that their clients tell them.

Community attitudes towards confidentiality and privacy are contradictory. On the one hand advances in technology are generally welcomed even though they favour disclosure and openness over confidentiality and privacy.[2] Depending on the circumstances, the public and lawyers are pleased or disturbed. When young people are groomed on the internet by paedophiles, Nigerian scammers steal from unsuspecting web users, or Russian mafia hijack thousands of credit card identities, the dangers of internet transparency are obvious. But when Julian Assange's *Wikileaks* publishes huge volumes of secret diplomatic communications, reactions are far more mixed. Depending on who is embarrassed, there is both public approval and political condemnation for breaching confidentiality.

Lawyers are involved in these debates at every level. Is national security endangered by the disclosure of classified military information on a publicly accessible website? Or is the resilience and strength of that society actually improved by such disclosures, because greater public discussion will make it less likely that its key institutions – parliament, courts and media – will be undermined from within?

Confidentiality (privacy) is important to the reality of individuals' humanity and freedom. We all deserve to keep some secrets – that is, to have a private life – if

2 See Jane Lee, 'You're Being Closely Watched', *The Age* (Melbourne), 17 September 2012, 4.

we are to remain psychologically healthy and effective. Sissela Bok[3] has suggested that there are three ethical principles that generally require us to preserve the confidences of others:

1. *Respect for individual autonomy over personal information*: People should generally be able to keep control over whether they want to keep their own thoughts, plans and actions secret or open, and others should respect this.

2. *Respect for the secrets of intimates*: Human relationship and intimacy in which secrecy can be shared is a good thing which should be respected.

3. *A pledge of silence (maintaining confidentiality) creates an obligation beyond the respect due to personal autonomy and relationships*: Where one person has promised secrecy to another then extra weight is added to the obligation of confidentiality beyond the respect due to individual autonomy and relationship.

Bok also points out, however, that each of these ethical principles has its limits and there can be ethical reasons to override the force of any of these reasons. The first two principles have limits, such as when secrecy would allow violence to be done to innocent persons or turn someone into an unwitting accomplice to crime. The third principle, where secrecy has been promised, adds moral weight, but should still only be a prima facie ground of obligation. We need to go on to ask whether one was right to make the pledge to start with, whether the promise is binding and if so what circumstances might nevertheless justify overriding it.

According to Bok, a fourth basis for confidentiality applies only to professional confidentiality and assigns weight beyond ordinary loyalty to professional confidentiality because of some utility to persons and society – that is, some public interest in confidentiality above and beyond ordinary obligations of confidentiality. In the case of the legal profession, the duty of confidentiality at general law and in professional conduct rules is said to exist to encourage full and frank disclosure between client and lawyer, so that clients can seek and obtain legal advice without apprehension of prejudice by disclosure. This is said to be necessary: (1) for effective legal representation to protect clients' rights; and (2) so that lawyers get enough information to advise clients as fully as possible on how to comply with the law.

A lawyer's role as representative and advocate for their client within the legal system, and as one who cares for the client, will often carry with it a particular obligation to maintain the confidentiality and privacy of what their clients tell them. This 'confidence' that the client must have in their relationship with their

---

3 See Sissela Bok, *Secrets: On the Ethics of Concealment and Revelation* (Random House, New York, 1983).

lawyer is fundamentally important for the client, and necessary to encourage the client to tell their lawyer as much as possible so that they can receive accurate and sensitive legal advice. The obligation of confidentiality and its rationale can be simply stated, but its practical and relational implications are not so easily comprehended. When a client comes in to see their lawyer, or telephones them late at night, they almost always mention something, or hint at something, that they are embarrassed about. Often these disclosures can seem minor on first telling – for example, a client mentioning that they are very late in paying a significant debt or are having difficulty in getting planning permission for a contentious subdivision. But from time to time there is immediately more at stake. Consider, for example, this true story told by criminal lawyer Bill Potts:[4]

CASE STUDY 4.1   THE CLIENT WITH A TERRIBLE SECRET

Many years ago a young man came to see me. He was charged with relatively minor property offences involving possession of stolen tools, parts from cars and various pieces of property that had been stolen from various places. The offences of themselves were not serious and, as he was a young man with no previous convictions, he was more likely than not to get a sentence of probation or community service.

But he was very, very worried, and kept hinting to me that there was something more serious going on. He told me that he was afraid that the people who owned the property, who had in fact stolen the property, would harm him, in fact [that] they were going to kill him. All of this just seemed to be the normal hysterical nonsense that you sometimes get from clients. But he had a very serious edge of worry about him. After some time in getting to know him, I eventually tried to get to the nub of what his real problem was. And what he revealed to me, haltingly, was that he was in fact in possession of a stolen car, and not just any stolen car, this was a car that had been on the front page of the local paper for weeks. The police were calling for whoever had it in their possession to come forward, because this was the key piece of evidence in a murder investigation.

Another young man, who had gone to a police station, and after some ten hours of being in the police station, admitted killing his father, told the police during the same interview that he had in fact taken the car down to a car park and left it there with the engine running. This young man went on to draw a

4 *The Law Report*, ABC Radio National, 26 March 2002. Reproduced here with permission.

picture of a knife blade and went on to describe how he'd cut his father's throat and stabbed him four times through the heart.

My client came to me and told me that he in fact had the car, and then told me a story that was entirely different. In fact he told me that he in fact had been at the deceased man's house earlier in the evening, and that the deceased man had given him the car to take away and store. Now if what my client was telling me was true, then the young man, the son who in fact had admitted killing his father, had told a story that was entirely incorrect, and could be proven so.

Now the difficulty I faced was that my young fellow who told me these things, told me that he was going to destroy this piece of evidence, and this thing that could literally have got a young man off a very serious murder charge. And he told me when he was going to do it, and how he was going to do it. And the ethical dilemma I faced was 'Do I in those circumstances contact the police with a view to effectively putting my client in?' The effect of me telling the police these things is that he would have been charged with offences relating to the murder vehicle, and indeed it may well have been that there were other more serious charges in the background. So the other alternative was to do nothing, in which case a young and possibly innocent man could have stayed in jail for the rest of his life, because the case was certainly overwhelming, given his written and signed admissions.

DISCUSSION QUESTIONS

1. What would you do in these circumstances? How would you decide what to do?

2. The lawyer narrating this story says: 'After some time in getting to know him, I eventually tried to get to the nub of what his real problem was'. In this situation, would you have probed into what your client's real worries were, or would you have let 'sleeping dogs lie'?

In situations like Case Study 4.1 the lawyer must offer advice, but is immediately confronted with the classic conflict between 'knowing too much', which might prevent them from advising a client to plead not guilty to any later charge, and knowing too little, which makes them ineffective as a client representative. It is arguably unethical to be willfully blind to a situation in which the client may be breaching their duty to the court and the law, because it means that the lawyer is assisting in the breach. It may also be a breach of the duty to the client to not be fully aware of the client's situation, as a matter of care to the client.

The law of confidentiality is the tool that the law has developed to guide lawyers through this maze, but its interpretation is still subject to lawyers' overriding awareness of whose interests are most important when secrets are kept or disclosed. Consider the following examples:

- Alton Logan was released from an Illinois prison in 2009 after being imprisoned for 26 years for a murder he did not commit. The fact that he was and always had been innocent was known by two lawyers, who had no doubts about this fact. At the time of Logan's original trial they had acted for another man who confessed to them that he was the real murderer, but they kept their knowledge secret for the entire 26 years because they considered themselves bound by the local Illinois Bar (and American Bar Association) rule of attorney-client privilege (or client confidentiality). Their own client had been convicted of another murder and had been sentenced to death, and they feared his chances of being executed would increase if the crime for which Logan was convicted were to be attributed to him. Subsequently, the lawyers said they would have spoken up if a *future* serious crime was intended by their client, because that disclosure was permitted as an exception to the rule, but could not bring themselves to make their own exception in relation to this past crime, even *after* their client's life had been saved by the commutation to life in prison of his own death penalty. They spoke and allowed Logan's release only after their own client had died.[5]

- In 2011, News Corporation's London newspaper *The News of the World* was closed by Rupert Murdoch after it became obvious that key employees of the paper had authorised the hacking of the message banks of people they considered to be newsworthy. Over many years, the paper selectively printed whatever they discovered. One of the message banks that was hacked belonged to a young girl who had been kidnapped and, it was later revealed, murdered. Because the newspaper journalists who hacked her phone also deleted some messages, this gave her parents the impression that she was still alive and using her phone.

  The case showed how technology can facilitate major breaches of confidentiality, particularly when there is media interest. When the hacking scandal was eventually uncovered, a House of Commons committee called the then CEO of the newspaper's English holding company, James Murdoch, to give evidence of his knowledge of the purpose and date of a large 'hush money' payout to individuals who could have provided even more information to the media if they wished. Murdoch said he remembered the payment,

---

5 See 'After 26 years, 2 Lawyers Reveal a Killer's Secret', *USA Today*, 13 April 2008, at <www.usatoday.com/news/nation/2008-04-13-murder-silence_N.htm%3F;csp=34> at 4 January 2010. See also Peter A Joy and Kevin C McMunigal, 'Confidentiality and Wrongful Incarceration' (Summer 2008) 23(2) *Criminal Justice*.

which was in the vicinity of £700,000, but did not know or suspect that it was in any way inappropriate. The newspaper's in-house lawyer (Tom Crone) also gave evidence to the Commons' committee and contradicted (his client) Murdoch's evidence about the latter's knowledge of what was really a bribe for silence. It is not clear whether or not Crone had warned Murdoch about the real nature of the payment, but Crone did subsequently decide to breach his client's confidences in his evidence to the Commons' committee. The unanswered questions are: Could that breach have been avoided? Was Crone's later disclosure an appropriate disclosure in the public interest? If it was an improper breach of confidence, why was he not disciplined by the *Law Society of England and Wales* or the UK *Solicitor's Regulation Authority*?[6]

- There are a number of other examples given throughout this book of lawyers and clients using the cloak of confidentiality to cover up misconduct and obstruct justice. These include the way in which tobacco industry lawyers in the United States devised schemes to try and claim client legal privilege over reports that showed smoking was dangerous (Case Study 4.4 in this chapter); and the response by AWB, which controls the export sale of all Australian wheat, to an Australian government commission of inquiry into whether it paid 'kickbacks' (a form of bribe) to former Iraqi dictator Saddam Hussein in order to make sure the Iraqi government bought wheat from Australia under the United Nations' Oil-for-Food Programme, which operated while trade sanctions were in place against Iraq (Case Study 4.5 in this chapter; see also Case Study 1.3 in Chapter 1, and Case Study 10.1 in Chapter 10), as well as the role of Enron's lawyers in doing this (discussed in Chapter 10 and also in Case Study 10.2).

In this chapter, we explore how tentative the concept of confidentiality has become in a world of surveillance, wired for instant disclosure and based on a communication and business model which feeds on demolishing all secrecy. Lawyers as much as anyone are caught up in the demand for instant, widely accessible and therefore transparent communication, and can forget that their primary stock-in-trade is that secrecy. In the next section we discuss cloud computing as a case in point, and explain how to limit the risk of disclosure of cloud-stored information. Using more case studies, we then examine the proper ideals of confidentiality and client privilege. We evaluate them both as an essential support for the process of legal representation, and as a tool of some unscrupulous lawyers, and perhaps of

6 See Nick Davies and Amelia Hill, 'Missing Milly Dowler's Voicemail Was Hacked by *News of the World*', *The Guardian*, 5 July 2011. See <www.guardian.co.uk/uk/2011/jul/04/milly-dowler-voicemail-hacked-news-of-world>; and <www.theaustralian.com.au/business/media/the-former-lawyer-for-news-of-the-world-says-james-murdoch-knew-extent-of-hacking-in-2008/story-e6frg996-1226131068694>. In-house lawyers owe the same general duties of confidentiality to their corporate client as does any private lawyer to their client.

other lawyers who lose sight of their need for courage and independence and fall into meek compliance. Finally, we examine how confidentiality is affected by the legitimate role that appropriate whistleblowing could play in balancing an otherwise unquestioned need for secrecy.

CASE STUDY 4.2   LIVING IN THE CLOUDS: THE REAL LEVELS OF CONFIDENTIALITY AND PRIVACY

As technology advances, computing in 'the cloud' is probably inevitable. Where libraries used to be only physical structures for paper-based books and a few hard drives on detached computers, we now have fewer of both. They are being rapidly replaced by anonymous servers located who-knows-where and controlled by global corporations. Yet despite the fairly obvious risks, many of us are choosing to deposit our documents, photographs and drawings through our mobile phones and internet-connected tablets onto the servers of any number of social and other media providers. Lawyers are also depositing client information on the servers of commercial providers, often located in developing economies. Our access devices, the mobiles clutched to the ear, have relatively small internal storage capacity – most of what we really value goes straight to cyberspace. That information is then no longer in our physical control, though we convince ourselves that that does not matter. The important thing is convenience of access, and such access is still more-or-less 'guaranteed' anywhere on the planet where the internet is available.

But the internet is not a benign environment and while access may be relatively certain, confidentiality is not. It seems that both our own and foreign security services record and analyse enormous numbers of voice communications. Apart from whatever protection we derive from the law of contract, there is no inherent reason to believe that anything placed in cloud 'care' will be retained, remain uncorrupted and, most importantly, remain private and confidential. The internet is now so embedded in our consciousness that criticism of its risks for lawyers' duty of confidence seems redundant. This is especially so where major hardware-software providers normalise cloud usage. Nevertheless, the following are the short- and medium-term legal ethics issues that arise, relating to the capacity of cloud computing to protect both professional and personal secrets:[7]

---

7 Michael Park (Partner, Norton Rose) and Ka-Chi Cheung (Snr Associate, Norton Rose) raised these issues in a presentation on 'The Ethics of Cloud Computing' to the Law Institute of Victoria, May 2012.

- Data containing client confidences is still commonly sent by lawyers to the cloud through unencrypted email and as such, is normally available to both the cloud provider and its outsourcing contractors. Arguably, unencrypted cloud storage *per se* means disclosure and waiver of client privilege, even if lawyers use local, on-the-ground data backups to guard against data destruction or corruption.

- Even when client data is encrypted both for transmission and cloud storage, it is protected for only as long as the integrity of the encryption and the pace of computing innovation allow. As quantum computing initialises and expands over the next few years, it will massively increase processing power to the point that stable encryption (that is, confidentiality) may become increasingly illusory.

- The cloud provider will routinely sub-contract cloud control, perhaps to a jurisdiction with a deserved reputation for corruption and bribery.

- Cloud providers and their sub-contractors, often located in corruption-prone economies, must screen their employees for past breaches of security. This process is technically difficult, easy for employees to subvert, and expensive to operate on an ongoing basis. Employee screening is therefore likely to be very porous.

- The initiating lawyer is completely reliant on their head contract with the cloud provider. They have no privity of contract with the sub-contractors who actually operate the cloud and hence only indirect access to those contractors when problems occur. Discovery processes are difficult to guarantee in a cloud.

- There is a risk of extra-jurisdictional legislation (for example, the United Kingdom *Bribery Act 2010* or the United States *Patriot Act 2001*) and foreign security services rendering cloud provider contracts redundant.

- Because lawyers' cloud storages are well known to contain information that is likely to be commercially valuable, their servers are 'high risk' hacking targets. As such, clients need to be *fully* informed of the firm's cloud provider details and the reality of their lawyer's actual supervision of their head contractor.

- Since cloud servers are by definition controlled outside the firm, and from time to time administered and segmented by 'uncontrolled' individuals, a proportion of any cloud-based information barriers that might be kept intact if controlled directly by the firm will inevitably disintegrate.

- It is consequently important that clients be told that their information is being stored in the cloud and local storage alternatives be discussed if concerns are raised.

DISCUSSION QUESTIONS

1. Since the cloud is now embedded in current generation IT/software products, and lawyers use it without realising, how should lawyers handle client confidences received through a mobile or tablet? Is this information really confidential? What risks are there? What safeguards are available? For example, would it be wise to override the default storage settings of the IT products used?

2. How should lawyers discuss these issues with their clients? Would you see it as sensible to discuss the risks with every client, or just to gloss over the risks of cloud storage since it is ubiquitous anyway?

3. If you were a client with highly confidential information, would you be comfortable about placing that information in the cloud?

Contemporary Confidentiality and Client Privilege

Clients may not initially appreciate the realities of the (lack of) privacy of much of their information, but lawyers carry a heavy obligation of confidentiality, and therefore ought to be particularly conscious of both the practical problems of security of information and of wider social issues that may justify disclosure. It is best practice for lawyers to be respectful but clear with their clients from the beginning about the balancing act that must be performed, explaining what can be kept secret and what might be disclosable in some future court or hearing, should government, media, competitors, whistleblowers or police learn of their actions. This is a difficult but necessary discussion between lawyer and client and requires character and several virtues – courage, respect and determination. A lawyer may need to show courage in warning their client that their current or proposed practices are illegal or immoral and may not remain confidential. They will have to choose their words carefully, arguing that their clients' business or safety is better served in the long run by avoiding questionable behaviour, and the lawyer may need to be determined not to back down if threatened with 'find yourself another job'. Lawyers truly do their clients a service when this kind of advice is listened to. When they do not offer this advice, or are not listened to, the results are sometimes very ugly.

William Simon commented in 2006 that:

> … lawyer-client confidentiality cannot play an important role in contemporary business regulation. Corporate confidentiality is dead and the Bar's attempt to suggest that things could be otherwise is an exercise in myth-making.[8]

---

8 William Simon, 'After Confidentiality: Rethinking the Professional Responsibilities of the Business Lawyer' (2006–7) 75 *Fordham Law Review* 1453, 1454.

He was writing prophetically just before the global financial crisis. That crisis was still depressing economic activity across the planet six years later. His analysis would be essentially the same now as then: that certain lawyers and accountants could not or would not say 'no' to their clients, and facilitated the crisis by disguising or hiding the huge debts of both corporations and some governments; and that they did so because of greed, implicitly justifying their actions as the proper dominance of client priorities, and all of it underpinned by the traditional culture of lawyer-client/accountant-client privacy. Stated more carefully, influential securities lawyers and accountants have become so conditioned to the culture of zealous advocacy that they have transformed appropriate lawyer-client confidentiality (a traditional loyalty) into anti-social secrecy. This secrecy has become so bad that these professionals' perceptions of what is in clients' interests, protected by that secrecy, became literally destructive to much of wider society. And all of this occurred without any alarm bells ringing in the lawyers' minds. They could see no proper limits to their obligation of confidentiality. Simon sums up his view:

> In the debate about Vinson & Elkins' (V&E) work for Enron, Lawrence Fox of the ABA Ethics 2000 Commission insisted, 'Clients are entitled to know there are loopholes…If you want to stop that, you have to rewrite the law.' Stephen Gillers of New York University Law School said, 'The job of a lawyer is to figure out how to accomplish the client's objectives within the law and if that can be done only through a technicality, that is not the lawyer's fault.' There is, of course, another view. It was concisely expressed by the Enron accountant Sherron Watkins in her famous memo to Ken Lay. She made no mention of any of the accounting rules Arthur Andersen and V&E relied on. Instead, she noted that '[t]he overriding basic principle of accounting is that if you explain the "accounting treatment" to a man on the street, would you influence his investing decisions? Would he sell or buy the stock based on a thorough understanding of the facts? If so, you best present [such facts] correctly…'.[9] [references omitted]

In the Enron aftermath, the global representative body of the legal profession, the International Bar Association, began to look carefully at the whole of lawyers' collective impact on issues of business integrity. In 2006, the IBA offered some guidance on professional expectations regarding confidentiality through its *International Principles on Conduct for the Legal Profession*:[10]

> A lawyer shall at all times maintain and be afforded protection of confidentiality regarding the affairs of present or former clients, unless otherwise allowed or required by law and/or applicable rules of professional conduct.[11]

---

9 Simon, 'After Confidentiality', 1457.

10 The *IBA International Principles* were adopted by the International Bar Association on 20 September 2006. This wording is taken from the 2011 revision. See <www.ibanet.org/ Publications/publications_IBA_guides_and_free_materials.aspx%23;ethics> accessed 9 May 2013.

11 See *IBA International Principles*: 4. Confidentiality/professional secrecy.

This language is formal and predictable, but the *Commentary* which accompanies the *Principles* makes it clear that:

> ... no statement of principles or code of ethics can provide for every situation or circumstance that may arise. Consequently, lawyers must act in accordance with the *dictates of their conscience*, in keeping with the general sense and ethical culture that inspires these International Principles.[12] [our emphasis]

That the IBA recognises the importance of conscience for lawyers faced with deciding matters of confidentiality is significant, because it supports the fundamental obligation of all lawyers to look to their own internal morality in weighing up the ethical alternatives that may be before them. In respect of confidentiality, the *Commentary* goes on to remind lawyers that confidentiality is always conditional, and that there '... are manifest situations in which the principles of confidentiality and professional secrecy of lawyer-client communications no longer apply in full or in part'.[13]

An important initial question is: What do Australian courts and conduct rules say about the limits to confidentiality and client privilege? In relation to client privilege, Deane J stated:

> That general principle is of great importance to the protection and preservation of the rights, dignity and freedom of the ordinary citizen under the law and to the administration of justice and law in that it advances and safeguards the availability of full and unreserved communication between the citizen and his or her lawyer and in that it is a precondition of the informed and competent representation of the interests of the ordinary person before the courts and tribunals of the land. Its efficacy as a bulwark against tyranny and oppression depends upon the confidence of the community that it will in fact be enforced. That being so, **it is not to be sacrificed even to promote the search for justice or truth in the individual case** or matter and extends to protect the citizen from compulsory disclosure of protected communications or materials to any court or person with authority to require the giving of information or the production of documents or materials.[14] [emphasis in the original]

---

12 See *IBA International Principles*, Commentary to International Principle: Introduction, #7.
13 See *IBA International Principles*, Explanatory Note to International Principle #4. This note goes on to deal with the approach to be taken where national systems differ in their approach to confidentiality: 'Generally, the national rules of all relevant jurisdictions must be complied with ('Double Deontology'). But national rules sometimes do not address the issue of how to deal with conflicting rules. If the conflicting rules are broadly similar, then the stricter rule should be complied with'.
14 Deane J, *A-G (NT) v Maurice* (1986) 161 CLR 475, 490.

Because of its significance, client legal privilege was recognised by the High Court of Australia as a fundamental common law principle, not just a rule of evidence.[15] This means that the privilege applies in all settings where some authority desires disclosure of information (orally or in writing). This rationale sees truth and justice in a particular case as subordinate to the protection of client confidences via the overall system of privilege. That is, the existence of the privilege protecting confidentiality of lawyer-client communications is considered such an essential bulwark against tyranny and oppression in the justice system as a whole that it is *more important than truth and justice in a particular case.*

Sissela Bok argues that we need to look at the roots of professional confidentiality in order to spell out the limits of its application. She argues that confidentiality should only extend as far as necessary to achieve the benefit the profession is supposed to secure, and that it cannot in any case override greater injustice. She takes an essentially moral activist approach, arguing that the role-based morality of professional confidentiality can be overridden where there is a higher public interest.[16] One legal ethicist has argued:

> Part of the difficulty [with confidentiality] lies in the tendency of lawyers to present and of courts and commentators to accept that confidentiality is some kind of absolute, preferably never to be overridden and pragmatically to be overridden rarely and then only in cases where the justification is little short of overwhelming. Given self-regulation by the legal profession, the ethos of those charged with the duty of maintaining ethical standards is likely to share and reflect the general respect for confidentiality as some kind of absolute. On that view, the professional duty of confidentiality necessarily restricts access to information about lawyer conduct including lawyer misconduct, if any. Socially responsible and effective regulation of lawyers' conduct requires not only balancing of confidentiality and access to information but also devising and sustaining institutional arrangements that permit critical and informed scrutiny of lawyer conduct where appropriate without damaging the legitimate interests of clients.

> In addressing these issues, legal education and theory should resist the lawyer's ideological and self-serving account of confidentiality as some kind of absolute and demonstrate that the doctrines of confidence and privilege in a society at any one time represent a compromise between conflicting principles and values ... A recognition that confidentiality and disclosure are of equal status leads to serious questions about limiting confidentiality in the interests of disclosure. Both confidentiality and disclosure can reasonably lay claim to being essential to the interests and administration

---

15 *Baker v Campbell* (1983) 153 CLR 52.
16 Bok, *Secrets.*

of justice ... Confidentiality does not necessarily mandate non-disclosure: it merely provides a reason for non-disclosure which may or may not be outweighed by other considerations.[17]

This suggests that we should direct attention to the goal of confidentiality obligations – that is, the public interest in the administration of justice – and what it requires, not just certain means of attaining it (that is, the privilege and confidentiality rules).

The Australian Approach to Confidentiality

Subject to some significant exceptions, Australian lawyers have obligations to:

- keep their clients' affairs *confidential*; and also
- to preserve their clients' *legal privilege*, that is to decline to reveal the contents of 'confidential communications' made between themselves and their clients that were made for the dominant purpose of obtaining legal advice, or for use in current or anticipated litigation, even to a court or investigatory authority that would otherwise have power to compel disclosure.

These two obligations are discussed in turn below. It is useful to keep in mind that confidentiality deals with the broad class of secrets, whereas privilege is a narrower sub-set of those secrets (confidential communications for the purposes of legal advice or litigation) that are often particularly related to court proceedings. The distinction between the two concepts is important and although the terms are often used interchangeably, they should never be equated.

The technological and cultural developments described in this chapter mean that as time goes by, much information that would otherwise be both confidential and privileged is likely to have been disclosed publicly or privately to others, without the permission of those directly affected. However, a party who seeks to deny confidentiality or client privilege must *prove* that the information in question is public knowledge. Only then are these concepts effectively removed as barriers to disclosure.[18] If that public knowledge is only likely or suspected, the concepts remain relevant and need to be understood at a detailed level. Importantly, while material that is merely confidential is certainly defended from frequent attack in the circumstances described above, material that is or might be privileged is even more vigorously protected by the courts when efforts are made by opposing parties of governments to discover its content.

---

17 Richard Tur, 'Confidentiality and Accountability' *Griffith Law Review* 1 (1992) 73, 83–4.
18 *LSC v Tampoe* [2009] LPT 14; *LPCC v Trowell* [2009] WASAT 42.

Confidentiality

The duty of confidentiality is based first in contract law and secondly in the fiduciary relationship between a lawyer and their client. It requires all lawyers to keep secret all information received in the course of acting for their client. The duty is subject to many exceptions, and the contractual and fiduciary obligation may end when the client retainer ends. Thirdly, however, the law of equity also classes information as confidential if communicated for a limited purpose, providing it is not public knowledge. This equitable obligation is likely to continue after the retainer ends, that is, after the employment ceases, or the file closes or even after the client dies.[19]

Australian Solicitors' Conduct Rule (ASCR) 9 (shown below) uses mandatory language in its primary prohibition of disclosure of confidential information ('must not disclose'); however, it uses permissive language for its exceptions ('may disclose'). That is, the exceptions are available to lawyers if they feel the need of them, but do not compel disclosure. The distinction between the two illustrates the fact that, from the profession's point of view, loyalty to clients (confidentiality) tends to weigh more heavily in the balance than wider public responsibilities (disclosure, especially for the purposes of whistleblowing).

ASCR 9 states as follows:

> 9.1   A solicitor must not disclose any information which is confidential to a client and acquired by the solicitor during the client's engagement to any person who is not:
>
> > 9.1.1   a solicitor who is a partner, principal, director, or employee of the solicitor's law practice; or
> >
> > 9.1.2   a barrister or an employee of, or person otherwise engaged by, the solicitor's law practice or by an associated entity for the purposes of delivering or administering legal services in relation to the client,

EXCEPT as permitted in Rule 9.2.

> 9.2   A solicitor may disclose confidential client information if:
>
> > 9.2.1   the client expressly or impliedly authorises disclosure;
> >
> > 9.2.2   the solicitor is permitted or is compelled by law to disclose;[20]
> >
> > 9.2.3   the solicitor discloses the information in a confidential setting, for the sole purpose of obtaining advice in connection with the solicitor's legal or ethical obligations;[21]

---

19 See generally Dal Pont, *Lawyers' Professional Responsibility*, Pt 10.

20 For example, the permission specified by the *Legal Profession Act 2004* (Vic) s 4.2.15 allowing a lawyer to disclose to regulators the details of a file, when their client makes a complaint against them.

21 This exception is new to the *Rules* and is intended to encourage lawyers to keep themselves out of potential ethical trouble before it becomes a reality, or at least before it becomes too damaging.

9.2.4 the solicitor discloses the information for the sole purpose of avoiding the probable commission of a serious criminal offence;

9.2.5 the solicitor discloses the information for the purpose of preventing imminent serious physical harm to the client or to another person; or

9.2.6 the information is disclosed to the insurer of the solicitor, law practice or associated entity.

The references to 'permitted... by law' to disclose (*ASCR* 9.2.2), 'commission of a serious criminal offence' (*ASCR* 9.2.4) and 'preventing imminent serious physical harm' (*ASCR* 9.2.5) all involve lawyers considering a wider public interest when discharging their duty of confidentiality. Implied authorisation by the client under *ASCR* 9.2.1 is important because it permits a lawyer to make a judgement about circumstances that might justify disclosure. For example, when a client goes missing in the middle of a difficult and financially damaging negotiation with other parties of dubious motives, their lawyer might go to the police with more confidence if they thought that their discussion of the background with detectives would be sanctioned by the client, given they might have met with 'foul play'. Note that this situation is not as obvious or compelling as that envisaged by *ASCR* 9.2.5 ('imminent... physical harm'). *ASCR* 9.2.2 is particularly vague, but its preparedness to allow disclosure permitted by law necessarily involves the law of equity, which can permit confidential information to be revealed where its source is the equitable doctrine of confidence, and disclosure would be in the public interest. *ASCR* 9.2.3 wisely encourages lawyers to seek confidential advice about their obligations and their options, where needed.

There are indications from the profession that public interest considerations are vital to professional judgements about confidentiality and must be taken seriously. The earlier equivalent exception to *ASCR* 9.2.4 (the former Law Council of Australia *Model Rule* 3.1.3) provided that commission *or concealment* of a serious criminal offence could justify disclosure. It is not certain why disclosure where 'concealment' (of a past crime) is an issue was removed from the list of exceptions, but some insight may be gained from commentary in a 'Draft Consultation Paper' released by the Law Council of Australia (LCA) in 2009. The Consultation Paper had no formal status and is frustratingly vague in respect of this rule, but indicates that the LCA was well aware of the public dismay that would occur should an *Alton Logan* situation (summarised above) occur in Australia. It is unfortunate that the LCA lacks the professional courage to proclaim a morally confident position – that is, to take a virtuous stance – especially as it knows full well what is at stake. Although the LCA declined to include an exception that would deal with the issue directly, the Consultation Paper timidly asserted that the client's interests '...always have to be considered', and that it was not possible to give enough specific guidance about '…balancing of client and public interests and other considerations, as always so much would depend on individual circumstances'.[22]

What the LCA would not say openly it nevertheless made clear by default: 'Individual circumstances' can be compelling of disclosure even when there is no conduct rule specifically authorising that disclosure. This concession reinforces the IBA *International Principles* (summarised earlier). In this implicit admission, the way is open for a practitioner to consider the public interest in relation to confidences, not just as an application of the law of equity or of personal conscience. Providing a lawyer makes a disclosure with a *bona fide* desire to 'balance the circumstances', as it were, it is very likely that their decision will be defensible if challenged.

This point about balance and fairness was forcefully illustrated in the case of Stephen Keim QC, who represented Indian doctor Mohammad Haneef in Queensland when he was charged by the Australian Federal Police (AFP) with terrorism-related offences in 2007. Glasgow airport had just been bombed by a distant cousin of Haneef. The AFP case against him was weak and, *before* the case was decided, the AFP leaked to the media selected and misleading extracts of their record of interview with him, in order to sway public opinion against him.

Keim faced the equivalent of *ASCR* 28.1, which states that 'A solicitor must not publish or take steps towards the publication of any material concerning current proceedings which may prejudice a fair trial or the administration of justice'. He nevertheless decided to publish the *full* record of interview (which showed how unlikely it was that Haneef was connected to his terrorist cousin), to balance the adverse effects of the AFP's selective publication, asserting later that his decision was essential to a fair trial and the administration of justice. The prosecution case against Haneef was withdrawn and although Keim was investigated by regulators after an AFP complaint was lodged against him, he (and his virtuous love of justice) was found to be justified.[23]

A lawyer's concern for the public interest and disclosure even to their own client can, however, be hard to identify, particularly if they are not sure who really is their client and to whom their duty of confidentiality is really owed. This uncomfortable realisation was brought home in 2012 in relation to the then Australian Prime Minister.

---

22 Law Council of Australia, Australian Solicitors' Conduct Rules, *Draft Consultation Paper*, 16 October 2009, 19.

23 See the LCA summary of the case at <www.lawcouncil.asn.au/programs/criminal-law-human-rights/anti-terror/haneef.cfm accessed> 19 April 2013.

CASE STUDY 4.3   THE TOO-SILENT PARTNER?: JULIA GILLARD AND THE AUSTRALIAN WORKERS' UNION SLUSH FUND

Early in the 1990s, former Prime Minister Julia Gillard was a salaried partner in Slater and Gordon, which represented a number of prominent trade unions. The Australian Workers' Union (AWU) was among these. In 1992, Ms Gillard had a personal romantic relationship with the AWU state secretary, Bruce Wilson, and she took him at face value as representing the AWU. On his instructions, she helped to establish an AWU fund, 'The Australian Workplace Reform Association', which she believed was to be used for workplace safety campaigns. In fact, $400,000 was fraudulently diverted from the fund and used by Wilson and another person to pay for real estate purchases for other unauthorised purposes.[24] Ms Gillard (as a representative of Slater and Gordon) was in effect used for her and her firm's legitimacy and reputation, and kept in the dark.

In 1995, other union officials raised their concerns about the slush fund with the firm and Ms Gillard was interviewed by the then senior partner Peter Gordon about the matter. It then emerged that Ms Gillard had '…drafted the rules for the association – without opening a formal file, without consulting the senior partners and without taking advice from expert lawyers within the firm'.[25] More importantly, by then Slater and Gordon and Ms Gillard clearly understood that the fund had been a slush fund, but remained silent for over 17 years about what could only have been fraud. Silence in these circumstances was not a crime, but the decision to stay silent was nevertheless deliberate.

In 2012, Prime Minister Gillard, as she then was, stated that, 'Those allegations came to my attention. I formed a view that I had not been dealt with honestly and based on that view I ended a relationship I then had with him'.[26] But if Ms Gillard was so concerned in 1995 that she had been used by Wilson, why was she not similarly concerned about his theft of union funds, to the point that she required Slater and Gordon to go to the Union or to the police, or independently took that action herself? If Gillard or Slater and Gordon had gone to the police, the AWU's affairs would have been subject to external scrutiny.

24 See Mark Baker, 'Letter Contradicts PM', *The Age* (Melbourne), 29 November 2012, at <www.smh.com.au/opinion/political-news/letter-contradicts-pm-20121128-2aegm.html>
25 Baker, 'Letter Contradicts PM'.
26 Marcus Priest, 'Silence May Be Unwise, but No Crime', *The Australian Financial Review* (Sydney), 26 November 2012, 4.

In late 2012, an intense political debate occurred about what Ms Gillard knew and when. This debate was short-lived after it was generally accepted that she did not know of the fraud or appreciate at the time that she was being used. But former Slater and Gordon partner Nick Styant-Browne emerged as a whistleblower and provided information to the media about the 1995 internal investigation inside Slater and Gordon.[27] A claim by Slater and Gordon of client privilege in respect of that investigation would fail for several reasons, not least because of the public status of the information now revealed.

The Australian Financial Review (*AFR*) has suggested in relation to the silence of both Slater and Gordon and Ms Gillard, that if lawyers '... fail to take further action in such circumstances, they will be out of step with the community's expectations of the profession'.[28]

DISCUSSION QUESTIONS

1. Presumably, the duty of confidence, which ordinarily survives the lawyer-client relationship, was invoked by the Slater and Gordon leadership to stop Ms Gillard from blowing the whistle. Yet Wilson's actions were criminal, and individual unionists' trust – not just that of the AWU as a union – had been abused. At the time, Victoria's professional conduct rules permitted disclosure if the '... sole purpose [was one of] avoiding the probable commission *or concealment* of a serious criminal offence'[29] [our emphasis]. There is an illegality exception to client legal privilege which means that privilege does not apply where the communication to the lawyer has been for the purposes of using the lawyer's advice and services to facilitate criminal activity.[30] Did Slater and Gordon have a moral and/or a legal obligation to go to the police when they first became aware of the fraud? Would the rules have permitted them to do so?

2. Independently of Slater and Gordon's position, did Ms Gillard have an obligation as a legal practitioner to inform the AWU or the police? Did

---

27 Priest, 'Silence'.
28 Priest, 'Silence'.
29 *Professional Conduct and Practice Rules*, (Vic) 2005, Rule 3.1.3. The rule allowed disclosure '... in circumstances in which the law would probably compel its disclosure, despite a client's claim of legal professional privilege, and for the sole purpose of avoiding the probable commission or concealment of a serious criminal offence'.
30 See Dal Pont, *Lawyers' Professional Responsibility*, 11.55.

she have a moral obligation to do so? Would the rules have permitted her to do so?

3. Should Mr Styant-Browne be praised for his whistleblowing (even if it was 17 years after the event) and protected by an indemnity against a disciplinary prosecution for breach of confidentiality (as is the case in legislation protecting whistleblowers in the public and corporate sectors in some jurisdictions)? Or should a different approach be taken to lawyers blowing the whistle?

If they think of it, lawyers can protect themselves in these situations by prior consultation with law society' ethics advisors pursuant to *ASCR* 9.2.3, if only because the fact of that consultation makes regulatory action less likely, should a client complain at a later date. It's not always a good idea just to take advice inside the firm. And in deciding where they stand personally on the choice they must make, lawyers will benefit from considering the various ethical categories and frameworks open to them, including virtue ethics, in considering the particular balance of private and public interests confronting them. In Chapter 11, an approach to making that judgement is discussed in detail.

Client Privilege

The law on client privilege is sufficiently broad to ensure that most confidential communications between a lawyer and their client remain private,[31] even before a court that would otherwise have the authority to compel disclosure. But there are a few caveats. The most important is that there be a clearly identified 'dominant purpose'[32] in the communication, and that that dominant purpose be either:

- to obtain legal advice (the 'advice privilege'); or

- for use in actual, pending or contemplated court proceedings (the 'litigation privilege').[33]

---

31 A lawyer who chooses to disclose privileged information faces a number of consequences, all designed to discourage such disclosure: injunction, liability for breach of contract, liability for equitable compensation and account of profits, an order to hand over or destroy materials, loss of clients, the loss of their job, damage to reputation, and even disciplinary proceedings. Whether any or all of these consequences actually occur depend on the circumstances and the presence of any mitigating factors.

32 See Dal Pont, *Lawyers' Professional Responsibility*, Pt 11.

33 *ASCR* 19.4 affirms, for example, that a lawyer seeking an interim order in the absence of the other party (that is, *ex parte*) must disclose all material facts and laws except those protected by client privilege.

In many cases, communications between lawyers and their clients will have *subsidiary* purposes – for example, to provide general assistance in the establishment of all manner of commercial transactions, or their restructure – but the relevant communications will remain privileged so long as a *bona fide* dominant purpose can still be identified.

There are, however, a number of subsidiary 'principles' that apply to privilege. All are important in understanding the limitations placed on the concept by the common law. The following paraphrased extract of those principles is from the judgment of Young J in a case concerning AWB's claims to privilege over various documents they were asked to produce for the Royal Commission inquiring into payments made by AWB to the Hussein regime (see Case Study 4.5 below and brief discussion above).[34] The original principles in the judgment are edited and dot-pointed here for ease of identification.

- The party claiming privilege carries the onus of proving that the communication was undertaken, or the document was brought into existence, for the dominant purpose of giving or obtaining legal advice.

- The purpose for which a document is brought into existence is a question of fact that must be determined objectively. Evidence of the intention of the document's maker, or of the person who authorised or procured it, is not necessarily conclusive. It may be necessary to examine the evidence concerning the purpose of other persons involved in the hierarchy of decision-making or consultation that led to the creation of the document and its subsequent communication.

- The existence of legal professional privilege is not established merely by the use of verbal formulae ... Nor is a claim of privilege established by mere assertion that privilege applies to particular communications, or that communications are undertaken for the purpose of obtaining or giving 'legal advice'.

- Where communications take place between a client and his or her independent legal advisers, or between a client's in-house lawyers and those legal advisers, it may be appropriate to assume that legitimate legal advice was being sought, absent any contrary indications.

- An appropriate starting point when applying the dominant purpose test is to ask what was the intended use or uses of the document which accounted for it being brought into existence.

- Legal professional privilege protects the disclosure of documents that record legal work carried out by the lawyer for the benefit of the client, such as research memoranda, collations and summaries of documents, chronologies and the like, whether or not they are actually provided to the client.

34 *AWB Ltd v Cole and Another* (No 5) (2006) 155 FCR 30, 44.

- Subject to meeting the dominant purpose test, legal professional privilege extends to notes, memoranda or other documents made by officers or employees of the client that relate to information sought by the client's legal adviser to enable him or her to advise … The privilege extends to drafts, notes and other material brought into existence by the client for the purpose of communication to the lawyer, whether or not they are themselves actually communicated to the lawyer.

- Legal professional privilege is capable of attaching to communications between a salaried legal adviser and his or her employer, provided that the legal adviser is consulted in a professional capacity in relation to a professional matter and the communications are made in confidence and arise from the relationship of lawyer and client.

- Legal professional privilege protects communications rather than documents, as the test for privilege is anchored to the purpose for which the document was brought into existence. Consequently, legal professional privilege can attach to copies of non-privileged documents if the purpose of bringing the copy into existence satisfies the dominant purpose test.

In the dominant purpose issue and in these secondary principles lie much ongoing disquiet about the proper limits to client privilege, as some of the case studies in this chapter demonstrate. It is clear that some clients do seek to keep out of court advice received that was not *bona fide* within the privilege 'protection zone' when first provided. For example, lawyers provide advice that is not necessarily legal advice. It may be financial planning advice, or accounting advice, or even strategic business advice that is only secondarily of a legal nature. In these cases they may provide legal advice, but not as the dominant purpose of the communication.

- For example, a client may ask for an analysis of the best capital market on which to issue a prospectus for a new manufacturing process to 'print' machinery in China. Their lawyer may offer an opinion which prefers the Shanghai stock exchange to the New York exchange because there is more capital available in China. At the time that opinion is provided, the lawyer may also comment that the manufacturing regulatory environment is less restrictive in Shanghai, and that specific environmental rules which apply in the United States do not apply in China. The latter piece of advice is legal in nature, but might not be privileged if it is clear that the lawyer was primarily retained for their overall capital market opinion. The distinction would be important and embarrassing for the client and their lawyer if, in later proceedings concerning pollution caused by the laser-printing process, it were alleged that their lawyer had encouraged location in China because, so stated, pollution of the Chinese environment was less important than that of the United States.

Although the central protections of privilege are reinforced by the law of evidence,[35] there are also some more general exceptions to the veil of silence erected around otherwise privileged communications. Importantly, privilege is the right of the lawyer's client and can be demolished by the client, even if their lawyer simultaneously takes other action on their behalf. Privilege does not cover confidential communications:

- directed *against* the public interest;[36]
- when legislation has specifically removed the privileged status of those communications,[37] for example where the Federal Parliament considers there is a risk that some lawyers will connive at setting up tax evasion schemes;[38]
- where the client has acted inconsistently (even on a single occasion) with the exercise of that privilege;[39]
- where the client knowingly and voluntarily disclosed the substance of the communication;
- where the communication is disclosed with the express or implied consent of the client; or
- if the client has acted in a way that would make it unfair to then claim privilege.[40]

For all purposes, while the *communication* is privileged, the information it contains is not. Accordingly, if that information is available elsewhere, a claim of client privilege is irrelevant. The following case study illustrates this point.

CASE STUDY 4.4   BIG TOBACCO PRIVILEGE

Tobacco industry lawyers in the United States devised schemes to ensure that it was lawyers who commissioned and controlled scientific evidence about the health effects of smoking. They then claimed client legal privilege over reports that showed smoking was dangerous, when litigants sought discovery in suits against tobacco companies. However, they made sure that reports prepared

35 For example, see *Evidence Act 2008* (Vic). For litigation privilege, see s 119 (*Mitsubishi v VWA* [2002] VSCA 59) and for advice privilege, see s 118. See also s 131A, which deals with pre-trial processes.

36 See *Evidence Act 2008* (Vic) s 125.

37 There must be a clear, unambiguous statutory intention to remove the exception. See *Daniels Corporation v ACCC* [2002] HCA 49.

38 See generally Stephen Barkoczy, *Foundations of Taxation Law*, 5th edn, CCH Australia Ltd, 2013, 752–6.

39 See, for example, *Evidence Act 2008* (Vic) s 122.

40 See Dal Pont, *Lawyers' Professional Responsibility*, 275–81.

by 'sympathetic' scientists that were positive for the tobacco industry were well publicised. Eventually, the claim of privilege over these reports was struck down as an abuse of privilege. But in the meantime lawyers had kept hidden for years scientific reports showing the dangers and addictiveness of smoking, and showing that the tobacco companies knew this. It was not until whistleblowers alerted plaintiff lawyers to the existence of these reports and devices that these claims of privilege could be attacked.[41]

In Australia, a court has heard the evidence of former British American Tobacco (BAT) Australian Services in-house legal counsel, Fred Gulson, that BAT and law firm Clayton Utz participated in a 'contrivance' to hide evidence behind client legal privilege. BAT would give Clayton Utz copies of its documents (including those that might harm it if discovered in litigation), ostensibly for legal advice. The originals were destroyed under the document retention policy while Clayton Utz kept the copies, but claimed that they were protected by privilege.[42] The court found that there was evidence that BAT had dishonestly concealed the true nature of its document policy from the other side, and ordered disclosure of the documents.[43]

The Australian Law Reform Commission later commented in respect of this case:

> The Victorian Court of Appeal held, however, that the decision at first instance was flawed and allowed the defendant's claim of client legal privilege. This meant that the documents had not properly been admitted into evidence and thus the basis of Eames J's conclusion – that there was a deliberate strategy to destroy disadvantageous documents – even if correct, could not stand.
>
> Although the outcome of the appeal was to put the documents back behind the cloak of privilege, the fact that the contents had been revealed brought certain practices into the spotlight...[44]

41 Ralph Nader and Wesley J Smith, *No Contest: Corporate Lawyers and the Perversion of Justice in America* (Random House, New York, 1996) 18–31; Richard Kluger, *Ashes to Ashes: America's Hundred-Year Cigarette War, the Public Health, and the Unabashed Triumph of Philip Morris* (Alfred A Knopf, New York, 1996).

42 Susannah Moran, 'Cloaks of Privilege and Smoking Guns', *The Australian Financial Review* (Sydney), 19 May 2006, 57; Vanda Carson, 'Smoke Clearing on Big Tobacco as Insurers Fight' and 'Policy Failed the Smell Test: Whistleblower', *The Australian* (Sydney), 19 May 2006, 24.

43 Elisabeth Sexton, 'Ifs, Butts and Big Bucks', *Insight, The Age* (Melbourne), 3 June 2006, 4. The case, however, then settled and the documents therefore did not have to be disclosed: Vanda Carson, 'Tobacco Company Sidesteps Ruling', *The Australian* (Sydney), 6 July 2006, 8.

44 ALRC, Report 107, Chapter 9, paragraphs 9.10 and 9.11.

DISCUSSION QUESTION

1. The experience of a number of Big Tobacco law firms was damaging to their brand in the aftermath of the *McCabe* case. Part of that negative experience arose from adverse judicial reflection on the firms' use of privilege. They hoped to keep secret their knowledge of earlier scientific reports on the toxic effects of smoking.

   Other large industries and sectors, for example fast food, confectionery, gaming and alcohol, are likely to be sued in future in respect of the effects of their products on consumers, particularly very young consumers. These large industry sectors will have the results of numerous internal marketing polls about how best to target advertising directed at children. Should you be acting for these sectors in the future, how will you advise them when they seek to exert claims to privilege in respect of that polling information?

The Australian Law Reform Commission (ALRC) has identified a number of possible problems in relation to lawyers' involvement in claims of privilege by their clients. Among them are:

- a lack of transparency in claims;
- the need to address blanket claims of privilege;
- over-claiming of privilege;
- over-use of masking of documents;
- 'warehousing' – placing prejudicial documents in the hands of third parties and beyond the power of a party to litigation;[45]
- 'privileging' – placing prejudicial documents in the hands of lawyers under cover of spurious requests for legal advice so as to permit a claim for privilege.[46]

Diplomatically, the ALRC has been cautious in commenting on the substance and scale of these possible problems, but claims of privilege are now treated warily because of the perception that clients' lawyers are responsible for its abuse, even when the client happens to be a major corporation in a position to dictate litigation strategy. Emphasising again its view that lawyers, not clients, are responsible for

---

45 The practice of warehousing was discussed in the aftermath of the *McCabe* case and other Big Tobacco litigation. Evidence has emerged that certain law firms physically moved potentially incriminating client documents to other law firms in other jurisdictions in order to frustrate court-ordered discovery processes. See the discussion of this case in Chapter 6.

46 Australian Law Reform Commission, *Privilege in Perspective: Client Legal Privilege in Federal Investigations* (ALRC Report 107), published 27 February, 2008, 30. See <www.alrc.gov.au/report-107>.

the abuse of privilege, the ALRC in its final report devoted an entire chapter to 'ensuring professional integrity' in claims of privilege.[47] The Commission therefore recommended better legal education and general enforcement of existing disciplinary standards by the courts and regulators, rather than specific penalties for abuse of privilege, but it was sufficiently concerned to observe as follows:

> The ALRC acknowledges that identifying when the assertion of a claim of client legal privilege amounts to 'abuse' may be problematic…[W]here a lawyer is testing the boundaries of the doctrine of privilege with an arguable case, this is different from maintaining a hopeless claim as a tactic in order to frustrate or delay an investigation. While there is no clear evidence of chronic abuse of claims of client legal privilege, there are some cases that cause concern, and also evident distrust on the part of federal investigatory bodies that claims are not being made legitimately in every case.[48]

It is likely that the problem of regulatory and judicial scrutiny of client privilege is inevitably and perennially insoluble, not least because

> …[t]he difficult issue of weighing up when an expansive claim of privilege becomes an improper one…is compounded by potential breadth of a test which requires the assessment of the 'dominant purpose' of the communications in question.[49]

Some groups of lawyers are being encouraged to shift away from excessive confidentiality, and to that extent there is less need to consider when client privacy should be challenged. The trend within civil and family justice to early and full disclosure of otherwise 'secret' evidence in the interest of fairer, cheaper dispute resolution is being embraced by courts and governments. Neither can afford to keep funding an expensive trial system where lengthy disputes about privilege are tolerated for many months. But courts and governments are also interested in shorter, more principled dispute resolution because it is perceived to be fairer to the parties. As discussed in Chapter 6, the concept of an 'overarching obligation' on lawyers and their clients to conduct civil proceedings with integrity signifies, in part, a policy-driven frustration with the inappropriate recourse to privilege by some lawyers and their clients.

Where the processes of justice are improving there is cause for optimism, but where those processes are corrupt or unresponsive, or simply inaccessible because of cost, as in many jurisdictions, there are understandable frustrations which lead some individuals to go to the media. More often than not, these whistleblowers

---

47 ALRC Report 107, Ch 9, 'Ensuring Professional Integrity: Accountability and Education'.
48 ALRC Report 107, 33.
49 ALRC Report 107, 493, para 9.19.

are not lawyers, but sometimes there is a convincing case for lawyers themselves to breach confidentiality regardless of conduct rules or the law of privilege. When they do so, there ought to be careful reflection on the ethical basis for the disclosure and a solid, pragmatic strategy to survive the experience.

Blowing a Careful Whistle

Although lawyers will increasingly find that what they thought was private has leaked into the public domain, there remains plenty of client information that clients and lawyers at least *believe* is private. Most law students and new lawyers progress through the early years of private practice increasingly conscious that they are expected to keep things that way, even if they know some of their clients are breaking the law or are behaving immorally. In the face of the primary and usually legitimate requirement for lawyers to keep client information confidential, and to preserve client privilege where appropriate, it would be remarkable if many lawyers considered that they were able to or should engage in 'pro-social behaviour'[50] as 'internal witnesses' or whistleblowers against their clients for any reason. But the United States *Sarbanes-Oxley Act*[51] grew out of the *Enron* crisis at the start of the millennium, and requires exactly that from in-house lawyers who know or strongly suspect that their client corporation is breaking the law. That pressure has not reduced. If anything there is now, in the aftermath of the global financial crisis, more public pressure to limit corporate confidentiality and more pressure on private lawyers to look carefully to their conscience in supporting such clients.

Corporate lawyers have a considerable obligation to blow the whistle on corporate wrongdoing under current rules and law. The obligation of confidentiality is not owed to individual managers, but only to the corporation as a whole. Logically, if individual managers are breaching the law, or even acting unethically, then a lawyer's obligation to the corporation as a whole means that they should first try to dissuade the manager they are dealing with from engaging in the misconduct, and then disclose the problem up the decision-making hierarchy within the organisation to someone who can authoritatively decide the matter – all the way to the board if necessary. Where shareholders' interests in a large public company are at stake, and the board itself is corrupt or ineffectual in resolving the issue, the lawyer might even have a duty to report to a regulator or to the public what the problem

---

50 A J Brown, *The Whistling While They Work Project; Whistleblowing in the Australian Public Sector: Enhancing the theory and practice of internal witness management in public sector organisations* from <http://epress.anu.edu.au/anzsog/whistleblowing/mobile_devices/ch01s03.html> accessed 26 Sept 2012.

51 HR 3763, 107th Cong. 2002.

is – in the interests of the corporation as a whole. This would be because this was the only effective way to serve the interests of the whole corporation – when the board is corrupt or ineffectual, the corporation as a whole must rely on the relevant regulator, or some other public authority, to protect it from illegal and damaging behaviour.[52]

The principle is that the lawyer should start by raising issues of ethics and misconduct with the person concerned in a private and confidential way, and move on to more public and coercive ways of resolving the issues only gradually as each previous option fails. This process respects the confidentiality and sensitivity of the information – by only revealing the information to the extent absolutely necessary to prevent unethical conduct. Nevertheless, the process is likely to be emotionally and professionally draining for the lawyer, since it will involve sensitive, often tense, communications and negotiations, and the constant possibility of open conflict. Figure 4.1 provides a short checklist of issues to take into account before becoming an internal witness.[53]

The Australian Corporate Lawyers' Association (ACLA) 'best practice guidelines' on ethics for in-house lawyers reflect this understanding that the law and professional conduct rules require lawyers to report unethical conduct up the corporate hierarchy. They state that where an in-house lawyer needs to be a whistleblower, 'they should make the appropriate disclosures first to the company's Senior Legal Officer and then, if still necessary, to the company's Chief Executive Officer. If required, the disclosures should then be made to the company's Chairman [of the Board]'.[54] This whistleblowing pathway is equally valid for external lawyers advising the company. It is also consistent with the 2004 amendments to the *Australian Corporations Act* which protect corporate employees and service-providers from civil or criminal liability, or victimisation, where they disclose in good faith information relating to a possible breach of the corporations legislation within the company to the board or to the corporate regulator.[55]

However, the national disdain for 'dobbing' and lawyers' conditioning remains strong, and a lawyer who finds their conscience troubled by client behaviour still faces an uphill internal battle in deciding what to do. They will need to weigh up the strength of their ethical preferences – for example, for either *responsible lawyering*

---

52 Simon, 'Wrongs of Ignorance', 18–19; see also Simon, 'Whom (or What) Does the Organization's Lawyer Represent?'.

53 This list is adapted by the authors from Peter Bowden's 'ten point process' for maximising chances of successful whistleblowing. See <http://whistleblowingethics.info> accessed 17 Sept 2012.

54 ACLA, *Ethics for In-House Counsel*, 6. They go on to say 'Subject to any overriding legislation, disclosure beyond that level is not required'. We do not agree with this rider, as the text above makes clear.

55 *Corporations Act 2001* (Cth) Pt 9.4AAA (commenced 1 July 2004).

Figure 4.1   Checklist of Issues to Consider Before Blowing the Whistle

1. Find out if the local (State-based) whistleblower legislation protects you. This legislation could cover public sector lawyers in certain States (*not* the Commonwealth) and private sector lawyers where the *Corporations Law* protection can be invoked. The local legislation ideally will protect you from retribution. Make sure that, when ready, you are revealing something that is sufficiently in the public interest and that you are revealing it to the designated person/authority.

2. See if you can find others in the organisation who will support you, and get them to come to any meetings that are called to discuss the matter.

3. Talk the issues over first with family and close friends, and then gather as much independently supported evidence of the wrongdoing as you can, before you reveal anything.

4. Use *ASCR* Rule 9.2.3 (permitting disclosure '…for the sole purpose of obtaining advice in connection with the solicitor's legal or ethical obligations'.) to get confidential advice from your local law society or legal ethicist on the right course of action and its implications.

5. Prepare a 'script' and raise the issue internally with a sense of personal confidence, in the presence of a trusted witness. Send a record of the discussion to an appropriate superior(s).

6. Be prepared for rejection and retaliation inside the organisation. It will be very unusual if it does not come. Senior managers will resent the implication that they have been ineffective (some of them may even be involved in the wrong doing), and colleagues will resent you as a threat to the security of the organisation. If the harassment continues, record all details and threaten legal action. If necessary, take legal action. Most State Acts give you the right to do so. Or seek a new job. Early consideration of this possible need will probably be in your best interests.[1]

7. Keep notes.
8. If the harassment continues, determine what other relief your act offers you (relocation, for instance). Complain to a higher level if possible, but in the final analysis, seek legal advice and take action for damages. If you complain about harassment, place your emphasis on the public interest disclosure; any harassment or ill-will is a result of that disclosure. Also follow up on the investigation of your complaint, as most jurisdictions are obliged to tell you what the outcome is. And finally, if you do not win, if the wrongdoing is covered over, and no action is taken, try not to allow any sense of injustice to dominate your life. Remember that you have had a personal moral victory in making the disclosure. Attempt, as far as is possible, to recreate a new life and a new job.[2]

9. Try to take into account that, should you do nothing and the wrongdoing is eventually revealed, the loss to your personal reputation may be irrecoverable.

---

[1] See Bowden's 'ten point process'.
[2] See Bowden's 'ten point process'.

or *moral activism* – before determining whether the circumstances justify blowing the whistle. The content of the current law on confidentiality gives ample room to corporate lawyers to fulfil their ethical duties. But knowing when to breach confidence requires ethical judgement (again an element of *moral activism*), not just legal knowledge, as the circumstances in which the public interest or a client's 'fraud on justice' might justify and, indeed, demand whistleblowing can never be fully specified in the law. So it is appropriate to suggest that lawyers know something of the wider public debate about whistleblowing.

Bowden defines public whistleblowing as '…the exposure, made in the public interest…of significant information on corruption and wrongdoing…that would not otherwise be available'.[56] The conditions are important: the public interest has to be at stake, not just personal interests; the information must be significant rather than trivial; major crimes such as corruption must be involved; and there must be no other way for the information to be made available. As can easily be seen from our earlier discussion about the limits of client confidentiality, these requirements are broadly similar to those for lawyers who decide to speak out.

The general law on confidentiality recognises that disclosure of confidential information to an appropriate authority that can do something about it might be necessary in the public interest. A person who discloses someone else's confidences will therefore be protected from liability by the *public interest defence* if a court decides that the interest in maintaining the confidence is outweighed by a higher public interest, such as the prevention of wrongdoing or harm to others or to national security.[57] *ASCR* 9.2.2 also makes an exception to the professional duty of confidentiality where the lawyer 'is permitted or compelled by law to disclose'. These words import the public interest defence (as part of the general law's definition of when it is permitted to disclose otherwise confidential information) into professional conduct obligations, and therefore allows a lawyer to disclose confidential information if a court would find it was in the public interest to do so.

Corporate lawyers often act as if confidentiality is an absolute value that must be protected at all costs. Indeed William Simon talks about the legal profession's 'confidentiality fetish'.[58] But the public interest defence to confidentiality at common law and the illegality exception to client legal privilege mean that there is

---

56 Peter Bowden, University of Sydney. See <www.whistleblowingethics.info> accessed 17 Sept 2012.

57 See Paul Finn, 'Professionals and Confidentiality' (1992) 14 *Sydney Law Review* 317, 323; Karen Koomen, 'Breach of Confidence and the Public Interest Defence: Is It in the Public Interest?' (1994) 10 *Queensland University of Technology Law Journal* 56. For cases that may be examples of the public interest defence (or very similar principles) being applied to lawyers, see *Finers v Miro* [1991] 1 All ER 182; *R v Bell; Ex parte Lees* (1980) 146 CLR 141.

58 Simon, 'The Confidentiality Fetish'.

no obligation to maintain confidentiality where a corporation is acting illegally, or perhaps unethically, and the conduct is likely to physically or economically harm people, or the public interest demands it be disclosed.

CASE STUDY 4.5   AWB

AWB (formerly the Australian Wheat Board) (Case Study 1.3 in Chapter 1, and also Case Study 10.1 in Chapter 10), offers the clearest possible example of the abuse of client privilege. After briefly reviewing the discussion of the AWB case in Case Study 1.3, consider the following.

According to newspaper reports of evidence given at the Cole Royal Commission, as soon as AWB became aware of allegations of corruption and bribery in June 2003, two months after the fall of Saddam Hussein, the company set up an internal investigation into the allegations, codenamed 'Project Rose', under the control of their in-house lawyer. He in turn called in three external law firms and two barristers to review emails and documents and to advise on whether AWB had paid illegal bribes. At the Australian government's commission of inquiry in 2006, the AWB Board then claimed privilege over all the legal advice they had received, and also all internal minutes and records that related in any way to the advice received from external lawyers. AWB's in-house lawyer also claimed privilege to prevent him from answering any questions about his own opinion about any of the documents the external lawyers had been asked to advise on since, he said, even his own opinion would be based in part on the outside advice, which was privileged. Since hundreds of emails and other documents had been handed over to the external lawyers, this left very little that the in-house lawyer could be questioned about. Other AWB Board members and staff also refused to answer questions on the basis of similar claims of privilege.[59]

AWB also tried (unsuccessfully) to claim privilege over a document accidentally given to the commission which recorded a draft 'statement of contrition' prepared in a teleconference with external lawyers, and a corporate image and crisis management consultant.[60] This consultant had advised that AWB should apologise 'sooner rather than later', and an apology had been drafted. But AWB decided it did not want to admit that level of responsibility. Some of the statements

---

59 Richard Ackland, 'That's Privileged, Sir, and Go Scratch', *The Sydney Morning Herald*, 3 March 2006, 13; Marian Wilkinson, 'Lawyers Swept Up Files, Inquiry Told', *The Sydney Morning Herald*, 24 February 2006, 1.

60 *AWB Ltd v Cole* [2006] FCA 571 (Unreported, Young J, 17 May 2006).

made by the AWB chief executive in the draft apology were inconsistent with what he later told the commission about AWB senior management's awareness of, and responsibility for, bribery.[61]

During the AWB inquiry, Commissioner Terence Cole commented that, although it might have been *legal* to claim privilege in some of the circumstances in which AWB claimed privilege, the AWB Board should be careful to consider the 'wisdom' of making the claim, from a 'corporate governance' point of view.[62] In other words, clients always have a choice about whether to claim privilege or enforce confidentiality, or not. There may be a number of considerations in deciding whether to do so, other than the mere fact that it is legally possible. For example, it might be desirable to not claim privilege so as to fully co-operate with a Commission or regulator in order to indicate an attitude of taking ethical responsibility for past wrongdoing.

Commissioner Cole also made this comment regarding AWB's claims for client legal privilege:

> The claim for legal professional privilege [by AWB] in respect of the Project Rose brief to Mr Tracey QC, abandoned on day 62 of the hearings, resulted in great delay and expense to the Inquiry. Had AWB produced the brief earlier, with most of the relevant documents contained in it, the course of this Inquiry would have been different, and its duration and expense much less. Whatever may be said about legal professional privilege flowing from the skill of compiling a brief, it is plain that the original documents copied in the brief were all material to this Inquiry, would have had to be produced in response to notices, and would, after the expenditure of significant time and money, be compiled by the Inquiry to give a chronological picture of the involvement of AWB and its officers in the payment of monies by way of trucking fees. Had there been frankness or real cooperation on the part of AWB, most material documents could have been produced in November 2005.[63]

61 Caroline Overington, 'I'm Deeply Sorry: AWB Chief's Apology', *The Australian*, 19 May 2006, 1, 8. In the Supreme Court of Victoria, the former AWB chief executive Andrew Lindberg was fined $100,000 and disqualified from being a company director until 1 September 2014. See Ben Butler, 'Iraq Scandal: Former AWB Boss Fined', *The Age* (Melbourne), 10 August 2012, 2.

62 Statement in a hearing for the Inquiry into Certain Australian Companies in Relation to the UN Oil-For-Food Program, Sydney, 6 March 2006, 4042 (TRH Cole, Commissioner) <www.ag.gov.au/agd/WWW/UNOilForFoodInquiry.nsf/Page/Transcripts> at 2 June 2006. Subsequently the Federal Court decided that a number of the documents over which AWB claimed privilege were not privileged: *AWB Limited v Honourable Terence Rhoderic Hudson Cole (No. 5)* [2006] FCA 1234 (Unreported, Young J, 18 September 2006).

63 ALRC, Report 107, Chapter 9.

DISCUSSION QUESTIONS

1. ASCR 17.1 states: 'A solicitor representing a client in a matter that is before the court must not act as the *mere mouthpiece* of the client or of the instructing solicitor (if any) and must exercise the forensic judgments called for during the case independently, after the appropriate consideration of the client's and the instructing solicitor's instructions where applicable' [our emphasis]. If you were an advocate representing a large corporation such as AWB, and believed that your claim of client privilege (on behalf of your client) was spurious and could result in very critical comment by a judge at a later date, would you be prepared to make that claim, as the 'mere mouthpiece' of your client?

2. As advocate for BHP-Billiton, for example, would you feel able to argue with your instructing solicitors and BHP that your reputation is worth as much if not more than their own?

3. Would you be prepared never to receive a brief from BHP again, as a consequence of a single instance where you considered a claim for client privilege to be disingenuous and not to be pursued?

To be clear, a lawyer can choose to report criminality or client corruption. This right, and perhaps moral obligation, is now accepted by *ASCR* 9.2.4[64] – that is, where serious crimes are contemplated. There are also limits to client privilege. The *illegality exception* referred to above allows a lawyer to report criminal activity. It does not matter whether the lawyer knew at the time what the client's purpose was, nor whether the lawyer joined in that purpose. The High Court of Australia has defined the scope of this exception broadly. It is not 'confined to cases of crime and fraud...unless the meaning is extended to anything that might be a fraud on justice'.[65]

Conclusion

Although it is easy to recognise that actual privacy is increasingly unlikely for those without power or influence (especially low income earners, the aged and all categories of disabled persons), it is critical for lawyers to recognise that

---

64 *Australian Solicitors' Conduct Rules*, Rule 9.
65 *A-G (NT) v Kearney* (1985) 158 CLR 500, 514.

impoverished clients are entitled to no less and no more privacy than those whose relative wealth, position or power allows them to contest intrusion into their private lives. Appropriate privacy and the confidentiality which supports it is essential to individuals' health and wellbeing, yet not at the cost of secrets which pervert the course of justice. The task of judging which secrets are appropriate falls to lawyers on an everyday basis, and *who* each lawyer is, at an ethical level, is central to that task. As law students and lawyers, we must contemplate who we are (or would be) in these crises. Will we be unthinking *zealous advocates* for wealthy governments and corporations seeking to evade disclosure through excessive claims to client privilege, or to Freedom of Information requests on the basis of 'cabinet papers' or claims of 'commercial-in-confidence'? If zealous advocacy is our strongest instinct, we will have to decide on the limits to our zealotry and ask: 'Who benefits and who suffers if the claim is pursued?', and how the counter-balancing call of responsible lawyering can assist us. Then we must apply our conscience to the integrity of those claims. The lawyers acting for the clients discussed in the case studies above had such an obligation. Consider how they discharged it and how you would wish to behave in a similar situation, should it arise.

RECOMMENDED FURTHER READING

Andrew Alexandra and Seumas Miller, *Ethics in Practice: Moral Theory and the Professions* (UNSW Press, 2009).

Sissela Bok, *Secrets: On the Ethics of Concealment and Revelation* (Random House, New York, 1983).

Peter Bowden and Vanya Smyth, 'Ethics, Good Governance and Whistleblowing' in *Contemporary Issues in International Corporate Governance* (Tilde University Press, 2009).

Selene Mize, 'Should the Lawyer's Duty to Keep Confidences Override the Duty to Disclose Material Information to a Client?' (2009) 12 *Legal Ethics* 171.

William Simon, 'The Confidentiality Fetish' (2004) 294(5) *The Atlantic Monthly* 113.

ETHICS IN CRIMINAL JUSTICE: PROOF AND TRUTH

Introduction

Television and movies often portray criminal practice as the most glamorous speciality within the legal profession. In fact it is among the least attractive to most new lawyers – probably because defending accused criminals can be seen as repulsive and unremunerative. Yet it is for these very reasons that the criminal defence advocate is usually taken as the paradigmatic example of the reason why *adversarial advocacy* is necessary and ethically justified. As one senior barrister puts it:

> The quality of the system is tested by how it treats the worst … The worst, most revolting criminal or terrorist or whoever it happens to be, if you can get a fair trial for them then everyone else is guaranteed a good run. But if the system starts taking short cuts because somebody is so bad, then it's the system that's coming apart.[1]

Because the potential sanctions for criminal offences, such as deprivation of liberty, are so serious and the resources and capacity of the state to investigate and prosecute crimes so vast, our system assumes that an accused should always have the opportunity to 'put the Crown to proof' of any charges brought against the accused. In other words, the strength of the Crown must be able to be put to the test in the adversary system. This effectively holds the state (including the police and other prosecutors) accountable by making sure that they have strong enough evidence to justify a court deciding to convict. It also maintains the integrity of the criminal justice system by making sure that the accused is treated fairly.

A similar rationale also applies to advocacy in other areas where the state has the power to deprive people of their liberty:

> I do refugee work because it cries out to be done. I was deeply offended by the way this country was treating refugees. I wanted to make amends for the country and try to make things better for them. It was the simple fact of locking up innocent people indefinitely that hit me like a thunderbolt … I saw a Holocaust documentary after taking on the Tampa case. There was a Berlin lawyer talking about Germany in the mid-1930s. He said they passed a law locking up innocent people, and that, in itself, is a terrible crime. I thought it was just plain wrong to hold innocent people on the deck of a ship in the tropics … The law was grossly stacked against the people I represented.[2]

To advocate effectively, it is often argued that the defence lawyer must argue passionately, as if they really believe in their client's case.[3] On the other hand,

---

1 Lex Lasry QC in Gary Tippet, 'Counsel for the Condemned', *Insight, The Age* (Melbourne), 26 November 2005, 12; cited in Abbe Smith, 'Defending the Unpopular Down Under' (2006) 30 (2) *Melbourne University Law Review* 495.
2 Julian Burnside quoted in ibid.
3 Smith, 'Defending the Unpopular'.

the prosecutor in the criminal trial is probably the clearest example in the law of lawyering, of lawyers being required in principle at least to act as *responsible lawyers* – as 'ministers of justice' – rather than *adversarial advocates*:

> The role of defence counsel in defended criminal proceedings is usually to seek an acquittal by any legitimate means; but the role of the prosecution is by evidence to prove all relevant facts to the court and (if appropriate) by moderately presented and reasoned steps to argue that by application of the law to those facts, the rational conclusion beyond reasonable doubt must be that the accused is guilty … The prosecution must assist the court to arrive at the truth. It is probably the *only* role that an advocate can perform that is dedicated to the ascertainment of the truth.[4]

Prosecutors have special duties of fairness because the prosecutor is an agent of the state, and it is not 'seemly' for a prosecutor to be adversarial in pressing for conviction in that position. As a state agent, the prosecutor generally has greater capacity and resources for investigating and prosecuting their case than the defence has for their case.

The prosecution often has greater credibility with the jury. As representative of the state, it is the prosecutor's job to present a fair case for conviction based on good evidence, not to argue for conviction, and a high sentence, with adversarial zeal (*Australian Solicitors' Conduct Rules (ASCR)* 29.1–29.3). Indeed the prosecution could be expected to have a role in checking the misconduct of the police or other state agents, by making sure that their own assertions are reasonably capable of supporting a finding of guilt and carry weight (*ASCR* 29.4). Prosecutors also have various duties to share the evidence collected by the state with the accused in order to assist the accused and their lawyer to prepare a defence to the charges (*ASCR* 29.5–29.6, 29.8).

Thus the prosecution and the defence have essentially complementary roles as 'officers of the court' in criminal trials – the prosecution's role is to present a fair case while the defence's role is to test and probe it adversarially. It is the combination of both responsible lawyering and adversarial advocacy that make for a fair trial and a fair justice system more generally.

The Criminal Trial

Defence lawyers see the criminal trial as being about putting the Crown to proof, but the general public often think that criminal trials (and lawyers' role in those trials) should be about discovering the truth. Public criticism of criminal trials is often uninformed and unfair. Nevertheless, there is a rarely discussed undercurrent

---

4 Nicholas Cowdery (NSW Director of Public Prosecutions), *Ethics and the Role of a Prosecutor* (New South Wales, 1997) 32.

of injustice endemic in criminal practice (assisted by some rules of conduct). This is the procedural trend towards 'managing' criminal justice systems so as to maximise the efficiency of the process and control costs by encouraging the accused to plead 'guilty' as early as possible, and make it easier to achieve convictions.

Unfortunately this risks achieving less justice for individual defendants.[5] Cost control is the mantra. But it is also obvious that pressure from politicians and the media to try to achieve security from public-execution-style murders of gangland members, large-scale drug distribution and the possibility of terrorist attack are leading to a culture of diminished personal freedoms and fewer rights for defendants generally.

The most established examples of this trend are plea discussions and judicial incentives to change pleas from 'not guilty' to 'guilty'. Plea discussions – under which a prosecutor and defence counsel agree to withdraw some charges in exchange for a 'guilty' plea on others – are of long standing in Australia. Most observers think this process is acceptable, provided it does not degenerate into something like the US system where the court agrees to a definitive sentence without presiding over a proper test of the evidence.[6] Efforts by the court system to formally 'encourage' 'guilty' pleas are far less satisfactory. Magistrates and local courts now commonly schedule so-called 'contest mention' or 'sentence indication' hearings at which the evidence is summarised by the advocates on both sides, and the defendant is then put under some pressure by the court to reflect on the likely outcome and sentence, if the plea is changed to 'guilty'. Governments argue that precious court time is otherwise wasted by the need to schedule a lengthy defended hearing, only to leave the magistrate and prosecutor idle when defendants change a plea to 'guilty' at the last minute. There is an attractive offer of relative certainty of outcome, but a defendant must pay for a lawyer for *two* appearances if they insist on a contest (the contest mention and then the actual hearing), effectively compelling many defendants to convert to 'guilty' and avoid the cost of the second appearance. A significant part of the cost of the criminal justice process – which is likely to include some inefficiencies if justice is to be served – is therefore shifted from the state to the defendant.

---

5 Arie Freiberg, 'Managerialism in Australian Criminal Justice: RIP for KPIs?' (2005) 31 *Monash University Law Review* 12; Mike McConville et al, *Standing Accused: The Organisation and Practices of Criminal Defence Lawyers in Britain* (Clarendon Press, Oxford, 1994); Mike McConville and C Mirsky, 'Guilty Plea Courts: A Social Disciplinary Model of Criminal Justice' (1995) 42 *Social Problems* 216. See also Russell Hogg and David Brown, *Rethinking Law and Order* (Pluto Press, Annandale, NSW, 1998).

6 Kathy Mack, 'Balancing Principle and Pragmatism: Guilty Pleas' (1995) 4 *Journal of Judicial Administration* 232. Plea negotiations should be distinguished from 'plea bargaining'. The latter practice is well-known in the United States as a bargaining process between prosecution and defence under which a defendant agrees to plead 'guilty' to one charge in exchange for the withdrawal of other charges and the certainty of a specific sentence.

In his snapshot ethics survey of twenty Australian criminal advocates published in 2003, Ben Clarke observed that there are many other indications of ethical malpractice in criminal justice, but few lawyers prepared to talk extensively about the problems.[7] Clarke's study provides a number of examples of lawyer practices that the public would see as reducing the ability of the courts to find out the truth in criminal cases:

- How does a lawyer defend the guilty client? Public incredulity over this issue usually points to a narrower question: Can a lawyer ethically argue a 'not guilty' plea for a guilty client? The profession says 'yes' on the basis that: First, in very few circumstances will a defence lawyer, faced with their client's denial, be able to be absolutely certain of the client's guilt. Secondly, even if they are so certain, it is still possible to play a limited, legitimate role designed to put the prosecution to their proof beyond reasonable doubt. The question in the mind of the community is nevertheless insistent: Why spend time, court resources and/or public money (if the matter is legally aided) on a 'not guilty' plea if the best judgement of defence counsel (even though this judgement may be slightly short of certainty)[8] is that their client is criminally responsible for the alleged crime? The final response by the profession – that guilt or innocence is for the court to determine – may be reasonable, but critics then ask why advocates are allowed by the rules to make outrageous allegations in court about others in order to defend someone, taking refuge in the principle that they do not *know*, as a fact, whether their allegations are true or false or if their client is criminally responsible? The answer is that the rules on this point are in place to ensure that fairness towards (or compassion for) the defendant prevails. But the contrary view is that compassion should never mean unbalanced favouritism.

7 Ben Clarke, 'An Ethics Survey of Australian Criminal Law Practitioners' (2003) 27 *Criminal Law Journal* 142. Clarke's study received considerable media attention because of its findings: See Kate Marshall, 'Ethical Dilemmas Keep Criminal Lawyers Awake', *The Australian Financial Review* (Sydney), 13 September 2002, 56; ABC Radio National, 'The Ethics of Criminal Lawyers', *The Law Report*, 12 November 2002 <www.abc.net.au/rn/talks/8.30/lawrpt/stories/s724128.htm> at 19 July 2006.

8 The alternative possibility – lying by counsel to ensure that an innocent client is acquitted – is less likely but not altogether unheard of. For example, in the book and film *To Kill a Mockingbird*, defence attorney Atticus Finch's decision to tell a lie to ensure that an innocent man is saved from death exposes the case of justification for lying because knowledge of innocence is *certain*: See Tim Dare, '"The Secret Courts of Men's Hearts", Legal Ethics and Harper Lee's *To Kill a Mockingbird*' in Kim Economides (ed), *Ethical Challenges to Legal Education and Conduct* (Hart Publishing, Oxford, 1998) 39. One view is that there ought to be an ethical rule that says lying by counsel is punishable no matter what, because as soon as any exceptions are allowed, the way is open to all sorts of normative situations that reduce the value of honesty to a functional zero: See T A Zlaket, 'Conference Proceedings on Professionalism' (Paper presented at the Conference on Professionalism, Savannah, Georgia, 20–21 October 2000) 535, 536–8 (arguing that the 'noble lie' example bears little relationship to the day-to-day problems in court: once exceptions are allowed, 'you can kiss the rule goodbye').

It has been suggested that experienced counsel are in an excellent position to make not just informed but the *best informed* judgements as to the truth or otherwise of their client's assertions, and therefore should not be ethically permitted to run a 'not guilty' plea when that judgement convinces them that their client is criminally responsible. There may be no really satisfactory answer to this issue except to allow for the possibilities of misunderstanding by advocates as to what is said to them, different cultural and religious understandings of guilt that allow a defendant to say one thing while meaning another, and the fact that what a client thinks of as guilt will occasionally be otherwise, as in the case of someone who commits a criminal act (*actus reus*) but has insufficient *mens rea* (generally because of some form of diminished mental responsibility). While it is therefore almost certainly risky to alter the Law Council's *Australian Solicitors' Conduct Rules* (especially *ASCR* 19–20, discussed below) which seek to balance the ethical obligations of counsel in this area of criminal defence, it is surely appropriate to require a positive educative process in values awareness among criminal counsel, to improve the chances that they will give serious consideration as to what they actually *know* about their clients' actions and what they should actively enquire about.

- In practice, clients are often deliberately silenced by a lawyer when it is likely that they are about to be 'told something privately' (that is, the client is about to confess) which might set up a conflict between their duties of candour (to the court) and confidentiality (to their client). Despite *ASCR* 19.1 ('A solicitor must not deceive or knowingly or recklessly mislead the court') and 19.2 ('[and must]…correct any misleading statement…'), 70% (fourteen) of Clarke's respondents admitted to this practice of passive deception and *thought it ethical*. Clarke is possibly over-generous in his comment that the practice is 'complex'.[9] In fact, pretending to ignorance among defence counsel is likely to be a major ethical failing by the profession. Clarke describes lawyers silencing their clients as the avoidance of 'precluding a client from running a successful defence'.[10] However he does acknowledge that this practice might prevent the taking of full instructions. In fact, experienced practitioners, having been caught out early on in their careers, and possibly feeling guilty for past silence, usually do not even allow the situation to arise. They inform a new client in a general introductory statement that the client is not to say anything or volunteer any information, apart from answering the lawyer's questions. If a lawyer learns, after an acquittal of murder, of the guilt of a client, most (75%) in Clarke's study would consider they are bound to keep the confidence. In other words,

---

9 Clarke, 'An Ethics Survey', 148. See also Kenneth Mann, *Defending White-Collar Crime: A Portrait of Attorneys at Work* (Yale University Press, New Haven, 1985) 103–18 (evidence of US lawyers in white-collar criminal defence doing the same thing).

10 Clarke, 'An Ethics Survey', 148.

Clarke's survey discloses lawyers' comfort with technical adherence to the rules in the hope that the court will be perceptive enough to recognise any deception by the client. Are lawyers risking subversion of the court with this practice in order to preserve client confidentiality? In Chapter 4 we mention the United States' *Alton Logan* case, where a considered concern for the confidences of a confessed murderer led to the imprisonment of an innocent person for 26 years, in exactly these circumstances. Is the risk of another similar case acceptable?

- Another recurring problem is that some advocates lengthen cases to an extraordinary degree, without concern for the process of justice. In *R v Wilson*,[11] for example – the trial and re-trial of two businessmen charged with corporate fraud – the delaying actions of counsel for the defendant Wilson were considered responsible by the court for the bulk of *22 months'* court time, while the prosecution was 'deplored' in the re-trial [for *reading* to the jury], '…over some ten calendar weeks', the evidence of the defendants at their first trial.[12] This is surely one of the worst cases of *adversarial advocacy* dominating *responsible lawyering*.

- Aggressive tactics are not uncommon – for example, undue pressure is put on witnesses by insulting them (contrary to *ASCR* 21.2 'making allegations or suggestions under privilege…[that are not] reasonably justified or are inappropriate for the robust advancement of the client's case on its merits…[or are] made principally in order to harass or embarrass').

- A variation on this problem is that of the incompetent or lazy defence, where advocates, for their own reasons, and despite *ASCR* 4.1.1 ('must…act in the best interests of a client…'), are clearly unconcerned to attend properly to their client's defence. In *R v Kina*,[13] for example, there was a complete failure of defence counsel to aggressively or competently represent an Aboriginal woman who had killed her de facto husband after shocking and sustained provocation.

- Coaching witnesses is routine, despite *ASCR* 24.1.1 ('[must not]…advise or suggest to a witness that false or misleading evidence should be given…') and 24.1.2 ('…coach a witness by advising what answers the witness should give…'): 35% (seven) of Clarke's respondents admitted to these practices.

- Jury nullification is used as a defence tactic – that is, juries are distracted from considering cogent prosecution evidence by focusing them on emotive issues such as personal or racial intolerance of a prosecution witness or remote possibilities of crime-scene contaminants. Case Study 5.1 below, *R v Neilan*, illustrates how this problem can occur in practice. 'Demolition' of rape victims

---

11 [1995] 1 VR 163.
12 David Parsons and Mark Taft, 'Review of Judgments' (1994) 68(9) *Law Institute Journal* 863.
13 [1993] QCA 480 (Unreported, Fitzgerald P, Davies and McPherson JJA, 29 November 1993).

still occurs in the witness box, though more judges are wary of the practice. The Victorian Law Reform Commission has recommended changes to case procedure such as '…judges should have a duty to protect children and people with cognitive impairment from misleading, confusing and intimidating questioning'.[14]

Abbe Smith quotes the following defence lawyers discussing some of the tactics they use to try to 'get their clients off':

- One lawyer was sceptical about her fellow lawyers' regard for the truth when it comes to advocacy: 'I think lawyers are kidding themselves when they say they care about truth. If someone has a drop of Aboriginal blood, I'll milk it in court for all it's worth. I will play on female stuff. I will use stereotypes as part of advocacy.…I know I'm not alone in this'.
- … [Another lawyer], and quite a few others, indicated that, as an advocate, he 'would do everything allowed by law', including 'exploiting prejudice on behalf of a client'. He saw this as a '"tactical decision" not an ethical one': 'If it was a weak, piddling point, I wouldn't make it. But if it was a decent point I would. … If there were blacks or Asians on the jury I would exploit a point to get to them – if the facts were there. I wouldn't make it up. It's not my concern whether I am perpetuating prejudice or misogyny or whatever. Political correctness is not an issue for the Bar'.
- [A third lawyer acknowledged] that there is a 'battle of prejudices' in trial lawyering, and that, in the Ramage murder case [in which a husband was accused of strangling his separated wife], he 'tossed the fact that Mrs Ramage was menstruating out there' to suggest 'gently' that she may have been hysterical and helped bring about her own death. … 'I would use any perceived notion or stereotype. I would throw it out there.'[15]

DISCUSSION QUESTIONS

1. Do any of these tactics break any rules? What principles might apply to this situation?

2. How do these practices fit with the idea of being an officer of the court and *responsible lawyering*?

The former *Model Rules* (insofar as they related to advocacy) began with an impeccable general statement which encouraged both competence and best ethical practice in all advocates:

---

14 Victorian Law Reform Commission, *Sexual Offences Final Report: Summary and Recommendations in Plain English* (Victorian Law Reform Commission, Melbourne, 2004) 8.
15 Smith, 'Defending the Unpopular'.

> Practitioners, in all their dealings with the courts, whether those dealings involve the obtaining and presentation of evidence, the preparation and filing of documents, instructing an advocate or appearing as an advocate, should act with *competence, honesty and candour*. Practitioners should be frank in their responses and disclosures to the court, and diligent in their observance of undertakings which they give to the court or their opponents.[16] [our emphasis]

Honesty and candour are the core concepts in this general statement, but many of the *Rules* and the common law, and the way they are applied in practice, do not obviously or consistently endorse these priorities in criminal advocacy. Also, the more recent *ASCR* have replaced this list of three essential personal virtues with a pared back and formulaic statement of objectivity (*ASCR* 3.1: 'A solicitor's duty to the court and the administration of justice is paramount and prevails to the extent of inconsistency with any other duty'.). The difference between the two rules suggests a lack of appreciation of the importance of personal professionalism in lawyers' professional conduct. In the following subsections we consider the rules for defence and prosecution advocates in more detail.

The Defence

Although many of the Law Council's 'Advocacy and Litigation Rules' (*ASCR* 17–29) do not expressly refer to the prosecution or defence of criminal cases, or to 'advocates', their context and application make it clear that the obligations of defence counsel in criminal trials are their primary concern.

ASCR 17.1 refers to the need for candour in its requirement for 'independence':

> A practitioner must not act as the mere mouthpiece of the client or of the instructing practitioner and must exercise the forensic judgments called for during the case independently [of the client] ...

This means that it is not permissible to simply do as the client wants – for example, lead evidence of an alibi which counsel thinks is very likely to be false – if the effect of that action would be to ignore the requirement for candour with the court. As far as it goes, this rule is credible and reflects the proper priority of *responsible lawyering* over *adversarial advocacy*.

Similarly, *ASCR* 17.3 requires a practitioner to avoid making any submissions or expressing any views to a court '... on any material evidence or material issue ... which convey ... the practitioner's personal opinion on the merits of that evidence or issue'. This rule also supports lawyer independence by prohibiting lawyers from giving

---

16 From the preamble to 'Advocacy and Litigation Rules', *Model Rules*.

personal opinions about cases. It is no surprise that such a rule is needed, since we are all familiar with the stereotypical (and usually foreign) attorney who comments 'zealously' on witnesses and their evidence in closing addresses to a jury. But it is perhaps not so clear that there is a fine line between negative comment on witnesses or evidence, having regard to objective criticisms that can be made of their credibility or recollections, and reflections on witnesses or their evidence that appear to target irrelevant matters or come from the private views of the advocate. The problem arises here not from the rule itself, but from its implementation.

One of the criticisms of this rule, and similar local versions in each jurisdiction, is that it is increasingly ignored and rarely enforced. Senior advocates comment that there is a tendency not only to cross the line by implying a negative personal opinion of a witness, but also to undermine an opposing police witness in front of a jury – 'to play the man, not the ball', as the (sexist) phrase goes – by repeatedly asking them to give opinions on matters of fact and then self-righteously correcting the process by insisting that they did not intend to put any opinion in front of the jury. On occasion, an appeal court will comment negatively on this tendency, but by then the consequences for the advocate concerned are minimal and only those with an intimate knowledge of the case are aware of the possible transgression. Since the values of the Bar do not yet support whistleblowers, *ASCR* 17.3 suffers from a lack of comprehensive enforcement.

The conduct in the following Case Study is probably an example of this approach to the defence.

CASE STUDY 5.1   R v NEILAN[17]

In the late 1980s, Mark Neilan was a successful veterinary surgeon in the Victorian town of Drouin, where he lived with his wife Kathryn and a young daughter, Sheridan. One night, according to Neilan, intruders broke in, took him outside and, while bundling him into the boot of his car, went to the main bedroom and apparently shot Kathryn, then four months pregnant, in the head. Sheridan was left undisturbed in bed. A neighbour found Neilan locked in the boot of his car the following afternoon. As soon as he was released from the boot, he entered the house and exclaimed, 'Oh Kathy, oh no', when he saw her body. A search for the intruders or any physical evidence of their presence in the house revealed nothing, though a break-in at Neilan's nearby veterinary practice in the town, which apparently occurred on the same night, resulted in some money and a small quantity of Valium disappearing.

17 [1992] 1 VR 57.

Neilan later made various inconsistent statements about when he had first seen the intruders on the night of the murder. The police came to disbelieve his version of events, and charged him with his wife's murder. He was bailed, and then two strange things happened. First, some weeks after his release on bail, Neilan claimed to have positively identified one of the intruders at Chadstone shopping centre, prepared a sketch of the sighting at his own expense and advertised for anyone who might know the face. Secondly, about nine days after the advertisement appeared, one of Neilan's dogs, a Border Collie, was shot and killed while Neilan was apparently away from home. The bullets came from a semi-automatic .22 rifle, the same type of gun that had been used to kill Kathryn – a gun that had not then and has never since been found. Neilan asserted that his advertisement had provoked the murderers into killing his dog as a warning to him to leave the murder alone, but the police believed that the incidents were manufactured by Neilan to support his story that the intruders, looking for drugs and money in the area on the night of the offence, were responsible for the killing. The major difficulty for the police, however, was that they could not suggest, let alone prove, any motive at all for Neilan to murder his wife.

When Neilan was eventually brought to trial, he asserted through his counsel that he knew nothing more about the death of his wife than he had already indicated. Significantly, he declined to give personal evidence in his own defence, but did call other evidence. His counsel relied on the lack of motive, witnesses or confession, and concentrated on characterising the prosecution case as entirely circumstantial, even prejudicial and vindictive on the part of the police. Nevertheless, Neilan was convicted.

Of ethical significance in this case is the effort to which defence counsel went to criticise the police witnesses. Neilan was facing the real hurdle of persuading the jury that he was innocent, while at the same time declining to give evidence about a matter that only he could clarify: what happened on the night. A formidable task therefore lay ahead of defence counsel and a device of some sort was needed to capture, or rather divert, the jury's attention. Counsel attempted to persuade the jury that the police, lacking a motive, had been engaged in nothing more than a series of speculations about what really happened, leaving them with the impression that no one could be certain of events on the night of the murder. In the event, however, this strategy failed – probably because the silence of the defendant was just too much for the jury to swallow.

Neilan unsuccessfully appealed his conviction on a number of grounds and in the course of the Court of Criminal Appeal's judgment, their Honours referred to the defence strategy of distraction or nullification:

A very strong attack was made by the defence on Noonan [a police witness]. It was suggested to him that he had shut his eyes to everything that was in favour of the applicant and assumed his guilt ... that he had put forward and acted upon theories with regard to the crime which were far-fetched ... It was not that Noonan sought argumentatively to support the Crown case or attempted to introduce tendentious matter: senior counsel for the applicant forced him to express opinions and in effect to debate with him a number of questions ... The cross-examination was highly unusual, amounting as it did on occasions to a debate between the police officer and counsel, and moreover a debate which was of counsel's making.[18]

There is a rule of evidence that witnesses, other than experts (and the police witness Noonan did not qualify as an expert in this case), must confine their evidence to factual observations of which they have personal knowledge. Knowing this rule only too well, counsel for Neilan invited the police witness to express an opinion on an issue of fact and, when the witness, after having been exposed to earlier questions of this type, duly provided that opinion, counsel immediately applied for discharge of the jury.[19] Although the request was refused by the trial judge, the seed could have been sown with the jury that, on the basis that opinion evidence had been given, there were other police theories about the crime and any of these theories, in the 'real' minds of the police, were all contenders. In other words, the jury was invited to reflect on the possibility that the police were not certain if the defendant was the murderer.

The Court of Criminal Appeal considered whether the trial judge ought to have reined in defence counsel or done more to counter the effects of the cross-examination, before deciding on balance that the jury had other bases on which to determine that the defendant was guilty. However, the Court was most critical of the strategy of the defence and said so at length, because this strategy of persistent invitation to the police to give opinion evidence, knowing such evidence was arguably inadmissible, was designed only to poison the jury's mind as to the motives of the prosecution.

As with so many other cases where counsel take an ethically suspect stance, however, appeal courts tend to confine themselves to criticism within the case context, and rarely refer matters to the regulators – the legal professional associations – for investigation as to whether any misconduct that may warrant disciplinary action has occurred.

---

18 In the reported decision of *Neilan* (ibid), the comments of the Court of Criminal Appeal as to the conduct of defence counsel were edited out. However, the unreported decision explains the matter fully: See *R v Neilan* (Unreported, Supreme Court of Victoria, Court of Criminal Appeal, Young CJ, Brooking and Marks JJ, 5 April 1991) 67.

19 See *R v Neilan* (Unreported, Supreme Court of Victoria, Court of Criminal Appeal, Young CJ, Brooking and Marks JJ, 5 April 1991) 68.

DISCUSSION QUESTIONS

Imagine you were defence counsel for Neilan:

1. Given the facts set out above, what instructions do you think it is likely you would have received from your client?

2. What would have been your advice to the defendant as to the best approach to take to the defence of his case?

Assuming your client was insistent on pleading 'not guilty':

3. Would you decide to criticise the police for their lack of a motive for the killing?

4. Would you think it appropriate to try to persuade the jury that the police were targeting your client unfairly or casting around for a defendant – any defendant – without any real idea as to who was responsible?

If you thought it appropriate to point out to the jury that the police had nothing absolutely 'concrete' on your client:

5. Would you think it acceptable to point to an ulterior motive by the police, and to do so by highlighting their opinions, rather than the facts, about the evidence?

6. In representing Neilan, would you see yourself as an *adversarial advocate* (and obliged to make serious allegations about the police in order to create doubt in the mind of the jury), or someone concerned to ensure that the jury deals only with admissible evidence in making their decision? Why? What difference would each make to your strategy in the case?

Advocates are also not supposed to knowingly mislead a court (*ASCR* 19.1). They may be excused from doing so 'unknowingly', if correction is made 'as soon as possible' (*ASCR* 19.2). But an advocate '... will not have made a misleading statement to a court simply by failing to correct an error in a statement made to the court by the opponent or any other person' (*ASCR* 19.3). This rule is most often used to advantage by defence counsel when a prosecutor fails, usually because their information is incomplete, to mention relevant prior convictions to a judge, and the judge gives a lighter sentence to a defendant as a result. Case Study 5.1 below is an example of this occurring. In fact, there is a specific reference to the prior conviction circumstance in *ASCR* 19.10, which permits silence by defence counsel, providing they truly remain passive and do not specifically ask a prosecution witness whether there are relevant 'priors', in the expectation of receiving a negative answer. These 'mere silence' rules are so well-established that they are unlikely to be overturned by any court, but there is a real case to review *ASCR* 19.10.

Since the modern trend in legal ethics gives primacy to the duty to the court (the *responsible lawyer*) – with the duty to the client increasingly taking second place – the notion that mere silence is still acceptable, in the face of error by the other side, ought to be re-examined by the regulators.

Similarly, on the surface, *ASCR* 20.1 seems to make a mockery of any sense of truth and justice in criminal trials by providing that counsel should keep a confession by a defendant secret from the court when it is made in the course of a trial, unless the client agrees to its disclosure:

> 20.1 A solicitor who, as a result of information provided by the client or a witness called on behalf of the client, learns during a hearing or after judgment or the decision is reserved and while it remains pending, that the client or a witness called on behalf of the client:
>
> > 20.1.1 has lied in a material particular to the court or has procured another person to lie to the court;
> >
> > 20.1.2 has falsified or procured another person to falsify in any way a document which has been tendered; or
> >
> > 20.1.3 has suppressed or procured another person to suppress material evidence upon a topic where there was a positive duty to make disclosure to the court;
> >
> > must –
> >
> > 20.1.4 advise the client that the court should be informed of the lie, falsification or suppression and request authority so to inform the court; and
> >
> > 20.1.5 refuse to take any further part in the case unless the client authorises the solicitor to inform the court of the lie, falsification or suppression and must promptly inform the court of the lie, falsification or suppression upon the client authorising the solicitor to do so but otherwise may not inform the court of the lie, falsification or suppression.
>
> 20.2. A solicitor whose client in criminal proceedings confesses guilt to the solicitor but maintains a plea of 'not guilty':
>
> > 20.1.1 may cease to act, if there is enough time for another solicitor to take over the case properly before the hearing, and the client does not insist on the solicitor continuing to appear for the client;
> >
> > 20.1.2 in cases where the solicitor continues to act for the client:
> >
> > > (i) must not falsely suggest that some other person committed the offence charged;
> > >
> > > (ii) must not set up an affirmative case inconsistent with the confession;

          (iii)   may argue that the evidence as a whole does not prove that the client is guilty of the offence charged;

          (iv)   may argue that for some reason of law the client is not guilty of the offence charged; and

          (v)   may argue that for any other reason not prohibited by (i) and (ii) the client should not be convicted of the offence charged;

    20.1.3   must not continue to act if the client insists on giving evidence denying guilt or requires the making of a statement asserting the client's innocence.

In fact there is a cogent *responsible lawyering* justification for this restriction on the truth, as illustrated by the Northern Territory case of *Tuckiar v The King*[20] decided more than seventy years ago. In that case an Aboriginal elder was charged with the murder of a policeman in Arnhem Land. Tuckiar, or Dhakiyarr as he was and is now known in his community, had come upon the policeman as he (the policeman) was taking Dhakiyarr's wife away in chains, during a search for other Indigenous people who were suspected of killing some Japanese fishermen. According to tribal law, the action of the policeman was probably a 'taking' and therefore Dhakiyarr's intervention was justified.[21] Dhakiyarr speared the victim, narrowly missing his own wife and young child in the process.

He was captured and tried in Darwin. However, it was only during his trial that Dhakiyarr communicated to his counsel, through an interpreter, enough of the circumstances of the spearing to produce a hasty and uninformed reaction in the lawyer. The now infamous advocate immediately got to his feet in front of the jury and stated that he was in '... the worst predicament he had encountered in all his legal career' (code for 'my client did it') and needed to speak to the judge.[22]

Counsel did not argue any defence on Dhakiyarr's behalf throughout the case, and his client was subsequently convicted.

On appeal to the High Court, there was a unanimous decision that advocates are bound to keep silent in such circumstances and continue with fully testing the prosecution case, although they must avoid putting their clients in the witness box to give affirmative evidence of innocence. Dhakiyarr won his appeal on the basis that his advocate's statement to the court had produced a substantial

---

20 (1934) 52 CLR 335.

21 As explored in the documentary *Dhakiyarr vs The King* (Film Australia, 2004). See also Tom Murray, *Dhakiyarr vs The King: Study Guide* (Film Australia, 2004) <http://sa-staging.com/programs/teachers_notes/8660_dhakiyarrnotes.pdf> at 25 August 2013. The documentary makes the point that 'two laws' operated in Arnhem Land at the time and that Dhakiyarr did not realise that his 'law' was no longer dominant.

22 *Tuckiar v The King* (1934) 52 CLR 335, 341.

miscarriage of justice (not that Dhakiyarr's actions were, by the standards of the day, acceptable). He was released, never to be seen again.[23] As a result of the appeal, however, it is clear that the duty of confidentiality binds advocates' actions, providing that no active misleading of the court occurs. In other words, fairness does dominate. The irony of Dhakiyarr's case, apart from the tragedy of the clash of two uncomprehending cultures, is that his own evidence, had he been allowed to give it, might have caused a modern jury to think he was not guilty, though this result was probably most unlikely before a jury in 1930s Darwin.

As the High Court explained in the *Tuckiar* case, the principles set out in *ASCR* 20 are designed to retain, for even the 'guilty' client, some representation before the court, in the interests of ensuring that the continuing prosecution is as fair as possible. This objective is achieved by the practical difficulty in which defendants find themselves if their advocate withdraws because they have lied to the court, a circumstance which is carefully explained to them by the (majority of) advocates who take the rule seriously. Even hesitant clients usually consent to disclosure and rectification of the lie when they realise that the effective penalty for non-co-operation will be the withdrawal of their advocate from the trial (*ASCR* 20.1.5 and 20.2.3), a circumstance which most quickly understand will communicate something of their guilt to the jury. The issue which the *ASCR* do not handle well is the possibility of some deceit upon the court, because the lawyer who withdraws must do so without formally advising the court of the reasons. Some juries may not understand what is happening and some judges, in their anxiety to avoid what they see as a likely guilty defendant escaping judgment, can misdirect juries and leave the verdict subject to appeal on that basis.

If a client calls the bluff of their lawyer and refuses to convert their plea to guilty after confessing to their lawyer that they have lied to the court, do all advocates simply depart from the case and keep silent? The answer is unknown, though Clarke's study suggests that some may stay. However, there may not be too many advocates who, once made aware of apparent lies by their client, are content to let that knowledge simply evaporate. Most experienced advocates realise only too well that criminal defendants have a habit of reappearing before courts from time to time and, facing custodial sentences for other offences, have little to lose and something to gain from reminding that advocate of their prior knowledge. Should an advocate pretend they know nothing after hearing a confession or learning from their client of falsified evidence by others, they would forever after leave themselves vulnerable to blackmail by that client. In short, the reputation of a criminal advocate within criminal circles is nearly always too important to leave to

---

23 Dhakiyarr's descendants have since claimed, though been unable to prove, that he was killed shortly after his release by those unhappy with the decision of the High Court: *Dhakiyarr vs The King*.

chance. *ASCR* 20.1 is generally an effective, but not always complete, antidote to the problem which *Tuckiar* exposed.

ASCR 20.2 deals with the necessary consequences for the trial when the advocate does not withdraw after hearing a 'confession' from their client. This rule properly allows such an advocate to continue to act providing they confine themselves to testing the prosecution's evidence (*ASCR* 20.2.2 (iii)–(v)) and avoid leading affirmative evidence of innocence (*ASCR* 20.2.2 (i)–(ii) and 20.2.3). Evidence (for example, DNA evidence of identity) must still be tested because it might be flawed. If such evidence is flawed, perhaps the alleged 'confession' was also contrived or misunderstood? Advocates are also supposed to avoid putting such clients in the witness box and asking them whether they are innocent or not, knowing their assertion of innocence will be false, because that is equivalent to actively misleading the court. Of course, the fact that the defendant does not give evidence is likely to be seen by most juries as a sign of guilt. If defence counsel cannot simply 'run out' on a difficult client or on an unwelcome development in a case, then neither can they simply decline to represent a defendant who is unpopular in the wider community or whom they find personally distasteful. Paedophile and rape prosecutions are the obvious examples. Many lawyers are reluctant to defend people charged with these and similar offences involving gross abuse and violence. That reluctance is understandable. In the Indian rape case mentioned in Chapter 1, an entire bar association refused to represent a group of alleged rapists and murderers, but this was an extreme case and, as soon as that decision was announced, many lawyers offered their services and were observed to do so in order to take advantage of the opportunity for publicity.[24]

Recognition of the social evil which would arise from undefended criminal trials – even if the courts would allow them – lies in large part behind the strength of *zealous advocacy*. The paradoxical cultural reverence for the unflinching and fearless defence counsel who takes on the very unattractive or vulnerable client is cited again and again.[25] It is no surprise therefore that lawyers often think that *zealous advocacy* is the preferred ethical type.[26] At its core, *zealous advocacy* embodies a deep professionalism for which lawyers are often justly praised. The so-called 'cab rank rule' which obliges barristers to defend anyone charged with a criminal offence if they are competent in the area, available, and their fee can be met,[27] is so strong that the principle that full-time advocates shall accept all

24 Reported to the authors on 2 March 2013 by Prof John Flood, who was in Delhi at the time of these events.
25 See Smith, 'Defending the Unpopular'.
26 In trials of the ethics self-assessment tool set out in Chapter 11, a small majority of respondents indicated a preference for *zealous advocacy* over other types. See further, Evans and Forgasz.
27 See, eg, r 87 of the Victorian Bar Council, *Practice Rules* (The Victorian Bar Inc, Melbourne, 2005) 16.

comers as clients in all matters (civil as well as criminal) is so well ingrained that it is regarded as a norm of practice.

Case Study 1.1 in Chapter 1 explored the case of the philanthropic QC who argued for a tobacco company's interests despite his concurrent membership of a cancer hospital's board. Part of the justification for barristers who choose to represent, for example, tobacco, gaming, liquor or armaments companies is to be found in the cab-rank rule, even though that rule grew out of the need to protect relatively powerless defendants from the resources of a state prosecution. In Chapter 6 we discuss in more detail whether the cab-rank practice norm should extend to civil matters where there are no criminal defendants and no connection to the resources inequality that continues to justify its use in criminal defence practice.

Significantly, there is no equivalent cab-rank rule for solicitors set out in the *ASCR* and the validity of this ethical norm is not as easily justified as it used to be, even when defending alleged criminals. In practice, a barrister who finds a defendant unattractive will be tempted to pretend that they are unavailable in order to avoid the cab rank rule. A few barristers will openly say that they find the case repulsive and simply defy the rule, risking a disciplinary prosecution. But bar associations in Australia do not want to proceed against their members for this type of offence, judging the publicity to be unfavourable. So the cab rank rule is really a guideline, even if its fundamental importance remains.

Barristers who are compelled by their character to say that their values or ethical preferences would not allow them to represent a particular client to the best of their ability, are put in an unenviable position by the cab rank principle. Would it be psychologically and ethically healthier for the bar and barristers to formally allow exceptions to the cab rank rule where a barrister has a conscientious objection to representation of a particular defendant?

The Prosecution

The focus of criminal justice has for a very long time culturally favoured the nobility of the defence role. Prosecutors, however, have lacked values-based scrutiny of their function. As noted in the Introduction, however, the times are changing.

Recognition of the penetration of organised crime into the Australian community and the politicisation of the so-called 'war on terror' have produced a climate where the role of 'protector of the state' (for want of a better phrase) is now rapidly acquiring a desirable status that has previously been confined to the United States. In Victoria, for instance, where public consciousness of the impact of organised crime has grown rapidly, the general prosecution function is now more powerful than ever with the advent of police powers that permit indefinite detention of witnesses who will not answer questions – a function previously thought safe only in the hands of Crime Commissions.[28] Similarly, the ability of the Australian government to detain anyone incommunicado for up to a week of interrogation when they are suspected of having information regarding terrorist activities[29] may or may not be justified, but such powers indisputably add to the moral authority of the prosecution function. Where once law students would see a decision to become a prosecutor as inexplicable, there are now many who are excited by the prospect. As will be seen in Case Study 5.3, prosecutors do face tactical choices in the exercise of the prosecution function and, as always, those choices are value-driven and ought to reflect the Rule of Law. It is still essentially the prosecutor's duty to hold the police accountable for the way they use their powers, all the more so now that police and other state instructors operate with ever-widening coercive powers of investigation.[30] In a changing balance of power between prosecution and defence, it is proper to spend a little time understanding prosecutors' current value structures, before moving to the possible alternatives.

ASCR 29 deals specifically with prosecutors' duties. *Rules* 29.1–29.4 set out the approach that the prosecutor should take in arguing their case:

> 29.1   A prosecutor must *fairly* assist the court to arrive at the truth, must seek *impartially* to have the whole of the relevant evidence placed intelligibly before the court, and must seek to assist the court with adequate submissions of law to enable the law properly to be applied to the facts.
>
> 29.2   A prosecutor must not press the prosecution's case for a conviction beyond a *full and firm* presentation of that case.
>
> 29.3   A prosecutor must not, by language or other conduct, seek to *inflame or bias* the court against the accused. [our emphasis]

When students and even new lawyers first contemplate these rules they are often slightly amused at their quaint expression and more than a little frustrated. If the defence can argue for extreme positions or interpretations of the evidence, why can the prosecution not do so? Certain news and current affairs media appear to reinforce the view that a successful defence of almost any defendant is part of a social disease rather than a check on over-zealous state power. Are these principles

---

28 See, eg, *Major Crime (Investigative Powers) Act 2004* (Vic) (giving the Victorian Chief Commissioner of Police powers previously only possessed by crime commissions in other States).

29 *Australian Security Intelligence Organisation Legislation Amendment (Terrorism) Act 2003* (Cth) s 3, sch 1, amending *Australian Security Intelligence Organisation 1979* (Cth) pt III, div 3.

30 David Brown, 'Breaking the Code of Silence' (1997) 22 *Alternative Law Journal* 220, 222 (asking why prosecutors and lawyers did not speak up about massive police corruption in New South Wales during the 1980s and 1990s).

of restraint too old-fashioned to worry about? After all, the interests of the state and the safety of its citizens have never been so threatened, or so it is argued.

Whatever the current cultural push to achieve convictions at all costs, whatever the personal attraction of a successful prosecution, and regardless of popular pressure to 'safeguard' person and property, there is no alternative in a democratic environment to a balanced prosecution process. If the prosecution function is allowed to become partisan, the burden of proof will subtly shift to the defence and the power of the state will prove inexorably more difficult to check. Prosecutors are supposed to stop at a 'full and firm' presentation of the case; they must not 'inflame or bias the court' (including the jury) against a defendant; and must 'believe on reasonable grounds' in the propriety of their arguments. All of these safeguards have been put in place because earlier generations have seen what can happen to individual autonomy and freedoms once the court system becomes just the instrument of the government of the day.

The stereotypical pressure to get a conviction at all costs is not endorsed by the *ASCR* and is therefore completely unacceptable in the Australian legal system. Just how careful a prosecutor must be to remain a prosecutor and – as cultural pressure can increasingly dictate – avoid becoming a *persecutor*, is made clear by the *ASCR* in the context of sentencing:

29.12   A prosecutor:
29.12.1   must correct any error made by the opponent in address on sentence;
29.12.2   must inform the court of any relevant authority or legislation bearing on the appropriate sentence;
29.12.3   must assist the court to avoid appealable error on the issue of sentence;
29.12.4   may submit that a custodial or non-custodial sentence is appropriate; and
29.12.5   may inform the court of an appropriate range of severity of penalty, including a period of imprisonment, by reference to relevant decisions.

All of these 'informing the court' functions are to be performed by prosecutors without inflaming the situation, that is, without becoming vindictive. Courts are not empowered by the Rule of Law to seek revenge, which is by definition a personal reprisal, but to impose proportionate punishment in a dispassionate atmosphere. There is quite a difference between the two, and prosecutors are expected to model that distinction in their own behaviour, balancing personal detachment with controlled strength rather than snarling or sarcastic commentary on the morality of the defendant. Prosecutors with a clear sense of their role need to be wary of *adversarial advocacy* and pay consistent attention to nurturing alternative ethical values in their advocacy. This is all the more important given that prosecutors are rarely disciplined, let alone subsequently prosecuted themselves, for breaking the rules.

Ethics in Criminal Justice: From the Local Criminal Trial to Global Justice

Global Ethics and Criminal Justice

At the big picture level, the ethics of criminal justice has been challenged by many issues. Both defence and prosecution lawyers and those involved in drafting criminal laws and procedures play an important part in global, as well as national and local, security and justice. Their role is to make sure the law works fairly, legitimately and effectively according to the Rule of Law, without ignoring fundamental human rights. There are dangers when lawyers face pressures from morally corrupt regimes to be involved in legal systems that take away those rights. Lawyers have been in the past and will again often be required to draft evil laws and, as prosecutors, judges and even defence counsel, to implement those laws. This occurred in apartheid South Africa, Stalinist Eastern Europe and Nazi Germany.[31] Even acting as defence lawyers in such a system might be seen as 'legitimating' a system that should only be resisted.

In liberal democracies, the criminal justice system is under pressure as governments try to grapple with the threats of terrorism, transnational crime, and tax evasion. Ethical challenges for lawyers in these situations are numerous. For example, should criminal defence lawyers comply with government requirements that they get security clearances before *defending* people accused on security-related charges?[32]

The 'torture memos' scandal in the United States was a major indication, depending on the viewpoint, of the Rule of Law operating appropriately or else of its continuing decline. In the aftermath of the 9/11 disaster, government lawyers

---

31 On lawyers' role in apartheid in South Africa see David Dyzenhaus, *Judging the Judges, Judging Ourselves: Truth, Reconciliation and the Apartheid Legal Order* (Hart Publishing, Oxford, 1998). In the Nazi era trial in Munich of Hans and Sophie Scholl, accused of circulating anti-government leaflets, the government permitted the defendants '... to have an "approved" lawyer, but he was much too frightened and intimidated to put up any kind of real defence'. Both were guillotined. See Jacob G Hornberger, 'Comparing USA to Nazi Germany', The Jailhouse Lawyer <www.angelfire.com/az/sthurston/comparison.html> at 21 July 2006.

32 *National Security Information (Criminal and Civil Proceedings) Act 2004* (Cth) s 39.

were instructed to provide written memoranda stating that it was legal under United States law to conduct 'interrogations' of suspected terrorists in order to prevent further attacks. These memoranda were eventually disclosed[33] and were discredited when it became clear that the interrogators had used them to justify torture, but they indicate the pressure that government and military lawyers were under to come up with ways to justify practices that would otherwise be seen as human rights abuses.[34]

The US national psyche was so damaged by the Twin Towers attacks that some process of retribution was politically and perhaps socially inevitable, but the frustration with an apparent inability to successfully fight back meant that many essential elements of fairness in criminal process were deliberately set aside, in Australia as well as in the US.[35] The Law Council of Australia was, to its credit, particularly critical of the Australian government's acquiescence in arrangements to establish the subsequently discredited 'military commissions' by the US,[36] in order to deal with those detained. But this criticism had little effect. US government preference for an indefinite and judicially unsanctioned detention, agreed to by the Australian government, continues today and shows a seriously flawed approach to criminal justice and to ethical accountability.

The argument continues in the wider community as to whether public security is enhanced or undermined by treating alleged terrorists differently to 'normal' criminal defendants; but in ethical terms, it is a dangerous path to say that one class of defendant is entitled to more rights than another, or that some individuals, though not charged with anything, are nevertheless by mere implication 'guilty'

33 See for example Clare Keefe Coleman, 'Teaching the Torture Memos: "Making Decisions Under Conditions of Uncertainty"' (2012) 62 *Journal of Legal Education* 81.

34 For a brief summary, see W Bradley Wendel, 'The Torture Memos and the Demands of Legality' (2009) 12 *Legal Ethics* 107. See also Jane Mayer, 'Annals of the Pentagon – The Memo: How an Internal Effort to Ban the Abuse and Torture of Detainees Was Thwarted', *The New Yorker* (New York), 27 February 2006, 32; W Bradley Wendel, 'Legal Ethics and the Separation of Law and Morals' (2005) 91 *Cornell Law Review* 67.

35 *Australian Security Intelligence Organisation Legislation Amendment (Terrorism) Act 2003* (Cth) s 3, sch 1, amending *Australian Security Intelligence Organisation 1979* (Cth) pt III, div 3 (giving ASIO the power 'to obtain a warrant to detain and question a person who may have information important to the gathering of intelligence in relation to a terrorist activity': Australian Government, Australian Laws to Combat Terrorism, Australian National Security <www.nationalsecurity.gov>.au/agd/www/nationalsecurity.nsf> at 26 July 2006. Detention can last up to seven days, and access to lawyers is strictly regulated).

36 See Law Council of Australia, 'Government Must Do More Over Mounting Criticism of Military Commissions' (Press Release, 3 August 2005) <www.lawcouncil.asn.au/read/2005/2414848000.html> at 26 July 2006. Military Commissions took away many of the rights of defendants in normal criminal trials, eg, the prohibition on hearsay evidence and the right to silence, the denial of jury trial, even the basic requirement for commission members to be legally trained. In June 2006, despite both the Australian and US governments' insistence that these commissions were legitimate, the US Supreme Court finally ruled them illegal: *Hamdan v Rumsfeld*, 548 US (2006).

of something 'bad'.[37] What ethical approach guided the lawyers who helped to establish the Guantanamo incarceration and advised the governments on the repatriation of detainees returned to their communities without charge?

The phenomenon of terrorism raises an essential ethical issue for lawyers, and especially criminal lawyers: If dominant western states, pursuing policing exercises around the planet without a United Nations consensus, do not unconditionally accept the principle of fairness in all adjudication regarding alleged terrorists (entrenching unfairness, in fact), what message is sent to practitioners of the justice systems in those nations? What political guidance is offered to those lawyers in both government and private practice as to the ethical principles that ought to govern them? What is the point, in fact, of demanding due process in an individual trial, when tarnished global ethics are setting the pace? What institutional encouragement is there, in reality, for the individual values awareness of either prosecution or defence practitioners?

Global terrorism has made it clearer than ever before that the Rule of Law, under which *everyone* is supposed to be equally protected and accountable, and which underlies every piece of substantive law taught in law school, is only as good as is the will of each government and each lawyer to insist on continuing fairness in all trial processes. Without fairness, the Rule of Law becomes a hollow, even termited, edifice. Thus there may be an ethical duty upon prosecution and defence to protest and withdraw (as *responsible lawyers* and perhaps *moral activists*) when systemic political decisions have been taken to eliminate or limit overall fairness in the drafting of legislation or the management of a trial. Suspect processes emerge by inducing participation from the legal profession. If that participation is appropriately withdrawn by lawyers, in the name of fairness and compassion, legitimacy withers and that process will lose social and moral credibility as surely as night follows day.

What might happen to criminal justice if political agendas like the 'war on terror' are pushed too far? Consider the issue of genocide. Lawyers' ethics may be implicated in mass killings when lawyers (often employed by government) remain silent about or condone genocides and then participate in compromised prosecutions of the alleged perpetrators. The German state in the 1930s was perhaps the first to systematically involve elements of the legal profession in what we now know as 'ethnic cleansing'. Starting with the drafting of national legislation to progressively de-legalise 'non-Aryans' in the 1930s (as a precursor to the Holocaust), Germans were progressively acclimatised to categorising Poles,

---

37 One of the Australian detainees at Guantanamo Bay, Mamdouh Habib, was returned to Australia after being released from three years' detention without charge. The Australian government tried to discourage, under a hastily enacted law, receipt by Habib of any payment for telling his story of incarceration and alleged torture: see Michelle Grattan, 'Canberra Shackled and Shamed by Habib', *The Sunday Age* (Melbourne), 30 January 2005, 17.

Jews, Roma, homosexuals and others as less than human – that is, by degree, as 'cockroaches', 'insects' and finally, 'nothing'.[38] The apparatus of the German criminal law was completely subverted by a relentless legislative (and cultural) program so that, eventually, the Nazi transportation and extermination program became domestic, hygienic and even banal to the populace at large.[39] Lacking any institutional or global ethic of *moral activism*, and overwhelmed by the culture of obedience to National Socialist edicts, there were then many lawyers who were simply ethically overwhelmed.

That problem remains today. Consider how easy it is for legislation – drafted with the help of legal professionals – to begin the task of marginalising those who are thought to be different. What ethical approach dominated the thinking of the lawyers who drafted the recent Australian legislation describing those seeking asylum, and entering Australia as refugees, as 'unlawful non-citizens'? Or set up the statutory rules which seek to ensure that asylum seekers from Afghanistan, Iran or Syria never make it to Australia for assessment?[40]

Hans Guggenheim, the Holocaust anthropologist, has written:

> We have no right to forgive the suffering inflicted on others, but we can show compassion for the suffering experienced by our enemies and thus lay the foundation for a better future … The lesson of Auschwitz is that without compassion our world is doomed … that it is the only way we can control our technologies of war, our greed for gold, our lust for power and domination and above all, the only way we can administer our Laws with justice for all.[41]

Guggenheim considers that for justice to be possible it must be inter-generational, inter-personal – that is, as having two sides – and it must be based on compassion.[42] There must be a sense of responsibility to and for the past, so that lawyers' ethical consciousness is never just focused on how they behave here and now, but also on who they were. This is why it's important to ask today's lawyers who they are (on the inside); that is, what values do they have and what virtues are characterised

---

38 See Therese O'Donnell, 'Review – "Law After Auschwitz: A Jurisprudence of the Holocaust" by David Fraser' (2005) 15(6) *Law & Politics Book Review* <www.bsos.umd.edu/gvpt/lpbr/> at 19 July 2006.

39 See Hans Guggenheim, 'Lecture to GAJE at Auschwitz' (Paper presented at the Worldwide Conference of the Global Alliance for Justice Education, Krakow, Poland, 22 July 2004) (on file with the authors); Hannah Arendt, *Eichmann in Jerusalem: A Report on the Banality of Evil* (Viking Press, New York, 1964).

40 Julian Burnside, 'Bridging Visas Send Refugee Policy Further Down the Wrong Track', *The Conversation*, 30 November 2012, <http://theconversation.com/bridging-visas-send-refugee-policy-further-down-the-wrong-track-10944>

41 Guggenheim, 'Lecture to GAJE at Auschwitz'.

42 Ibid.

Source: Michael Leunig, *The Age* (Melbourne), January 2005

by their behaviour? Secondly lawyers can never forget that those to whom they are opposed have a right to be taken seriously. The key is for law students and then lawyers to see that all are or may become defendants themselves and experience the potential degradation of that position. Lawyers must be conscious not to regard themselves as 'good' and defendants as 'bad'. Only in self-identification with fear, with failure and even with their own potential for evil will lawyers realise their existential need (regardless of religious convictions) for a sense of compassion. Indeed, it is the quality of compassion which helps to identify the virtuous or 'good' lawyer and provides the ethical bridge between a global ethic and the criminal trial.

Further Case Studies

The values of criminal advocates are probably as diverse as those of the rest of the community. There is no empirical evidence to suggest that criminal advocates are all *adversarial* all the time or, on the other hand, all *responsible* all the time, let alone inclined to take a universal *morally activist* approach and decline to act for any clients who refuse to 'do the moral thing'.[43] It is more likely that experienced advocates will tend to take one ethical approach most of the time, varying their behaviour on occasion, when the complexity of the situation demands. It may be appropriate that the *ASCR* and the common law seek to strike a balance between duties to client and court, but they still give conflicting messages as to the values to apply in criminal advocacy. Rather than simply trying to rely on these, sometimes conflicting, rules it is therefore important to be aware of alternative ethical approaches to criminal trial work. Since the dominant ethic in criminal practice is adversarial, it will often be the case that the alternatives – *responsible lawyering* and *moral activism* – will be invisible, unless lawyers explicitly bring ethical reflection to the foreground of their minds.

Further, since the enforcement of rules of advocacy in Australia is more or less left by the courts to the legal professional associations, and advocates tend not to report one another, it is not unusual for their bad ethical decisions to go unnoticed by the wider community: advocates' ethical decisions are not very accountable. The case studies below each demonstrate the need for criminal advocates to remain alert to the risks of unquestioning *adversarial advocacy*.

CASE STUDY 5.2 PRIOR CONVICTIONS

If Case Study 5.1 was probably a case of excessive zeal, there are other examples of experienced criminal advocates who will identify an ethical line which advocates may go up to, but never cross. A former Victorian Supreme Court judge, 'A', cites this case from his own history while at the bar in the 1960s.[44]

Prior to the legislation prohibiting driving with a blood alcohol reading of more than 0.05, A had a client with a number of drink-driving convictions at a time when such a history, if proved, would result in a defendant going to prison for the next offence. However, most of these convictions were interstate, and therefore the prosecution could not then prove those convictions except through a long and complex process. Since defendants are entitled to insist that the prosecution be put to its proof beyond reasonable doubt in all matters, A stated to the Court, when his client was asked by the prosecution about the convictions, that 'on my advice, my client does not admit these convictions'. The prosecution did not wish to go to the expense of the formal proofs. The defendant was accordingly sentenced as if he did not have the previous drink-driving convictions, and therefore did not go to prison.

---

43 See Smith, 'Defending the Unpopular'.
44 Interview with 'A', former Victorian Supreme Court judge (Melbourne, 2004).

The former judge argues that his response was not unethical because of the overarching principle that obligates prosecutors to prove their case and defence counsel to insist on that process. The magistrate at the time was initially angry, but A believes he subsequently accepted the legitimacy of A's approach. This case study provides a good illustration of the requirement for 'complex judgement' in ethical decision-making. The values agenda embedded in this example is very stark: Is the more important value to support the social principle of the onus of proof upon the prosecution (for powerful systemic reasons represented by the *adversarial advocacy* approach), or is it more important to serve the (utilitarian and *moral activist*) value of ensuring that a multiple drink-driver is removed from society? Regardless of the correct view, the *process of weighing up* these alternative loyalties is to be commended and emulated consciously each time a hard case arises.

Discussion questions

1. If your client was facing sentencing for an excessive blood alcohol level and you knew that the prosecution was unaware that your client had some prior convictions for similar offences, would you consider yourself bound to advise the Court of the true position?

2. Would it make any difference to your decision if you had reached the conclusion that your client had little awareness of their behaviour and would offend again, unless they were ordered by the Court to undergo a medical assessment in response to your disclosure of the prior convictions?

3. Suppose you had just 'gone to the bar' and this brief was the only one you had been offered in the last three weeks. Would your decision be any different?

CASE STUDY 5.3   PROSECUTORS' VALUES

Former judge A also recalls a murder trial that relates to the duty upon prosecutors. In the trial, insanity had been raised as a defence, and a then renowned forensic psychiatrist was called to give evidence for the prosecution as to the mental state of the defendant. He said that 'on the balance of probabilities', the defendant was not insane. Counsel for the prosecution (a private barrister, *not* a full-time

Crown prosecutor) had in his possession, but did not disclose to the defence, a report from the psychiatrist in which he had said that the defendant was sane on a '51/49%' estimate of the probabilities: In other words, the defendant could just as well have been insane as sane.

The defendant was convicted but committed suicide shortly afterwards. The death exposed the forensic strategy of the prosecution as likely to have been flawed. Desire for conviction for its own sake, rather than for a finding of guilt mitigated by insanity, must have seemed a very hollow victory to the prosecutor, on learning of that death.

In the interests of justice, if not compassion, A considers that the report should have been made available to the defence by the prosecution. Today, prosecution pre-hearing disclosure rules (ASCR 20.5) would require disclosure of such a report. However, the thoroughness of prosecutors' compliance with this mandated disclosure is still a matter of concern to defence counsel.

On the other hand, former Liberty Victoria President and now Magistrate, Greg Connellan, cites a case he prosecuted of a truck driver accused of raping a hitchhiker. In the defendant's record of interview he had said 'I can't help myself'. His Honour was tempted to use this admission in his summing up to the jury and states that he could have got away with it, but decided against it because, in the context of the whole of the record of interview, the comment related only to the accused's homosexuality, not to the alleged assaults.[45]

These contrasting examples of prosecutors' values can be seen in the context of recent research into law students' values. Several hundred final-year law students from around the country were asked to imagine what they would do in the following situation:

> You are a DPP [Director of Public Prosecutions] prosecutor who has concentrated on drug trafficking cases. You have argued to many juries that every case of drug dealing harms society and must be reported and dealt with by the Police. You discover that your daughter has been selling cannabis to other students at her school. Your partner implores you not to report the matter and threatens to end your relationship (already strained by overwork) if you do. **Would you report the matter to the Police?**[46]

---

45 Interview with Greg Connellan of Counsel, former Liberty Victoria president (Olinda, Victoria, 2004). Connellan cites *R v Rugari* (2001) 122 A Crim R 1 as an example (with some arresting passages from the summing up of the Crown Prosecutor) of a case where an appeal against conviction was allowed because of the failure of the prosecutor to toe the line in his summing up.

46 Adrian Evans and Josephine Palermo, 'Australian Law Students' Perceptions of Their Values: Interim Results in the First Year – 2001 – of a Three-Year Empirical Assessment' (2002) 5 *Legal Ethics* 103, 112.

The results were neither surprising nor encouraging, with a large proportion of law students (78.1%) choosing to remain silent (see Figure 5.1 below).

Figure 5.1   Number of Respondents to the Australian Lawyers' Values Study Who Would Report Daughter's Drug Offence

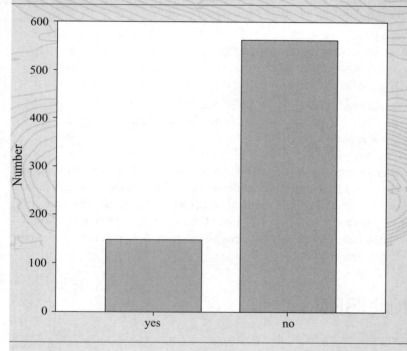

DISCUSSION QUESTIONS

1. If you had the choice, would you prefer to be a prosecutor or a defence advocate? If the former, would you see yourself as entitled to prosecute with as much vigour, energy and willingness to engage in personal criticism as an advocate for the defence?

2. As a prosecutor, would you see your role as being properly discharged if you simply set out the facts for a jury without emotion, without an attempt to accuse defence witnesses as biased or prejudiced, and without offering any opinion as to what the sentence upon conviction should be?

3. Would you be satisfied that you had done your job as a prosecutor properly if the defence were making all sorts of ridiculous allegations about the police witnesses but you declined to deliver personally damaging (and forensically irrelevant) insults about witnesses for the defence?

4. As a prosecutor with a teenage son or daughter, can you imagine being tempted to keep their transgressions secret? If you agreed to secrecy, would you consider yourself morally vulnerable?

5. Are you by nature more or less inclined to see the outcome of any contest as more important than the means used to get to that outcome? What implications does your answer have for the way in which you will tend to practise law?

6. Are you likely to have one set of values 'at home' and another set for 'the office'? If so, will the differences make it hard to lead an emotionally integrated life?

A large number of criminal accused are afflicted by mental health and drug and alcohol problems. Their actions reflect wider social problems as well as any criminal responsibility. In response, should criminal prosecution and defence be conceived as a matter of justice or as a matter of care? Or, to put it another way, would a 'therapeutic' jurisprudence[47] which balances justice with therapy have more impact on reducing recurrent crime?

Conclusion

Criminal justice in Australia is likely to retain its adversarial character, even if governments generally want to shift the goal posts in favour of greater prosecutorial power, heavier penalties and the criminalisation of more and more behaviour. The stakes for all lawyers involved in criminal justice are increasingly ethical stakes: Do they help draft repressive and de-humanising legislation? Do they exploit 'confessions' made by tired and fearful individuals after many hours of interrogation? Do they pressure defendants to simply plead 'guilty' and eliminate the stress of a trial on them and their families? Or, do they risk poisoning the minds of juries by belittling prosecution witnesses when there is no confession and no murder weapon?

47 See for example David Wexler and Bruce Winick (eds), *Law in a Therapeutic Key*, Carolina Academic Press, Durham NC, 1996; Susan Daicoff, 'The Role of Therapeutic Jurisprudence in the Comprehensive Law Movement' in D P Stolle, D B Wexler and B J Winick (eds), *Practicing Therapeutic Jurisprudence*, Carolina Academic Press, Durham NC, 2000.

In fact, an ethical approach to criminal justice has never been so important for social confidence in our courts. If there is a line somewhere between the approach of the *responsible lawyer* and the *adversarial advocate* inside a criminal trial (with prosecutors struggling to hang on to the former and defence counsel over-zealously defending the latter), both can stray over the boundaries in the quest for adversarial success.

The most effective approach may be to encourage criminal lawyers to examine their own motives – that is, to look at *who* they are and *what* they value – before they make a choice on a difficult ethical dilemma. The tendency for lawyers to personally invest in adversarial competition is the least attractive feature of the trial process, and is at the heart of public suspicion as to whether the system is really about truth *or* proof, rather than both.

RECOMMENDED FURTHER READING

ABC Radio National, 'The Ethics of Criminal Lawyers', *The Law Report*, 12 November 2002 <www.abc.net.au/rn/talks/8.30/lawrpt/stories/s724128.htm> at 19 July 2006.

Ben Clarke, 'An Ethics Survey of Australian Criminal Law Practitioners' (2003) 27 *Criminal Law Journal* 142. Ken Crispin, 'Prosecutorial Ethics' in Stephen Parker and Charles Sampford (eds), *Legal Ethics and Legal Practice: Contemporary Issues* (Clarendon Press, Oxford, 1995) 171.

G E Dal Pont, *Lawyers' Professional Responsibility* (Lawbook Co, Pyrmont, NSW, 5th edn, 2013) 'Prosecuting Counsel' [18.10]–[18.90] and 'Criminal Defence Lawyers' [18.100]–[18.125].

Peter Hidden, 'Some Ethical Problems for the Criminal Advocate' (2003) 27 *Criminal Law Journal* 191.

David Luban, 'The Fundamental Dilemma of Lawyering: The Ethics of the Hired Gun' in Richard Abel (ed), *Lawyers: A Critical Reader* (The New Press, New York, 1997) 3.

Abbe Smith, 'Defending the Unpopular Down Under' (2006) 30(2) *Melbourne University Law Review*, 495.

David Wexler (ed) *Rehabilitating Lawyers: Principles of Therapeutic Jurisprudence for Criminal Law Practice* (Carolina Academic Press, Durham NC, 2008).

Richard Young and Andrew Sanders, 'The Ethics of Prosecution Lawyers' (2004) 7 *Legal Ethics* 190.

6

CIVIL LITIGATION AND EXCESSIVE ADVERSARIALISM

Introduction

Lawyers in civil litigation are sometimes criticised for 'excessively' adversarial conduct.[1] On the one hand we might argue that clients are entitled to expect that their lawyer will represent them as zealously as possible within the bounds of the law. Any attempt by lawyers to moderate adversarial advocacy on behalf of clients in civil litigation might be seen as an unjustifiable usurping of the role of the judge in our adversary system. On the other hand, 'excessively' adversarial advocacy by their lawyer might be harmful to clients because it wastes their time, money and energy, and ruins important business or personal relationships. Moreover, as officers of the court, lawyers are considered to have responsibilities to truth and fairness in litigation that override clients' short-term self-interests.

The different roles of criminal defence and prosecution lawyers are clearly delineated by the very nature of a criminal trial as a public forum for determining guilt and innocence and upholding the rule of law. In civil litigation, however, it is not so clear where the public and the private aspects of the process begin and end. That is, to what extent is civil litigation a public process in which fairness and justice must be paramount, or to what extent is it a private dispute resolution process which the parties are free to control in their own interests?

CASE STUDY 6.1 EXCESSIVE ADVERSARIALISM

The following short case studies each set out examples of conduct that could be seen as excessively adversarial. For each case, consider the following questions: What consequences might the adversarial behaviour have for other parties? For the legal system as a whole? What about the pursuit of truth and justice? How would you feel about the outcome of each case if you were the client in that case? To what extent do you think lawyers are under any responsibility to curb the adversarialism of the process in each case? To what extent can parties (rather than lawyers) be seen as responsible for the way their case is run?

(a) Lawyers for a large multinational fast food chain routinely issue defamation writs against anyone who criticises the company on issues like its environmental responsibility, its labour standards and attitude towards union representation of its workers, the healthiness of its products, misleading and deceptive advertising, and advertising aimed at children. Most protestors faced with

---

1 Australian Law Reform Commission, *Managing Justice: A Review of the Federal Civil Justice System*, Report No 89 (Australian Government Publishing Service, Canberra, 2000) [3.30]–[3.41].

a defamation writ from the company agree to apologise and withdraw their protest activities. When two protestors in England choose to defend the writ, the company's lawyers spend four years on interlocutory applications aiming to have the protestors' defence struck out before the case can be heard on its merits. They then spend a further 314 trial days (a record for the longest trial of any kind in English legal history at that time) and £10 million on a trial in which the company is represented by a large team of barristers and solicitors, while the protestors represent themselves. The company is successful in relation to about half of the statements it alleged were defamatory. Later the defendants are successful in the European Court of Human Rights where they argued that they did not have a fair trial because they lacked legal aid, and that the outcome was a disproportionate interference with their right to freedom of expression.[2]

(b) In a nervous shock case, the plaintiff's psychologist and psychiatrist provide evidence that the plaintiff is still suffering from severe depression because of witnessing the aftermath of an accident in which two of his children were killed. This is used to bolster the argument that he should receive a large damages payout. In separate custody proceedings against the plaintiff's former wife, the same psychologist and psychiatrist provide evidence that in the same time period he had experienced a dramatic recovery. This argument is used to support his case that he should be granted custody of his children. Although the plaintiff is represented by different lawyers in each proceeding, the lawyers in the nervous shock proceedings are well aware of the expert witnesses' change of opinion, before judgment in the personal injury action is handed down, but advise that the court should not be informed of the change.[3]

(c) A tobacco company settles a suit alleging it is liable for negligence for selling addictive and cancer-causing cigarettes. Soon after the case is settled, lawyers for the tobacco company help draft a 'document retention policy' that leads to the destruction of thousands of documents setting out scientific evidence relevant to understanding the health effects of smoking cigarettes, in order to make sure those documents are not used against the company in any subsequent litigation by other plaintiffs. Later on when the tobacco company is sued by another woman dying of cancer, the company's lawyers

2 Based on the 'McLibel' case: at first instance – *McDonald's Corporation v Steel* [1997] EWHC QB 366 (Unreported, Bell J, 19 June 1997); on appeal – *Steel v McDonald's Corporation* [1999] EWCA Civ 1144 (Unreported, Pill and May LJJ, Keene J, 31 March 1999); at the European Court of Human Rights – *Steel and Morris v The United Kingdom*, no 68416/01 [2005] ECHR 103 (15 February 2005). See also <www.mcspotlight.org and John Vidal, *McLibel: Burger Culture on Trial* (Macmillan, London, 1997).
3 *Vernon v Bosley* [1997] 1 All ER 614; see also Richard O'Dair, *Legal Ethics: Text and Materials* (Butterworths, London, 2001) 176–86.

construe the court's orders for discovery in narrow and pedantic ways so as to avoid not only disclosing existing documents to the plaintiff, but also avoid admitting that thousands of relevant documents had been destroyed after the previous litigation. For example, tobacco company lawyers interpret the order to give discovery of 'documents *of* the defendant' company not to apply to documents held by the defendant company but authored by people who were not its employees or agents. This means that the company does not disclose research papers commissioned by them from external scientists, as well as documents authored by employees and agents of related companies. They do nothing to inform the plaintiff they are interpreting the order in this way.[4]

(d) A dispute over whether one of Australia's biggest and most profitable financial institutions insufficiently compensated an engineer for designing an online trading and financial advisory system was argued for 222 days in court, costing $80 million before the engineer's claim was thrown out of court because he could not raise $1.9 million security for costs if his case failed. The financial institution had a team of more than 30 lawyers that fought every step of the way. The cross-examination of one witness took 10 weeks. The nub of the case was never tested in court.[5] The costs of this one case amounted to more than one quarter of the total amount for legal aid funding for the whole of Australia in the 2003/04 financial year, which is enough to provide legal aid services for three-quarters of a million Australians.[6]

(e) A poorly educated manual worker's back and neck are badly injured in an accident at work. He does not seek legal advice or sue for damages at common law until after the limitation period for such actions has expired. He therefore needs to apply to the court for an extension of the limitation period. During the application for the extension, he endures a hectoring cross-examination designed to show that he has bad motives for bringing suit. The barrister for the other side repeatedly suggests that his injury is not the result of the accident at work, and that he is only suing at common law because he read in union newspapers and other places that high payouts could be achieved. The barrister also repeatedly gives the plaintiff various

4 *McCabe v British American Tobacco Australia Services Ltd* [2002] VSC 73 (Unreported, Eames J, 22 March 2002) (overturned *British American Tobacco Australia Services Ltd v Cowell* (2002) 7 VR 524). See Camille Cameron, 'Hired Guns and Smoking Guns: *McCabe v British American Tobacco Australia Ltd*' (2002) 25 *University of New South Wales Law Journal* 768; cf Martin H Redish, 'The Adversary System, Democratic Theory, and the Constitutional Role of Self-Interest: The Tobacco Wars, 1953–1971' (2001) 51 *DePaul Law Review* 359 (for an *adversarial advocacy* argument in favour of defensive tobacco litigation tactics).

5 A Stevenson, 'He's Mad as Hell, and He Still Wants the Bank's $56 Billion', *The Sydney Morning Herald*, 31 January 2002, 1, 6.

6 National Legal Aid, *About National Legal Aid* <www.nla.aust.net.au/> at 15 January 2006.

documents that the barrister refers to and asks questions about. But he never allows the plaintiff to explain that all the questions about what newspapers and magazines he has read are irrelevant because he is functionally illiterate. Although the plaintiff repeatedly tries to say so, he is always cut off. The plaintiff suffers severe stress because of this ordeal, feels 'like an idiot' because he cannot read the things counsel for the defendant shows him, cannot remember all the dates when he received different physiotherapy treatments and becomes very confused. He feels that the whole questioning process is too quick for him. The plaintiff receives permission from the court to go ahead with his action even though the limitation period has expired. But the plaintiff is so worried and depressed about how he will perform in court when the matter comes to trial that he commits suicide eight days after the hearing of the application for the extension. In an action brought by his widow, a court later held that the stress he suffered during the hearing was a cause of the depression that led to his suicide.[7]

In this chapter we first consider how and why problems of excessive adversarialism can occur in civil litigation when neither zealously *adversarial advocate* lawyers nor their clients see themselves as responsible for moral restraint in the conduct of litigation. In the next section we explore the extent to which lawyers should be held morally and legally responsible for the ethics of litigation, and use case studies to critically analyse the ways in which the law of lawyering attempts to give lawyers obligations to balance their *adversarial advocacy* with *responsible lawyering*. In Chapter 7, we will go on to consider attempts at alternative and more collaborative (*ethics of care*) forms of dispute resolution and legal practice.

Adversarial Advocacy: The 'Adversarial Imperative' and Excessive Adversarialism

The 'Adversarial Imperative'

According to the *adversarial advocate* approach, a lawyer's role is to advance clients' interests subject only to his or her duty to obey the law, including professional

---

7 *AMP General Insurance Ltd v Roads & Traffic Authority of New South Wales* (2001) 22 NSWCCR 247.

conduct rules and procedural rules that spell out the lawyer's duty to the court and the administration of justice. Although case law and professional conduct rules contain numerous statements that the duties of truth and fairness owed to the court override the duty to the client (see below), in practice, lawyers often feel that the adversarial system makes them subject to an 'adversarial imperative' which requires them to exploit any advantages the legal system allows for their clients:

> The adversarial imperative is the compulsion which litigants and especially their lawyers have to see the other side as the enemy who must be defeated; the 'no stone unturned mentality' is a compulsion to take every step which could conceivably advance the prospects of victory or reduce the risk of defeat. Both, in turn, increase the labour intensiveness and consequently the cost and delay of dispute resolution and, especially as between parties of unequal means, render it unfair.[8]

Although this 'adversarial mindset' has its roots in litigation, it also extends to most areas of practice. Lawyers have a 'pervading consciousness' that litigation is the potential conclusion of any contract, trust or deed of conveyance, or any legal advice tendered. Some lawyers operate on the basis that litigation is the *likely* outcome of each retainer. This leads to an attitude of precaution and anticipation of litigation directed at covering every circumstance and eventuality, which makes legal advice (even outside of litigation) time-consuming, complex and costly.[9]

Problems of 'Excessive' Adversarialism

The level of adversarialism engendered by this imperative can harm the client, the other side, and the legal system as a whole.

First, it *seems* obvious that zealous adversarial advocacy is always in the interests of clients. But this is not necessarily so. The *adversarial advocate* may feel that lawyers must do whatever they can to protect, advance and expand clients' legal rights in the short term. Yet *adversarial advocates* might not adequately take into account the costs of these actions to clients.[10] The financial costs of legal advice and action will often be greater, the longer and more adversarial the litigation. There will also be relational, emotional and reputational losses for the client in aggravating or

8 G L Davies, 'Fairness in a Predominantly Adversarial System' in Helen Stacey and Michael Lavarch (eds), *Beyond the Adversarial System* (Federation Press, Sydney, 1999) 102, 111.

9 Australian Law Reform Commission, *Review of the Adversarial System of Civil Litigation – Rethinking the Federal Civil Litigation System*, Issues Paper No 20 (The Commission, Sydney, 1997) [11.10]–[11.11].

10 David Wilkins, 'Everyday Practice *is* the Troubling Case: Confronting Context in Legal Ethics' in Austin Sarat et al (eds), *Everyday Practices and Trouble Cases* (Northwestern University Press, Evanston, Illinois, 1998) 68.

pursuing a dispute, and these too will be greater the longer the dispute continues. Clients are also often disappointed with the outcomes that lawyers, and the legal system, deliver – damages awards are lower than expected, the amount is eroded by costs, and cases are settled without the satisfaction of being morally vindicated in court. Where clients do go through the entire court process, that process is often alienating rather than empowering, and the financial and non-financial costs much greater than expected. Clients can feel cheated by their lawyer as a result (see discussion of fees and costs in Chapter 9). This is partly a matter of clients with unreasonably high expectations not 'hearing' lawyers' words of caution. One writer suggests that we might see the relationship between lawyers and clients as like that between a drug addict and their supplier.[11] The lawyer feeds off the misery of others by selling the promise that law will give clients some substantive good – a promise that many clients are eager to believe.

Second, adversarial behaviour by the lawyer on behalf of the client does not just affect the client and their rights. It also affects the other side, and other parties. As the case studies above illustrate, adversarialism can lead to various misleading and deceptive tactics such as failing to admit facts known to be true (putting the other side to the expense and trouble of proving them), arguing partial truths, choosing expert witnesses such as doctors and engineers on the basis of the evidence they are likely to give (and how favourable it is to the client's case), and 'burying' relevant and damaging documents in an avalanche of documents to be produced on discovery. It can also lead to highly technical and manipulative arguments about the facts or the law that evade the substance, while paying lip service to the letter of the law. There is also just plain aggressive and bullying behaviour that is not only unpleasant, but might be unfair to just claims. Some lawyers argue that each of these tactics is appropriate because each party is represented and can look after themselves. Excessive adversarialism, however, is dangerous where one side cannot afford as much, or as skilful, legal representation as the other side. Since large business enterprises dominate many economic and social relationships, the fact that companies' legal expenses are tax deductible and individuals' legal expenses generally are not heightens this type of inequality.[12]

This leads to a third concern – that overly zealous advocacy can damage the fabric of the legal system itself. Excessive adversarialism makes the whole system

---

11 Michael McChrystal, 'At the Foot of the Master: What Charles Dickens Got Right About What Lawyers Do Wrong' (1999) 78 *Oregon Law Review* 393 (describing Dickens' critique of lawyers in *Bleak House*).

12 See Australian Law Reform Commission, *Managing Justice*, [5.34]–[5.50]; Cameron Murphy, 'Tax Deductability [sic] and Litigation: Reducing the Impact of Legal Fees and Improving Access to the System' (2004) 27 *University of New South Wales Law Journal* 240.

more expensive and unfair for everyone since it constantly increases expectations about the minimal level of representation. It is like the Cold War nuclear arms race – the race by each side to have more weapons than the other so that each side would be deterred from actually using their weapons because the other side would then use theirs – eventually both sides had enough weapons to blow up the entire world several times over. Similarly, with adversarial advocates in an adversary system, each side always needs to do more to protect their own client because of what they believe the other side is going to do, until ultimately the more skilful the advocate, and the more money the parties have, the more the issues seem to revolve around procedure rather than substance, and the form of words rather than their purpose.[13] Excessive adversarialism can make the civil legal system more and more complex and expensive, yet more and more removed from the substantive justice concerns of ordinary people, and no one person can stop this.[14] We might even argue that in this context over-zealous lawyering could eventually lead to social breakdown rather than social justice.

These concerns raise the possibility of at least three different ways in which ethics might restrain the adversarialism of lawyers and their clients. First, lawyers and clients might consider alternative means of dispute resolution other than litigation in court – such as mediation, arbitration or restorative justice processes – that might be less expensive, less time-consuming and/or more likely to resolve the underlying conflict in a way that meets both parties' needs. This might encourage a broadly *ethics of care* approach to lawyering. The ethical issues raised by *alternative dispute resolution* (ADR) for lawyers are considered in Chapter 7. Second, lawyers and their clients might be expected to comply with certain legal and/or ethical obligations to *truthfulness* in litigation. Third, we might expect that lawyers and their clients should be legally and/or ethically obligated to use the processes of litigation *fairly*, not to invoke court processes unreasonably or for improper purposes, and not to unreasonably waste the court's time and run up costs for the other side.

Recently, some jurisdictions have enacted legislation to enshrine these ethical principles in law. In this chapter, those provisions appear where appropriate. The law of lawyering does indeed give lawyers (and their clients) some (*responsible lawyering*) obligations in relation to truthfulness in, and fair use of, legal processes. We critically examine the ways in which the law attempts to temper *adversarial advocacy* with *responsible lawyering* in the third part of this chapter below.

---

13 See William Simon, *The Practice of Justice: A Theory of Lawyers' Ethics* (Harvard University Press, Cambridge, Massachusetts, 1998) 138–69.
14 See Christine Parker, *Just Lawyers: Regulation and Access to Justice* (Oxford University Press, Oxford, 1999).

Mutual Avoidance of Ethical Responsibility for Litigation by Lawyers and their Clients?

The fact that lawyers engage in adversarial behaviour as agents for their clients makes it hard to pinpoint whether it is the lawyer, the client, or the adversarial court system itself that should be held responsible for any unethical conduct. Indeed *adversarial advocacy* can undermine the capacity of both the client and the lawyer to take moral responsibility for the way legal representation is carried out:

> Lawyers often justify their misdeeds as necessary to protect the interests of their client. Whether and when the adversary system or the protection of client rights can justify lawyers in committing lawful acts that would otherwise be unethical is a familiar subject of debate. If the justification holds, it transfers blame from the lawyer to the client. This presupposes the lawyer has actually placed the choice before the client. Too often, lawyers assume that clients would do anything lawful to prevail, while clients rely on their lawyers' judgment on the propriety of their tactics. The attorney-client relationship thus fosters mutual avoidance of responsibility, making it easier for lawyers to use professional rules unethically with a clear conscience.[15]

A purely *adversarial advocacy* approach to the lawyer's role in litigation suggests, first, that lawyers are under no obligation to encourage or equip clients to consider the ethical dimension of any potential courses of action in litigation beyond what the law requires. Second, it suggests that lawyers should not consider ethical matters beyond obedience to the law in considering what they can or cannot do for clients. The argument goes like this: For a lawyer even to advise a client as to the ethical aspects of proposed courses of action might be to discourage clients from fully exercising their rights, because a lawyer's warning about the ethical consequences of a course of action is likely to carry too much weight in the client's mind. It would be even worse, according to *adversarial advocacy*, for a lawyer to unilaterally decide to limit what they are willing to do for a client by reference to ethical considerations or the spirit of the law where the course of action is not clearly prohibited by law. In grey areas, *adversarial advocacy* sees it as up to the other side to complain, and for the courts to order the conduct to stop, if a lawyer is doing something wrong.

The client is expected to be able to bring ethical considerations to bear on deciding their own course of legal action without any help or encouragement from the lawyer, and the lawyer is expected to be able to delineate between where advice on the law stops, and ethical considerations begin.

---

15 John Leubsdorf, 'Using Legal Ethics to Screw Your Enemies and Clients' (1998) 11 *Georgetown Journal of Legal Ethics* 831, 836–7.

On the other hand, the client feels that they have handed the case over to their lawyer and that the lawyer is the expert who is best placed to choose the tactics and approach to dispute resolution (a perception that some lawyers may still wish to encourage). The client does not feel morally responsible for the tactics, nor even the whole approach to conflict resolution chosen, because it is the lawyer's role to advise those tactics or that approach. Indeed the client may feel they have no expertise or power to make ethical judgements about the appropriateness of the way their case is run. At the same time the lawyer feels it is not really their role to do so either. This can lead to a situation in which choices are made that neither lawyer nor client would have chosen by themselves on their own account, or that are in no one's longer term interests.

Consider as an example of how this can happen the reputed role of some lawyers in shaping the response of Anglican and Catholic church leaders to child sexual abuse, in Case Study 6.2 below.

CASE STUDY 6.2 PRIESTS AND LAWYERS[16]

In 2003, the Australian Broadcasting Corporation's current affairs show, *The 7:30 Report*, broadcast the story of Lucien Leech-Larkin. Leech-Larkin had been sexually abused in 1968 by a teacher at the Catholic school run by Jesuits that he attended. Lucien's parents had told the school, but Lucien was not believed. The teacher stayed on at the school and Lucien was asked to leave. Lucien had a breakdown before he turned sixteen and was admitted to hospital twice. Over the next thirty years he had three further breakdowns and attempted to take his own life several times. He now works selling train tickets at a Sydney station. Before the sexual abuse and the school's response to it, he had been a very bright student.

In the late 1990s, the teacher who had abused Lucien was charged with eleven child sex offences in New Zealand. But a magistrate decided he could not be extradited from Australia to New Zealand to face the charges because he was too sick. The New South Wales police then charged the teacher with seventeen child sex offences against three boys in New South Wales. But again the court decided that the teacher was so sick that as a matter of humanity he should not stand trial.

---

16 This case study is based on Richard Ackland, 'At Last, Some Understanding', *The Sydney Morning Herald*, 7 July 2003; and transcripts of two editions of the ABC's *7:30 Report* (23 June 2003 and 1 July 2003) where this story was televised: see <www.abc.net.au/7.30/ content/2003/s886452.htm> and <www.abc.net.au/7.30/content/2003/s892572.htm> (10 October 2006).

Lucien Leech-Larkin then wrote a series of letters to the headmaster of his old school and to the Jesuits seeking 'reconciliation' with his former schoolmasters (the Jesuits), and asking them to say that they would help him get 'justice' against the teacher. All he received were brief replies from the Jesuits' lawyers. He was also told that the Jesuits had refused to sign up to the Catholic Church's Towards Healing Program which is aimed at reconciliation with victims of abuse and providing assistance in helping them to overcome the effects of the abuse.

Leech-Larkin then commenced civil action against the Jesuits. As the head of the Jesuits later explained, their 'clear legal defence' was to 'fight this matter at every point ... to attempt to block it and until the point either that the complainant gives up from exhaustion or that we win the case or that we lose it'.[17] Reportedly some of the legal tactics that the Jesuits used to fight the case were to argue that because the teacher's 'assaults had not happened on school property and were outside school hours, the trustees of the order were not liable. There was also the proposition that the Jesuit Fathers are an unincorporated association and so it is the individual Jesuits who have to be sued, all of whom have taken a vow of poverty'.[18] It has also been reported that 'In Melbourne, where similar actions are under way against the Catholic Church, one response has been that the diocese is not a legal entity because Henry VIII abolished the Catholic dioceses. You are therefore 500 years too late with your legal action'.[19]

When the Jesuits heard that the ABC's *7.30 Report* was going to do a story on the Leech-Larkin case, the relatively new head of the Jesuits, Father Mark Raper SJ, promised to visit Leech-Larkin and his mother at their home, and to do an interview with the show. Within forty-eight hours, however, the home visit and interview were cancelled by Raper, after the Jesuits' lawyers advised him not to speak.

The day after the programme went to air, Raper decided to ignore the legal advice and wrote Leech-Larkin a letter:

I'm deeply sorry for the treatment you received while you were a student at St Aloysius in the 1960s. In addition, I offer you a profound apology on behalf of the Australian Jesuits. I'm also deeply sorry that I didn't keep the appointment we had made to meet, and discuss the issues face-to-face last Saturday. It was my decision to accept the advice not to proceed with our planned get-together, and I am sorry for the further hurt this caused you.[20]

---

17 Transcript of *The 7.30 Report* (1 July 2003).
18 Ackland, 'At Last, Some Understanding'.
19 Ibid.
20 The exact words of the letter are quoted from Ackland, 'At Last, Some Understanding'.

Raper also appeared on *The 7.30 Report* a few days later. On the programme he explained his change of mind, saying:

> I was moved by Lucien Leech-Larkin and also for me it was a moment of liberation, I must say, because I'd been accepting advice against my better judgement … Now it seems a sheer folly, but we – supposedly the experts in the pastoral area – allowed the legal area to dominate.[21]

Raper went on to say that he was reviewing the Jesuits' protocol for dealing with these issues and that this would 'certainly mean an end of the way in which the society follows legal advice'.[22] The reporter then asked him: 'But what if your approach means the Jesuits might be taken to the cleaners in a financial sense?'; Raper replied: 'Um, well, the assets are not as important as the people that we seek to serve'.[23]

DISCUSSION QUESTIONS

The ethical issues in this case are particularly salient because many people still expect religious leaders to be particularly careful to show moral responsibility. Yet the 2012 announcement of a Federal *Royal Commission into Institutional Responses to Child Sexual Abuse* suggest that legalistic defences were continuing into the present.[24]

1. Imagine that your firm must draft and argue defences like these to a claim against your church client and that you are allocated to the task: How would you justify yourself to the parents of an abused child? Assuming you decide you should stay in your job, which of the four ethical approaches to lawyering do you think is most appropriate in these circumstances?

2. In what circumstances, if any, do you think lawyers should help clients consider the ethical and relational dimensions of how to respond to legal problems? Does it make a difference what ethical stance the client has? Or should lawyers take some ethical responsibility for the advice they give regardless of the values and ethical positions of their clients? Why do you think the lawyers in these cases apparently

21 Transcript of *The 7.30 Report* (1 July 2003).
22 Ibid.
23 Ibid.
24 See <http://childabuseroyalcommission.dpmc.gov.au> accessed 9 January 2012.

advised their church clients not to apologise? What other options might they have discussed with their clients?

3. What, if anything, do you think the clergy representing the defendant church organisations in these cases would have thought about the ethical implications of their lawyers' advice and arguments? What sort of legal advice, if any, do you think the Jesuits would be looking for after the events described above? Could a lawyer help them in any way once the Provincial had apologised to the victim of abuse? In what circumstances do you think clients would value explicitly moral advice from lawyers? Do similar ethical issues arise in more 'mundane' matters of injury compensation and product liability?

If it wasn't for that horrible lawyer the really nice priest would have been a Christian.

Source: John Spooner, *Sydney Morning Herald*, 7 July 2003

Alternative Ethical Practices: Fostering Lawyer and Client Responsibility in Litigation

In order to address the potential mutual avoidance of ethical responsibility in litigation by lawyers and clients, lawyers would need to take responsibility, first, for *advising clients* in a way that helps or encourages them to make decisions about litigation on ethical grounds as well as legal and practical grounds. Second, lawyers would also need to take ethical responsibility for *their own conduct on behalf of clients* in litigation. In the following sections we critically consider whether lawyers *should* take on these *responsible lawyering* type of obligations to the court, and the extent to which current rules on lawyers' obligations in relation to litigation already *do in fact* temper obligations of *adversarial advocacy* with *responsible lawyering*. We argue that as a matter of ethics and good practice, lawyers certainly should advise clients as to the ethical dimension of their decisions about how to pursue litigation. The issue of the extent to which lawyers should take it upon themselves not to act unfairly or untruthfully on behalf of their clients, even where the client is instructing them to do so is, however, more complicated. We suggest that neither *adversarial advocacy* nor *responsible lawyering* is likely to be an infallible guide to how lawyers should behave in these situations. Much depends on context, as we shall see.

Should Lawyers Advise Clients to Consider Ethical Issues in Litigation?

It is generally accepted that good lawyer-client interviewing and advising (or counselling) means that lawyers should work through all the options for responding to legal issues with their clients, and also the potential legal and other consequences of each option – in terms of finances, time, emotions, business and personal relationships and so on. Lawyers should put clients in a position where they understand everything they can about the benefits and costs, risks and possibilities of each legal course of action they might take.[25] Although lawyers may not be psychological counsellors, they generally have a greater experience and knowledge of the wide-ranging costs and consequences of different legal strategies than their clients do, and therefore have a responsibility to explain these costs and consequences in a way that clients will listen to and understand. Moreover, the lawyer generally gets paid for his or her work, often on a 'time spent' basis, regardless of whether their client is happy with the process or the outcome. Therefore the lawyer is under a special responsibility to make sure that clients understand the costs of litigation, and do not even subconsciously push clients towards litigation for the sake of fees (see Chapter 9 for an analysis of this in terms of conflicts of interest principles).

Lawyers might also encourage their clients to seek other professional advice from counsellors, financiers and accountants, public relations people,

25 See David A Binder, Paul Bergman and Susan Price, *Lawyers as Counselors: A Client-Centered Approach* (West Publishing Co, St Paul, Minnesota, 2nd edn, 2004); Avrom Sherr, *Client Care for Lawyers: An Analysis and Guide* (Sweet & Maxwell, London, 2nd edn, 1999).

family and friends on the likely impact and the wisdom of different courses of action. A good oncologist will advise a patient to think about and discuss with family and counsellor the consequences of chemotherapy or radical surgery, in responding to a cancer, in relation to their total wellbeing. They do not expect patients to treat this type of decision as a purely medical matter. Good lawyers should be no less holistic in the way they advise their clients. Since legal options are generally about how to resolve disputes with other people, there is likely to be an ethical dimension to a holistic consideration of different options for litigating or resolving a dispute. This is true for all types of clients, individual or business. Business people and companies are, or should be, no less concerned about the cost of different legal options, in terms of their own individual ethics and the ethical reputation for corporate social responsibility of their businesses, than individuals are. (Indeed in Chapter 10 we argue that lawyers for companies have a particular responsibility to consider the ethical dimension of their advice.)

Both *ethics of care* and *moral activist* approaches to lawyers' ethics suggest, with different emphases, that ethics should explicitly be an important part of the conversation between lawyer and client. *Responsible lawyering*, too, suggests that at least as much as the law seeks to enforce certain obligations of truthfulness and fairness (as set out below), lawyers should, implicitly at least, try to help their clients understand and comply with those ethics. *Adversarial advocacy* includes contradictory views as to the extent to which lawyers should talk ethics with their clients. On the one hand, it might be easier for an *adversarial advocate* to advocate their clients' rights where they limit their knowledge of clients' potentially unethical or illegal behaviour. On the other hand, lawyers are likely to provide a better service and help their clients resolve their problems in a sustainable way the broader the context, including ethical context, that is discussed with each client.

Therefore there seems little justification for lawyers not to discuss with clients at least the ethical obligations of truthfulness and fairness in litigation in relation to different options, and to advise them of possible consequences of courses of action that are likely to be seen as unethical by the courts or other parties. A lawyer should also seek to establish with clients the ethical considerations that the clients themselves would see as important in resolving a dispute, and engage in dialogue with the clients about the lawyer's view of the situation including ethical, legal and practical dimensions.[26]

---

26 For a good case study and ethical analysis of this dynamic, see William H Simon, 'Lawyer Advice and Autonomy: Mrs Jones's Case' in Deborah L Rhode (ed), *Ethics in Practice: Lawyers' Roles, Responsibilities, and Regulation* (Oxford University Press, New York, 2000) 165.

Are Lawyers Responsible for the Ethics of Actions Taken in Litigation on Behalf of their Clients?

This still leaves open the question as to the extent of the lawyer's responsibility if the client wishes to go ahead with litigation or a litigious strategy that is in some way unethical or contrary to professional obligations: Is it enough that the lawyer has clearly advised a client that such conduct would be unethical or perhaps illegal? Must the lawyer withdraw from representation or can they continue to act? Can they, or should they, take it upon themselves to do the right thing regardless of client instructions?

Recent civil procedure reforms in some jurisdictions recognise that both the lawyer and their client are capable of behaving inappropriately in litigation. The *Civil Procedure Act*[27] (*CP Act*) prescribes an 'overarching purpose' for civil litigation in language that leaves no doubt that '...just, efficient, timely and cost-effective resolution of the real issues...' is the only valid objective.[28] The *CP Act* sets out a number of 'overarching obligations' – to act honestly; to proceed on a proper basis (that is not frivolous, vexatious or an abuse of process); to only take steps to resolve or determine the dispute; to co-operate in the conduct of the civil proceeding; not to mislead or deceive; to use reasonable endeavours to resolve the dispute; to narrow the issues in dispute; to ensure costs are reasonable and proportionate; to minimise delay; and to disclose the existence of documents[29] – with which all practitioners must comply regardless of any conflicting duties owed to their clients[30] or any 'orders' given by those clients.

The judiciary is right behind these initiatives:

> What s 14 highlights is that a practitioner under *this* Act is in a different position from a practitioner refusing to act on an instruction that conflicts with their duty to the court. At present the advice to the client in such a context is that the law does not allow the practitioner to follow the instruction. The advice under the new Act in such a circumstance will be that the instruction is contrary to the client's own obligations, with the secondary advice that the practitioner is bound to ensure that the client does not contravene the obligation.[31]

Only the lawyer's overriding duty to the court survives.[32] The *CP Act* recognises that some corporate clients are often in an economically powerful position and can

---

27 Provisions of the *Civil Procedure Act 2010* (Vic) are used as the paradigm example. References to other jurisdictions' legislation are appended where applicable.
28 *Civil Procedure Act 2010* (Vic) s 7(1).
29 *Civil Procedure Act 2010* (Vic) ss 17–26 respectively.
30 *Civil Procedure Act 2010* (Vic) ss 12–13.
31 Chief Justice Warren, Victoria, quoted in (March 2011) 85(3) *LIJ* 44.
32 *Civil Procedure Act 2010* (Vic) s 15.

exert inappropriate pressure on their lawyers. Accordingly clients (whether human or corporate), litigation funders, insurers and even expert witnesses are also bound by these provisions;[33] the parties must personally certify that they have read and understand the overarching obligations;[34] and lawyers must themselves personally certify in writing before cases commence that they and their clients assert that the litigation has a proper basis to proceed.[35]

Legislation such as the *CP Act* may change behaviours at least in the short term, but clients are (appropriately) reassured by their lawyers every day to 'sign here' and it is not really a given that they will make clear-headed decisions about a proper basis for commencing their own case, even if they must sign that that is the case. Further, all legislation must be interpreted, and it is legitimate to ask what are the limits to the phrase 'proper basis' for litigation? All litigation is contentious and the overarching obligations are qualitative in nature, without a binary function that has an obvious yes/no answer. Many vexed cases might be said only to have a proper basis after the court finds in favour of their proponents.

Once litigation commences, it is true that lawyers must not '…cause the client to contravene any overarching obligation'.[36] But if some lawyers do not understand what they truly value, and have not carefully contemplated their ethical preferences and weighed up their moral responsibilities, then some may still be tempted to subvert the process in a spirit of 'let's see what happens'. For these lawyers, ethics awareness could lead to more purposeful decisions with fewer adverse consequences for their clients and themselves.

Apart from jurisdictions where provisions similar to the *CP Act* are in force, some of the law of lawyering suggests that lawyers must make clients aware of situations in which they might be breaching the boundaries of fairness and adversarialism in the adversary system, and simultaneously distance themselves from that behaviour by resigning from representation if the client chooses to go ahead with unethical action. At other times, the rules suggest that as long as excessively adversarial, unethical (or even illegal) behaviour is the client's choice, that the client understands the dangers of so behaving, and that the relevant tactic or behaviour has not been initiated by the lawyer, the lawyer can continue to act without personal responsibility. In still other situations, the law suggests that a lawyer must not take on a case in the first place where the client is proposing to abuse court process or even just run a weak case, even though the client understands the ethical objections to, and is willing to take full responsibility for, their actions.

---

33 *Civil Procedure Act 2010* (Vic) ss 10 and 14.
34 *Civil Procedure Act 2010* (Vic) s 41(1).
35 *Civil Procedure Act 2010* (Vic) ss 41 and 42.
36 *Civil Procedure Act 2010* (Vic) s 14.

Why are the rules on the balance between lawyers' obligations to the court and the client so complex and contradictory? Even where specific ethical obligations exist for civil litigation, the interpretation of those obligations will be contested. A cynic might conclude that the legal profession has deliberately chosen to put in place rules that give lawyers the choice of using those rules to control or disengage from their clients, or continuing to make money from 'unethical' clients. Either way, lawyers are extremely unlikely to ever face disciplinary action for their choices on the basis of such unclear rules, unless a judge recommends such action. A more sympathetic view is that the complexity of these rules reflects the complexity of lawyers' different, and sometimes contradictory, moral obligations to client and to court in different situations.

As we have mentioned, it is extremely difficult to lay down 'bright line' rules as to when and how the duty to the court properly overrides the duty to the client without risking clients' access to justice. Contentious, heart-felt, emotional and even scandalous cases must sometimes be brought in order to achieve justice and advance the law. We can confidently state that the duty to the court is an important guarantor of justice, yet to lay out what that duty actually requires in the form of specific rules risks the possibility that lawyers will refuse to act for people who should be represented because the basis of the case is 'improper' in some eyes. In some cases the duty to the court rules can themselves become the subject of adversarial excess. The vagueness of even the rules about minimising delay, 'steps' to resolve, co-operation, reasonable endeavours, narrowing the issues, and reasonable cost[37] still require lawyers to take responsibility themselves for balancing the overriding duty to court against the duty to client in the context of the specific facts of each case.

General Principles

The law of lawyering is clear that lawyers in litigation have duties to the court and to the administration of justice that override their duty to their clients.

Adversarial advocacy sees the lawyer as obligated to follow these rules only to the extent that they clearly prohibit certain conduct. Yet the law of lawyering does not frame the lawyers' duty to the court and the administration of justice as a set of clearly defined rules, but rather as a set of broad principles that prescribe a *responsible lawyering* type role as officer of the court, independent from the client. The following statement by former Chief Justice Mason of the High Court of Australia exemplifies the way the law sees lawyers' ethical obligations to the court:

> It is not that a barrister's duty to the court creates such a conflict with his
> duty to his client that the dividing line between the two is unclear. The duty

---

37 These terms are all used in the *Civil Procedure Act 2010* (Vic) ss 17–26.

to the court is paramount and must be performed, even if the client gives instructions to the contrary. Rather it is that a barrister's duty to the court epitomizes the fact that the course of litigation depends on the exercise by counsel of an independent discretion or judgment in the conduct and management of a case in which he has an eye, not only to his client's success, but also the speedy and efficient administration of justice.[38]

Similarly, the Law Council of Australia's *Australian Solicitors' Conduct Rules* (*ASCR*) state as a matter of general principle that lawyers should not slavishly follow client instructions if this would involve injustice:

A solicitor representing a client in a matter that is before the court must not act as the mere mouthpiece of the client or of the instructing solicitor (if any) and must exercise the forensic judgments called for during the case independently, after the appropriate consideration of the client's and the instructing solicitor's instructions where applicable. (*ASCR* 17.1)[39]

A court can also use its own 'inherent' jurisdiction to control its 'officers' (that is, lawyers admitted to practice in that court) and its own procedure, in the course of each individual case, to prohibit lawyers from excessively adversarial conduct, to order them to take certain steps in litigation, to order them to personally pay costs associated with the litigation to the other side if they have behaved inappropriately, or to find them guilty of contempt of court where they have breached their duties to the court. The court of its own motion, or by the motion of parties, can comment on the behaviour of lawyers and make procedural and substantive decisions in a case on the basis of what they think the duty to the court involves. It is very rare for disciplinary action to be taken against a lawyer for breach of the duty to the court. But in recent years civil courts have increasingly used their inherent powers to control their own process to limit the level of adversarialism in the way parties and their lawyers run their cases.[40] It seems that disciplinary authorities and lawyers themselves have left it to the courts to rein in excessive adversarialism on the basis of case management and civil procedure rules. It has not, however, been seen as a matter for disciplinary action or voluntary ethical restraint.

In the following two sections we look at the legal principles governing lawyers' obligations of honesty and fairness as developed in disciplinary cases and the

---

38 *Giannarelli v Wraith* (1988) 165 CLR 543, 556 (sexist language in original). But note that *Giannarelli* was a case where the court was using lawyers' supposed duties to the court to defend advocates' immunity from accountability to clients for negligence in court. It was not a case where the duty to the court was enforced.

39 See also Australian Law Reform Commission, *Managing Justice* [3.41], stating that much excessive adversarialism would amount to misconduct.

40 Jill Hunter, Camille Cameron and Terese Henning, *Litigation I: Civil Procedure* (LexisNexis Butterworths, Chatswood, NSW, 7th edn, 2005) 10–18.

court's exercise of its inherent jurisdiction. We will focus particularly on the extent to which these principles see lawyers as ethically responsible for dishonest or unfair tactics taken on behalf of their clients.

Honesty – Misleading the Court

The clearest curb on lawyers' adversarial behaviour on behalf of their clients is the principle that practitioners must not mislead the court. Many instances of excessive adversarialism amount to misleading (or potentially misleading) the court either directly or indirectly. The *ASCR* state that:

> 4.1 A solicitor must…[4.1.2] be honest and courteous in all dealings in the course of legal practice;[41]
>
> …
>
> A solicitor must not deceive or knowingly or recklessly mislead the court. A solicitor must take all necessary steps to correct any misleading statement made by the solicitor to a court as soon as possible after the solicitor becomes aware that the statement was misleading. (*ASCR* 19.1–19.2)

Note that these rules define 'court' broadly to include tribunals, investigations or inquiries established or conducted under statute or by a parliament, royal commissions and arbitrations or mediations or any other form of dispute resolution.

The law of lawyering also makes it clear that where a legal practitioner knows that their client, or one of his/her witnesses, has perjured themselves, or has tendered evidence that is false, the lawyer must advise the client that the dishonesty must be corrected or else the lawyer will have to take no further part in the case, and ask the client for authority to inform the court of the correction. If the client refuses to permit the lawyer to make the correction, the lawyer can no longer continue to act, even if this means withdrawing representation in the middle of a trial – something that would generally be anathema to *adversarial advocacy* (see *ASCR* 20.1–20.2). Similarly it is clear that practitioners should 'not advise or suggest to a witness that false or misleading evidence should be given', nor 'coach a witness by advising what answers the witness should give to questions which might be asked' (*ASCR* 24.1.1–24.1.2). As well as being clearly prohibited in the *ASCR*, such conduct could amount to a criminal offence and contempt of court.

These appear to be 'bright line' rules setting out precisely how and when the duty of candour to the court (broadly defined) overrides the duty to the client. But what do they mean in practice? In each of the following situations, *would* a lawyer

---

41 *ASCR* R 4.1.2, 12–20.

be held legally liable for misleading the court? *Should* they be allowed to behave like this?

- One side makes a genuine mistake about the facts in court. The mistake favours the other side. (For example the lawyer for the plaintiff makes a mistake about the amount owing under a contract.) The lawyer for the other side knows it is incorrect, but does not correct the mistake.

- A lawyer makes a statement that is not incorrect, but leaves out further facts that are unfavourable to their client's case. (For example, a lawyer states that the client had not been drinking alcohol before a car accident, but does not mention that the client had been smoking marijuana.) The other side does not know about these additional facts.

- During lawyer-client interviews, a lawyer always needs to go to the bathroom or get a cup of tea when it looks like his or her client might be going to confess to liability for a crime or civil wrong.

- A lawyer withdraws from representing a client who perjured themselves because of the rule cited above, but does not inform anyone else, including the court, of the perjury because of the need to keep client information confidential. The client is much more convincing at lying to their new lawyer and the case is decided in the client's favour on the basis of their perjured evidence.

- An in-house lawyer for a corporation sends an email to an officer of the corporation asking them to come and see the lawyer before the officer gives evidence to a statutory inquiry on possible wrongdoing by the corporation. The email says that the corporation needs to 'make sure that everyone is inside the tent'.

- A lawyer explains to their defendant client what sort of documents the plaintiff on the other side might find helpful to discover. The lawyer explains to the client their obligation under the court rules of discovery to give the plaintiff on the other side access to all these documents if they still exist, but also points out that many of the relevant documents would probably be quite old now so it would be quite understandable if they had been destroyed in order to free up storage space. What if the lawyer waits until after the case has been settled and then suggests to their client that a cleanup of documents might be appropriate before anybody else sues?

- A lawyer informs a proposed expert witness (eg a doctor who is to write a medical report) which type of expert findings would be helpful to their client's case and which would not.[42]

The conduct in each of the first four bullet points above is clearly allowed by the law, yet seems contrary to the idea of the lawyer having a broad ethical obligation

---

42 See Garth Montgomery, 'Clayton Utz Trio Facing Inquiry', *The Australian* (Sydney), 16 September 2005, 25.

of honesty to the court. The conduct in each of these cases certainly does not assist the court to decide a matter justly on the facts. In the last three cases the conduct may also be within the letter of the law, depending on the intonation and context of the lawyer's statements, but is even more clearly outside the spirit of the rules prohibiting lawyers from interfering with witnesses' evidence. Case Study 6.3 below illustrates how subtle the process of interference with witnesses' evidence can be and how the independence of both witnesses and lawyers cannot be assumed.

CASE STUDY 6.3   COBAW COMMUNITY HEALTH SERVICES LIMITED v CHRISTIAN YOUTH CAMPS LIMITED[43]

A state-wide youth suicide prevention project targeting same-sex-attracted young people in rural areas sought to run a weekend forum for 60 young people and 12 workers from across rural Victoria involved in the project. A camp on Phillip Island run by the respondents, Christian Youth Camps Limited (CYC), which was in turn established by trustees of the Christian Brethren, was contacted by the applicants to provide the necessary facilities and associated activities on its 85 acre site.

The camp manager allegedly refused to take the booking because of the sexual orientation of the proposed attendees, and a complaint of discrimination was made to the Victorian Equal Opportunity and Human Rights Commissioner pursuant to s 104 of the *Equal Opportunity Act 1995* (the *EO Act*).

CYC denied that an application for a booking was made, or refused, but if found to have refused an application, sought to rely on ss 75(2) and 77 of the *EO Act*, which exempts from the operation of the legislation certain conduct based on religious doctrines or beliefs. One of the questions that had to be determined by VCAT was the meaning of the s 75(2) provision which allowed CYC to claim exemption provided it was a body established for religious purposes, whose conduct conformed with the 'doctrines of the religion'.[44]

During the course of the trial one of the issues in dispute was the meaning of the term 'doctrine' of the religion. CYC called as their principal expert witness Dr Peter Adam, an Anglican theologian who gave evidence that, in general terms, the term 'doctrine' had a wide meaning and covered all of the beliefs of the particular religion. In contrast, the applicants called Dr Rufus Black, a Uniting

---

43 *Cobaw Community Health Services v Christian Youth Camps Ltd & Anor (Anti-Discrimination)* [2010] VCAT 1613 (Judge Hampel).
44 *Equal Opportunity Act 1995* (Vic) s 75(2)(a).

Church theologian who preferred to confine the term doctrine to the essential beliefs arising from the New Testament, as interpreted by the large ecumenical councils (in 'creeds') that occurred over several hundred years in the first millennium. Dr Black said there was no statement dealing with homosexuality in any of these primary documents.[45]

VCAT accepted the evidence of Dr Black and found that the discrimination against the applicants was not excusable on the basis of a doctrine of religion. But in the course of its judgment, VCAT made some pointed references to the CYC approach to the case and in particular its willingness to persuade an already partisan expert witness to its own purposes so that the evidence given was no longer independent in the manner required of an expert:

> ...I have come to a very clear view that [Dr Adam's] independence and impartiality in respect of the evidence he gave was seriously compromised. As a result I am not prepared to accept him as an independent expert. He became in my view an advocate for the cause for which he had been retained and in which he believed. That cause was to advance the interests of those who hold the belief, based on their literal interpretation of certain passages from the scriptures, that homosexual sexual activity is forbidden by the scriptures, to engage in it endangers salvation, and that conduct motivated by those beliefs is justified.[46]

VCAT was particularly concerned that Dr Adam's preparation for the hearing was not all his own work and that the CYC solicitors had gone well beyond helping an expert clarify what his evidence would be:

> The reasons why I have come to this conclusion include the following matters. His two witness statements were the product of extensive collaboration between him and Mr George Morgan, the solicitor for the respondents, and to a lesser extent, counsel for the respondents. Dr Adam wrote the initial draft of each of his statements, but the many drafts which succeeded them before a final draft was filed were largely drafted by Mr Morgan. The statements were partisan and argumentative in tone. They contained expressions of opinion on matters well beyond his expertise as a theologian. Significant passages of his witness statements, although adopted by him, contained opinions of which he was neither the originator nor the author. Qualifications included in his initial draft about the extent of his expertise to express opinions were removed from the final draft. The final drafts expressed opinions on matters he had initially said he was not qualified to opine about.[47]

45 *Cobaw Community Health Services v Christian Youth Camps Ltd & Anor (Anti-Discrimination)* [2010] VCAT 1613 (Judge Hampel), 293.
46 Ibid para 280.
47 Ibid para 281.

Ultimately, VCAT reflected adversely on the fact that the CYC solicitors were also too closely connected to their clients to be able to best represent them:

> A number of…witnesses gave evidence that the author of [a key issue in the description of doctrine] as understood by the Christian Brethren which appeared in their statements was Mr Morgan, the solicitor for the respondents. Other evidence revealed Mr Morgan is a trustee of the Christian Brethren Trust, and a director of CYC, the first respondent.[48]

DISCUSSION QUESTIONS

The law surrounding opportunity and discrimination is both contentious and in a sense somewhat remote from everyday legal practice, but there are many social access issues in which lawyers will find themselves too closely identifying with their clients' views. This case involved a possible conservative bias, but other lawyers would take a (liberal) view in the opposite direction. Both entail risk of too much engagement.

1. Why do you think the solicitor, Mr Morgan, allowed himself to take on the case for CYC when he was already a director of the organisation? Could you 'act in your own case' with integrity, if the opportunity arose? Who was likely to be deciding on strategy in preparing the case – CYC or Morgan – or were the two functioning as one? Would the Christian Brethren as the parent body of CYC be entitled to complain about the lack of independence of the solicitors?

2. Were Morgan and CYC excessively adversarial in their attempted construction of the evidence supporting a doctrinal basis for opposing homosexuality, or was their action justifiable because they were doing so in order to defend what they saw to be important in maintaining and witnessing to their faith?

3. Is it ever morally acceptable to subvert a properly constituted judicial process by coaching or overbearing witnesses (whether willing or not), in the interests of a perceived need to deliver a greater justice?

The law is clear that for a lawyer to be responsible for misleading the court they must have been actively and knowingly involved in misleading the court. Lawyers can sit back and watch the court being misled (*ASCR* 19.3). As long as they have

---

48 Ibid para 283.

not knowingly and actively said anything themselves to mislead the court, their hands are clean, according to the law, at least.[49] Similarly they can fail to disclose the whole truth to the extent that this favours their client, as long as what they do say is correct and not misleading on its own terms (see *ASCR* 19.10).

Similarly, although the law requires lawyers to withdraw from representation if they know of their client's perjury and their client will not allow them to correct it, the same rule goes on to preserve client confidentiality above the duty of truthfulness to the court by providing 'but otherwise may not inform the court of the lie, falsification or suppression' (*ASCR* 20.1.5). The wider implications for client trust and confidentiality are discussed in Chapters 4 and 5, but these principles do not expressly mandate that a practitioner's duty of candour to the court *overrides* the duty to the client (including the duty of confidentiality). At best the rules cited here *balance* the duty to the court and the duty to the client by requiring the lawyer to withdraw themself from the morally distasteful situation of representing a client who the lawyer knows to be basing their case on perjured evidence. Because the lawyer withdraws without being able to alert the court to the deception, the best that can be said is that the lawyer is no longer directly a part of any deception of the court. Yet the lawyer has still allowed the court to be misled.[50] Many laypeople would view this sort of 'silent withdrawal' as damning for the client and morally weak on the part of the lawyer. The rule gives no definitive moral guidance towards either duty to the client (*zealous advocacy*) or duty to the court (*responsible lawyering*). Thus although the statements of principles cited above suggest that the duty to the court *overrides* the duty to the client, when we look at specific rules, this is not true. Yet simultaneously the rules do not unequivocally support *adversarial advocacy* either. Rather they support ambiguity and abrogation of responsibility by both lawyer and client.

The same is true where a lawyer does not allow him or herself to find out about a client's perjury or liability. The lawyer's conscience may be clear, but the court has still been misled. Can a lawyer really wash their hands of ethical responsibility for the client's dishonesty to the court so easily? Unless varying ethical approaches are actively compared, the rules can offer great scope for lawyers and their clients to avoid the letter of the law so that the court is misled, rather than being an appropriate 'balance' between lawyers' duties to the court

---

49 See, eg, *Tombling v Universal Bulb Company* [1951] 2 TLR 289; *Englebrecht* (LST (NSW), Disciplinary Reports No 5, 1995, 1); cf *Meek v Fleming* [1961] 2 QB 366; *Vernon v Bosley (No 2)* [1999] QB 18.

50 See the discussion of the 'perjury trilemma' (it is impossible for a lawyer to fulfil all three of their duties to know everything, keep it in confidence and reveal it to the court) in Monroe H Freedman and Abbe Smith, *Understanding Lawyers' Ethics* (LexisNexis, Newark, New Jersey, 3rd edn, 2004) 161.

and their clients. (See also Chapter 5 on defence ethics in criminal trials for further discussion of these issues.)

The principles and scenarios discussed so far each relate to misleading the court on the *facts*. In relation to making sure the court is fully and honestly appraised as to the *law*, however, lawyers' legal responsibilities are much more onerous. Lawyers are under an obligation to pro-actively inform the court of any binding authority, any authority decided by the Full Court of the Federal Court of Australia, a Court of Appeal of a Supreme Court, or a Full Court of Supreme Court (even if it is not binding on the court in question), and any decision (including first instance decisions) on similar legislation to that at issue in a case, as well as any applicable legislation 'which the practitioner has reasonable grounds to believe to be directly in point', against the client's case (*ASCR* 19.6). This obligation extends to authority that comes to the lawyers' knowledge after argument in a case has concluded and while judgment is pending (*ASCR* 19.8). In the case of perjury on the facts, lawyers must actually know that their client has perjured him or herself, and must then advise the client to correct the matter, and withdraw if they do not. In the case of legal authority against the client's case, however, there need only be 'reasonable grounds' to see the authority as relevant, the client's permission (or even knowledge) is not required, and the lawyer is under a pro-active duty to inform the court of the authority – they cannot wash their hands of the problem by withdrawal or by saying nothing. The principle does not, of course, prevent lawyers from arguing that a contrary authority should not be applied for some reason.

Apart from the provisions of the *CP Act*, as discussed above, there is only one area where the rules of conduct provide that lawyers are under a similarly pro-active obligation to disclose *factual* information to the court even though it goes against their client's case. That is where they are making an *ex parte* application for interlocutory relief, where the other side is not present to argue their side of the case in relation to an injunction or other order which might make a big difference to the way their case progresses (*ASCR* 19.4).[51] The law's allocation of responsibility for dishonesty sees lawyers as wholly responsible for the *legal* argument in a case while clients, not lawyers, are ultimately responsible for the *facts* advanced in a case. In practice this can often be an artificial distinction, as Case Study 6.4 illustrates. Why should the lawyer not be obliged to argue the client's case on the basis of the full *facts*, not hiding facts or misleading the court in their client's interests, in the same way that they must argue the case on a full view of the relevant *legal authority*?

---

51 A similar principle might apply where the lawyer is acting against a litigant who is not represented by a lawyer.

Fairness – Abuse of Process, Unsupported or Irrelevant Allegations, Unreasonable Delay and Expense, and Hopeless Cases

The principles relating to lawyers' obligations of fair use of court processes are more broadly defined than those relating to honesty to the court. There are four broad categories of conduct that can be seen as unfair uses of litigation processes for which a lawyer might be held responsible: (1) using legal processes for improper or ulterior purposes; (2) making unsupported or irrelevant allegations against a person; (3) entering into proceedings without proper consideration for the prospects of success; and (4) running a case in a way that gives rise to unreasonable delay or expense. These principles apply to the *parties* to litigation, not just their lawyers. But the focus here is on the extent to which *lawyers* can be held personally responsible for these types of conduct. Case Study 6.4 below, *White Industries v Flower & Hart*, illustrates lawyers involved in conduct that falls into a number of these categories.

CASE STUDY 6.4   *WHITE INDUSTRIES v FLOWER & HART*[52]

In 1986, 'colourful' Queensland property developer George Herscu (through his company Caboolture Park) was building a new shopping centre, and had hired White Industries to build it. After several months, Mr Herscu was running out of money and felt that the cost of the project was blowing out. He did not want to pay any more to White Industries. His solicitors, Flower & Hart, advised him that there were no grounds for refusing to pay any more money under the terms of the contract with White Industries. But they suggested a legal strategy for buying time: They advised that Mr Herscu had an arguable but weak case that the builders had deceived him (as to the costs of the project) and could therefore sue them for fraud. They also briefed Ian Callinan QC (who was later appointed to the High Court of Australia) and other junior barristers for the case. Flower & Hart wrote Mr Herscu a letter advising that:

> The strict legalities are against you and your contractual position is weak … Is there anything that can be done to try to give you, at the very least, *a temporary bargaining*

---

52 *White Industries (Qld) Pty Ltd v Flower & Hart* (1998) 156 ALR 169 (Goldberg J); affirmed *Flower & Hart v White Industries (Qld) Pty Ltd* (1999) 87 FCR 134.

stance? ... Ian Callinan and I think that you should immediately start Section 52 proceedings (under the Trade Practices Act) in the Federal Court alleging deceptive conduct ... Fraud on the ground of recklessness may also be available to be pleaded against the builder ... I do have to make it clear to you however that you could not win any litigation if put to the test ...[53] [emphasis in original letter]

The fraud case went ahead, with White Industries cross-claiming for the money due under the contract.

After 150 hearing days (more than a year of trial, and almost three years from when the action was commenced), Caboolture Park had gone into liquidation and Flower & Hart and Mr Callinan had withdrawn from the case. Judgment was entered in favour of White Industries for more than $5 million including costs that were awarded to White as well. But with Caboolture Park in liquidation, White Industries had no prospect of recovering the amount from them, and still had their own very large legal bill to pay. In a separate matter, George Herscu was later convicted and jailed for bribery of a government official.

Because of the liquidation, however, White Industries got access to the written advice and communications Flower & Hart and Mr Callinan had given Mr Herscu. White Industries therefore sued Flower & Hart (not Mr Callinan[54]) for the legal costs in the Federal Court. In 1998, Goldberg J held that Flower & Hart had alleged fraud without evidence to support it, that their purpose was to delay and frustrate the claims of their client's creditor for payment, and that 'abuse of process was exacerbated by the manner in which Flower & Hart conducted the proceeding and the obstructionist and delaying tactics in which it indulged'.[55] The obstructionist and delaying tactics had included making sure senior counsel was not present when White Industries tried to get a trial date set, so that 'awkward questions' could not be asked, and sending 700 pages of interrogatories to make matters more difficult for the other side.

Justice Goldberg observed that:

[t]he fact that [Mr Herscu] had a robust approach to litigation, did not believe anything was impossible and was unconcerned about entering into litigation with limited prospects made it all the more important for Flower & Hart to have regard to the manner in which it instituted and conducted proceedings on his behalf and on behalf of his companies and to be conscious of its duty to the Court. [56]

---

53 *White Industries (Qld) Pty Ltd v Flower & Hart* (1998) 156 ALR 169, 180–1.
54 This means Callinan was not a party and it was not necessary to make any determination about whether Callinan shared Flower & Hart's improper purpose in commencing the litigation: *Flower & Hart v White Industries (Qld) Pty Ltd* (1999) 87 FCR 134, 148, 149.
55 *White Industries (Qld) Pty Ltd v Flower & Hart* (1998) 156 ALR 169, 251.
56 Ibid 249–50.

Flower & Hart were ordered to pay White Industries $1.65 million in court costs.[57] The President of the Law Council of Australia asked the Attorney-General for an investigation into Mr Callinan's fitness to remain on the High Court.[58] The Attorney-General refused, saying, 'No inquiry into the conduct of the judge is warranted. Any inquiry held inappropriately can endanger the independence of the judiciary, damage the standing of the courts and do harm to an individual judge'. One prominent lawyer, Professor Greg Craven said, 'If this is proved misbehaviour then we've just disqualified 95% of the commercial bar from High Court appointment'. Ian Barker QC (then president of the NSW Bar Association) replied, 'I have perhaps led a sheltered, forensic existence, but everybody does not do it'.[59]

DISCUSSION QUESTIONS

1. If there ever was a client who was clearly capable of abusing the legal system, Mr Herscu was that client. Why do you think the lawyers acted as they did in this case? How would you relate to such a client? What if this client was responsible for 50% of your firm's fees – would you assert a *responsible lawyering* approach? A *moral activist* approach? Can you think of any ways in which you might demonstrate the *ethics of care* with Mr Herscu?

2. Flower & Hart were ordered to pay costs, but the solicitors involved were never disciplined. Justice Callinan was criticised in the media for his involvement, but did not suffer any legal consequences at all, since he was not a party to the costs order action and he had been appointed to the High Court by that time anyway. Do you think this sort of behaviour should be liable for professional discipline, in addition to or instead of wasted costs orders? Does it make any difference if 'everybody did it'? Why do you think the self-regulator in Queensland at the time (the Queensland Law Society) did not take action against the solicitors from Flower & Hart?

3. White Industries is an unusual case because the lawyers' communications with their client about the case became available to

57 *White Industries (Qld) Pty Ltd v Flower & Hart* (No 2) (2000) 103 FCR 559, 561.
58 See also *Flower & Hart v White Industries (Qld) Pty Ltd* (1999) 87 FCR 134, 148, 149.
59 Based on Margo Kingston, 'Callinan Casts a Long Shadow', *The Sydney Morning Herald*, 14 August 1998, 19; Margo Kingston, 'Judge Back in Hot Seat', *The Sydney Morning Herald*, 12 June 1999 , 1. See also ABC Television, 'His Honour', *Four Corners*, 14 September 1998 <www.abc.net.au/4corners/stories/s18184.htm> at 26 July 2006.

the other side for the court to consider (because of the liquidation of Mr Herscu's company). Usually such communications are protected by client legal privilege and so only available to the lawyer and their client. Even if the other side suspects a breach of the duty to the court they are unable to access communications between lawyer and client on the other side to prove their case. Most investigations of lawyer conduct arise from complaints by clients, in which case the client has impliedly waived privilege. What problems does this create in uncovering and sanctioning lawyer-client collusion in abuses of court process? How could courts and disciplinary authorities overcome this problem? Is there any other way in which lawyers could be encouraged or forced not to engage in such behaviour?

It is an abuse of process for a party to make allegations, bring proceedings, or argue a particular defence for an *ulterior purpose*; that is, for purposes for which they are not intended, or dishonestly. This is absolutely prohibited.[60] There does not have to be evidence of a malicious intent, as long as the party's purpose for using court proceedings and court processes is unrelated to the objectives the court process is designed to achieve. It is likely to be easier to prove an ulterior purpose where a case is 'arguable although weak',[61] but the prohibition applies also to stronger cases if the only purpose in bringing the case is an ulterior one. Lawyers for a party do not avoid responsibility for running cases for ulterior purposes where they knew that the proceedings were brought for an ulterior purpose, merely because the client also knew of and approved the ulterior purpose.[62]

Most of the cases where lawyers have been held liable for ulterior purposes in bringing litigation concern situations where the lawyer knew the cause was hopeless, and the proceedings were clearly designed for some purpose other than to establish the party's legal rights and achieve the remedy available within the proceeding. For example, in *Clyne v New South Wales Bar Association*,[63] baseless allegations were made against the solicitor on the other side in order to intimidate him into dropping the case and in the hope that the opposing client would then settle on favourable terms. Clyne was struck off for professional misconduct because of this behaviour. In *White Industries* the solicitors, Flower & Hart, were made liable for paying the costs of the other side because they helped Herscu

---

60 *Williams v Spautz* (1992) 174 CLR 509. For a reworking of the idea of abuse of process and how that might moderate the lawyer's obligation of zealous advocacy, see Tim Dare, 'Mere-Zeal, Hyper-Zeal and the Ethical Obligations of Lawyers' (2004) 7 *Legal Ethics* 24.

61 *White Industries (Qld) Pty Ltd v Flower & Hart* (1998) 156 ALR 169, 251.

62 *R v Weisz* [1951] 2 KB 611; *Ridehalgh v Horsefield* [1994] Ch 205; *Re G Mayor Cooke* (1889) 5 TLR 407; *Levick v Deputy Commissioner of Taxation* (2000) 102 FCR 155.

63 (1960) 104 CLR 186.

bring the proceedings for the ulterior purpose of gaining a 'temporary bargaining stance'.[64]

The case law and professional conduct rules are also concerned that lawyers not be involved in using court proceedings to harass or embarrass people either intentionally (which would amount to an ulterior purpose and therefore an abuse of process as in Clyne), recklessly (also grounds for a wasted costs order), or negligently (by making serious allegations against other people without there being an evidential basis for those allegations), or where the allegations are not necessary to the advancement of the case (*ASCR* 21.1).[65] This is considered especially important since advocates are privileged from liability for defamation for what they say in court. So the courts consider that lawyers need to take responsibility for the 'common decency and common fairness' of what is said.[66]

In 2012, a highly politicised example of abuse of process emerged. In *Ashby v Commonwealth of Australia*,[67] the plaintiff claimed he had been sexually harassed by the second defendant, who at that time was the Speaker of the Australian House of Representatives and an ally of the then Gillard Labor Government. The Federal Court found that the case was brought with the purpose of disqualifying the Speaker from his position, with the ultimate purpose of forcing the Gillard Government into a position where it could not pass legislation and might be compelled to call an early election. The incidents of harassment alleged were relatively minor, would result in only a small award of damages, if any, if found to be justified, and could have been dealt with through other processes. Moreover, some allegations that were later dropped had been included that were substantially irrelevant but designed to injure the second defendant. The Court left open the possibility that costs might be awarded personally against the plaintiff's lawyer for his part in this abuse of process. The plaintiff has appealed the decision.

Ulterior purposes and baseless allegations are two areas where lawyers do have a clear *responsible lawyering*, 'gate keeping' type of obligation to curb their clients' more adversarial tendencies by checking the truthfulness and purpose of client allegations before repeating them before the court. The *ASCR* provide that:

> 21.1 A solicitor must take care to ensure that the solicitor's advice to invoke the coercive powers of a court:
>> 21.1.1 is reasonably justified by the material then available to the solicitor;

---

64 *White Industries (Qld) Pty Ltd v Flower & Hart* (1998) 156 ALR 169, 180.
65 See also *Medcalf v Mardell* [2003] 1 AC 120; *Guo v Minister for Immigration & Multicultural Affairs* [2000] FCA 146 (Unreported, O'Loughlin J, 23 February 2000).
66 *Clyne v New South Wales Bar Association* (1960) 104 CLR 186, 200.
67 *Ashby v Commonwealth of Australia (No 4)* [2012] FCA 1411.

21.1.2   is appropriate for the robust advancement of the client's case on its merits;

21.1.3   is not made principally in order to harass or embarrass a person; and

21.1.4   is not made principally in order to gain some collateral advantage for the client or the solicitor or the instructing solicitor out of court.[68]

However, the *ASCR* do give lawyers a number of 'excuses' for avoiding these obligations. The rules provide that the practitioner must 'believe … on reasonable grounds that the factual material already available provides a proper basis to allege any matter of fact' (*ASCR* 21.3). In the same breath, the *ASCR* also state that solicitors can rely on the opinion of an instructing practitioner 'except in the case of a closing address or submission on the evidence' (*ASCR* 21.6). The rules also provide that practitioners must not 'allege any matter of fact amounting to criminality, fraud or other serious misconduct against any person unless the solicitor believes on reasonable grounds that … available material by which the allegation could be supported provides a proper basis for it' (*ASCR* 21.4.1). But this rule goes on to provide an exception where 'the client wishes the allegation to be made, after having been advised of the seriousness of the allegation and of the possible consequences for the client and the case if it is not made out' (*ASCR* 21.4.2) – an exception which seems quite contrary to the spirit of the rest of the rule and the case law on the issue.

The exceptions to the general principle and requirement to only make 'reasonable inquiries to the extent which is practicable' suggest that the rules give lawyers maximum room to move as *adversarial advocates*, rather than wholeheartedly putting the *responsible lawyering* approach into practice. There is considerable room for barristers to say that they relied on the instructing solicitor to check the motivation for, or evidential basis of, a client's claim, while the solicitor can say that they briefed counsel in order to get counsel's expert opinion on that very point. Similarly the rules start off by suggesting that it is ultimately the lawyer's responsibility to act as a gatekeeper on the client's invocation of the court's coercive powers. Yet they also provide that, at least at the beginning of the proceedings when the court documents to start a claim are being drafted, the duty to the client will override any duty to the court so long as the client understands that the claim may not succeed, or even might be struck out as an abuse of process.

---

68 A number of more specific rules apply the same principle to the practitioner opening 'as a fact any allegation which the practitioner does not believe on reasonable grounds will be capable of support by the evidence' (16.3), and cross-examination or an address on the evidence 'so as to suggest criminality, fraud or other serious misconduct on the part of any person' (16.4, 16.7).

The rules definitely apply where it is clear that there is absolutely no supporting evidence for a client's case (apart from the client's statement). In any other situation the rules do not give much guidance as to what level of active inquiry lawyers should make about the truthfulness of what their client tells them, in terms of the evidential basis for the allegations the client wishes to be made. There is even less guidance as to any inquiry that the lawyer should make into the client's motivations for making the allegations, and whether they are for 'some collateral purpose' or 'principally in order to harass or embarrass' someone. Both base fault on what the lawyer knows – but what if the lawyer purposely turns away from finding out? At what point should a lawyer be put on inquiry as to whether what the client is telling them is true?

As we have seen, in order to advise and represent a client well, a good lawyer would usually need to know all about their memory and records of events. A lawyer who wanted to give a client full advice on the strengths and weaknesses of their case (even on an *adversarial advocacy* approach) would need this information, as would any lawyer who wanted to help their client consider and address the ethical and relational aspects of their legal problem (using a *responsible lawyering, moral activist* or *ethics of care* approach). Yet the ethics of *adversarial advocacy* might sometimes pull in the other direction – they might motivate lawyers to try to limit their knowledge of any fault on the part of their client so that they are 'free' to advocate zealously for that client.

The obligations on lawyers to avoid making baseless allegations through the court process apply to allegations of fraud, crime and improper conduct. They do not state that the lawyer should be satisfied there is an evidential basis for more run-of-the-mill allegations and claims.[69] Nor do they apply to the situation where lawyers deny (or 'fail to admit') allegations made by the other side that they know are true (ie, 'put the other side to the proof'). Although professional conduct rules and disciplinary decisions do not give lawyers active obligations in these areas, the courts are now using practice directions, rules of court and interlocutory decisions on procedural matters to require 'truth in pleading'.[70] As we have seen, the professional conduct law that we have described is lagging behind legislation such as the *CP Act*. This reality of inconsistent law underscores the importance of lawyers' general willingness to reflect on *who* they are as moral agents and what type of practitioner they ought to be, before they make tactical decisions in litigation.

What obligations do lawyers have more generally to screen *weak or hopeless cases*, and to ensure that cases are conducted as efficiently and expeditiously as possible in order to avoid *unreasonable delay and expense?*

---

69 Although the overarching rule in *ASCR* 21.1–21.3 suggests caution in making any allegation.
70 Hunter, Cameron and Henning, *Litigation I: Civil Procedure*, 163–5.

ASCR 17.2.1 supports the independence of *responsible lawyering* in these circumstances by releasing practitioners from an obligation to look after their client when they decide to emphasise the 'real issues' only, or present a case in a concise manner, or actually inform the court of an authority that might persuade the court against their client. These 'freedoms' are important since each of them helps a court to get to a prompt and arguably correct result. But, with the exception of the last circumstance – the existence of the contrary authority or decision, which must be disclosed (see *ASCR* 19.6.1) – the rule contains no positive injunction to conduct the case having regard to these factors. It simply *permits* an advocate to take this approach, in the face of client demands to do the opposite. Accordingly, the rule operates in a passive, defensive role (primarily for the benefit of the advocate) rather than in active support of the court's function. As things stand, this rule does not require that an advocate conduct a case expeditiously.

The common law on payment of costs is more rigorous in its requirements. The party (that is, the client) whose case is ultimately unsuccessful must generally pay the legal costs of the other side, and greater costs can be awarded against a party if the court considers that party caused unnecessary delay or expense to the other side because of the way they argued their case. It is generally the party themselves, not their lawyer, who bears these costs. But there are a number of cases where the courts have held that where the 'wastage' of costs through unreasonable behaviour is the lawyer's fault, rather than their client's, the lawyer (or law firm) personally can be ordered to pay the other side's costs. These costs orders against lawyers are clearly available where the lawyer has been party to an abuse of process or something akin to an abuse of process, as in *White Industries*. But the courts have also held that 'wasted costs orders' are available against lawyers where the lawyer has commenced proceedings (or put forward defences) on behalf of a client '*without any, or any proper, consideration of the prospects of success*' [our emphasis],[71] that is the lawyer failed to 'give reasonable or proper attention to the relevant law and facts in circumstances where if such attention had been given it would have been apparent that there were no worthwhile prospects of success'.[72] They are also available where the lawyer has personally caused costs to be 'wasted by a *failure to act with reasonable competence and expedition*' [our emphasis].[73] This latter ground would include situations where the lawyer fails to

---

71 *Levick v Deputy Commissioner of Taxation* (2000) 102 FCR 155, 166; for an example where a costs order was made on such grounds, see *Cook v Pasminco Ltd (No 2)* (2000) 107 FCR 44.

72 *White Industries (Qld) Pty Ltd v Flower & Hart* (1998) 156 ALR 169, 239. The court is more likely to see the lawyer as unreasonable where there is no case on the law than where there is an unresolved issue of fact: *Levick v Deputy Commissioner of Taxation* (2000) 102 FCR 155, 166.

73 This wording is from the *Supreme Court (General Civil Procedure) Rules* (Vic), r 63.23. Similar provisions exist in other Australian jurisdictions. The rules also refer to 'incurring costs

file documents on time, to attend court, or to be properly prepared. Conducting a case with unreasonable delay or other obstructionist tactics on purpose (not through negligence or incompetence), in order to delay judgment or in the hope of wearing out the other side's resources so that they give up the fight, as in *White Industries*, would also amount to abuse of process. This is because the tactics are being chosen for an ulterior purpose, although it is likely to be difficult to prove this intention.

The availability of the costs orders against lawyers personally for failure of proper consideration of the prospects of success and unreasonable delay and expense is a matter of fairness to the lawyer's own client and the party on the other side. Why should either of the *parties* have to bear costs that were spent because a *lawyer* failed to give proper consideration to the prospects of success and accordingly advise their client, or acted negligently or inappropriately so that the case took longer than was necessary? In such circumstances the lawyer might also be liable for unsatisfactory professional conduct (failing to meet the standard of service of a reasonably competent practitioner), and the client might be able to contest their own legal bill and have it reduced as well. In other words, the problem is that the lawyer has breached his or her duty to the client by acting incompetently during the case,[74] or by taking a weak or hopeless case in the first place. This behaviour can reap fees for the lawyer without giving the client any benefit.

However, the courts traditionally made it clear that even if a case was weak or hopeless, if the lawyer had in fact fully advised the client of the prospects of success, *and* of the likely consequences to the client if the case went ahead (including that costs would likely be awarded against the client), *and* the client instructed the lawyer to proceed, then the lawyer would not breach any duty in proceeding with the case. Indeed, to say that the lawyers should not run cases or argue points merely because they are weak or hopeless would be for lawyers to improperly predetermine the extent of their client's legal rights. Absent an ulterior purpose, clients ought to have a right 'to have a case conducted in the courts irrespective of the view which his or her legal adviser has formed about the case and its prospects of success'.[75] On this view, the lawyer is under an obligation

---

improperly or without reasonable cause' which would reinforce the abuse of process, and failure to give proper consideration to prospects of success grounds at common law. See also *Whyte v Brosch* (1998) 45 NSWLR 354; J J Spigelman, 'Supreme Court: Just, Quick and Cheap – A New Standard for Civil Procedure' (2000) 38 *Law Society Journal* 24.

74 For example, for failing to advise the client that their case was hopeless: *Kolavo v Pitsikas* [2003] NSWCA 59 (Unreported, Stein, Santow JJA and Cripps AJA, 1 April 2003).

75 *White Industries (Qld) Pty Ltd v Flower & Hart* (1998) 156 ALR 169, 231; *Medcalf v Mardell* [2003] 1 AC 120, 143–4; *Orchard v South Eastern Electricity Board* [1987] 1 QB 565, 580–1. See also Bill Pincus and Linda Haller, 'Wasted Costs Orders Against Lawyers' (2005) 79 *Australian Law Journal* 497.

to advise the client of the prospects of success and the fact that the court may in the end consider it inappropriate to run the case, but not to impose on the client their own view of whether it should be run or not. If a lawyer takes seriously the *CP Act* requirements where they apply, those provisions will support rather than undermine these general precepts. In other words, the legal duties to give proper consideration to the prospect of success of a case and to avoid unreasonable expense and delay ought not generally be duties that override the lawyer's duty to follow client instructions.

In recent years, however, courts and governments have started to give lawyers an obligation to refuse to act in cases even where a client has instructed them to go ahead after being advised of the weakness of their position. The availability of personal costs orders against lawyers in these circumstances is expanding, and some reforms have also explicitly stated that lawyers can be found guilty of professional misconduct or unsatisfactory professional conduct in such circumstances:

- In New South Wales a 2002 law prohibits legal practitioners from providing legal services on a claim 'or defence of a claim for damages unless the solicitor or barrister reasonably believes on the basis of provable facts and a reasonably arguable view of the law' that the claim or defence has 'reasonable prospects of success'.[76] Breach may constitute the disciplinary offences of professional misconduct or unsatisfactory professional conduct and a personal costs order is also available against the lawyer.

- In a series of cases, the Department of Immigration (and also the Australian Taxation Office) have sought personal costs orders against lawyers acting for clients appealing decisions of these government agencies.[77] In most cases they were unsuccessful. In 2005 the federal government inserted into the Commonwealth *Migration Act* provisions stating that a person (including a lawyer) must not encourage another person to commence or continue migration litigation if it has 'no reasonable prospect of success'. A lawyer

76 *Legal Profession Act 1987* (NSW) ss 198J–198M; *Lemoto v Able Technical Pty Ltd* (2005) 63 NSWLR 300.

77 *De Sousa v Minister for Immigration, Local Government & Ethnic Affairs* (1993) 41 FCR 544; *Guo v Minister for Immigration & Multicultural Affairs* [2000] FCA 146 (Unreported, O'Loughlin J, 23 February 2000); *Money Tree Management Services Pty Ltd v Deputy Commissioner of Taxation (No 2)* (2000) 207 LSJS 287; *Gersten v Minister for Immigration & Multicultural Affairs* [2001] FCA 260 (Unreported, Lee, Carr and Sackville JJ, 19 March 2001); *SBAZ v Minister for Immigration & Multicultural & Indigenous Affairs* [2002] FCA 1280 (Unreported, Mansfield J, 25 October 2002); *Tanddy v Minister for Immigration & Multicultural & Indigenous Affairs* [2004] FCA 29 (Unreported, Mansfield J, 30 January 2004); *Buksh v Minister for Immigration & Multicultural & Indigenous Affairs* [2004] FCA 32 (Unreported, Mansfield J, 30 January 2004); *Kumar v Minister for Immigration & Multicultural & Indigenous Affairs (No 2)* (2004) 133 FCR 582.

who acts in contravention of this provision can be ordered to pay the costs of their own client and/or the other side (usually the government), or to pay back costs already received from their own client. Lawyers must not file any documents commencing migration litigation unless they certify in writing that there are reasonable grounds for believing it has reasonable prospects of success.[78] Public interest lawyers argued that these provisions would deter lawyers, especially those working pro bono, from assisting immigration clients to challenge Department of Immigration decisions.

One problem with this *responsible lawyering* approach (reinforced perhaps by *CP Act* provisions), as with *responsible lawyering* generally, is that it might unwittingly reinforce existing law and practices, even where those are unjust. It might discourage lawyers from taking on cases where they would have to argue novel interpretations of the law, challenge existing precedent or common conceptions of how the law should be interpreted, and causes where little evidence is available at the beginning of the case. It is one thing to argue that personal costs orders (and perhaps disciplinary sanctions) should be available against lawyers who are willing to assist a George Herscu to use the legal system as a way to buy time before paying a debt that would inevitably have to be paid. But what if personal costs orders or misconduct charges were pursued against *moral activist* lawyers, like those who sought to argue that the longstanding doctrine of *terra nullius* should be overturned in the *Mabo* case so that indigenous native title claims could be recognised in Australian law?[79]

Adversarial advocacy emphasises the importance of lawyers being free from the fear of government intervention and control of their activities so that lawyers can challenge government policies, laws and actions on behalf of their clients. The availability and use of personal costs orders and disciplinary sanctions might discourage lawyers from doing this. The abuse of process rules sanction lawyers for assisting in a misuse of the legal system. But from both an *adversarial advocacy* and *moral activist* perspective, it is quite proper for lawyers to use the legal system to help clients challenge perceived injustices, or to test government decision-making, even if there is little chance of success. On this view, proper but weak or hopeless cases cannot be said to 'waste' the court's and other parties' time and money, as the legal system is available precisely for that purpose. If there is an ulterior purpose to bringing the case, or for using delay and prolixity in the way it is run, then abuse of process principles may properly apply. But they

---

78 *Migration Act 1958* (Cth) ss 486E, 486F, 486I; Michael Stanton, 'Removing Voices from the Voiceless: The Migration Litigation Reform Act 2005' (2006) 31 *Alternative Law Journal* 25.

79 *Mabo v Queensland (No 2)* (1992) 175 CLR 1. See also Peter H Russell, *Recognising Aboriginal Title: The Mabo Case and Indigenous Resistance to English-Settler Colonialism* (University of New South Wales Press, Sydney, 2006).

should not be expanded to prohibit lawyers taking on cases with apparently little or no prospects of success where there is a genuine issue of justice or rights to be resolved.

The problem, as we have seen, is that proof of purpose is difficult. This is why the lawyer who has a virtuous track record – that is, they are known to be motivated by a desire to seek justice or by a compassionate concern for an individual's suffering, or even by a sense of public benevolence in running a case to clarify a 'bad' law – may have an advantage before the courts if their virtue is a matter of reputation. Judges need to know which advocates are, in effect, virtuous if they are to make appropriate decisions[80] and value having the right (that is, the good) advocate.

There is a second problem with expanding the availability of personal costs orders and disciplinary charges against lawyer behaviour in civil litigation: Rather than these measures curbing adversarialism, as hoped, paradoxically they often become new tools for excessive adversarialism in satellite litigation.[81] Rather than defending their position in the substantive dispute itself, parties can spend even greater time and money arguing costs order applications or even seeking to have disciplinary sanctions levied against the lawyers on the other side, rather than resolving the substantive dispute between them. Thus the original *White Industries* case took three years from initiation of the action to the trial collapsing, then a further six years in court and appeals on the litigation about the costs order against Flower & Hart. Several months after the introduction of the new law in New South Wales (briefly described above), the Law Society of New South Wales reportedly issued a statement asking lawyers to stop making threats of costs orders against each other and pointing out that it is more appropriate to make an application for dismissal or strike out if one side believes proceedings are so ill-founded as to warrant a personal costs order against the lawyer on the other side.[82] It was also reported that the New South Wales Legal Services Commissioner 'has been forced to reprimand and seek apologies and retractions from solicitors who use the threat of personal costs against other solicitors to put pressure on them to drop a case'.[83]

---

80 See the comments of Bergin J, Supreme Court of New South Wales, reported in *Lawyers Weekly*, 5 April 2013, 14. Bergin J said: 'My conduct and the integrity of the system…depends on you'.
81 See Stephen Parker, 'Islands of Civic Virtue: Lawyers and Civil Justice Reform' (1997) 6 *Griffith Law Review* 1.
82 'Hearsay', *The Australian Financial Review* (Sydney), 10 September 2004, 52. Also discussed in *Levick v Deputy Commissioner of Taxation* (2000) 102 FCR 155.
83 Marcus Priest, 'Costs Orders Wielded as Threat', *The Australian Financial Review* (Sydney), 10 June 2005, 55. See also *Lemoto v Able Technical Pty Ltd* (2005) 63 NSWLR 300.

Discussion questions

1. What justifications might there be for taking 'hopeless' public interest cases such as the Stolen Generation case? In that case, indigenous Australians who had been taken from their parents as children and adopted out to white families or put in orphanages as part of government policies of assimilation unsuccessfully sought compensation for their suffering.[84] Should lawyers in such cases be disciplined or made responsible for costs? Or should their motives first be examined and their character assessed before anything else is considered? If they are to be responsible for costs orders, under what conditions? If not, what, if any, is the difference between this and a case like *White Industries*?

2. A commentator on the New South Wales provision mentioned above has said that 'It is not difficult to imagine the Act being used against less empowered litigants, to further discourage them from bringing claims. It might also be a sword in the hands of effective legal representatives of such litigants'.[85] Should lawyers threaten applications for costs orders against each other in this way? Think about whether such action would be considered justified by each of the four ethical approaches to lawyering – *adversarial advocacy*, *responsible lawyering*, *moral activism*, and *ethics of care*.

3. What would you do if the lawyer on the other side was seeking such an order against you? Would you drop the client or fight? How would you decide what is more important to you? Should there be disciplinary or costs orders sanctions available against lawyers for inappropriately threatening costs orders against each other?

Conclusion

Litigation lawyers perform the frequently unattractive and uncomfortable work of advising and representing people as they try to resolve their conflicts. When a person needs to use a lawyer, they are often in the midst of conflict and not feeling the most altruistic: the work that they ask their lawyers to do is very likely to be aimed at cutting across the positions that other people have taken in relation to

---

84 *Cubillo v Commonwealth* (2000) 103 FCR 1; affirmed on appeal in *Cubillo v Commonwealth* (2001) 112 FCR 455. See also Pam O'Connor, 'History on Trial: *Cubillo and Gunner v The Commonwealth of Australia* ' (2001) 26 *Alternative Law Journal* 27.

85 Jane Stratton, 'Ethical Threshold for Litigation' (2002) 27 *Alternative Law Journal* 193, 194.

their own interests. People need lawyers precisely because of the conflicts we face as we live together in society.[86] Surveys show that people tend to be critical of lawyers in general but very favourable towards their own lawyer: They condemn lawyers for doing for others what they praise them for doing for themselves – being adversarial advocates.[87] We do not like the idea of lawyers being available as hired guns … until we feel we need a hired gun ourselves!

Adversarial advocacy argues that it is not for the lawyer to rein in the client's adversarialism – that would be for the lawyer to unjustifiably limit the autonomy and rights of the client. The legal advocate is not responsible for the conflict, nor even for making sure that it stays within ethical bounds. Rather, according to *adversarial advocacy*, it is up to the client to ethically limit their own case, if they wish to. If the other side sees their opponents' tactics as beyond the bounds, then it is up to them to complain about it to the court or the disciplinary authorities. It is for the courts and disciplinary authorities to clearly enforce the boundaries of adversarialism in response. This makes the proper boundary of adversarialism in litigation itself an issue that is often only decided via the adversarial process. Moreover, it gives lawyers little role in encouraging or equipping their clients to limit their own behaviour by reference to any duty to the court or to the legal system.

Justice Ipp has argued that a lawyer is only required to do for a client what the client might 'fairly' do for him or herself, not take every point and make every argument or allegation.[88] This is in tune with the Australian Law Reform Commission's recommendation some years ago that we should move 'away from the idea that litigation is only self-seeking activity in a private sphere with lawyers there merely to oil the wheels …' Rather, 'the central role of the court as "battleground" [should] be downplayed in favour of a notion of the court as a public forum in which, with the assistance of lawyers, rights and obligations of parties to litigation were determined according to law'.[89] Lately, over-arching purpose legislation is going in the same direction. All this suggests that it should always be part of the lawyer's role, as an officer of the court, to at a minimum *advise* the client as to the limits of appropriate adversarial behaviour in how they approach their case – in terms of both honesty to the court and fair use of process.

To what extent should lawyers go beyond this and screen their clients' cases? To what extent should they take it upon themselves to rein in adversarial

---

86 Robert Post, 'On the Popular Image of the Lawyer: Reflections in a Dark Glass' (1987) 75 *California Law Review* 379.
87 C Parker, *Just Lawyers*, 11.
88 D A Ipp, 'Lawyers' Duties to the Court' (1998) 114 *Law Quarterly Review* 63, 100.
89 Australian Law Reform Commission, *Review of the Adversarial System of Civil Litigation*, [11.17]; partially quoting Stephen Parker, 'Islands of Civic Virtue? Lawyers and Civil Justice Reform' (Speech delivered at the Inaugural Professorial Lecture, Griffith University, Nathan, 1996) 38.

behaviour by correcting client dishonesty, or refusing to act at all where a client is instructing them to action abuse of process or in a truly hopeless case? It is clear as a matter of both legal and ethical responsibility that lawyers must not be actively and knowingly involved in deception of the court, the use of legal processes for ulterior purposes, and making baseless allegations of serious misconduct. But different ethical approaches can give quite different answers as to whether lawyers should take it upon themselves to correct their client's dishonesty against client instructions, or to screen weak or hopeless cases so as to avoid wastage of court time. Where the law attempts to put more onerous *responsible lawyering* obligations on lawyers, as with the *CP Act*, the adversarial system itself seems to encourage lawyers to interpret those obligations narrowly and legalistically as they apply to *themselves*, and simultaneously use them as an extra adversarial weapon *against the other side* in a way that might chill appropriate adversarial representation by other lawyers.[90] This means that taking either a strictly *adversarial advocate* or *responsible lawyering* approach to ethics in litigation is likely to lead to injustice. Lawyers need to understand their own values and character before they make ethical decisions, in the contexts of specific cases, about whether duty to court or to client is more important in particular circumstances.

RECOMMENDED FURTHER READING

Camille Cameron, 'Hired Guns and Smoking Guns: McCabe v British American Tobacco Australia Ltd' (2002) 25 *University of New South Wales Law Journal* 768.

G E Dal Pont, *Lawyers' Professional Responsibility* (Lawbook Co, Pyrmont, NSW, 5th edn, 2013) 'Ch 17: Duty to the Court' 373–403.

Tim Dare, 'Mere-Zeal, Hyper-Zeal and the Ethical Obligations of Lawyers' (2004) 7 *Legal Ethics* 24.

D A Ipp, 'Lawyers' Duties to the Court' (1998) 114 *Law Quarterly Review* 63.

Carrie Menkel-Meadow, 'The Limits of Adversarial Ethics' in Deborah L Rhode (ed), *Ethics in Practice: Lawyers' Roles, Responsibilities, and Regulation* (Oxford University Press, New York, 2000).

Stephen Parker, 'Islands of Civic Virtue: Lawyers and Civil Justice Reform' (1997) 6 *Griffith Law Review* 1.

William H Simon, 'The Ideology of Advocacy: Procedural Justice and Professional Ethics' (1978) *Wisconsin Law Review* 30.

---

90 See Duncan Webb, 'Civil Advocacy and the Dogma of Adversarialism' (2004) 7 *Legal Ethics* 210.

7

ETHICS IN NEGOTIATION AND ALTERNATIVE DISPUTE RESOLUTION

Introduction

The standard conception of lawyers' role and ethics revolves around a combination of advocacy on behalf of clients and responsibilities to the court. Yet only a small proportion of lawyers devote a substantial amount of their practice time to litigation. Most disputes do not go all or even part of the way to trial. The vast majority of problems that could lead to legal proceedings are handled without recourse to law, lawyers or any other form of organised dispute resolution at all.[1] Even where people do seek legal advice and commence court proceedings, most civil disputes are settled or 'compromised' through negotiation before the dispute goes to trial.[2]

Most lawyers are not involved in litigation on a regular basis, but all lawyers are likely to negotiate on behalf of clients on a daily basis, whether to settle a dispute, or conclude a contract or deal. These negotiations can be a purely private affair between the parties and their lawyers. Or negotiation can occur through a variety of methods of 'alternative' or appropriate[3] dispute resolution (ADR). We use the term 'ADR' here to include any processes in which neutral third parties (other than courts) intervene to either help parties reach a settlement, or to determine a dispute. ADR can be aimed at avoiding the need to use lawyers or courts by helping people to settle their disputes as soon as possible after they arise – for example, customer or workplace complaints schemes within commercial and government organisations, external ombudsman schemes and complaints commissioners, neighbourhood or community justice centres, some commercial mediation and arbitration, and preventive dispute management systems. Or, ADR can be aimed at avoiding trial once lawyers have been hired and court processes invoked – for example, court-annexed or court-ordered mediation, diversionary restorative justice conferencing,[4] commercial conciliation and arbitration, and the mediation offered by government regulators such as Equal Opportunity Commissions and

---

1 See William Felstiner, Richard Abel and Austin Sarat, 'The Emergence and Transformation of Disputes: Naming, Blaming, Claiming…' (1981) 15 *Law & Society Review* 631; Hazel Genn, *Paths to Justice: What People Do and Think About Going to Law* (Hart Publishing, Oxford, 1999) 252.

2 Hilary Astor and Christine Chinkin, *Dispute Resolution in Australia* (LexisNexis Butterworths, Chatswood, NSW, 2nd edn, 2002) 44–6.

3 Tania Sourdin, *Alternative Dispute Resolution* (Thomson-Reuters, Sydney, 4th edn, 2012) 2. Sourdin does not express a clear view as between 'alternative' or 'appropriate' dispute resolution, but notes that any shift to the latter term is 'significant' because it recognises that non-court processes can be more effective than courts in resolving disputes.

4 '[R]estorative justice is a process whereby all the parties with a stake in a particular offence come together to resolve collectively how to deal with the aftermath of the offence and its implications for the future': John Braithwaite, *Restorative Justice and Responsive Regulation* (Oxford University Press, Oxford, 2002) 10.

Legal Services Commissioners.[5] In addition to the fact that many lawyers now represent clients during mediation and other ADR processes, increasing numbers of lawyers also practise as ADR facilitators – such as mediators, arbitrators, and in positions such as ombudsman roles.

What ethical standards should apply to lawyers when they are involved in negotiation and ADR, rather than litigation, on behalf of clients? Does the fact that negotiations often occur privately and away from the supervision of the court mean that lawyers should bargain even more aggressively on behalf of their clients as *adversarial advocates* free of the constraints of court? On the other hand, if the purpose of negotiation is for the parties to conclude a deal together, or to come to a consensual agreement about how to resolve a dispute, then perhaps a completely different set of values, more informed by the *ethics of care*, should guide lawyers' role in negotiation? Where ongoing relationships between the parties are at stake, it is likely that zealous approaches based on rights will miss the mark completely. As Sourdin comments: '… a rights-based [approach] is increasingly clumsy in managing conflict that involves continuing relationships or interests that lie outside a clearly articulated rights-based framework'.[6]

In this chapter we will explore these questions by reference to lawyers' ethics in the negotiation of settlement of disputes, and in mediation. We focus on mediation, rather than any other ADR processes, since mediation is the ADR process that lawyers are likely to be most commonly involved in as representatives of clients, or as facilitators.[7] This is because as part of the pretrial process of case management, courts now frequently order parties (and their lawyers) to take part in mediation to try to reach a settlement before trial.[8]

First, we consider the ethical issues that are likely to, and commonly do, arise for lawyers in negotiation and mediation, and how current professional ethical standards and the conventional *adversarial advocacy* approach to lawyers' ethics would apply to these concerns. In the second part of this chapter, we outline an

---

5 For brief descriptions and definitions of ADR and of a range of alternative dispute resolution processes, see Astor and Chinkin, *Dispute Resolution in Australia*, 77–95; National Alternative Dispute Resolution Advisory Council ('NADRAC'), *Dispute Resolution Terms: The Use of Terms in (Alternative) Dispute Resolution* (2003) <www.ag.gov.au/agd/WWW/disputeresolutionhome. nsf/Page/Definitions2> at 10 March 2006.

6 Sourdin, *Alternative Dispute Resolution*, 4th edn, ix.

7 Other ADR processes in which lawyers are often involved include arbitration (where the impartial third-party arbitrator makes a determination of the issue), conciliation (where the impartial third-party conciliator can take an advisory role on the content of the dispute and outcomes) and combined processes such as 'med-arb' in which the third party uses first mediation then arbitration.

8 Jill Hunter, Camille Cameron and Terese Henning, *Litigation 1: Civil Procedure* (LexisNexis Butterworths, Chatswood, NSW, 7th edn, 2005) 48–56; Kathy Mack, 'Court Referral to ADR: The Legal Framework in Australia' (2004) 22 *Law in Context* 112.

alternative *ethics of care* approach to what lawyers' ethics should be in negotiation and mediation, as reflected in various proposed ADR standards, and consider the difficulties that this is likely to raise.[9] In each section we divide our discussion into a consideration of ethics for lawyers *representing* parties in negotiation or mediation, and those issues facing lawyers acting as *facilitators* of ADR (focusing on mediation), since lawyers' roles are quite different in these two situations.

Current Ethical Practices and Standards for Lawyers in Negotiation and Mediation

'Litigotiation'? Representing Parties in Negotiation and Mediation

It has often been commented that when lawyers use negotiation to settle disputes, negotiation is not a separate process to litigation. Rather both are part of 'a single process of disputing in the vicinity of official tribunals that we might call *litigotiation*, that is, the strategic pursuit of a settlement through mobilizing the court process ...'.[10] This means that lawyers are likely to use legal rules and norms to shape the substance of the outcomes they seek to negotiate on behalf of their clients. It also means that they may be likely to conduct negotiations as *adversarial advocates*, consistent with the way they would operate in litigation. Conventional advice on negotiation tactics for lawyers (and often for business people) suggests that they should see their role as to represent their client's position as aggressively as possible, using posturing (emotional displays and manipulation) and other misleading or bullying tactics as required (see the case studies below for examples), and making concessions only to the extent necessary to get greater concessions

---

9 For standards of ethical conduct for lawyers and others in ADR see the Law Council of Australia, *Ethical Standards for Mediators* (2000) <www.lawcouncil.asn.au/policy/1957353025. html> at 20 March 2006; Law Society of New South Wales, *The Law Society Guidelines for Those Involved in Mediation* (1993) <www.lawsociety.com.au/page.asp?partid=3779> at 20 March 2006; NADRAC, *A Framework for ADR Standards* (NADRAC, Barton, ACT, 2001) 40–7 <www.nadrac.gov.au/publications/PublicationsByDate/Pages/FrameworkforADRStandards. aspx>. See also Astor and Chinkin, *Dispute Resolution in Australia*, 220–4; Sourdin, *Alternative Dispute Resolution*, 4th edn, Appendices E–F.
10 Marc Galanter, 'Worlds of Deals: Using Negotiation to Teach About Legal Process' (1984) 34 *Journal of Legal Education* 268, 268; see also Hazel Genn, *Hard Bargaining* (Oxford University Press, Oxford, 1987) 15.

from the other side.[11] It has also been suggested that negotiation is all about finding out as much as possible about the other side's case and position while hiding the strengths and weaknesses of your own case and preferred outcomes: '…the negotiator's role is at least passively to mislead his opponent about his settling point while at the same time appearing to engage in ethical behaviour'.[12]

This raises two questions about lawyers' ethics in negotiation. *First*, to what extent *do* current *professional conduct standards* that seek to curb excessive *adversarial advocacy* apply to negotiation and mediation? Or are these private processes outside of the court room unregulated? *Second*, to what extent *should adversarial advocacy* and/or *responsible lawyering* values apply to lawyers' behaviour in negotiation, mediation and other ADR processes? Or should different values guide lawyers' behaviour in these processes?

CASE STUDY 7.1   ETHICS IN NEGOTIATION

Consider the following descriptions of lawyer behaviour and possible tactics that could be used in negotiations. All of the practices recounted here are either based on real cases, or have been recommended as tactics for success in business negotiation.

Thinking about each one, consider the following questions: Which of these behaviours or tactics are in breach of professional conduct standards? Which would you personally use and not use in negotiation? Why or why not? How do you think the other side would view your use of each behaviour or tactic in each situation if and when they found out about it?

1. In negotiations for the sale of a licensed restaurant, the lawyer for the vendor tells the potential purchaser that the restaurant can seat 120 people at 39 tables. In fact, the Liquor Licensing Authority has approved only the seating of 84 people at 26 tables in the restaurant. The vendor has been illegally seating 120 people at the restaurant for the last two years, and the figures for the restaurant's takings given to the other side are based on this. Both the lawyer and the vendor know all this.[13] As an alternative, what if the vendor simply

---

11 See Albert Z Carr, 'Is Business Bluffing Ethical?' in Carrie Menkel-Meadow and Michael Wheeler (eds), *What's Fair? Ethics for Negotiators* (Jossey Bass, San Francisco, 2004) 246; Jim Parke, 'Lawyers as Negotiators: Time for a Code of Ethics?' (1993) 4 *Australian Dispute Resolution Journal* 216.

12 James White quoted in Richard O'Dair, *Legal Ethics: Text and Materials* (Butterworths, London, 2001) 298 (sexist language in original).

13 Based on *Collins Marrickville Pty Ltd v Henjo Investments Pty Ltd* (1987) 72 ALR 601; *Henjo Investments Pty Ltd v Collins Marrickville Pty Ltd (No 1)* (1988) 39 FCR 546. See

overstated the average takings of the restaurant and the lawyer, knowing the truth, sat and watched silently?[14]

2. In the course of a mediation, the client instructs the lawyer in a private meeting that the client is willing to pay anything up to $200,000 to the other side to settle the matter. The lawyer then tells the other side, 'My client has instructed me that she will not pay a cent more than $150,000. That's our final offer'.

3. It has been suggested that '[t]he art of compromise centres on the willingness to give up something in order to get something else in return. Successful artists get more than they give up. A common ploy is to exaggerate the importance of what one is giving up and to minimise the importance of what one gets in return. Such posturing is part of the game'.[15] Tactics that might be used to achieve this include: acting as if I am very disappointed with how things are going (even if I am not); acting as though I am very angry about the situation; appearing to move in one direction to divert the other party's attention from my real goal; introducing imaginary issues into the negotiation to disguise my real intentions.[16]

4. Consider also the following tactics:[17]

   a. 'Coercion: Use threats to force the other side to accede to your demands.' For example: Say that I will use negative personal information about the other party to their detriment, although I am just bluffing; Threaten to leave the negotiation permanently unless the other party offers me some concessions now, even though I will stay; Tell the other party that if they do not answer my request by a deadline that I will never do business with them again.[18]

   b. 'Quick thrust: Try to force a settlement within a short time frame, giving the other side inadequate time to strengthen their case.'

Warren Pengilley, '"But You Can't Do That Anymore!" – The Effect of Section 52 on Common Negotiating Techniques' (1993) 1 *Trade Practices Law Journal* 113, 118–19.

14 See *Sutton v AJ Thompson Pty Ltd (in liq)* (1987) 73 ALR 233. Described in Stephen Corones, 'Solicitors' Liability for Misleading Conduct' (1998) 72 *Australian Law Journal* 775, 784.

15 H Raiffa quoted in Michelle Wills, 'The Use of Deception in Negotiations: Is It "Strategic Misrepresentation" or Is It a Lie?' (2000) 11 *Australian Dispute Resolution Journal* 220, 224.

16 From the survey described in Cheryl Rivers, 'What Are They Thinking? Considerations Underlying Negotiators' Ethical Decisions' (Paper presented at the 2004 Annual Meeting Academy of International Business Conference, Stockholm, Sweden, 13 July 2004) <http://eprints.qut.edu.au/archive/00000366/> at 1 May 2006.

17 These strategies for negotiation identified in College of Law Pty Ltd, *Negotiation Strategy: Participants' Manual* (College of Law Pty Ltd, Sydney, 1999).

18 From Rivers, 'What Are They Thinking?'.

   c. 'Prolonged pressure: Try to prolong the process over periods of time, using extended time to weaken the other side's case as resolve, memories and witnesses slowly fall away.'

5. The lawyer for Company A negotiates an 'in principle' agreement with Company B in which Company A and Company B will work together on a joint venture and appoint directors to each other's boards. Lawyer A agrees to the terms unconditionally on behalf of Company A. But Company A has not given Lawyer A authority to agree the matter unconditionally. As far as Company A is concerned, the real agreement could only be agreed in detail if they had an adequate cash flow later on, which is unlikely. This has not been revealed to Company B and the in principle agreement means that Company B misses out on the opportunity of negotiating a similar arrangement with a third party because they believe that their arrangement with Company A will work out.[19]

6. Finally, consider the following quotation from a 'chief claims inspector' for a British insurance company. His job is to negotiate and settle personal injury claims (eg motor vehicle accidents and workers' compensation) against the insurance company, and he has the resources and experience to thoroughly investigate each claim and decide what it is worth.[20] This quotation describes his approach to negotiating a settlement in situations where it is obvious to him that the solicitor for the plaintiff does not know as much about the strengths of their own client's case as the chief claims inspector for the defendant does:

> You're going into a discussion to feel your way. After all, if all you're going to do is make an offer, there's no point discussing it anyway. You may as well write him a letter … The object of a discussion is to try and find out whether the judgment which you have formed is a sound one … and you've got to be prepared to modify your own assessment in the light of what you hear (and that can be up or down). It's not uncommon to think, 'Right if I can get out of this at £5,000 I'll think it's good. I don't want to have to pay more than £6–6,500 …' Now, when you get in discussion with a solicitor you find that your case improves – because he hasn't done the depth of work that you've done. He hasn't interviewed the independent witnesses and so doesn't know that the evidence is dead against

19 Based on *Poseidon Ltd v Adelaide Petroleum NL* (1991) 105 ALR 25. See Pengilley, '"But You Can't Do That Anymore!"', 119–20. Consider this issue as an ethical one without regard to whether a court would find that the lawyer had ostensible or actual authority to act in this way.

20 Based on material in Genn, *Hard Bargaining*, 132–3, 163–4. Note that the capacity for individuals to take common law actions for personal injuries is now curtailed in Australia. But this was not true in the UK at the time of this quotation.

you. He hasn't been to see the scene of the accident. And very often you become a bit more optimistic when you get in discussion…You realise that the judgment which you were forming had no need to be as pessimistic as it was. I mean, you're not taking advantage of any situation, you are merely altering your own views that you had previously formed.[21]

Do you agree that this is not 'taking advantage' of the situation? Would you do it?

DISCUSSION QUESTION

1. Research has shown that when there is the likelihood of a future long-term relationship with the other party, negotiators are less likely to believe in using marginally ethical tactics such as many of those set out here.[22] Why do you think this is so? How might the use of each tactic affect the way the parties view each other or carry out their agreement later?

Current Professional Conduct Standards for Lawyers in Negotiation and Mediation

Current professional conduct law contains little that *explicitly* sets out specific standards for lawyers' behaviour in negotiation and ADR processes, although a variety of standards for ADR practitioners (of all backgrounds, not just lawyers) have been proposed.[23] We discuss these proposed conduct standards for negotiation and ADR in the second half of this chapter. Here, however, we briefly consider the extent to which current professional conduct rules already regulate lawyers' behaviour in negotiation and mediation, even though those rules were formulated primarily in relation to litigation.

It is sometimes suggested that tactics such as posturing, strategic misrepresentation, taking advantage of the other side's mistakes or ignorance and even bullying and threats are just part of the 'rules of the game' for *negotiation*, as if negotiation has a different set of ethics to everyday life, or even to court. In fact the law of lawyering as it currently stands assumes that lawyers owe similar obligations of

21 Ibid 133.
22 Rivers, 'What Are They Thinking?', 6.
23 See the sources listed above, n 9.

truthfulness and fairness in negotiations with other parties as they owe in litigation. Thus 'court' is defined in the glossary of the Law Council of Australia's *ASCR* to include 'an arbitration or mediation or any other form of dispute resolution' – a definition that is probably broad enough to include settlement negotiations between the parties. This means that all the rules discussed in Chapter 6 concerning misleading statements to 'the court', client perjury, and the need to have evidence before making serious allegations, apply equally to lawyer behaviour on behalf of clients in all ADR processes and negotiations.

The *ASCR* also include a rule specifically prohibiting practitioners from 'knowingly' making 'a false statement to the opponent in relation to the case (including its compromise)' and requiring practitioners to correct any false statements made as soon as possible (*ASCR* 22.1 and 22.2). Thus the situation in paragraph 2 in the case studies section (where the lawyer lies about client instructions) is certainly a breach of professional conduct standards that could lead to disciplinary action. Many of the tactics described in paragraphs 3 and 4 would also fall foul of the spirit of the *ASCR*, although one can also imagine most lawyers being capable of legalistic arguments for why they should not be construed as having knowingly made a false statement in such circumstances. As with the rules relating to misleading statements in court, however, *ASCR* 22 (making a false statement to the opponent) explicitly provides that it is not making a false statement 'simply' to 'fail to correct an error on any matter stated to the practitioner by the opponent' (*ASCR* 22.3). On this principle, 'taking advantage' of the other side's ignorance of the facts, as in paragraph 6, is not against the rules. (But this does not mean that it is conducive to collaborative problem-solving.)

Furthermore, misleading and deceptive conduct and bullying behaviour in negotiating contracts will generally be contrary to federal and State legislation as well as general principles of contract and tort law. If lawyers knowingly participate in such misbehaviour on the part of their clients, they (as well as their clients) can be liable under general principles of law.[24]

The *ASCR* also include a general provision that 'A solicitor must not take unfair advantage of the obvious error of another solicitor or other person, if to do so would obtain for a client a benefit which has no supportable foundation in law or fact' (*ASCR* 30.1).

The lawyer in the two versions of the scenario in paragraph 1 and the lawyer in the scenario in paragraph 5 might both argue that they have not made a false statement to the other side. They have simply omitted to mention facts and circumstances that might have been relevant. All three scenarios are, however, based on general law cases in which similar behaviour was held to amount to misleading and deceptive conduct.

---

24 Pengilley, '"But You Can't Do That Anymore!"'; Corones, 'Solicitors' Liability'.

Thus many ethically questionable tactics used in negotiation, particularly those that are misleading, are in fact already outlawed under current law and professional conduct standards.

Mediation is essentially a form of assisted negotiation. Therefore the same ethical issues are likely to arise in mediation as in unassisted negotiation, and these same rules will apply to mediation as to negotiation.

It has been observed that some lawyers (and clients) use ADR processes, such as court-ordered mediation, as 'just another stop in the "litigotiation" game', another 'opportunity for the manipulation of rules, time, information and ultimately, money'.[25] As one experienced mediation practitioner in Australia has commented:

> Regrettably, many litigators use ADR as an adversarial tool to gain an advantage in the litigation rather than to resolve it. Such parties unashamedly use ADR as a fishing expedition. It can take many forms. Through the careful use of interrogation (in the nature of cross-examination at a case appraisal) or a question and answer session at a mediation, a party can use the process to weed out weaknesses in an opponent's case. It can be used to test the demeanour or frailty of material witnesses or decision-makers. It can be used for fact-finding and accumulating undisclosed information that may not have been available through interlocutory processes such as discovery or interrogatories. It may be used to test an opponent's susceptibility to admissions or to ascertain how vigorously a point of law will be contested or conceded.[26]
>
> There may be several other reasons why a party would use ADR process for an ulterior purpose. If there is a power imbalance, a financially stronger party may use the process and its accompanying expense for the purpose of draining the funds of a poorer litigant. ADR may be used as a delaying tactic[27] or to 'mask' and contain wider social and political conflicts.[28]

Where court-ordered ADR is being used for ulterior purposes such as these, then the party, and their lawyer, could be subject to sanctions for abuse of process and contempt of court under the same principles as discussed in Chapter 6.[29] Costs sanctions may also be available and, as we saw in Chapter 6, these may also be available against the lawyer, not just the party, where the conduct is the lawyer's fault, or the lawyer was knowingly involved in improper conduct.[30]

---

25 Carrie Menkel-Meadow quoted in Sourdin, *Alternative Dispute Resolution* (Lawbook Co, Sydney, 2nd edn, 2005) 235.

26 Grant Dearlove, 'Court-Ordered ADR: Sanctions for the Recalcitrant Lawyer and Party' (2000) 11 *Australian Dispute Resolution Journal* 12, 14.

27 Ibid 16.

28 Sourdin, *Alternative Dispute Resolution*, 4th edn, 84.

29 ibid.

30 Scott Crabb and Natalie Tatasciore, 'Costs Consequences for Failing to Participate in ADR' (2003) 30 *Brief* 27.

Lawyers as Third Party Mediators and Facilitators of ADR Processes

So far we have considered the ethics and conduct of lawyers as *representatives* of parties in negotiation and mediation. Many lawyers are now also acting as third party *facilitators* of ADR processes, especially as mediators. Mediation can be defined as:

> the process by which the participants, together with the assistance of a neutral person or persons, systematically isolate disputed issues in order to develop options, consider alternatives and endeavour to reach an agreement. The mediator has no advisory or determinative role in regard to the content of the dispute or the outcome of its resolution, but may advise on or determine the process of resolution whereby resolution is attempted. Mediation may be undertaken voluntarily, under a court order, or subject to an existing contractual agreement.[31]

Looking at this definition, it is clear that the role of facilitator of ADR differs greatly from the role of lawyer acting as a representative for a party. Current professional conduct rules are only addressed to lawyers in their representative role. Many current conduct rules will be irrelevant or inappropriate for lawyers acting as mediators or other facilitators of ADR, and new and different ethical principles will be necessary to guide their conduct.

It might not even be possible to lay out one set of ethical principles for ADR facilitators since ADR processes range from those that are purely *facilitative* – 'processes in which a dispute resolution practitioner assists the parties to a dispute to identify the disputed issues, develop options, consider alternatives and endeavour to reach an agreement about some issues of the whole dispute' – through to those that are *advisory* – where 'a dispute resolution practitioner considers and appraises the dispute and provides advice as to the facts of the dispute, the law, and, in some cases, possible or desirable outcomes, and how these may be achieved'.[32] There is also the possibility of arbitration where the dispute resolution practitioner makes a determination, and 'conciliation' which can include advisory elements as well as facilitative ones.

In theory, mediation is generally considered to be a purely facilitative process. But in practice, many lawyer-mediators combine advisory elements with their

---

31 NADRAC, *Dispute Resolution Terms.*
32 Ibid.

mediation role. This may be formalised in 'hybrid' processes such as 'med-arb' where the ADR facilitator first uses mediation, and then arbitration to resolve the dispute.[33] Any set of ethical standards for ADR facilitators will need to cover all these different roles, and even the use of multiple roles within the one process.

To further complicate matters, many ADR practitioners are not lawyers at all. Should lawyer-facilitators of ADR have additional legal professional obligations that non-lawyer facilitators of ADR may not have? Or, when lawyers act as ADR practitioners, do they cease being lawyers (since they are no longer acting within the adversarial paradigm) and therefore stop being bound by lawyer professional conduct rules?

The Commonwealth's National Mediation Accreditation System (NMAS) Practice Standards require that accredited ADR practitioners, whether facilitative, advisory or determinative, aspire to a professional impartiality – that is, that they be known for their sensitivity to possible current or future conflicts of interest; for an obvious detachment; for the need to avoid any unprofessional relationship with one side or the other; and for the respect that they demonstrate towards the parties.[34] NMAS Standard 4 also introduces a concept unknown to the *ASCR*, requiring practitioners '…to recognise power imbalance and issues relating to control and intimidation and take appropriate steps to manage the mediation process accordingly'.[35] In this respect, mediators' professionalism identifies some elements of *responsible lawyering, moral activism* and an *ethic of care,* but not *zealous advocacy.*

A lawyer who represents individual clients in some cases and acts as an ADR facilitator in other cases will eventually be confronted with perceived conflicts of interest. Can a lawyer-mediator or their firm *later* represent one of the parties to a mediation that the lawyer-mediator had facilitated? Who will have access to the previous facilitation file? Can they later act against a party to the mediation? What will one or even both parties think of that lawyer's professionalism if they do so act, and what might those parties do about it?

The NMAS Standards suggest that the combination of representation and mediation roles in the one person will be ethically problematic, but these standards apply to accredited mediators and, significantly, are unlikely to be enforced against lawyers by State law societies or any future national lawyer regulator. What if the lawyer-mediator or their firm has *previously* acted for or against a party to a proposed mediation – can the lawyer-mediator take on the job of facilitating the

---

33 ibid.

34 Sourdin, *Alternative Dispute Resolution*, 4th edn, 83, citing *National Mediators Standards: Practice Standards* (September 2007) s 5, available at Mediator Standards Board on <http://www.msb.org.au/mediator-standards/standards>.

35 NMAS Practice Standards. The Standards set out some key principles which include that a mediator must conduct the dispute resolution process in an impartial manner and adhere to ethical standards of practice, particularly in respecting the confidentiality of the participants.

mediation? The law of lawyering guides lawyers extensively as to what amounts to a conflict of interest in relation to concurrent or successive *representation* of clients by the same lawyer or the same law firm (see Chapter 8). But it does not specifically address the issue of when facilitating resolution of a dispute might conflict a lawyer from acting for or against a party to the mediation. Nor does the law of lawyering address what personal interests, associations, or previous representation of parties on the part of the proposed mediator might prevent that mediator from facilitating resolution of a dispute. It is also conceivable, even predictable, that a litigation lawyer will be so steeped in an adversarial instinct that the alternative mindset of a lawyer-mediator is beyond their competence, and vice versa.

The case studies below illustrate some of the ethical issues that commonly arise for mediators. In the next section of this chapter, we consider what alternative, or new, ethical principles should be applied to mediators, as well as lawyers representing parties in negotiation or mediation.

CASE STUDY 7.2   MEDIATORS' ETHICS

1. Consider again the scenario at paragraph 2 of Case Study 7.1: Ethics in Negotiation, above, where the lawyer lies about their client's instructions. Assume that the mediator is a lawyer and is aware of the truth about the client's instructions because the mediator was present in a private caucus with the lawyer and client immediately beforehand when instructions were discussed. (It is common during mediations for each party and their lawyer to have private meetings with the mediator.) The mediator is also present when the lawyer makes the false statement to the other side. Does the mediator have a duty to do anything about this? (Bear in mind that mediators almost always promise confidentiality to both parties in relation to everything said during the mediation in private caucus or in the presence of the other side.[36]) Should the mediator withdraw? The Law Council of Australia's *Australian Solicitors' Conduct Rule* (*ASCR*) 32.1 permits lawyers to report to the relevant regulatory authorities any misconduct by a practitioner, providing the report is made *bona fide* and it is supportable with evidence: Should the mediator utilise this rule and report the lawyer's breach of professional conduct standards to the disciplinary authorities? Or does the need for the mediator to be impartial, and the confidentiality of the mediation process mean that the mediator should

---

36 Astor and Chinkin, *Dispute Resolution in Australia*, 178–86. Indeed confidentiality of what occurs in mediation is often required under statute or court rules for court-annexed schemes as well as the common law privilege for 'without prejudice' communications.

not report their own judgments of a lawyer's or party's conduct outside of the process?[37]

2. The facilitator of a mediation is an experienced lawyer in the relevant area of practice. The mediator knows that the deal about to be voluntarily concluded at the mediation is much worse for one party than if they took their case to court. This party is either not represented by a lawyer, or, their lawyer seems to be unaware that their client could do better in court. The mediation has been set up as a purely facilitative process. Can or should the mediator advise the parties that the proposed settlement does not fairly represent the way the dispute would be decided in court? Do you think the parties (especially an unrepresented or poorly represented party) might expect a mediator who they know is a lawyer with expertise in the area to give some advice as to the law relating to their matter? Is there anything else the mediator could or should do in this situation?[38]

3. A very senior barrister and mediator is facilitating a mediation between two sisters in relation to a dispute over the multi-million dollar estate of their late mother. Each sister is represented by at least one solicitor and one barrister, and the husband of one sister is also present. One sister is participating via phone and fax from Israel, while the other is present at the mediation in Australia. Because of the time difference, the mediation starts in the middle of the day and continues into the evening. At 8 pm 'in principle' agreement is reached as to the distribution of the assets under dispute. Some of the lawyers present point out that it is late, and knowing that there are still fine details of finances to work out, they would like to go home and work out the final settlement later. The mediator, however, forcefully insists that no one should leave until the agreement is written down by saying: 'You have got to stay, you have got to do the terms of settlement tonight'; 'No, we are doing it now. We are signing up tonight as that is the way that I do it, that's how I conduct mediations'; 'Given the acrimony between the two sisters we must go away with something that is written. It is in the interests of all parties to sign up tonight'. The lawyers interpret this 'as a direction from the mediator about which, effectively, [we] did not have any choice'.

The mediator dictates the terms of settlement and one of the people present writes them down. Later it turns out that no clause has been included making the agreement about the transfer of a bundle of shares from one party to the other

---

37 Interview with James Leach, Ethics Office, Law Institute of Victoria (Melbourne, 8 March 2006).

38 Scenario from Camille Cameron on the basis of her research into the experience of unrepresented litigants: interview with Camille Cameron (Melbourne, 9 March 2006).

subject to advice about the impact of tax. Earlier in the day it had been agreed that such a clause should be included, but it was forgotten in the rush to get the settlement agreement written down at the last minute. In fact the transfer attracts capital gains tax and this substantially alters the financial position between the parties as agreed in the settlement.[39]

Has the mediator done anything wrong? Should the mediator have any ethical responsibility or legal liability to the parties for the missing term in the settlement agreement? Would it make any difference to your answer if one or both of the parties had not been represented by lawyers? Would it make a difference to your answer if the parties had not reached an 'in principle' agreement at 8 pm when people wanted to go home and the mediator insisted that they stay until agreement was reached? For mediators the measure of their 'success' and reputation is whether the disputes they mediate end up with final settlement agreement or not. Future mediation work and funding will often depend on success measured in this way. Is this a conflict of interest?

All three of these case studies raise issues about exactly what the role of the mediator is. It is generally accepted that mediators are responsible for the process of dispute resolution, but not for the outcome. They are supposed to facilitate the process, but not advise the parties, nor prejudice their neutrality and impartiality by judging the parties and issues in dispute in any way, or appearing to do so. However, the line between facilitation and advice, between ensuring parties participate in the process in the way they are supposed to, and taking a role in the outcome of the process, can be difficult to discern in practice. We shall consider these problems in more detail below as we discuss the alternative values that could guide mediators' ethics.

Alternative Values for Negotiation and ADR

What Ethics 'Fit' ADR?

Current professional conduct rules only minimally limit untruthfulness and unfairness. As we have seen, they provide that a lawyer cannot actively and knowingly make a misleading or deceptive statement to the other side in negotiations, or to a third

---

39 Based on the allegations in *Tapoohi v Lewenberg* [2003] VSC 410 (Unreported, Habersberger J, 21 October 2003). See John Wade, 'Liability of Mediators for Pressure, Drafting and Advice: *Tapoohi v Lewenberg*' (2004) 16 *Bond Dispute Resolution News* 12 <www.bond.edu.au/law/centres/drc/newsletter.htm> at 19 March 2006.

party ADR facilitator, just as they cannot do so in litigation. The rules assume that apart from these minimal *limits*, lawyers should be free to act as adversary advocates even in negotiation. They do not give lawyers any *proactive* obligations to act collaboratively in good faith where they are not engaged in adversarial litigation.[40]

On the other hand, many practitioners and theorists argue (and we agree) that the purpose of negotiating a settlement to a dispute is to avoid the adversarialism of a trial in which each side defends a position, and one side's position must win. The advantage of negotiating is that parties can come to a voluntary, mutually agreed resolution in which the interests of both (or multiple) parties in solving the problem efficiently, practically and fairly are recognised and any ongoing relationship (for example, business relationships, neighbours, divorced parents) can be maintained, rather than handing their dispute over to a court that will generally make one party the winner in terms of a financial award, while both parties might be losers when it comes to time, cost, and stress.[41]

For example, Roger Fisher and William Ury's leading model of 'principled negotiation' in their book, *Getting to Yes*, proposes that negotiation should not be a matter of hard bargaining over positions, nor should it consist of soft and gentle offers and concessions with the aim of staying friends. Rather 'principled negotiation' means that parties should separate the people, their egos and emotions from the substantive merits of the problem. They should focus on identifying interests rather than taking positions, consider a variety of possible solutions to the problem that 'advance shared interests and creatively reconcile differing interests' before deciding what to do, and 'insist that the result be based on some objective standard'.[42] It is assumed that although parties have different positions, they are

---

40 Note that recent legislation, eg, the *Civil Procedure Act 2010* (Vic) is impacting on practitioners' obligations to act in good faith immediately prior to the commencement of civil proceedings – see Ch 6 above. Note also that in some cases the parties (and their lawyers) may have a legal obligation to participate in court-ordered mediation or mediation that is required as a term of a contract in good faith. But it is currently uncertain to what extent the courts are able to enforce this obligation, whether it has any precise legal meaning, and if so if it requires lawyers and parties to take pro-active steps or whether it only provides sanctions for actions that unequivocally demonstrate bad faith. See Sourdin, *Alternative Dispute Resolution*, 4th edn, Ch 8; David Spencer and Tom Altobelli, *Dispute Resolution in Australia: Cases, Commentary and Materials* (Lawbook Co, Pyrmont, NSW, 2005) 489; and the discussion of *Gannon v Turner* (Unreported, District Court of Brisbane, Ford DCJ, 28 February 1997) cited in Dearlove, 'Court-Ordered ADR', 14–15.

41 See, eg, Roger Fisher, William Ury and Bruce Patton, *Getting to Yes: Negotiating Agreement Without Giving In* (Penguin Books, New York, 2nd edn, 1991); Carrie Menkel-Meadow, 'Whose Dispute Is It Anyway? A Philosophical and Democratic Defense of Settlement (In Some Cases)' (1995) 83 *Georgetown Law Journal* 2663; Jennifer J Llewellyn, 'Dealing with the Legacy of Native Residential School Abuse in Canada: Litigation, ADR, and Restorative Justice' (2002) 52 *University of Toronto Law Journal* 253.

42 Fisher, Ury and Patton, *Getting to Yes*, 10–11.

also likely to share some common interests, and if they explore these they are likely to be able to develop options and solutions that benefit all parties.

Similarly, Carrie Menkel-Meadow, one of the most influential and prolific writers on lawyers' practices and ethics in relation to ADR, argues that negotiation should be a process in which the parties can choose how they want their dispute resolved, with the possibility of a broad range of possible solutions that may be more responsive to their needs and take into account a wide range of principles outside of legal principles. She argues that ideally it 'can be defended as being participatory, democratic, empowering, educative, and transformative for the parties'.[43] There is certainly evidence that going through litigation can have ill effects on people's health and mental state, and that people who resolve their disputes on the basis of a negotiated agreement are more likely to be satisfied with the resolution they have achieved, and to feel that they have achieved their objectives than those who go to court.[44] There is also evidence that truthful, open negotiating behaviour can spur others to act similarly, making collaborative negotiation possible.[45]

Many ADR processes, including mediation, are aimed at facilitating this vision of principled, collaborative or problem-solving negotiation. The mediator or ADR facilitator is supposed to help the parties identify their interests and to see the problem from the other side's point of view and work together to identify options and creative solutions. The policy statements and contracts governing many ADR processes usually explicitly state that it is expected that the parties and their lawyers will enter into the process in a 'good faith' effort to work together to identify interests and options and resolve their dispute.[46] Even court rules and court decisions requiring court mediation as part of the pre-litigation process recognise that the object of mediation is that the parties should 'communicate effectively with each other about the dispute' in an 'endeavour to resolve their differences'.[47] Or in the memorable words of Justice Gray to the litigants in one case, 'you can go and make love before you make war'.[48]

---

43 Menkel-Meadow, 'Whose Dispute Is It Anyway?', 2693.
44 On the physical and mental stress effects of litigation, see Brent K Marshall, J Steven Picou and Jan R Schlichtmann, 'Technological Disasters, Litigation Stress, and the Use of Alternative Dispute Resolution Mechanisms' (2004) 26 *Law & Policy* 289; Genn, *Paths to Justice*, 194.
45 See Rivers, 'What Are They Thinking?'; Michelle Wills, 'The Negotiator's Ethical and Economic Dilemma: To Lie, or Not to Lie' 2001 (12) *Australian Dispute Resolution Journal* 48, 54.
46 David Spencer, 'Requiring Good Faith Negotiation' (1998) 1 *ADR Bulletin* 37; Spencer and Altobelli, 'Dispute Resolution in Australia', 485–93.
47 *Australian Competition & Consumer Commission v Lux Pty Ltd* [2001] FCA 600 (Unreported, Nicholson J, 24 May 2001) [26], [28]. See also Hunter, Cameron and Henning, *Litigation I: Civil Procedure*, 48–56.
48 Transcript of Proceedings, *Australian Competition & Consumer Commission v Cadbury Schweppes Pty Ltd* (Federal Court of Australia, Gray J, 22 April 2002). See also Hunter, Cameron and Henning, *Litigation I: Civil Procedure*, 51.

We might therefore expect that where parties are using negotiation or ADR to resolve their dispute, their relationship should be more open and collaborative than in litigation. The ethical standards that apply to their conduct (and that of their lawyer representatives) ought to reflect this. *Ethics of care* type values, such as good faith, fair dealing and open disclosure, are likely to be more appropriate than the conventional combination of *adversarial advocacy* and *responsible lawyering* reflected in the professional conduct standards.[49] In other words problem-solving negotiation and mediation assume certain standards of behaviour to achieve their purposes, and these standards will be different to those that apply in litigation. This will be more important the more explicit the goals of collaborative problem-solving are in the negotiation or the ADR process. It is also more important for lawyers acting as third-party facilitators of the negotiation or mediation to promote these values than it is for lawyers who are acting as representatives for the parties.

Carrie Menkel-Meadow has suggested that any ethical rules applying to lawyers' conduct in ADR (as representatives or facilitators) should reflect five generally accepted underlying goals of ADR.[50] These goals are different to and complementary to adversarial litigation:

1. 'Party consent' – 'outcomes should not be coerced' and 'parties should be given a fair chance to make their own choices';

2. 'Democratic participation (of clients vis-à-vis lawyers and multiple parties when disputes involve more than two dyadic players)' – parties should be given a fair opportunity to participate in their own dispute resolution, and third parties should be neutral and show no partisanship;

3. 'Responsive and particularized solutions to legal disputes and transactions, which do no worse harm to the parties (or other parties) than non-resolution of the dispute';

4. 'An orientation to joint, not individualized, problem-solving'; and

5. '"Problem-solving," rather than "adversarial" orientation to legal disputes and transactions'.

These principles reflect the ideal of ADR as an equitable process where people communicate freely, understand each other, settle differences and perhaps even

---

49 Carrie Menkel-Meadow, 'The Limits of Adversarial Ethics' in Deborah L Rhode (ed), *Ethics in Practice: Lawyers' Roles, Responsibilities, and Regulation* (Oxford University Press, New York, 2002) 123; Wills, 'The Use of Deception in Negotiations'.

50 Carrie Menkel-Meadow, 'Ethics in Alternative Dispute Resolution: New Issues, No Answers from the Adversary Conception of Lawyers' Responsibilities' (2004) 38 *South Texas Law Review* 407, 453.

change their behaviour rather than have a judgment (usually financial damages) imposed on them in the alien, adversarial setting of the court.[51]

In the following two subsections we consider what this might mean for lawyers acting as representatives of parties in mediation or in negotiation, and lawyers acting as mediators. As we have seen, the Commonwealth Government's NMAS Standards apply to accredited mediators. Some ethical standards have also been proposed for lawyers and other ADR practitioners in these roles – most significantly the National Alternative Dispute Resolution Advisory Council's (NADRAC) proposed 'framework' for ethics standards for ADR practitioners[52] and the Law Council of Australia's best practice model entitled *Ethical Standards for Mediators*.[53] We shall use these as our starting point. In the final subsection we consider what role if any (*moral activist*) concerns about harm to third parties and public interests ought to have in ethics standards for ADR and private negotiations.

What Ethics Are Appropriate for Lawyers as Representatives of Parties in Negotiation and ADR?

One outcome of the Australian Law Reform Commission's inquiry into adversarialism, ADR and the federal civil justice system was that lawyers' professional conduct rules were changed to make it clear that solicitors have a duty to inform the client about 'the alternatives to fully contested adjudication of the case which are reasonably available' (*ASCR* 7.2). The existing principles of lawyers' duties to act in the interests of their clients mean that this obligation should go further than this anyway. Lawyers should thoroughly assess with their clients what dispute resolution option is likely to best suit the client's needs and circumstances. An astute lawyer knows that a focus on cost-effective outcomes is the only way to keep clients over the long term. However, the adversarial mindset (discussed in

---

51 Christine Parker, *Just Lawyers: Regulation and Access to Justice* (Oxford University Press, Oxford, 1999) 36–8, 60–1; Genn, *Paths to Justice*, 225 (on the anxiety and stress people feel on 'entering the alien world of the court').

52 NADRAC, *A Framework for ADR Standards*, 110–14, April 2001. The ethical issues covered by the framework are: promoting services accurately; ensuring effective participation by parties; eliciting information; managing continuation or termination of the process; exhibiting lack of bias; maintaining impartiality; maintaining confidentiality; and ensuring appropriate outcomes (with particular reference to statutory and other frameworks).

53 Law Council of Australia, *Ethical Standards for Mediators*.

Chapter 6) means that lawyers do not always naturally think about the possibility that non-adversarial dispute resolution might suit their clients better than litigation.

Lawyers should also help clients to prevent disputes arising in the first place. As the Law Council of Australia has suggested in its *Policy on ADR*, '… they should assist their clients who are about to enter upon commercial or other relationships to put in place, whenever appropriate, machinery which is aimed at preventing disputes from arising and, where disputes nevertheless do arise, to procure resolution of them as soon as possible otherwise than by litigation'.[54] Such 'machinery' could include setting up ADR processes at the beginning of major projects even before any disputes have arisen (eg 'project alliancing'[55]), including mediation or arbitration clauses in contracts and, for organisational clients, setting up internal dispute-resolution schemes and joining up to external complaints resolution and ombudsman schemes.

Each of these obligations is broadly consistent with the *adversarial advocacy* emphasis on the paramount duty to the client. But instead of assuming that the client's interests are always likely to be furthered by advocacy in the adversarial system, these obligations require lawyers to help clients consider their broader *ethics of care* concerns to prevent disputes arising in the first place, and to resolve them in a way that does less damage to themselves and to their relationship with the other party.

Once a client's matter does actually proceed to negotiation or ADR, the appropriate ethics for the process should relate to the purpose of the process. A lawyer's role in ADR is not to aggressively represent the client's position. It is to assist the client in working with the other side to attempt to solve their problem through open (fair and honest), interest-based (based on interests and principle, not on adversarial positions) negotiation. Our concern in this book is with the ethics of lawyers – but when it comes to collaborative negotiation and, especially, ADR processes, one of the main purposes of these processes is to allow the parties (clients) to participate directly in resolving their own disputes. This means that it is the ethics and conduct of the parties that is more important in many ways than the ethics and conduct of their lawyers. Indeed many ADR processes stipulate that parties may not be represented by lawyers at all. Where parties are represented, it is a very important part of a lawyer's role to explain to their clients how the ADR process will work, what their obligations are in that process and to prime them to participate effectively.[56]

---

54 Law Council of Australia, *Law Council Policy on Alternative Dispute Resolution* (1989) <www.lawcouncil.asn.au/shadomx/apps/fms/fmsdownload.cfm?file_uuid=239B985C-1E4F-17FA-D2E4-8BCF725655D8&siteName=lca> at 29 January 2013.

55 Greg Rooney, 'Mediation and the Rise of Relationship Contracting – A Decade of Change for Lawyers' (2002) 22(6) *Proctor* 18.

56 See the Law Society of New South Wales, *Law Society Guidelines*, '2. Professional Standards for Legal Representatives in Mediation' for a helpful guide as to what the lawyer's role in preparing a client for mediation involves.

During mediation and other collaborative negotiation or ADR processes, it is the duty of the lawyer, as the Law Society of New South Wales suggests, 'To participate in a non-adversarial manner... A legal adviser who does not understand and observe this is a direct impediment to the mediation process'.[57] Indeed in order to make the mediation and collaborative negotiation processes work as intended, lawyers (and parties) would need to have pro-active obligations to co-operate with one another. Thus leading US legal ethicist Robert Gordon has suggested the following standard for lawyers' ethics in conducting settlement negotiations:[58]

(A)   A lawyer shall at all times act in good faith and with the primary objective of resolving the dispute without court proceedings;

(B)   A lawyer shall not

    a.   Knowingly make any statement that contains a misrepresentation of material fact or law or that omits a fact necessary to make the statement considered as a whole not materially misleading;

    b.   Knowingly fail to

        i.   Disclose to opposing counsel such material facts or law as may be necessary to correct manifest misapprehensions thereof; or, alternatively,

        ii.   Give reasonable indication to opposing counsel of the possible inaccuracy of a given material fact or law upon which opposing counsel appears to rely. Such indication may take the form of statements of unwillingness to discuss a particular matter raised by opposing counsel.

The first part gives a different role to the lawyer than the conventional one of zealous *adversarial advocacy*. The second part gives lawyers more pro-active obligations to avoid misleading and deceptive conduct than the rules that apply in litigation (discussed above). They give lawyers an obligation to actually disclose facts to correct mistakes or ignorance on the other side, or at least refuse to take advantage of mistakes or ignorance of the other side. It certainly makes sense for the parties, and their lawyers, to take a fair and truthful approach to negotiation so that the parties can trust each other and co-operate to strike a bargain. As Wills puts it, 'If a negotiator's opening gambit to a fellow negotiator was, "I wish to make it clear that it is accepted that we will both lie to each other in the course of these negotiations", how many people would continue to do business on this footing?'[59]

57 Ibid.
58 Robert Gordon, 'Private Settlement as Alternative Adjudication: A Rationale for Negotiation Ethics' (1985) 18 *University of Michigan Journal of Law Reform* 503, 530.
59 Wills, 'The Negotiator's Ethical and Economic Dilemma', 48–9.

It is also likely to be good for the long-term reputation of both the lawyer and their client, and the maintenance of a good relationship with the other side, if parties and their lawyers engage honestly and fairly in negotiation.

If we expect lawyers (and parties) to co-operate with one another, this will also have implications for other aspects of lawyers' professional conduct obligations. Firstly, conventional lawyer-client confidentiality and privilege rules assume that every client has an interest in keeping many aspects of their case confidential. In mediation, however, the parties are encouraged and expected to 'lay bare their souls' and their cases to the other side. Disclosing documents and facts to the other side, and making admissions, could mean that confidentiality in any such admissions, statements and documents would be lost, and that the other side could use them in any subsequent litigation. This creates a problem for lawyers deciding how to advise their clients to behave in mediation or negotiation. On the one hand, they might feel that they should advise clients to keep as much confidential as possible to preserve their rights in any later litigation. On the other hand, lawyers might realise it is more conducive to a negotiated resolution to disclose certain confidential information, and advise their clients accordingly. In order to encourage parties to feel free to be open and honest in mediation, everything said and revealed in mediations (and many other ADR processes) is usually subject to confidentiality under the terms of the contract setting up the mediation and, for court-annexed schemes, the legislation or court rules under which the mediation takes place. Similarly there is a common law privilege for 'without prejudice' communications made in the course of genuine settlement negotiations that prevents them from later being disclosed. But the exact limits of these protections of confidentiality are not clear.[60] For example, will a lawyer be bound to keep confidential information which suggests that child abuse has occurred or will occur, or that an adult is at risk of serious assault?[61]

Moreover, there are further problems if parties attempt to settle a matter at negotiation or mediation, fail to reach a resolution and then proceed to litigation. How can a lawyer who has tried to genuinely work together with the other side on behalf of their client and who has heard and seen much confidential information subsequently act for their client against the other side?[62] Similarly, how can a

---

60 See discussion accompanying n 31 above and also n 93 below.

61 The NMAS Practice Standard 6 'Confidentiality' defers to the *ASCR* and permits disclosure where the mediator is '(6.1(c))... required to do so by law; or (d) where permitted by existing ethical guidelines or requirements and the information discloses an actual or potential threat to human life or safety.' Sourdin deals extensively with these mediator issues, particularly for family lawyers, in *Alternative Dispute Resolution*, 4th edn, Ch 12.

62 It may even be possible for a party to mediation to prevent lawyers who had acted for the other side in that mediation from acting against them in a future case on the basis that the lawyers had been privy to confidential information from the other side: *Williamson v Schmidt* [1998] 2 Qd R 317; *Carter Holt Harvey Forests Ltd v Sunnex Logging Ltd* [2001] 3 NZLR 343.

lawyer be required to help a client come to a resolution with the other side, with one of the principles of the negotiation being that they will work towards their joint interests and 'do no worse harm to the parties (or other parties) than non-resolution of the dispute' (as suggested by Menkel-Meadow in the quotation above), but also keep an eye on the possibility that there might be litigation in the future where that lawyer will need to act as an *adversarial advocate* for their client against the other side? Some of these conflicts may be so intractable that, in tune with the *ethics of care*, the only ethical practice is for the lawyer who unsuccessfully represents a client in an ADR to withdraw from subsequent litigation.

The candour and co-operation required in collaborative negotiation do not fit well with traditional adversarial roles and ethical expectations governing lawyers. Therefore groups of lawyers who are interested in taking a more collaborative, problem-solving approach to practice have developed various alternative methods and ethical expectations for lawyering. One of these alternatives is 'collaborative law'. It was started in the United States, but has now spread to Australia, where it is becoming popular with family law specialists.[63] Collaborative law is one way in which practitioners who want to act according to *ethics of care* values have tried to specify what this might mean in practice by setting out a precise protocol for how they should behave. In the case study below we evaluate these alternative ethics.

CASE STUDY 7.3   COLLABORATIVE LAW

Consider the following description of 'collaborative law' from a leader of the collaborative law movement in the US:

> Collaborative law consists of two clients and two attorneys, working together toward the sole goals of reaching an efficient, fair, comprehensive settlement of all issues. Each party selects independent collaborative counsel. Each lawyer's retainer agreement specifies that the lawyer is retained solely to assist the client in reaching a fair agreement and that under no circumstances will the lawyer represent the client if the matter goes to court. If the process fails to reach agreement and either party then wishes to have matters resolved in court, both collaborative attorneys are disqualified from further representation. They assist in the orderly transfer of

---

63 Mary Rose Liverani, 'Collaborative Law Practice Shaping Up as the Primary Dispute Resolution Mode' (2004) 42 *Law Society Journal* 24; Marilyn Scott, 'Collaborative Law: A New Role for Lawyers' (2004) 15 *Australian Dispute Resolution Journal* 207; Pauline Tesler, 'Collaborative Law: What It Is and Why Family Law Attorneys Need to Know About It' (1999) 13 *American Journal of Family Law* 215.

the case to adversarial counsel. Experts are brought into the collaborative process as needed, but only as neutrals, jointly retained by both parties. They, too, are disqualified from continuing work and cannot assist either party if the matter goes to court. The process involves binding commitments to disclose voluntarily all relevant information, to proceed respectfully and in good faith, and to refrain from any threat of litigation during the collaborative process … The process moves forward via carefully managed four-way [ie two lawyers and two clients] settlement meetings …[64]

One key feature of collaborative law is the agreement that the lawyers will withdraw from the case if the process breaks down and does not achieve resolution. This gives lawyers a powerful incentive to 'find a good solution for the other party's legitimate needs that is also acceptable to my client'.[65] In traditional practice, if lawyers fail to help their clients negotiate a settlement, they just go on to represent their client in court – charging the appropriate fees.

The second important feature of collaborative law is the promise to negotiate in good faith and voluntarily share information. In some protocols for collaborative law in Australia this has been spelt out to mean that lawyers are required to point out to the other side any mistakes they have made, or matters they have overlooked, rather than taking advantage of mistakes or ignorance.

DISCUSSION QUESTIONS

1. How do the two key features of collaborative law described above fit with traditional conceptions of the lawyer as *adversarial advocate* and traditional professional conduct rules? How does it change the conventional expectations of whose interests lawyers should be considering? How does it change the relationship between the lawyer and their own client?

2. The disqualification requirement in collaborative law is not only useful as an incentive to lawyers to come up with creative solutions to settle the parties' dispute. It also avoids some ethical problems of protection of confidential information and, possibly, conflicts of interest, where lawyers act co-operatively to try to resolve a problem but know that adversarial litigation is still a possibility. How does it do that?

64 Tesler, 'Collaborative Law: What It Is', 219.
65 Ibid 221.

3. What are the disadvantages of the collaborative practice protocols? What complaints might a client have if their lawyer is acting as a collaborative lawyer?[66] How would each of the four different ethical approaches – *adversarial advocacy, responsible lawyering, moral activism* and *ethics of care* – evaluate the practice of collaborative law? Would each see it as ethically justified? Why?

Lawyers' awareness of the potential of mediation and negotiation in a collaborative law setting has steadily widened so that the term now used is 'collaborative practice'.[67] Increasingly, lawyers with an *ethic of care* preference are recognising that the collaborative model can apply well beyond family law – and that they can still earn a significant income without propelling their clients into litigation.[68] Such lawyers see that, provided their clients are willing to share confidential information and agree to their lawyers' withdrawal if the collaborative mediation and negotiation is unsuccessful, then both clients' and lawyers' interests are advanced without significant conflicts of interest developing.

Attempts to mediate disputes involving, for example, employment law, medical negligence and some types of commercial disputes are all slowly expanding as more lawyers recognise these realities.[69] Civil and commercial lawyers can actively care for their clients using a collaborative practice model without being seen as 'soft' or litigation averse by their peers. Significantly, the confidential information that clients must share in a collaborative approach will often be disclosed later on in any event, if the dispute continues to litigation (with new lawyers) under the 'overarching obligation' regime now increasingly required in Australian civil litigation (see Chapter 6 above). The Law Council of Australia considers there is so much potential in collaborative practice that it has issued ethical guidelines for those who seek to work as collaborative lawyers.[70] These guidelines substantially repeat the cautions given to mediators generally about abuse of power and the need for impartiality among collaborative lawyers.[71]

---

66 See John Lande, 'Possibilities for Collaborative Law: Ethics and Practice of Lawyer Disqualification and Process Control in a New Model of Lawyering' (2003) 64 *Ohio State Law Journal* 1315; John Lande, 'The Promise and Perils of Collaborative Law' (2005) 12 *Dispute Resolution Magazine* 29; Julie Macfarlane, *The Emerging Phenomenon of Collaborative Family Law (CFL): A Qualitative Study of CFL Cases* (Department of Justice, Canada, 2005) <www.justice.gc.ca/en/ps/pad/reports/2005-FCY-1/index.html> at 26 July 2006.
67 Sourdin, *Alternative Dispute Resolution*, 4th edn, 103.
68 Ibid.
69 See generally Sourdin, *Alternative Dispute Resolution*, 4th edn, Ch 4.
70 Law Council of Australia, *Australian Collaborative Practice Guidelines for Lawyers* (Law Council of Australia Ltd, Canberra, March 2011); See <www.lawcouncil.asn.au/shadomx/apps/fms/fmsdownload.cfm?file_uuid=48054DBF-0CDC-95F8-9F3D-6B645E96D004&siteName=lca> accessed 30 January 2013.
71 Law Council of Australia, *Australian Collaborative Practice Guidelines for Lawyers*, Guidelines 18–25.

What Ethics Are Appropriate for Lawyers Acting as Mediators (ADR Facilitators)?[72]

A mediator's role is to be a neutral facilitator of collaborative, interest-based negotiation between the parties to resolve their dispute. Neutrality and impartiality of the mediator towards the parties is crucial. It is usually suggested that mediators who cannot be impartial should withdraw from the mediation process.[73] Some might suggest that a lawyer whose main work is in litigation should not also attempt the very different role of mediation. At the very least, lawyers ought to be aware of the different mindsets appropriate to the two different settings and identify their own dominant value approach before choosing to act in either litigation or ADR.

At the minimum, mediators should be free of any association with either party, or their case, that could mean they have an interest in the way the dispute is resolved. The relevant principles should be similar to those concerning how an *adversarial advocate* lawyer should handle any conflict of interest that might interfere with them zealously advocating on behalf of a client. But the objective is different – the purpose is to ensure that the mediator is free of any interest that could impact on being completely neutral towards *either* party's case (like a judge), whereas for conventional lawyering the objective is that they should be free of any interests except the need to zealously represent their *own client*. Thus NADRAC suggests in its framework standards for ADR practitioners:

> ADR practitioners need to demonstrate independence and lack of personal interest in the outcome, so that they approach the subject matter of the dispute with an open mind, free of preconceptions or predisposition towards either of the parties. The importance of exhibiting lack of bias is that the parties can be satisfied that they can trust the ADR practitioner to conduct the process fairly. This has usually been referred to as a requirement of neutrality. In NADRAC's view neutrality requires that the ADR practitioner disclose to all parties: any existing or prior relationship or contact between the ADR practitioner and any party; any interest in the outcome of the particular dispute; the basis for the calculation of all fees and benefits accruable to the practitioner; any likelihood of present or future conflicts of interest; personal values, experience or knowledge of the ADR practitioner which

---

72 For an excellent account of ethical issues in mediation practice, see Astor and Chinkin, *Dispute Resolution in Australia*, 224–31.

73 See for example Principle 2 ('Impartiality') of the Law Council of Australia, *Ethical Standards for Mediators*.

might substantially affect their capacity to act impartially, given the nature of the subject matter and the characteristics of the parties.[74]

As with the general law on conflicts of interest, these principles recognise that full disclosure to the parties and their consent can 'cure' conflicts of interest so that the mediator is free to continue to act. It also recognises the possibility of future conflicts – if the mediator, or their firm, might act for one of the parties in the future, this is a potential conflict of interest that would detract from the mediator's neutrality. For that reason, some commentators have suggested that mediators, and their firms, should not act for parties to any mediation in the future in relation to similar issues, or there should at least be a certain period of time (eg five years) before the mediator or their firm can do so.[75] Note also that the 'basis for calculation of fees and benefits' for the mediator is a matter that should be disclosed because it could lead to conflicts of interest. If, for example, the mediator's fee depends on the success of the mediation, this ought to be disclosed because this makes it more likely the mediator might pressure parties into a false harmony.[76]

There will almost certainly be a range of minor, and perhaps not so minor, factors that arise as the mediation progresses that potentially make a mediator less than completely neutral in their attitude to the parties, whether it is personal dislike of the way a party presents themselves, or deep-rooted values and assumptions that affect their opinion about the rights and wrongs of the parties' cases.[77] The mediation process, however, requires that the mediator conduct the whole process 'in a fair and even-handed way'. They should 'generally treat the parties equally', for example by 'spending approximately the same time hearing each party's statement or approximately the same time in separate sessions' and 'ensure that they do not communicate noticeably different degrees of warmth, friendliness or acceptance when dealing with individual parties'.[78] This is likely to require considerable self-awareness, as well as training and practice. Indeed discussion of the appropriate *ethics* of mediators often shades into discussion as to the character, skills and techniques that mediators should have.

---

74 NADRAC, *A Framework for ADR Standards*, 112. See also Law Council of Australia, *Ethical Standards for Mediators*, Principle 3 ('Conflicts of Interest').

75 See Menkel-Meadow, 'Ethics in Alternative Dispute Resolution', 432–41. Note that the commentary to Principle 3 of the LCA's *Ethical Standards for Mediators* says that 'The mediator should not establish a professional relationship with one of the parties in relation to the same dispute': Law Council of Australia, *Ethical Standards for Mediators*.

76 Also the commentary to Principle 6 ('Quality of the Process') of the LCA's *Ethical Standards for Mediators* says that 'A mediator's conduct should not be influenced by a desire to achieve a high settlement rate': Law Council of Australia, *Ethical Standards for Mediators*.

77 See Astor and Chinkin, *Dispute Resolution in Australia*, 228. Note that the NADRAC principle quoted in the text above suggests that the ADR practitioner should disclose any 'personal values, knowledge or experience' that might affect their capacity to act impartially.

78 NADRAC, *A Framework for ADR Standards*, 113.

It is part of the purely facilitative, impartial role of the mediator as a neutral third party that they are not to advise the parties on the content of the dispute. Thus the Law Council of Australia's *Ethical Standards for Mediators* states that:

> Even if all the disputants agree that they would like the mediator to express an opinion on the merits, there is a substantial risk in giving such an opinion that the mediator may no longer appear to be impartial. As a result the mediator may be obliged to withdraw.[79]

The reason for this is that mediation is intended to be a process in which the parties come up with their own solution to their own problem. ADR facilitators are supposed to facilitate parties reaching a voluntary agreement. They are not to advise or guide the parties towards any outcome.

But what capacity or obligation does this imperative impose on mediators to correct any unfairness they observe in the way the parties negotiate with one another, and the outcome by which they resolve their dispute?[80] The case studies on mediators' ethics above included situations where one party was not represented, or was poorly represented, and therefore did not understand their own legal rights sufficiently, and also where the mediator was aware that one side's lawyer was lying in the mediation. Negotiations in a mediation process might also be unfair where there is a power imbalance between the parties, for example, husband and wife where there has been domestic violence; or business and individual consumer where the allegations concern the business taking advantage of a disability on the part of the consumer; or where one side is seeking to abuse the mediation process to cause the other side additional expense or get a foretaste of the other side's evidence, and has no intention to resolve the dispute. Even where there is no specific unfairness or power imbalance, there is always the constant danger that one or both of the parties will simply feel pressured into coming to a 'voluntary' resolution of their dispute, despite misgivings, in order to avoid trial and further conflict.

The mediator may also become aware of unfairness to third parties or the public interest. For example, two parents might agree to shared parenting arrangements in circumstances where one has admitted during mediation to physical or sexual abuse of the children in the past. Or an aspect of the arrangements agreed in a commercial dispute might amount to illegal conduct: for example, backdating a document to avoid stamp duty, or making part of the settlement payment in cash to avoid income tax. Someone who has been injured by a faulty product might agree

---

79 Law Council of Australia, *Ethical Standards for Mediators*, commentary on Principle 2 ('Impartiality').
80 See Astor and Chinkin, *Dispute Resolution in Australia*, 229–31.

not to warn anyone else of the danger in return for a larger settlement amount (see also Case Study 7.4 on the Cape asbestos settlement on page 236).

Consistent with the mediator's role in facilitating party participation, ADR practitioners and commentators generally suggest that it is the mediator's role to do what they can to ensure the integrity of the process, but not to interfere in the outcome. It is clear that a large part of the mediator's role will often be educating the parties as to what the process requires of them and guiding them through the steps of a collaborative interest-based negotiation. Thus:

- It is the mediator's responsibility to ensure as much as possible that the parties are entering into a voluntary agreement, for example by giving parties the opportunity and recommendation to seek independent advice before signing any agreement.
- Mediators should also have a responsibility to notice whether parties are participating freely, equally and in good faith in the negotiation process.
- They should make suggestions as to how the mediation *process* should unfold in order to address any inequality or unfairness they have noticed, and prevent it tinging the outcome.
- The mediator's ordinary role of suggesting and facilitating processes such as private caucuses, reality testing, identifying interests and generating options should also help to even out less substantial power imbalances and engage reluctant parties in good faith negotiation.[81]

Where power imbalances and inequalities are more entrenched, the mediator should have the responsibility to make more substantial suggestions about changes to the process. The NADRAC *Framework for ADR Standards* suggests that where issues arise:

- The mediator 'may then consider' including an interpreter, support person, adviser, or representative in the process to even up any power imbalance; or
- Enabling the provision of technical assistance, information or expert advice to even up any knowledge and expertise imbalance.[82]

Thus the mediator would have the responsibility to recommend that the parties expand the number and range of people participating in the process in order to make sure that the parties have adequate support to participate effectively.

Other ethicists and commentators have gone even further and suggested that mediators (and facilitators of other ADR processes) have a responsibility to make sure that all the parties who have an interest in a particular dispute should be present (or represented) in any ADR process, so that the issues can be comprehensively

---

81 Dearlove, 'Court-Ordered ADR', 17.
82 NADRAC, *A Framework for ADR Standards*, 110–11.

settled.[83] For example, consider the situation where one victim of child sexual abuse by a teacher in a church school sues the church, and it is known that many other children were abused as well. If the school wants to resolve the matter without litigation, then the ADR process should include any other victims that could be identified, rather than leaving each one to negotiate or sue individually without knowing what has happened in the other cases.[84] This partially addresses the possibility of negotiated resolutions creating unfairness or harm to third parties by making sure that third parties who have an interest in the way the dispute is resolved participate in its resolution. There are also more practical reasons for including third parties who have an interest in the dispute resolution process since it means that any solution agreed to is likely to be more sustainable in the long term, because people who participated in negotiating the solution are less likely to challenge it.

In cases where it is impossible to address problems of power imbalance, lack of good faith by the parties, or structural inequality within the mediation process, where the parties refuse to follow the mediator's lead on process issues, or where the parties simply cannot communicate effectively (perhaps because one party is not physically present), it is generally accepted that the mediator's ethical responsibility is to terminate the process and withdraw.[85] If the problem, and the fact that it cannot be remedied, is evident beforehand, the mediator could and should refuse to take on the mediation in the first place. The mediator's duty is to ensure integrity of the mediation process, so where integrity cannot be ensured, termination of that process seems an appropriate response.

The standard view of ADR practitioners and commentators is that the mediator cannot, however, suggest a different *resolution* to that which the parties come up with.[86] Nor can the mediator *breach confidentiality* by reporting party or lawyer misconduct to regulatory authorities, or by blowing the whistle on any illegal or unethical aspects of agreements reached in mediation, unless there is a law

---

83 Making sure that all those affected by a dispute or crime are present when the matter is discussed in 'conferences' is a hallmark of the 'restorative justice' approach to diversionary conferencing in the criminal justice system and other disputes. See Braithwaite, *Restorative Justice*.

84 Example based on Llewellyn, 'Dealing with the Legacy'.

85 Dearlove, 'Court-Ordered ADR', 18; Law Council of Australia, *Ethical Standards for Mediators*, Principle 7: 'A mediator may terminate the mediation if the mediator considers that: (i) any party is abusing the process; or (ii) there is no reasonable prospect of settlement'.

86 The Law Council of Australia's *Ethical Standards for Mediators* also recommends that '[t]he mediator ought to be cautious about direct involvement in drafting the terms of agreement, as their involvement in drafting may be construed as providing legal advice': Law Council of Australia, *Ethical Standards for Mediators* commentary to Principle 8 'Recording Settlement'.

specifically authorising such disclosure.[87] The rationale is that if parties and their lawyers believe that mediators are judging their conduct with a view to reporting any ethical misconduct or illegality afterwards, this would destroy their trust in the impartiality of the process.[88] Thus the mediator's role is to protect the ADR *process* and its integrity, but not to worry about any *substantive* illegality or injustice as seen by criteria external to that process, unless a law clearly requires them to do so. This raises the issue of the role, if any, of considerations of public interest, potential harm to third parties, and legality in negotiated resolutions to disputes that could otherwise have been litigated. These issues can be equally significant for lawyers representing parties in ADR and indeed in negotiations not assisted by a third-party neutral. We consider these issues in the next, and final, subsection of this chapter.

Protecting Third Parties and the Public Interest in Negotiated Settlements and ADR?

While collaborative negotiation and ADR are put forward as means for people to resolve their disputes to meet their own needs in their own way, critics argue that they are just as likely to perpetuate the domination and oppression of everyday life as they are to empower disputants to participate in resolving their own problems. Inappropriate mediation in family law and domestic violence can return disputes to families already imbued with imbalances of power between men and women, give unaccountable power to mediation professionals, and detour women away from enforceable decisions of courts. Consumer complaint schemes in a bank or phone company can send pacified customers away unaware that their problem confronts thousands of others who may or may not complain, and leave exploitative company policies untouched. Internal dispute resolution in a workplace can change issues of institutional bias and discrimination into individual management problems for particular work areas to deal with.[89]

We have seen above that collaborative negotiation and mediation require lawyers representing parties, and especially those acting as mediators, to be centrally

---

87 Dearlove, 'Court-Ordered ADR', 18–19. Note that mediators employed by the Family Court of Australia have a legislative obligation to report suspected child abuse: see Astor and Chinkin, *Dispute Resolution in Australia*, 182–3.

88 See Law Council of Australia, *Ethical Standards for Mediators*, commentary to Principle 5.

89 C Parker, *Just Lawyers*, 61–3; Genn, *Paths to Justice*.

concerned with doing what they can to ensure that *processes* of negotiation are open, honest, fair and co-operative.[90] Should lawyers and ADR facilitators also be concerned about whether the *outcomes* decided in ADR processes are fair as between the parties, and whether the interests of third parties and the public interest are appropriately protected?

Where settlements are negotiated between the parties and their lawyers without third-party assistance, the lawyers will often be 'god' in deciding what an appropriate settlement is. As one of the specialist plaintiff's solicitors in Hazel Genn's research said:

> The fact is, when you settle a case, who can argue? The client's happy. I mean, most clients will settle for tuppence. You know, you tell them that that's all they're going to get – they'll settle…So all you've got is you and your conscience to actually play with and it depends where your conscience leads you.[91]

The standard *adversarial advocacy* conception of lawyers' ethics and professional conduct obligations says that lawyers have a responsibility to make sure their own clients get the best deal they can in negotiations. But how do they balance the desire to get justice for their client against the need to compromise in order to get anything at all? The client will generally rely on the lawyer to advise them as to whether to accept a deal that gives them less money than they think they deserve (that is, less than justice), or whether to risk getting nothing at all, except a huge bill for legal costs, if they go to court. A lawyer might also have considerable discretion as to how hard to press the other side in negotiations for a public apology or admission of liability, as opposed to a confidential settlement. A good lawyer should not simply advise their client to agree to anything that gets the matter resolved co-operatively. But nor should they refuse any deal that does not conform exactly with what they believe the courts would, or should, give their client. Lawyers will often need to take responsibility for developing their own ethical opinion about what is a 'good' deal for their clients – taking into account their duty to represent their client's needs and desires, the other side's interests, and legal principle. Case Study 7.4 on the Cape asbestos settlement illustrates some of the issues that might be relevant in such a decision.

The issue of whether lawyers ought to take ethical responsibility for the justice of the outcome of negotiation becomes even more pressing when we consider their role as mediators.[92] The Law Society of New South Wales has argued that

---

90 Note however that this does not necessarily require that they follow legal standards or procedural fairness.

91 Genn, *Hard Bargaining*, 129.

92 Note that for ADR practitioners who have a role in evaluating and determining the dispute, such as arbitration, this is less of a problem, as they clearly have a role in advising the parties as to what an appropriate outcome would be.

lawyers (and others) acting as facilitators of ADR should have no role at all in evaluating, or trying to influence, the fairness of an outcome agreed in ADR:

> To promote fairness and justice for the parties, we prefer the test of the 'satisfaction of the parties'...We would not like to see dispute resolvers intervene on the basis of 'We have to protect you from your own values' or 'We know what's best for you'...[P]arties have a right to enter into agreements that may be perceived as 'unfair' by an uninvolved person's yardstick.[93]

By contrast, Astor and Chinkin take the *moral activist* view that:

> There are clearly some situations where the agreement that the parties propose is repugnant and the mediator can, and should, withdraw...because, although they recognise that the parties are free to make an agreement, the mediator finds it ethically unacceptable that she or he has anything to do with arriving at that agreement.[94]

Mediators cannot hide behind their role where they can see that social structural inequalities make mediation unfair. They should withdraw if the solution proposed by the parties to a mediation is morally repugnant or creates some injustice such as prejudicing the safety or welfare of a party, a third party or the public. A *moral activist* approach would argue that the same should be true for lawyers representing parties. The NADRAC *Framework for ADR Standards* is consistent with this view stating that, in cases of grave injustice, mediators and other ADR practitioners retain a discretion to refuse to take part in that injustice and to do what they can to remedy it. The *Framework for ADR Standards* states that even in non-determinative cases ADR facilitators

> may need to consider and get advice on whether: the interests of third parties are appropriately protected, or at least not unnecessarily or unjustifiably threatened;...an agreement condones an illegal activity; an agreement is legally void or voidable;...any advice, agreement or decision does not involve unlawful or unjustifiable discrimination.[95]

A *responsible lawyering* perspective might argue that this means that lawyers, as officers of the court, have a fundamental duty to law that means that whether they are acting as representatives of parties in negotiation and ADR, or as ADR facilitators, then they ought to have regard to whether the deals agreed to in negotiation and ADR meet the requirements of legal fairness both in terms of

93 Law Society of New South Wales, *Submission on NADRAC Paper: Issues of Fairness and Justice in Alternative Dispute Resolution* (1997) National Alternative Dispute Resolution Advisory Council <www.ag.gov.au/adr/Lawsocnsw.htm> at 5 March 2006.

94 Astor and Chinkin, *Dispute Resolution in Australia*, 230–1.

95 NADRAC, *A Framework for ADR Standards*, 113–14.

process and substance.[96] Moreover they might have a duty to make sure that disputes are resolved publicly, and in a way that sets precedent, and is subject to precedent.[97]

But to take this approach would be to give up the idea of the distinctiveness of ADR and negotiation – that they provide an opportunity for doing justice and resolving disputes in ways other than those traditionally envisioned by law. Proponents of ADR argue that parties should be free to choose to settle matters in ways that they are happy with even if this means agreeing to something less than, or different to, what the law might strictly require, as long as they are not actually agreeing to break the law, and provided they have fully and freely participated in the process and consented to the outcome.[98] Yet, how are we to know what full and free participation and consent mean, without recourse to legal principle? There are no easy answers in exploring lawyer and ADR practitioners' ethical responsibilities for the justice of negotiated settlements. There is likely to always be a space in which lawyers and others will need to choose for themselves how to balance legal principle, client interest and justice for third parties or the public in a particular set of circumstances. The following case study is designed to help identify how these issues might arise and what considerations might be relevant.

CASE STUDY 7.4   THE CAPE ASBESTOS SETTLEMENT[99]

A South African company, Cape Plc, had mined and crushed asbestos in South Africa for decades. In March 2003 Cape (and an associated company, Gencor, another asbestos mining company) finally settled a long-running compensation claim in the UK courts made by 7500 largely poor, black and illiterate South Africans who had worked for the company or been affected by its operations because they lived nearby and now suffered from various diseases caused by exposure

---

96 It has been argued that the empirical research on party satisfaction with ADR shows that the most important thing is people's sense of procedural fairness in the process, whether litigation or ADR: JustBalstad, 'What Do Litigants Really Want? Comparing and Evaluating Adversarial Negotiation and ADR' (2005) 16 *Alternative Dispute Resolution Journal* 244.

97 For discussion of arguments for and against this approach see David Luban, 'Settlements and the Erosion of the Public Realm' (1995) 83 *Georgetown Law Journal* 2619.

98 See Menkel-Meadow, 'Whose Dispute Is It Anyway?'.

99 See Richard Meeran, 'Cape Plc: South African Mineworkers' Quest for Justice' (2003) 9 *International Journal of Occupational & Environmental Health* 218. Some of this material is based on an interview with Richard Meeran, former Leigh Day partner (Melbourne, 7 March 2006).

to asbestos. Over the seven years of litigation and settlement negotiations in relation to the group action by 7500 claimants, about 1000 of them died. An earlier settlement in 2001 in which Cape agreed to pay a total of £21 million to the claimants collapsed in late 2002 when Cape's financial difficulties meant that their bankers would not release the money needed to pay the agreed amount. Gencor was joined to the action and the matter was eventually settled for £7.5 million to be paid by Cape for the claimants, and about another £40 million to be paid by Gencor in relation to the claims against Cape as well as claims against Gencor in its own right, including £3 million for environmental rehabilitation.

The law firm that represented the plaintiffs in the group action was Leigh Day, a well-known law firm with a history of taking on public interest cases on behalf of disadvantaged people. Richard Meeran, the partner who ran the case, has commented that:

> The settlement terms represented a pragmatic solution to the financial reality of Cape's position rather than reflecting any relation to the true value of the case…Although the evidence justified the claimants' confidence of winning the trial…Cape's financial position was such that it would probably have gone into liquidation if it lost…the only achievement of a court victory might have been to set a precedent for claims against multinationals. Victims would receive only what was available on the break-up of the company. The claimants could also have lost what was, after all, a cutting-edge case. Furthermore, judgment was at least seven months away and the process could be drawn out by appeals…So there was a serious risk that an award would not have translated into real money.[100]

The Leigh Day team of lawyers (up to 42 of them at one stage) developed a database and formula to determine what amount of compensation each individual claimant would get, depending on their exposure, development of the disease and so on. Many of the claimants did not even have up to date medical records. The lawyers knew that not only was the settlement amount less than a court might have judged to be appropriate, but also there were likely to be many individual cases where claimants actually had a more or less deserving case than the scant evidence available suggested. But it would have cost much more money to make the necessary assessments to make a fairer distribution and this would have just eaten into the settlement amount (which was already lower than the claimants legally deserved). Just as importantly, undertaking more evidence-gathering and analysis would have taken time, which was most undesirable given the claimants' financial predicament, and the rate at which the victims were dying uncompensated.

---

100 Meeran, 'Cape Plc', 225.

The law firm Leigh Day agreed to destroy all the documents they had received from Cape in discovery relating to Cape's liability in relation to the matter (but Cape agreed to keep their copies of the same documents until 2011) and also agreed not to act for any future claimants against Cape. Cape insisted that this was a precondition for any settlement, what lawyers call a 'deal-breaker'. An additional condition of the first (failed) settlement, but not the second (successful) settlement was that the South African government agreed not to fund any future claims against Cape, and that it would not pursue Cape in relation to its environmental law obligations for any of the cost of rehabilitating its former asbestos mines.

DISCUSSION QUESTIONS

1. In group actions such as this the lawyers for the plaintiffs negotiate the terms of any settlement and also the arrangements for sharing out the settlement amount, and then advise the claimants on whether or not to accept the settlement package. (In group or class actions the court will also need to approve the settlement, but the court will not generally suggest changes to particular terms.) What factors do you think the lawyers took into account in recommending this settlement to their clients? Was a settlement on these terms the only way to meet their clients' needs? What would have been the arguments, if any, in favour of going to court even if Cape was bankrupted? Do you think lawyers for the parties have too much discretion in deciding these matters? Is there any alternative?

2. It is not uncommon for a plaintiff's lawyers (and their firm) to be asked to agree not to represent any future plaintiffs against the defendant in relation to the same issue where there are likely to be multiple people with the same complaint against the defendant. In this case there were another couple of thousand potential claimants who had not signed onto the action.[101] Why would the defendant want such a clause? Is it in the plaintiff's lawyers' interests to sign up to such a clause? Is it in their client/s' interests? It might be argued that such clauses prevent lawyers acting according to the fundamental rules of the adversary system of being available to any client who comes along. Is it ethical for the defendants' lawyer to ask for such a clause in a settlement

---

101 The earlier settlement agreement (that collapsed) had actually included provision for these potential future claimants, but the second one did not.

agreement? Should the courts approve agreements that include such clauses?[102] Do the plaintiffs' lawyers and their clients have any duty to consider and protect other potential plaintiffs' interests?

3. Leigh Day were criticised by one group of asbestos activists for agreeing to destroy the documents received from Cape on discovery, although two other prominent asbestos support groups, and also the Premier of the Northern Cape province supported Leigh Day.[103] But there is a rule of law ('the rule in Harman') that means that those discovered documents would be subject to an implied undertaking not to disclose them, or use them for any other purpose, without the leave of the court (which will only be given in special circumstances) anyway.[104] Why do you think this principle exists? Why do you think asbestos activists might have been angry about this aspect of the agreement?

4. Firms like Leigh Day would generally be seen as *moral activist* in their ethical orientation. To what extent do their actions described above fit with *moral activist* values in lawyering? To what extent do they not? Are their actions ethically justified on other bases?

Conclusion

When lawyers *represent* clients in negotiation, mediation or other ADR processes, they are usually not acting primarily as *adversarial advocates*. Nor is it in their clients' interests that they act as *adversarial advocates*. Rather they act in collaborative, problem-solving mode to help their clients prevent or resolve disputes. When lawyers act as ADR *facilitators*, their role is even further from traditional *adversarial advocacy*. They are third-party neutrals with an obligation to impartially help both parties co-operate to resolve their problems. The processes of negotiation and ADR themselves assume that practitioners' ethics and practices should be informed by *ethics of care* values, rather than *adversarial advocacy*. This assumption does not

---

102 See David A Dana and Susan P Koniak, 'Secret Settlements and Practice Restrictions Aid Lawyer Cartels and Cause Other Harms' (2003) *University of Illinois Law Review* 1217; Luban, 'Settlements and the Erosion of the Public Realm', 2624–5; cf Stephen Gillers and Richard W Painter, 'Free the Lawyers: A Proposal to Permit No-Sue Promises in Settlement Agreements' (2005) 18 *Georgetown Journal of Legal Ethics* 291; Yvette Golan, 'Restrictive Settlement Agreements: A Critique of Model Rule 5.6(b)' (2003) 33 *Southwestern University Law Review* 1.

103 Kevin Maguire, 'Law Firm Was Ready to Shred Data on Asbestos Claims', *The Guardian Weekly* (London, UK), 1–7 October 2004 , 12; unpublished letters to *The Guardian* from these parties on file with the authors.

104 Matthew Groves, 'The Implied Undertaking Restricting the Use of Material Obtained During Legal Proceedings' (2003) 23 *Australian Bar Review* 1.

apply only to lawyers. The parties themselves and non-lawyer ADR practitioners should demonstrate similar ethics.

If the role and ethics of lawyers in ADR and interest-based negotiation are so different from the traditional role and ethics of adversarial lawyering, we might question whether lawyers should be encouraged or allowed to be involved in collaborative negotiation and ADR at all. Indeed some ADR processes have rules that state that parties are not allowed to bring lawyers into the process, or that lawyers may be present but cannot speak. The reason is the danger that where lawyers are allowed to participate freely, they will tend to dominate the process so that parties do not feel empowered to take responsibility for their own dispute. Lawyers' interventions can also mean that the process becomes excessively concerned with legal and procedural rights. Some commentators have also argued that when lawyers act as mediators, their training makes them inclined to be too opinionated and directive of the parties, rather than facilitate the parties' own development of solutions to their problems.

At the same time many lawyers have themselves become disillusioned with traditional legal practice based on *adversarial advocacy*, and the way it requires them to behave as aggressive warriors rather than problem-solvers for their clients. Many lawyers see the possibility of being involved in collaborative negotiation and ADR as a welcome broadening of conventional practice. But lawyers who are used to conventional adversarial practice will need to be aware of the change they need to make to their own adversarial instincts, values and practices in order to practise appropriately in ADR and negotiation processes. Rules alone are unlikely to be able to enforce such a change in culture and mindset. Ethics self-assessment (see Chapter 11) may increase the chances that a lawyer has sufficient awareness of any preference for adversarial advocacy to allow them to responsibly act on behalf of the many clients whose cases will benefit from collaborative, interest-focused and purposeful mediation.

It is important to note again the fact that legal professional practice inspired by the *ethics of care* can be criticised because it is not primarily aimed at protecting people's rights (unlike *adversarial advocacy*) or advancing legal or social justice (unlike *responsible lawyering* and *moral activism*, respectively). It will not be desirable to encourage *all* lawyers to act according to *ethics of care* values *all* the time, if this means abandoning these other roles. Even the strongest advocates of the use of *ethics of care* values and ADR by legal practitioners emphasise that ADR and co-operative negotiation can only work fairly where people still have realistic access to courts and lawyers to vindicate their rights if necessary, and law and lawyers are vigilant in promoting justice more broadly.[105] But in the end it is likely

---

105 Menkel-Meadow, 'Whose Dispute Is It Anyway?'; Parker, *Just Lawyers*.

that those lawyers who seek to develop a close understanding of *who* they are in a virtue ethics context will be best placed to balance these complementary ethical values and in so doing, make that vigilance more conscious and deliberative.

RECOMMENDED FURTHER READING

Hilary Astor and Christine Chinkin, *Dispute Resolution in Australia* (LexisNexis Butterworths, Sydney, 2nd edn, 2002).

Michael King, Arie Freiberg, Becky Batagol and Ross Hyams, *Non-Adversarial Justice* (Federation Press, Sydney, 2009).

Law Council of Australia, *Ethical Standards for Mediators* (2000) <www.lawcouncil. asn.au/policy/1957353025.html> at 20 March 2006.

Carrie Menkel-Meadow, 'Whose Dispute Is It Anyway?: A Philosophical and Democratic Defense of Settlement (In Some Cases)' (1995) 83 *Georgetown Law Journal* 2663.

—— 'Ethics in Alternative Dispute Resolution: New Issues, No Answers from the Adversary Conception of Lawyers' Responsibilities' (1997) 38 *South Texas Law Review* 407.

—— 'The Limits of Adversarial Ethics' in Deborah L Rhode (ed), *Ethics in Practice: Lawyers' Roles, Responsibilities, and Regulation* (Oxford University Press, New York, 2002) 123.

Carrie Menkel-Meadow and Michael Wheeler, *What's Fair?: Ethics for Negotiators* (Jossey Bass, San Francisco, 2004).

National Alternative Dispute Resolution Advisory Council, *A Framework for ADR Standards* (NADRAC, Barton, ACT, 2001) <www.ag.gov.au/agd/WWW/ disputeresolutionhome.nsf/Page/Standards> at 20 March 2006.

Jim Parke, 'Lawyers as Negotiators: Time for a Code of Ethics?' (1993) 4 *Australian Dispute Resolution Journal* 216.

Tania Sourdin, *Alternative Dispute Resolution* (Thomson-Reuters, Sydney, 4th edn, 2012).

Michelle Wills, 'The Negotiator's Ethical and Economic Dilemma: To Lie, or Not to Lie' 2001 (12) *Australian Dispute Resolution Journal* 48.

8

CONFLICTING LOYALTIES

Introduction

The profession has traditionally seen it as a cornerstone of *adversarial advocacy* that lawyers serve each client's interest loyally, confidentially and carefully. As we saw in Chapter 4, the touchstone of lawyers' professional obligations of devoted service to their clients is the trilogy of duties – loyalty, confidentiality and care; and the most strict and onerous rules in the law of lawyering relate to these duties.[1] This chapter is concerned with the first of those duties – loyalty.

The duty of loyalty requires lawyers to avoid situations involving a *conflict of interest* between a lawyer's personal interest and their duty to a client; or, a *conflict of duties* owed to two or more clients. It also requires lawyers to refrain from using their relationship with the client as a means of making any personal gain; and they must fully disclose to their client any conflicts of interest or personal gains that do arise. These obligations apply not just to the individual lawyer but to the whole firm: if one lawyer cannot act for a potential client because of a conflict of interest, then usually the whole firm cannot act. These are 'fiduciary' obligations set out and enforceable in the law of equity and also reinforced in professional conduct rules and disciplinary decisions. In addition to being sued by their clients for breach of these obligations at general law, lawyers can also be disciplined.

The duty of loyalty can be based in either or both adversarial advocacy and responsible lawyering. *Adversarial advocacy* assumes that clients need to be able to trust their lawyers to provide advice and represent them in the legal system completely uninfluenced by any concern other than the client's interests. A narrow adversarial advocacy conception of the duty of loyalty would see the client's interest as the touchstone of the duty. This means that as long as the client's interests are not actually harmed, then it might be possible to 'cure' a potential conflict through measures such as client consent or information barriers (discussed further below). On an adversarial advocacy approach, the duty of loyalty also might not survive the ending of the lawyer-client relationship to the extent that the lawyer is no longer obligated to further the client's interests.

An alternative conceptualisation of the duty of loyalty as based on a combination of *adversarial advocacy* and *responsible lawyering* sees the lawyer's role in advancing the client's interest (as advocate) as stemming from (and therefore tempered by) their role as officer of the court. In this conception, the appearance of bias or disloyalty is considered important because of its implications as to whether justice is done and seen to be done, even if the client consents to the conflict and there is no evidence that their interest has in fact been harmed. That is, the lawyer's

---

1 For a thorough account see G E Dal Pont, *Lawyers' Professional Responsibility* (Lawbook Co, Pyrmont, NSW, 5th edn, 2013) 'Part II: Lawyers' Duty to the Client'.

role as officer of the court is seen as requiring a broader obligation to justice than merely serving this client in this case according to what this client will consent to. When we think about the duty of loyalty in terms of both *adversarial advocacy* and *responsible lawyering* together, we can see that the lawyer and their duty of loyalty is both to be a partial advocate or representative of the current client, and also to not be too heavily identified with any one client and merely what their interests demand (or do not demand) at any one time. On this view, the lawyer's role as an advocate or representative of their client stems firstly from their role as officer of the court, not merely from the interests of the client. It is a role that is given to them as part of their purpose in the legal system and the adversarial court system, and this is so central that the higher duty to the court and the law has to define what adversarial advocacy and therefore the duty of loyalty actually means. This allows the lawyer to take account of the other approaches to lawyering, rather than merely allowing adversarial advocacy and client interest to define their ethical obligation.

The implications of this approach to conflicts of interest are considerable. Large and increasingly global law firms have multiple clients in commercially similar industries, long histories of complex representation, interlocking subsidiaries, and partners with potentially prohibited information operating all over the planet that all practically undermine the efforts of the courts to affirm the pre-eminence of the administration of justice. As we will suggest below, the recent *Australian Solicitors' Conduct Rules (ASCR)* have been developed with the interests of such firms in mind and do not necessarily reflect an adequate synthesis of *adversarial advocacy* and *responsible lawyering*. In particular, lawyers need to be sensitive to the fact that zeal on behalf of clients cannot be the highest ethical goal – a delusion that is especially likely to occur where the client's interests (in unethical or illegal behaviour) coincide with the lawyer's own interests (in making money and keeping a client that produces steady and interesting work).

In practice, it is part of the nature of legal practice that lawyers will inevitably face conflicting pressures and loyalties that might *interfere with* the performance of their duty of loyalty. The ethically significant thing is how each lawyer responds to these conflicting pressures and loyalties when they occur, or whether they even notice them. Case Studies 8.1 and 8.2 give examples of law firms that, arguably, did not adequately respond to conflicts of duties to different clients. Consistent with the combined *adversarial advocacy* and *responsible lawyering* conceptualisation of the duty of loyalty, there should be ethical *constraints* on the extent of lawyers' duties of loyalty arising from the lawyer's duty to the court and the law, to the public interest and perhaps, in some circumstances, even to the lawyer's own family and self.[2]

---

2 As we shall see below, the *ethics of care* would certainly say that it is a lawyer's obligation to themselves not to ethically debase themselves in the interests of a client. An *ethics of care*

In the first part of this chapter, we critically analyse the principles of professional conduct set out in the *ASCR* that relate to conflicts between lawyers' own interests and their duty to their clients, conflicts between the duties owed to two or more current clients, and the situation where a lawyer proposes to act against a former client for a new client. As we shall see, some of these obligations are not set out as clearly, nor enforced by professional regulators as strictly, as we might expect, given the emphasis which the dominant *adversarial advocacy* ideal gives to devoted client service. There are grounds to criticise the *ASCR* for a tendency to strengthen lawyers' capacity to generate additional fees by defining unacceptable conflicts in the narrowest possible terms. We question whether clients' interests are the actual priority of the *ASCR* insofar as conflicts are concerned. In the second part of this chapter we consider how using the three alternative ethical approaches introduced in Chapter 2 – *responsible lawyering*, *moral activism* and *ethics of care* – would change our view of the extent and limits of a lawyer's duty to their client in the face of various conflicting pressures and loyalties and inadequate conduct rules.

How Far Does Loyalty to Client Extend? The Values in the Conduct Rules

The *ASCR* reflect the major value of loyalty to the client over lawyer self-interest in general terms. They also, however, temper and even undermine that loyalty with specific rules (and exemptions to the general rules) that appear designed to provide opportunities for lawyer self-interest to hold sway. In this section we look firstly at the rules concerning lawyer-client conflicts of interest, and ask how broadly defined are the conflicting 'interests' that lawyers must avoid. Does and should the prohibition only extend to lawyers' financial interests that conflict with their client's interests, or does it also extend to 'fuzzier' conflicts of interest such as conflicting social or political ties that might temper a lawyer's zeal on behalf of their client?

Next, we consider the situation where lawyers owe duties of loyalty, confidentiality and care simultaneously to two or more clients who might have conflicting interests in a matter. We ask whether the nominal position in the *ASCR* that lawyers must *avoid* acting simultaneously for two or more clients with conflicting interests, but can act for clients with *potentially* conflicting interests makes any ethical sense.

---

might also argue that in some circumstances the obligation to spend time with one's family should trump the obligation to serve a client zealously.

Finally, we critically consider the situation where a lawyer or law firm proposes to act for one client against a former client. The dominant view is that the lawyer's obligation of loyalty and care to the former client stops when the retainer stops, but the ongoing duty of confidentiality often might prevent the law firm from acting for the new client. We ask whether this confidentiality-based approach to deciding when lawyers and law firms can act against former clients is ethically adequate. This question is especially pertinent in the context of the widespread use of information barriers (often known as 'Chinese walls') within law firms in an effort to continue acting against former (or even current) clients, even where the law firm does hold relevant confidential information.

Lawyer-Client Conflict

ASCR 12.1 formally insists that lawyers[3] 'must not act for a client where there is a conflict between the duty to serve the best interests of the client and the interests of the solicitor...' *ASCR* 12.2 is clear that a lawyer must not 'exercise any undue influence intended to dispose the client to benefit the solicitor in excess of the solicitor's fair remuneration for the legal services provided to the client' and provide that 'an associate' of the lawyer is also unable to benefit from conflicts (*ASCR* 12.1).[4]

Underlying all lawyer-client relationships, as *ASCR* 12.2 implicitly recognises, is the fact that a lawyer's interests are in conflict with their client's interests 'the minute they begin work for a client, since their interest in making a larger income conflicts with the client's interest in paying as little as possible for solving his or her legal [problems]'.[5] Moreover, the fact many lawyers are employed by law firms means that their interest in serving their employer law firm (by clocking up billable hours) may well conflict with their fiduciary duty to their client.

The courts have recognised that a lawyer's interest in receiving a higher fee from the client is a conflict of interest that should be handled carefully. In *Council of the Queensland Law Society Inc v Roche*,[6] for example, a practitioner negotiated

---

3 Note: The *ASCR* are largely addressed to 'solicitors', but in the interests of consistency we use the term 'lawyer' throughout our commentary in this chapter as this is the term we use generally throughout the book.

4 An 'associate' of a solicitor is defined very broadly (in the glossary section of the *ASCR*) to include 'a partner, employee, or agent of the practitioner or of the practitioner's firm', 'any corporation or partnership in which the practitioner has a material beneficial interest', 'a member of the practitioner's immediate family' or 'a member of the immediate family of a partner of the practitioner's firm'. 'Immediate family' is defined in turn to mean 'the spouse (which expression may include a de facto spouse or partner of the same sex), or a child, grandchild, sibling, parent or grandparent of a practitioner'.

5 Larry May, *The Socially Responsive Self: Social Theory and Professional Ethics* (University of Chicago Press, Chicago, 1996) 126.

6 [2004] 2 Qd R 574.

a substantial increase in fees with an existing 'no win, no fee' client in a personal injuries matter. The client was in financial difficulties, did not fully understand how charges were being incurred under the original fee agreement, and was anxious for the legal practitioner to take on a second case on his behalf. The court found the practitioner guilty of professional misconduct for 'preferring his own interest to that of his client'. He had breached his fiduciary obligations to the client by failing to fully inform the client of the way the client's rights under the fee agreement and the fees payable would change. He should also have advised the client to obtain independent legal advice before signing the new agreement, even though the client gave evidence that he would not have sought out that independent advice.[7] (See Chapter 9 for further ethical analysis of lawyers' fees and billing arrangements.)

On the other hand, there are many lawyer-client conflicts where an uncompromising stand is resolutely (and properly) applied. The courts and legal profession regulators consistently denounce and sanction obvious, direct conflicts of interest such as financial or property dealings between lawyers and clients, including borrowing or lending money to one another, as well as situations where the client invests in a scheme or business run by the lawyer.[8] *ASCR* 12.1 and 12.2 support these prohibitions in general terms. *ASCR* 12.3 and 12.4, however, provide for a number of exceptions that appear designed to permit, tolerate and regulate conflicts rather than to prohibit and prevent them.

ASCR 12.3 expressly permits lawyers to borrow from clients who are trustee companies, managed investment schemes, 'associates' of the lawyer, or their employer. But a lawyer who enters into financial dealings with these types of clients may not be able to consider their *responsible lawyering* obligations. How can a lawyer who owes money to a client, particularly a client in one of these commercially powerful categories, discharge their duty to provide independent advice to them (*responsible lawyering* and *moral activism*) when problems arise?

Lawyers have been disciplined for receiving a profit or commission for referring clients to other service providers (eg to a financial adviser or real estate agent) if that has not been fully disclosed to the client and the client's fully informed consent has not been provided. Indeed receiving a secret profit in this way can even amount to a crime being committed by the lawyer (see *ASCR* 12.4.3–12.4.4).[9]

ASCR 12.4 addresses the conflicts of interest inherent in lawyers earning fees from their clients in the specific environment of will-making – an area where there is a timeless concern about temptation overtaking lawyers acting for elderly, well-resourced and unsupported clients. *ASCR* 12.4.2 generally prevents a lawyer from

7 Ibid 576 (de Jersey CJ).
8 See, eg, *Law Society of New South Wales v Harvey* [1976] 2 NSWLR 154; *Maguire v Makaronis* (1997) 188 CLR 449; Dal Pont, *Lawyers' Professional Responsibility*, 209–32.
9 Dal Pont, *Lawyers' Professional Responsibility*, [6.115].

drafting a will 'under which the practitioner or the practitioner's firm or associate will, or may, receive a substantial benefit...' in addition to normal fees and any executor's commission. *ASCR* 12.4.1 also requires lawyers to disclose in writing to the client any commission or fee they will be entitled to claim under the will, for example for being appointed executor and administering the estate, and to inform the client that they could appoint as executor someone else who would charge no fee. This rule recognises a long tradition of lawyers acting both as executors (when no suitable family members exist) and solicitors for deceased estates, and so there is no prohibition on these additional benefits accruing to the lawyer. But it is increasingly doubtful whether a lawyer's right to claim a sizeable executors' commission from beneficiaries' shares in the estate is a good thing. The beneficiaries often have no connection to the lawyer at all but commonly have to pay 3–4% of the gross value of a deceased estate to them. Do such large commissions recognise the lawyer's work at the cost of reducing loyalty and increasing tension between those beneficiaries and the solicitor-executor?

Most cases of enforcement of lawyer-client conflicts have been concerned with *direct* conflicts of *financial* interests. What about more *indirect* conflicts of interests? The rules quoted above define it as a conflict of interest where the lawyer, or any immediate family member of the lawyer, or a partner in the lawyer's law firm, or any immediate family of the partner, have any interest that conflicts with that of the client. This could include any of these people holding shares in a company that is in dispute with, or possibly even on the other side of a proposed transaction with, the client. Most lawyers would probably consider it ethical practice to disclose to a client any interests of their own of this nature, and perhaps any immediate family member's interests that they are aware of, and allow the client to decide whether the lawyer can continue to act. The *ASCR* seem to expect lawyers to have a high level of awareness of potentially conflicting interests among a wide range of 'associates', defined broadly.[10]

Moreover, *financial* conflicts of interest between lawyer and client are only the most obvious of the many ways in which a lawyer's personal interests are likely to diverge from pure client loyalty. There is also the question of whether lawyers must avoid or discontinue acting where there are conflicting interests that are not financial, but more personal, social or political. For example, what about the situation where the lawyer on the other side is a close friend or family member, or where the client asks the lawyer to do work for them to advance a social or political cause to which the lawyer is opposed? It is only fairly recently that there has been some suggestion in the disciplinary cases, and in commentary on the rules of professional conduct, that even something as obviously fraught with the potential for conflict of interest as a sexual relationship between a lawyer and client

---

10 See n 3 above.

is, or should be, prohibited.[11] There is no rule in the *ASCR* explicitly prohibiting it, and professional associations have been very slow to take any action in this area.[12] Case Study 8.1 below (based on Case Study 4.3 in Chapter 4) was an unfortunate example. Similarly, there are no rules addressing situations where the lawyer's own client, or one of the other parties to a matter (either a client or lawyer on the other side) is a relative, friend or social associate of some kind (whether spouse or indeed enemy). Although generally advised to avoid these situations as a matter of common sense, many lawyers act for a friend or relatives at least once and then regret it.

Ethicist Larry May has commented on a number of other types of conflict between a lawyer's personal interests and their client's interests:

> [T]he lawyers I have known are often highly ambitious individuals who see the pursuit of a particular client's case as a means of furthering their own careers. Furthermore, lawyers also have political agendas. As Wolfram and others have pointed out, 'Even in pro bono representations, the ideological or altruistic motives that induce a lawyer to offer legal services' can often obscure the pursuit of the client's interests.[13]

The lawyer's personal interest in receiving a higher fee, pursuing satisfying and career-enhancing cases, or advocating certain political, ethical or ideological interests might have a tendency to influence the way the lawyer performs their duty to the client. Yet the potential for these conflicts is unavoidable. Lawyers naturally have their own concerns and interests that they bring to the lawyer-client relationship. It would be naive to assume that complete client loyalty in all one's thinking and acting as a lawyer can be guaranteed, and that all conflicts can be completely avoided. Indeed the more broadly we define the lawyer's 'interests', beyond the direct financial interests of the lawyer personally, the more likely we are to discover other conflicts between the lawyer's interests (and their associates' interests) and their duty to the client. Lawyers cannot be expected to be completely immune to these other interests or pressures. The real ethical issue is whether a lawyer is able to:

- *identify* their own motives (virtues), values and interests and those of their 'associates' (including colleagues and their immediate families) and the way those interests might affect their judgement and actions on behalf of clients;
- *avoid* or rid themselves of those conflicts that can be avoided; and

---

11 *Legal Practitioners Conduct Board v Morel* (2004) 88 SASR 401; Dal Pont, *Lawyers' Professional Responsibility*, [6.105].

12 Dal Pont, *Lawyers' Professional Responsibility*, [6.135]; John Ellard, 'Sex and the Professions' (2001) 75 *Australian Law Journal* 248.

13 May, *The Socially Responsive Self*, 132 (footnote reference omitted).

- *fully and clearly explain* any remaining conflicts, and their possible effects, to the client in a way that ensures the client properly understands what the limits of their lawyer's loyalty will be, and can make up their own mind about whether to continue with that lawyer or not – which may involve strongly suggesting that the client seek independent legal advice on the issue.

The existing rules give lawyers little indication of the degree of openness and honesty about their own interests that might be required to fully apprise the client of the extent of lawyer-client conflicts of interest.

Consider for example the situation where a lawyer has a personal or political commitment that goes against a position they are asked to argue: perhaps a committed animal lover and vegetarian is asked to defend a fast food company that claims it has been defamed by suggestions that the chickens it cooks have been treated inhumanely. The law of lawyering generally seems to assume the *adversarial advocacy* view that a lawyer will automatically be able to do his or her best for the client regardless of their personal opinion of them and their case. But a broader, more holistic view of the principle of avoiding lawyer-client conflict suggests that the lawyer ought to disclose to their client their personal position and opinion and the way these might affect the lawyer's representation of the client's case. The first case study in Chapter 1 might be seen as this type of lawyer-client conflict of interest, but consider also the following.

CASE STUDY 8.1   ROMANTIC LIAISON BECOMES A CLIENT

'Imagine for a moment you are the managing partner of a well-known firm. One of your solicitors comes to you with a bombshell. They have provided advice to their girlfriend/boyfriend and their mates on the incorporation of a "slush fund" named after one of the firm's key clients. It was a freebie and they didn't open a file on the matter. To make matters worse, it turns out that money paid to the new association – ostensibly for one purpose but in reality for something else – has been used fraudulently. What do you do?'[14]

This level of disclosure requires lawyers to be brutally honest with themselves (before they can be honest with their clients) about their own character, the interests they might have that will interfere with their duty to each client, and the

---

14 Quotes from Marcus Priest, 'A dud is no sacking offence', *Australian Financial Review* (Melbourne), 30 November 2012. See also *Legal Practitioners Complaints Committee v Pepe* [2009] WASC 39; Linda Haller, 'Chambers should be off duty to bedfellows', *The Age* (Melbourne), 24 August 2012.

human impossibility of being absolutely and completely loyal to any client. Is it possible for a lawyer to be so candid with their client? Perhaps only if they have first examined their own character and explored their preferences for different ethical types. In the second half of this chapter, we will return to this issue as we consider the different ethical approaches that lawyers might take to obligations, interests and loyalties beyond pure zealous advocacy of clients' interests.

In the following two subsections we consider conflicts between the duties owed to two clients. As we shall see, lawyer-client conflicts can magnify client-client conflicts, since it will often be in the interests of a lawyer or law firm to keep acting for two clients with conflicting interests – so as to earn more fees or maintain a relationship with a client who provides steady and interesting work – and this may influence lawyers' ethical judgement about how to handle the equally difficult client-client conflicts.

Clients, Confidentiality, Loyalty and the Duty to the Administration of Justice

There are two main situations where client-client conflicts can arise:

> *Current client conflicts*: The lawyer or law firm has two current clients with conflicting interests. This can be especially common for large law firms, where different practitioners in a single firm can easily engage in work raising a conflict, for example, where someone in the banking section acts for a bank suing a building firm in liquidation, and someone in the insolvency section acts on behalf of that building firm. Concurrent conflicts can also arise in specialist firms or small firms in country towns – in each instance the limited number of practitioners can easily give rise to concurrent conflicts.

> *Former client conflicts*: The lawyer faces a conflict between the interests of a current client and a former client.

> Classic examples include a firm that previously held a general retainer to provide legal work for a large corporate client in many areas. It is common for a retainer to be moved to another firm over time. The firm may then be offered work that essentially requires it to act against the corporate client with whom it had the retainer.

These do not, however, exhaust the situations where a court may decide that there is a conflict of interest that prevents a lawyer from acting, as illustrated in some of the scenarios and cases below.

There are up to three *rationales* for a court to intervene to prevent a lawyer from acting in a conflict of interest situation. These rationales will apply differently depending on the situation.

First, it is clear that the court will intervene *to protect the obligation of confidentiality* that the lawyer owes a client in equity (as discussed in Chapter 4). This will generally mean that a lawyer cannot be allowed to act for both clients in a current client conflict scenario. In a former client conflict scenario, where there has been actual communication of confidential information, the obligation to maintain confidentiality remains beyond the particular lawyer-client relationship and even after the client has died. An injunction is therefore available to protect the former client against the serious and sensible possibility of misuse of the confidential information previously given.

Second, in a number of cases, the courts have stated that they will intervene *where that is necessary in order to further the administration of justice* and ensure that justice is done and is seen to be done, even though there is not necessarily any confidential information at risk of being disclosed. This jurisdiction is based on the court's inherent jurisdiction to control its own officers. This administration-of-justice grounds for preventing a lawyer from acting in breach of a conflict is very broad, and the court will make a contextual judgement regardless of whether both parties were clients or not. It can apply in current client conflict scenarios, former client conflict scenarios, and also other situations such as where a lawyer has acted repeatedly against one party.[15]

Third, the courts in Victoria at least have decided that an injunction is available to prevent a lawyer from acting in a former client conflict situation, even where no confidential information is at risk of disclosure but rather merely *in order to enforce an ongoing duty of loyalty that the lawyer owes the former client in equity*, even after the lawyer-client relationship has ended. There is conflicting authority in different jurisdictions over whether there is a separate obligation of loyalty that continues to apply after the lawyer-client relationship has ended.[16] It may be better to conceptualise the ongoing obligations of a lawyer in relation to a former client either in terms of the obligation to maintain confidentiality (the first rationale) or the duty to the administration of justice (the second rationale).

Finally, *client consent and 'Chinese walls' or information barriers* may 'cure' client-client conflicts in certain situations, but generally only where the issue is the potential misuse of confidential information. Information barriers are arrangements within a firm supposedly designed to manage or minimise conflicts so that a

---

15 See *Bracewell v Southall* [2008] FamCA 687 (13 August 2008); *Grimwade v Meagher* [1995] 1 VR 446.

16 See *Spincode Pty Ltd v Look Software Pty Ltd* (2001) 4 VR 501; *Contrast Asia Pacific Telecommunications Limited v Optus Networks Pty Limited* [2007] NSWSC 350 (18 April 2007).

law firm can continue to act where there is a successive or concurrent client-client conflict. Many firms use Chinese walls but many also question if they are effective, and indeed whether they are appropriate in the context of the duty to the administration of justice and the ongoing duty of loyalty.[17]

Current Clients

The *ASCR* provisions as to whether lawyers can act where there is a conflict between two clients are confused. *ASCR* 11.1 requires a practitioner to '*avoid* conflicts between the duties owed to two or more current clients' [our emphasis]. But it is immediately followed by several other rules which *allow* legal practitioners to act for more than one party in a matter, even though this might give rise to conflicts of interest:

> 11.2   If a solicitor or a law practice seeks to act for two or more clients in the same or related matters where the clients' interests are adverse and there is a conflict or potential conflict of the duties to act in the best interests of each client, the solicitor or law practice must not act, except where permitted by Rule 11.3.
>
> 11.3   Where a solicitor or law practice seeks to act in the circumstances specified in Rule 11.2, the solicitor may, subject always to each solicitor discharging their duty to act in the best interests of their client, only act if each client:
>
> > 11.3.1   is aware that the solicitor or law practice is also acting for another client; and
> >
> > 11.3.2   has given informed consent to the solicitor or law practice so acting.

The values expressed in *ASCR* 11.1 and 11.2–11.3 are contradictory. On the one hand, *ASCR* 11.1 requires lawyers to avoid *any* conflict of interest, however insignificant the practitioner, or even the client, thinks it is. One might expect that if it is the lawyer's purpose to *avoid* conflicts of interest between clients, they should also avoid situations, such as joint representation, that are likely to give rise to a conflict of interest. The joint representation of criminal accused is a case in point. It may be convenient for the one lawyer to represent both accused, but the danger is that facts and arguments that emerge during preparation and trial mean that the two clients may benefit from having inconsistent defences argued on their behalf,

---

17 Law Institute of Victoria, *Information Barrier Guidelines*, <www.liv.asn.au/regulation/ethics/pdf/guide_infobarrier.pdf>; *Prince Jefri Bolkiah v KPMG* [1999] 2 AC 222; *World Medical Manufacturing Corp v Phillips Ormonde & Fitzpatrick Lawyer's* [2000] VSC 196 [1]–[135]; *Australian Liquor Marketers Pty Ltd v Tasman Liquor Traders Pty Ltd* [2002] VSC 324.

or even blaming each other for the crime. Yet *ASCR* 11.2–11.3 implicitly allow a firm to act for two or more clients to a matter, even though this joint representation could involve a conflict of interest. Indeed, *ASCR* 11.3.1 contemplates that the lawyer, or law firm, may well already be in possession of information which will benefit one client and hurt the other, but they are still allowed to represent both.

ASCR 11.3 attempts to reconcile the inconsistency by allowing joint representation only where the lawyer has disclosed the (potential) conflict to both clients, and both clients consent. In effect, the Law Council has 'avoided' the inconsistency between *ASCR* 11.1 and 11.3, by decreeing as a matter of expediency that a conflict of interest will be disregarded, providing the clients agree. Some clients do want the same lawyer to represent them both in relatively simple transactions, because they see it as more convenient and less expensive. Even in more complicated, commercial transactions two clients may well be happy for different partners (in different offices) of the same large law firm to represent them both – perhaps a lawyer who is familiar with their business, or a lawyer who specialises in a particular area.[18]

ASCR 11.2–11.3 see client consent as the 'cure-all' for a potential conflict in joint representation. The consent process appears to be tight and protective: it insists on a high level of disclosure of the (potential) conflict, and its likely impact, to both clients, followed by their informed consent. However, a client's understanding of the potential conflict, its likely impact on them, and whether they should consent to it will depend very much on what their lawyer tells them. Even so-called 'sophisticated' clients are prepared to rely on advice that they are paying for. The whole point of prohibiting conflicts of interest is that the lawyer's own judgement, and ability to fully inform and advise the client about the conflict, might be clouded by the conflict. The case law on breach of fiduciary obligations generally requires that independent advice be obtained before someone can consent to a conflict of interest. For lawyers and clients, this means that the client should be advised to go to a second, independent lawyer in order to receive reliable advice as to whether to consent to the first lawyer acting in a potential conflict situation.[19] Yet the professional obligations of the *ASCR* do not appear to reflect this requirement of the general law. Instead, they seem to suggest that it can be left completely up to the lawyer's judgement when and how to inform clients of potential conflicts and obtain consent, and when to withdraw.

ASCR 11.4 seeks to go even further and challenges the general law by permitting a firm to act for two or more clients where they hold confidential information for

---

18 See Elizabeth Nosworthy, 'Ethics and Large Law Firms' in Stephen Parker and Charles Sampford (eds), *Legal Ethics and Legal Practice: Contemporary Issues* (Clarendon Press, Oxford, 1995) 57.

19 See *Clark Boyce v Mouat* [1993] 3 NZLR 641; Dal Pont, *Lawyers' Professional Responsibility*, [7.80].

one or more that is material and adverse to the interests of another client, providing there is informed consent from all parties and an 'effective' information barrier is established. It is clear that in nearly every conceivable case, a firm that acts for two clients in contention with one another should be and will be restrained from so acting in these circumstances when one or the other client changes its mind and asks a court to so order.[20] Frequently, this will mean that the firm must withdraw from acting for both clients, at great cost to all concerned. Yet again, the *ASCR* are constructed so that the very few cases[21] of joint contentious representation that might be sustainable can proceed, encouraging lawyers to look for opportunities to get around the primary requirement to avoid a conflict.

These provisions of the *ASCR* seem to suggest that there is a difference between an 'actual' conflict, which must be avoided, and a 'potential' conflict (*ASCR* 11.2), that may be tolerated so long as it does not crystallise into an actual conflict. But the purpose of rules requiring lawyers to avoid conflicts of interest is to avoid the need to make such mental contortions in the first place. Justice Cummins of the Victorian Supreme Court has commented at an ethics seminar:

> What bedevils the prohibition of a conflict of interest is a confusion of purposes. The purpose of prohibition of conflict of interest is not to remedy an offence or a failure. The purpose of prohibition of conflict of interest is to prevent an offence or a failure. Prohibition of conflict operates upstream of offence or failure. It is preventative. It is prophylactic. Thus it is no answer to breach of conflict to say that in fact no harm occurred, that the client was not harmed. If harm, a loss, a failure, an offence occurred, you would be dealt with for a consequential matter. Prohibition of conflict is an antecedent matter. That also is why the phrase 'potential conflict of interest' is tautologous.[22]

---

20 *Prince Jefri Bolkiah v KPMG* [1999] 2 AC 22.

21 Thus in *UTi v Partners of Piper Alderman* [2008] NSWSC 219, an application for an injunction made by the client UTi (a customs agent and cargo forwarder) restraining Piper Alderman (PA) was denied where PA acted in a contractual matter *for* UTi, but at the same time was acting *against* UTi and for a number of plaintiff exporters in claims for damages where goods were destroyed in a warehouse fire at UTi's Sydney premises. The apparent anomaly is explained by the fact that the insurers for UTi were in fact controlling the litigation (rather than UTi itself) and it was the insurers who objected to the joint representation, not UTi. The NSW SC held that the two retainers were 'not the same or related matters' (no duty of loyalty), only generic confidential information was at stake, and no threat to the administration of justice was involved because UTi was (itself) perfectly happy to see PA continue to act, it having effectively consented to same by failing to object when made aware of PA's intent by the partner involved.

22 Justice P D Cummins, 'An Ethical Profession: Dealing with Ethical Dilemmas' (Speech delivered at a Law Institute of Victoria Continuing Legal Education seminar, Melbourne, 28 February 2002).

The last part of *ASCR* 11, subsection 11.5, expressly permits the existence of a potential conflict inside the regime of *ASCR* 11.3 and 11.4 and only requires a lawyer to withdraw if that conflict becomes an 'actual' conflict. But prevention of conflict in the sense identified by Justice Cummins is not the Law Council's priority. The subsection seems to assume that both clients will be willing to agree to just so much loyalty – or agree to tolerate as much infidelity – as may be necessary for them to enjoy access to the same lawyer. But why is it felt necessary at all to endorse joint representation of two clients involved in the same matter? It is often suggested that clients should be able to have their 'lawyer of choice', or might even need access to a particular lawyer in order to obtain adequate representation at all, especially where there might be a shortage of lawyers with relevant specialist expertise. Chief Justice Young of the New South Wales Supreme Court, however, has recently commented that 'lawyers generally are a pretty able lot and it usually does not take long for someone to develop the skills and experience which places him or her among the major league in particular fields of little competition'.[23] To the public it might look more like the rules have been crafted expediently to make sure that lawyers and law firms can preserve their ability to earn fees from multiple clients, rather than being intended to assist access to rare expertise. To the extent that *ASCR* 11.3 and 11.4 enshrine a mechanism for tolerating conflict without first ensuring that the mechanism (consent) operates independently of the practitioner, the prevailing values might relate more to business efficacy, than the loyalty to one client required by *adversarial advocacy* combined with the responsible lawyer's sense of obligation to the justice system. This does not imply that all lawyers behave badly in this environment, but rules are there to deal with those practitioners who have no other conscious values base from which to operate, and no great inclination to examine the case law.

Competing loyalties between clients can occur in respected and respectable law firms. The very *size* of large law firms – each with hundreds of partners and employee practitioners – requires that they be constantly on guard in case one of those partners takes on a client who is involved in a dispute or transaction with a client already represented by another partner. Often, there is no intention for such 'joint representation' to occur, it is simply a case of one partner not being careful enough to check out the proposed retainer with the partner (often described as the 'conflicts partner') designated to keep a list of all current clients and, especially, their opposing parties. This situation is not so much an occasion of conflicting loyalties as inattention. More problematic is the situation where the partners concerned realise that they each have a client opposed to the other (or in negotiation with the other) and decide to try and 'manage' the situation so that

---

23   *British American Tobacco Australia Services Ltd v Blanch* [2004] NSWSC 70 (Unreported, Young CJ in Eq, 20 February 2004) [142].

no 'material' conflict of interest emerges. This approach can be a slippery slope to either breach of obligations, or a situation where the law firm has to cease acting for both clients. In Case Study 8.2 (Allens Arthur Robinson and the Drug Companies) at the end of this chapter, we see how easily conflicts of interest can arise in the large law firm context.

In the next subsection we consider how the *ASCR* apply to situations where the conflict is between a former client and a current client – an even more common scenario in the context of large commercial law firms.

Former Clients and Information Barriers

Where a lawyer or law firm is considering representing one client in a matter where they would be acting against a former client, *ASCR* 10 provides that:

10.1   A solicitor and law practice must avoid conflicts between the duties owed to current and former clients, except as permitted by Rule 10.2.

10.2   A solicitor or law practice who or which is in possession of confidential information of a former client where that information might reasonably be concluded to be material to the matter of another client and detrimental to the interests of the former client if disclosed, must not act for the current client in that matter UNLESS:

10.2.1   the former client has given informed written consent to the solicitor or law practice so acting; or

10.2.2   an effective information barrier has been established.

In this rule, which closely reflects the position at common law,[24] loyalty to a former client is only required where there is confidential information that is both 'material' to the matter, and that could be used to the detriment of the former client. If so, then in the leading House of Lords decision in *Bolkiah's* case, and also in a series of Australian cases, the courts have held that the former client can get an injunction to prevent their former lawyer, or their former lawyer's law firm,[25] acting against them unless there is *no* risk, or no 'real' risk, of disclosure.[26] *ASCR* 10.2 reflects this by suggesting that the lawyer cannot act if confidences 'might reasonably be

---

24   *Prince Jefri Bolkiah v KPMG (a firm)* [1999] 2 AC 222; Dal Pont, *Lawyers' Professional Responsibility*, [8.05]–[8.265]. This means that in addition to a lawyer being liable to disciplinary action for breach of this rule, the former client can seek an injunction to prevent their former lawyer acting against them on this basis.

25   This can even include their former lawyer's new law firm, where the lawyer has switched firms in the meantime: see Dal Pont, *Lawyers' Professional Responsibility*, [8.235].

26   *Prince Jefri Bolkiah v KPMG* [1999] 2 AC 222. For a good summary of the law, see *World Medical Manufacturing Corp v Phillips Ormonde & Fitzpatrick Lawyers* [2000] VSC 196 (Unreported, Gillard J, 18 May 2000).

concluded to be material to the matter of another client and detrimental to the interests of the former client'.

Here the *ASCR* convey a certainty or simplicity that is not present in the common law. Again, the *ASCR* take the issue only so far. There is no indication in the rule at all that the practitioner should actually consult the former client for their opinion or permission. Nor is it suggested that the lawyer, or law firm, should refer the matter to any other authority for decision. The *ASCR* contemplate that the lawyer may in fact come to their own decision about whether they hold 'material' confidential information, the likelihood that it will be prejudicial to the former client's interests, and whether there is a risk of disclosure, without reference to anyone else. Yet the lawyer themself will generally have a material interest in the outcome – to decide that they can take on the new case and earn fees – that might influence their thinking on these issues.

ASCR 10.2 attempts to brush over a subjective conflict for the lawyer in such a way that their loyalty to the former client is permissively disregardable in all but the most obvious cases. Even the consent of the former client can be dispensed with, without even cursory enquiry of the former client in an effort to obtain that consent, if the firm can set up an 'effective information barrier'. The value expressed by this and most of the other relevant conduct rules (which generally reflect the common law) is a conditional loyalty only. Many former clients might feel that *any* confidential information their lawyers acquired from them could be material, and it will not matter much to them if their lawyer thinks otherwise. They might expect that the value of loyalty inherently requires that if a lawyer or law firm holds confidential information from a former client, they should not act against them. Even the remote possibility that their former lawyer might not need to ask their permission before acting against their interests would give most former clients pause to reflect on the character and values of their former lawyer and the profession in general. This reality would seem to be inconsistent with the very strict, almost sacrosanct, protections for lawyer-client confidentiality that lawyers argue for in all other circumstances, especially when any court or other external authority seeks access to any information that might prejudice the confidentiality of communications between lawyer and client.[27]

Indeed we might question whether lawyers only have a duty of loyalty to a former client to the extent that this is necessary to protect confidential information received from the former client, suggested by *ASCR* 10.2. Should lawyers have more wide-ranging duties to remain loyal to their former clients? In the Full Court of the Victorian Supreme Court's decision in *Spincode Pty Ltd v Look Software*

---

27 See William Simon, 'The Confidentiality Fetish' (2004) 294(5) *The Atlantic Monthly* 113; Richard Tur, 'Confidentiality and Accountability' (1992) 1 *Griffith Law Review* 73.

Pty Ltd ('Spincode'),[28] Brooking JA somewhat controversially stated that case law and legal principle suggest they do. The facts of that case concerned the not uncommon problem of a lawyer who was supposed to be acting for a company, but in fact preferred the interests of one individual officer of the company with whom he presumably had a good working relationship.

Figure 8.1 sets out the relationships between the law firm and its clients. The law firm McPherson + Kelly (sic) acted for Look Software. The McPherson + Kelly lawyer helped set up Look as a joint venture when businessmen Robert Moore and Gavin Rogers decided to join their existing businesses, Spincode and G-Wiz, together into one business. McPherson + Kelly continued to act for Look in relation to all its ongoing legal matters. A little while after setting up the business, Moore and Rogers invited three more men to join the venture, and work for Look, promising that each of them would get shares in Look in addition to the shares already held

Figure 8.1 Relationship between Law Firm and Clients in *Spincode* Case

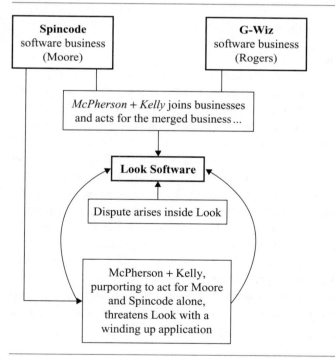

by Spincode and G-Wiz. But these shares were never issued. Later they began to disagree as to what each was entitled to in terms of remuneration and shares.

All the participants in Look went to their (that is, Look's) lawyer for advice as to how to resolve their disagreements. Their McPherson + Kelly lawyer set up a mediation to try to resolve the issues, but this collapsed. A few days later the managing director of Look was surprised to find Look's own law firm McPherson + Kelly sending a fax purporting to act on behalf of Moore (and Spincode), which made a series of allegations and complaints, and raised the possibility that Moore would sue to have Look wound up. McPherson + Kelly later denied that they had been acting for Look at all throughout the dispute, despite the fact that Look was paying their bills. Instead McPherson + Kelly claimed they had been acting for Moore only all along.

The Supreme Court of Victoria made it very clear that the relevant McPherson + Kelly solicitor was Look's lawyer and should have behaved that way. His conduct was heavily criticised: 'One would have expected a solicitor acting for the company in an attempt to sort out disagreements among those who were or intended to become shareholders in it to act as an "honest broker" and not to seek to advance covertly the interests of one person at the expense of another'.[29] The court gave an injunction to prevent McPherson + Kelly acting for Moore against Look.

The court granted the injunction on the basis that the law firm did have confidential information from Spincode that was at risk of being disclosed to their detriment. But Brooking JA also stated that case law suggested that lawyers have an ongoing obligation of loyalty not to act against a former client and in the interests of a preferred client in relation to the same matter in which the solicitor had acted for both, regardless of whether there is any issue about confidential information. Brooking JA argued that this was because, first, a solicitor's obligation of loyalty cannot be 'extinguished by the mere termination of the period of [the lawyer's] retainer' and, second, because public policy 'gives a special relationship to the relationship of solicitor and client that the law will not generally permit to be stained by the appearance of disloyalty'. He went on to say there was a 'public interest in reassuring the community…that even the appearance of improper behaviour will not be tolerated', and that the lawyer's conduct in this case was 'offensive to common notions of fairness and justice'.[30]

Courts in other jurisdictions outside of Victoria have so far not accepted Brooking JA's suggestion that a solicitor can be restrained from acting against a

---

29 Ibid 507.
30 All quotes in above paragraph from ibid 517 (Brooking JA). Note that Brooking JA is not the only judge to have emphasised the importance of the impropriety of a lawyer being seen to 'change sides' as important in this context. See, eg, *Carindale Country Club Estate Pty Ltd v Astill* (1993) 42 FCR 307, 311–12 (Drummond J) and the other judicial statements cited in Dal Pont, *Lawyers' Professional Responsibility*, [8.35]–[8.40].

former client on the basis of the obligation of loyalty alone, but do accept the *responsible lawyering* perspective of the courts' inherent jurisdiction over solicitors as officers of the court to prevent the appearance of impropriety.[31] They have seen the existence of confidential information, its relevance to the new matter, and its risk of disclosure as the only basis for restraining a lawyer from acting against a former client. This tends to focus attention on technical legal arguments between the former client and their lawyers as to the existence and nature of the confidential information, and of the arrangements within the firm that might lead to its disclosure. It might be more in keeping with the expansive way in which the profession usually expresses its value of loyalty to clients, to see lawyers' obligations more broadly as refraining from acting at all against former clients, at least in relation to the same or similar matters.

This is, broadly, the approach that the American Bar Association's *Model Rules of Professional Conduct* take regarding when a lawyer can act against a former client. The American *Rules* do not limit themselves to where confidential information exists, but instead provide that lawyers cannot represent 'another person in the same or a substantially related matter' as a former client, if the former client's interests will go against the new client's interests, unless the former client consents.[32] This would see the lawyer's obligation of loyalty to the client as coming out of the lawyer's role in the justice system (as advocate for the client), rather than being purely a matter between the lawyer and client relating to the confidential information that has passed between them. It also sees the privilege of being an advocate for a client as carrying with it responsibilities to preserve that loyalty, and the appearance of loyalty, rather than being able to take any client at any time. While the profession might consider this approach to be commercially naive, loyalty to clients is a basic value which the courts lean towards, leaving behind the evasiveness of the *ASCR*.

A final problem with the approach of the existing law and *ASCR* concerning when lawyers can act against former clients is the problem of *information barriers* (sometimes called 'Chinese walls'; and also, disparagingly, known as 'dingo fences' or 'Dutch dykes'). It will usually be impossible for the same lawyer to act against a former client, since they personally will know any confidential information from the former client, or even if they believe they have forgotten it, might subconsciously use that information. But law firms sometimes argue that other individuals within the law firm, who had nothing to do with the representation of the earlier client,

---

31 See the NSW Supreme Court decisions in *Belan v Casey* [2002] NSWSC 58 (Unreported, Young CJ, 4 February 2002); *British American Tobacco Australia Services Ltd v Blanch* [2004] NSWSC 70 (Unreported, Young CJ in Eq, 20 February 2004).

32 American Bar Association, *Model Rules of Professional Conduct* (2004) Rule 1.9 <www.abanet. org/cpr/mrpc/mrpc home.html> at 13 June 2006. See Richard O'Dair, *Legal Ethics: Text and Materials* (Butterworths, London, 2001) 466.

should be able to act for the new client, as long as adequate ('effective') safeguards are in place to make sure they cannot access any confidential information from those who did act for the former client. On the other hand, the law provides that generally if one lawyer is disqualified from acting, the whole firm is disqualified. Nevertheless the courts have held that, in exceptional cases, a law firm may be able to show that there is 'no real and serious possibility of misuse' or risk of detrimental disclosure to the lawyers acting for the new client against the old client, by showing that it has in place an effective information barrier between those lawyers (and other staff) who worked on a case for the former client, and know or have access to the former client's relevant confidential information, and those working for the new client.[33]

According to the courts, an effective information barrier should include established, documented protocols for setting up and maintaining barriers or screens between those with relevant confidential information from former clients and those working on new matters. These would include undertakings and procedures to ensure people on either side of the information barrier have no, or limited, contact with one another, as well as physical separation of people and files on each side of the information barrier from one another, restricted access to electronic files, programmes to educate all staff on their responsibility in relation to confidentiality and the firm's protocols for information barriers, monitoring of effectiveness of the protocols by a compliance officer, and disciplinary sanctions on any staff who breach the protocols.[34] Yet all these precautions may not be enough to prevent inadvertent slips in discussion, especially in those firms that cultivate a 'work and play together' attitude among their staff.

As with the decision about whether the lawyer holds material, confidential information, one of the potential problems with the use of information barriers is that lawyers and law firms are likely to have an interest in believing that there will be an effective way of 'managing' potential conflicts in a much wider range of circumstances than is appropriate. For example, in the case law, the courts have generally said that information barriers are only relevant for protecting the confidential information of *former* clients who are no longer clients of the firm.[35] They are not appropriate where there is an active duty to promote the interests of two current clients in contentious cases (see Case Study 8.4), though as we

---

33 See Lee Aitken, "Chinese Walls", Fiduciary Duties and Intra-Firm Conflicts – a Pan-Australian Conspectus' (2000) 19 *Australian Bar Review* 116; Law Society of New South Wales in consultation with the Law Institute of Victoria, *Information Barrier Guidelines* (2006) Law Society of New South Wales <www.lawsociety.com.au/page.asp?partID=15645> at 2 June 2006.

34 See *Prince Jefri Bolkiah v KPMG (a firm)* [1999] 2 AC 222; Law Society of New South Wales, *Information Barrier Guidelines*.

35 But see *Australian Liquor Marketers Pty Ltd v Tasman Liquor Traders Pty Ltd* [2002] VSC 324 (Unreported, Habersberger J, 14 August 2002).

have seen in relation to *ASCR* 11.4.2 above, the Law Council has not expressly discouraged their use in those situations. But many law firms also extensively use information barrier arrangements to allow them to represent clients with potentially conflicting interests at the *same time* in transactional work, as is illustrated in Case Study 8.2 (Allens Arthur Robinson and the Drug Companies) at the end of this chapter.[36] Although this was not the case with Allens, it is particularly dangerous where law firms simply assume that these arrangements will be acceptable without even consulting affected clients or former clients. Case Study 8.3 (Blake Dawson Waldron and the Share Buy-Back) gives another scenario in which a law firm, belatedly, found out that it had a conflict problem between a current client and a former client. It informed its current client about the problem and how it could deal with it, but did not inform the former client.

Conclusion: Client Loyalty and the Ideal of Adversarial Advocacy

The *ASCR*'s approach to client loyalty is based on the ideal of *adversarial advocacy* alone. Adversarial zeal for single clients is, however, undermined by efforts to generate fees from multiple clients. In relation to *lawyer-client conflicts*, *adversarial advocacy* assumes that in their role as professional advocates, lawyers can and should divest themselves of human temptations and all other concerns apart from their obligation to further their client's interests. But this is more difficult than the *ASCR* assume. Some conflicts – such as lawyers writing wills for clients which include bequests to the lawyers themselves – can be readily evaded under the rules. But some conflicts are not addressed in the *ASCR* at all, such as avoiding sexual relationships with clients. Other conflicts cannot be so easily prohibited and avoided: for example, the inevitable conflict of interest between lawyer and client in negotiating the lawyer's fee, and the time and priority devoted by the lawyer to clients' work as against personal and family commitments. Handling these sorts of conflicts well is likely to be more a matter of lawyers being aware of their innate character and of the influences on their own thinking and action, rather than merely following rules.

In relation to *client-client conflicts*, the *ASCR* themselves undermine their own apparently absolute commitment to client loyalty. The duty to avoid conflicts between current clients or former and current clients are expressed subject to conditions and qualifications that appear based on commercial expediency, rather than principle. Lawyers and law firms often seem to be able to decide for themselves which clients will receive their loyalty. As we have seen previously, the ideal of

---

36 See Janine Griffiths-Baker, *Serving Two Masters: Conflicts of Interest in the Modern Law Firm* (Hart Publishing, Oxford, 2002) 148–57.

adversarial advocacy developed particularly as a rationale for the role of lawyers representing individual (not corporate) clients in criminal proceedings. The *ASCR* have not adequately dealt with the current context of large commercial, growth-oriented law firms with many large clients, often including many in the same industry, some of whom are likely to come into conflict with one another at some point in time. It is hard to see how allowing law firms to act in these situations really demonstrates the ideal of zealous advocates' devotion to the client's best interests. But the pressure to allow this to occur seems to have affected the content of the *ASCR*.

Alternative Ethical Approaches to Client Loyalty

In the next three sections we consider how the *adversarial advocacy* picture of unadulterated loyalty to client is made richer, and more complex, by considering the insights of the other three ethical approaches introduced in Chapter 2 – *responsible lawyering*, *moral activism* and *ethics of care*, respectively. We also touch briefly on how an awareness of personal character is needed to underpin and strengthen our preferences for one or more of these approaches, and to choose between them or to reconcile them. We have argued above that the *Model Rules*, or at least the way they have been applied, seem to allow exceptions to the *adversarial advocacy* duty of pure loyalty to clients for *practical and commercial* reasons. The other three approaches give *principled and ethical* justifications as to the extent and limits of lawyers' loyalty to clients that challenge the current rules and the way they are applied to legal practice. Following this, we set out three case studies that can be used to explore in more depth the application and implications of the dominant *adversarial advocacy* approach, and three alternative ethical approaches to the problems of lawyers and law firms facing conflicting loyalties.

The Responsible Lawyer

The *responsible lawyering* approach takes the lawyer's obligation of loyalty to the client very seriously because it is derived from the lawyer's role as an officer of the court who must be available to represent and advocate for clients. Client representation and advocacy is seen as a public obligation, not just a private matter between lawyer and client. But the private quality of loyalty must be present in a lawyer as an everyday character trait if it is to be evident in their public actions. A *responsible lawyering* approach to conflicts between clients would therefore likely be consistent with Brooking JA's view in *Spincode* that a lawyer should not act in a situation where there would be an appearance of impropriety in the administration of justice, regardless of whether there was a risk of the detrimental disclosure of confidential information from one client to another.[37] Similarly, *responsible lawyering* would see the lawyer's obligation to avoid personal conflicts as absolute and going well beyond the current concern only with avoiding direct, financial conflicts.

Responsible lawyering would also suggest that, since loyalty to the client is part of the public role of the lawyer and must be strictly protected for that reason, lawyers and clients should not be allowed to make private arrangements in which clients consent to waive their rights to full loyalty. Arguably, it is not up to clients to decide how much loyalty they are willing to accept from their lawyer. There is also a public interest in requiring lawyers to show full loyalty to the first client every time – in effect, to demonstrate that they do live by the virtue of loyalty – so as not to damage the appearance of justice being done by lawyers performing their role properly in the legal system.[38] *Responsible lawyering* is therefore highly suspicious of information barriers and other arrangements by which law firms try to garner client consent for continuing to act in conflict situations.

However, for the *responsible lawyer*, alongside the duty of loyalty to the client there will also always be an equal ethical concern that lawyers not show 'too much' loyalty to clients. According to the *responsible lawyer*, because the duty of loyalty to clients is derived from the lawyer's role as officer of the court, the lawyer's loyalty to the client must be confined and constrained by the lawyer's loyalty to the court and the legal system. Loyalty to the client cannot be carried out in a way that is inconsistent with the lawyer's duty to the court or the law. We have already considered what this might mean in the litigation context (in Chapter 6) in terms of the lawyer seeking to dissuade a client from any action that goes against the lawyer's duty to the court, withdrawing from acting for the client if they refuse, and perhaps informing an appropriate authority of the issue. In Chapter 10 we will also consider lawyers' responsibilities in relation to legal or ethical misconduct by corporate clients, including lawyers' whistleblowing capacities and obligations. Discerning at what point the duty to the court overrides the duty to the client is not always easy. The virtue of judgement – that is, the lawyer's inherent willingness and capacity to seek a balance between these different types of loyalties – becomes critical here. This discernment is even more difficult where lawyers have become so used to seeing things from their client's point of view – and profiting from the

37 It is also important to remember that one reason the law so strongly protects the confidentiality of information communicated between lawyers and clients is also because of the lawyer's role as officer of the court: see, eg, *A-G (NT) v Maurice* (1986) 161 CLR 475, 490 (Deane J); *Baker v Campbell* (1983) 153 CLR 52, 120 (Deane J).

38 See Duncan Webb, 'Autonomy, Paternalism, and Institutional Interest: Why Some Conflicts Can't be Waived' (2005) 12 *International Journal of the Legal Profession* 261.

fees obtained – that they have lost touch with ordinary ideas of fairness. Even more difficult issues are raised if we consider that lawyers, in at least some circumstances, might also owe an obligation of loyalty to the public interest that overrides their duty to their client, and perhaps even to the court. This is the concern of the *moral activist*.

Moral Activism

Moral activism encourages lawyers to have other ethical priorities beyond their loyalty to the client which may impinge on what those lawyers will and will not do for their clients. This does not mean that *moral activism* gives lawyers an excuse for allowing self-interest or personal taste to limit their loyalty to client interests. The grounded moral activist will know and be nurturing the personal characteristics that drive their positions and opinions – for example, a concern for fairness in the distribution of public resources – and is likely to be protected from too much self-interest. Rather, *moral activism* says that lawyers must critically examine their own inclinations and commitments in each situation in terms of what justice requires. Without a similar concern for private virtue, *adversarial advocacy* and *responsible lawyering* can encourage lawyers to put their own ethical commitments out of their mind when acting for clients. *Moral activism* on the other hand provides an intellectual framework for the private virtues and values that lawyers need if they are to identify what justice requires. When private virtue and rational commitment are in harmony in the moral activist lawyer, they are often particularly effective in generating the public actions that distinguish the whole of the legal profession.

The *moral activist* celebrates the lawyer who integrates their other ethical loyalties into their professional role. For example, the *moral activist* might say that instead of lawyers being required to show loyalty to whichever client comes along first, regardless of that client's cause, lawyers should be encouraged to actively seek out and choose clients and causes to whom they can ethically devote their services. A *moral activist* approach would also urge lawyers to explicitly discuss their own values and ethical commitments with their clients, to inform the client as to the likely limits of their loyalty, but also more importantly to try to persuade the client to share their ethical commitment. This general virtue of compassion for the wider community and humanistic responsibility for the body politic would also allow *morally activist* lawyers to support causes and individuals who are either ahead of or well outside mainstream sympathies, policies and even fair procedures. *Moral activist* lawyers will support the law if, in their opinion, it is just, but will dispense with it also when justice demands. The key to their determination is their sense of an internal moral compass. Thus, for example, environmentalist lawyers and those with a Gaia-like sense of 'deep ecology' for the exploited and degraded environment might in extreme circumstances determine to act outside the law and disable timber-cutting equipment adjacent to national parks, if they considered that long-term environmental concerns justified their stance.[39]

In serious circumstances, where a client cannot be persuaded to do what the lawyer believes (on principled grounds) to be the right thing, the *moral activist* would consider breaching client loyalty and confidentiality to prevent harm.[40] For the *moral activist* this in itself would be a difficult decision that must be taken after due ethical examination. The *moral activist* does not discount the importance of loyalty and confidentiality to clients as an important part of the way justice is usually achieved in our legal system. But where a client's actions are likely to physically or financially harm third parties, or put some other public interest at serious risk, then a *moral activist* could decide that ethical regard for client loyalty and confidentiality is outweighed by the need to do what is necessary to stop the client harming others or the public interest. Normally this would mean informing an appropriate authority (the police or a regulator) of the client's intended actions. There may even be situations in which informing the media at large, or some other drastic measure, might be justified.

As discussed in Chapter 4, the *ASCR* and the law itself do recognise that there are exceptions to lawyers' obligations of confidentiality where clients are acting illegally or unethically. These exceptions give lawyers some legal discretion and even permission to behave in a *moral activist* way to blow the whistle and breach confidentiality and loyalty where a greater public interest demands it.[41]

The Ethics of Care

The *ethics of care*, like *moral activism*, encourages lawyers to be aware of, critically examine and act on their own ethical commitments in the practice of law. But the *ethics of care* will embrace more personal and relational ethical commitments than *moral activism's* focus on what justice requires. For example, the other three ethical approaches might each see a lawyer's commitment to maintain a healthy family life by getting home every day in time to eat dinner with the children and put them to bed as a personal concern that might interfere with doing one's best for one's clients in some situations. Rather, the *ethics of care* see personal

---

39 See Bradley Wendel, 'Civil Obedience' (2004) 103 *Columbia Law Review* 363, 418.

40 Sissela Bok, *Secrets: The Ethics of Concealment and Revelation* (Pantheon Books, New York, 1983) 129–30; David Luban, *Lawyers and Justice: An Ethical Study* (Princeton University Press, Princeton, 1988) 177–205; Donald Nicolson and Julian Webb, *Professional Legal Ethics: Critical Interrogations* (Oxford University Press, Oxford, 1999) 'Ch 9: Confidentiality' 253–76; Tur, 'Confidentiality and Accountability', 83–4.

41 Dal Pont, *Lawyers' Professional Responsibility*, [10.100]–[10.130]. See also Paul Finn, 'Professionals and Confidentiality' (1992) 14 *Sydney Law Review* 317, 323; Karen Koomen, 'Breach of Confidence and the Public Interest Defence: Is It in the Public Interest?' (1994) 10 *Queensland University of Technology Law Journal* 56, 86–8.

ethical commitments as a desirable and legitimate part of the way the lawyer cares for themselves and their client in the practice of law. Similarly a lawyer's personal commitment to a 'healing' practice, that as much as possible helps clients to resolve disputes amicably rather than adversarially, would be an appropriate influence on the way a lawyer interprets and represents their clients' interests, according to the *ethics of care*.[42] But it may well be seen by the other three approaches as an illegitimate conflicting interest that might distract the lawyer from zealously and responsibly considering what the client's interests justly require (as we have seen in Chapter 7).

The *ethics of care* approach also recognises lawyers' humanity, fallibility and susceptibility to pressure and temptation, even when trying to act ethically. Conflicting interests and obligations will inevitably be a part of the lawyer-client relationship, for good and for ill. According to the *ethics of care* therefore, lawyers need to be completely open and honest with their clients about the factors that might influence their judgement, so that clients can judge their lawyer's advice for themselves, and even persuade their own lawyer to a different point of view on ethical issues.[43]

An *ethics of care* approach would see a client as able to consent to their lawyer continuing to act in a situation of conflict of interests, or potential conflict, as long as the lawyer has put the client in a position to fully understand the conflict and its possible implications for them. Indeed the *ethics of care* approach sees it as possible and desirable that two or more clients will want the same lawyer or law firm to act for them both on the same matter. The *ethics of care* will focus on the clients' potential to harmonise their interests and work together to a 'common goal' – for example, in putting together a deal, arranging matters amicably after a separation or divorce, or mediating a dispute between business partners.[44] Here the *ethics of care* suggests that it might be quite appropriate for a lawyer to act as 'lawyer for the situation' and disregard the traditional adversarial advocate ideal of pure loyalty to just one client's interests.[45]

---

42 See Steven Keeva, *The Healing Practice* (Contemporary Books, Chicago, 1999).

43 See, eg, Nicolson and Webb, *Professional Legal Ethics*, 146–56, on the concept of 'autonomy-in-relation'.

44 Griffiths-Baker, *Serving Two Masters*, 115, cites solicitors' firms as differentiating 'common goal' conflicts as one type of conflict.

45 See Richard Tur, 'Family Lawyering and Legal Ethics' in Stephen Parker and Charles Sampford (eds), *Legal Ethics and Legal Practice: Contemporary Issues* (Clarendon Press, Oxford, 1995) 145; Richard Tur, 'Legal Ethics, Overview' in Ruth Chadwick (ed), *Encyclopedia of Applied Ethics* (Academic Press, San Diego, 1998) vol 3, 59, 67–9; Milner S Ball, *Called By Stories: Biblical Sagas and Their Challenge for Law* (Duke University Press, Durham, 2000) 'Ch 3: Counsel for the Situation' 22.

However, joint representation can only be justified by an *ethics of care* approach where the clients genuinely want to work together, can be equal partners without power imbalances, and are in a position to understand what that involves. If that is so, then it seems unlikely that the lawyer or law firm would be using information barriers and other arrangements to maintain confidentiality and the appearance of separation. For if clients truly want to work together, then they will need to do so on the basis that they are going to be completely open and honest with each other, and go to completely new, separate lawyers if they fail to work together effectively (as in the discussion of collaborative lawyering in Case Study 7.3 in Chapter 7). The *ethics of care* cannot be used merely as a justification for arrangements that seem to promise clients complete loyalty, while risking breach of confidential information and disloyalty. If the clients are not willing to agree to the proposal that the lawyer help them work together completely openly and honestly, then under an *ethics of care* approach it is questionable whether they have given their true consent to the arrangement at all.

CASE STUDY 8.2   ALLENS ARTHUR ROBINSON AND THE DRUG COMPANIES

Large national law firms with many partners in different offices, and many clients, frequently find themselves in situations where different partners are acting, or proposing to act, for clients with conflicting interests. Often conflicts between existing clients only emerge incrementally. It is tempting to assume that these conflicts can be 'managed', rather than avoided, so that the firm can continue to earn fees from two clients. This is a case study of a potential conflict that a large firm tried to manage, but eventually a decision to drop at least one of the clients became inevitable.

The Melbourne branch of major national law firm, Allens Arthur Robinson, found itself acting for three drug companies with potentially conflicting interests. Two, Pfizer and GlaxoSmithKline, were 'originators', major multinational pharmaceutical companies that invent, develop and manufacture new drugs. They had been Allens' clients for many years, and Allens acted for them on many issues.

The third was a 'generic' manufacturer, Mayne. Generic drug companies do not develop their own drugs, but manufacture drugs developed by other companies by waiting until originator companies' patents expire, or by successfully challenging originators' patents. Generic and originator drug manufacturers are strong commercial competitors, and also routinely engage in disputes and litigation over intellectual property rights. The Allens partner who acted for Mayne had previously acted for them from time to time when he had had his own small firm. That firm, and its practice, was then acquired by Allens.

For several years Allens maintained both Mayne and its originator clients on its books. Allens judged that this was appropriate, as there was no actual conflict of interest between the clients – the firm held no specific confidential information on the operations of each client that was of specific relevance to the matters they handled for other clients. Allens also put in place internal procedures (information barriers) to make sure that any confidential information that did exist would not pass between the lawyers acting for the different clients.

However, five years after the partner representing Mayne had joined Allens, 'it became increasingly clear there was a real potential for conflict'.[46] By this stage, Allens had already been acting for both GlaxoSmithKline and Mayne in relation to the same transaction (with the consent of both). Now, after five years, another client, Pfizer, was likely to sue Mayne in relation to a patent dispute, and was not happy that Allens also acted for Mayne.

It was considered necessary to cease acting for both Pfizer and Mayne, and Allens decided to 'let go' one client – Mayne. Mayne took action against Allens for breach of retainer, alleging, among other things, a conflict in Allens' continued representation of Pfizer, an action which was settled on undisclosed terms with Pfizer remaining an Allens client.[47] The partner and his team who had represented Mayne, however, also left Allens and joined another firm where, presumably, they could continue to act for Mayne.

Allens believed that the context and history of their relationship with both sets of clients made their decision to dispense just with Mayne appropriate. Mayne were recent clients, brought into the Allens fold only as a result of a firm merger. Further, Allens' representation of Mayne was sufficiently limited so that a degree of consensual separation akin to an information barrier had been constructed for the specific purpose of enabling that representation to occur. The originators, GlaxoSmithKline and Pfizer, were clients of much longer standing and had been represented by Allens in litigation as well as in a wide range of transactional matters. Allens believed that their loyalty to Mayne was in these circumstances limited.

---

46 Quotation from an Allens spokesperson reported in 'Mallesons Prospers from Allens IP Conflict', *Lawyers Weekly* (Sydney), 11 September 2003.

47 Christopher Webb, 'Dramatic Exile on Mayne Street', *Strictly Private, The Age* (Melbourne), 18 June 2003, 4.

DISCUSSION QUESTIONS

1. Suppose you were making the decision as to which client was owed the most *loyalty* and you were 'interviewing' both clients to determine their likely reactions to your withdrawal from acting for one of them before making a decision: Which issues do you think that GlaxoSmithKline and Pfizer would raise with you? What matters would be stressed by Mayne?

2. Imagine you are the Allens partner who does work for Pfizer. In what way would you respond to a request from Pfizer that you go to your fellow partner (working for Mayne) and ask them to stop acting for Mayne? What would the four different ethical approaches – *adversarial advocacy*, *responsible lawyering*, *moral activism* and the *ethics of care* – suggest about how you should handle this situation?

3. Allens decided to withdraw from representing its more recent, smaller client[48] in preference to its larger, longer-standing clients, when faced with a looming concurrent conflict involving litigation. A spokesperson from Allens was reported as saying, 'Decisions such as these are never easy, but we had longer standing relationships with those originator companies, those were better established'.[49] Is this an ethically justified reason to decide which client to continue representing? Which values, among those espoused by the four ethical approaches as discussed above, would most appeal to you in making your decision about who to 'let go' as a client? What would be the consequences of applying your chosen values? What would be the consequences of applying the alternative values? What would you do?

4. In hindsight, was Allens' initial reaction of setting up a device like an information barrier a good one? What other options were available to the firm and to the partner who represented Mayne when Allens first hired Mayne's lawyer? Would there still have been a conflict problem if the partner from the acquired law firm had ceased all representation of Mayne after joining Allens and then later Allens had planned to act against Mayne?

5. Do the conflicts of interest rules unjustifiably restrict the opportunity for individuals and smaller businesses or new entrants to a market to obtain access to lawyers with experience and expertise in a particular

---

48 Mayne is a large company by Australian standards, but not as large as the multinational drug companies Allens was representing. And it appears Mayne was not giving Allens as much work as these other clients.

49 'Mallesons Prospers from Allens IP Conflict'.

area of law (because they are all likely to already be acting for larger incumbents in the market)? Do the conflicts of interest rules unjustifiably restrict lawyers' capacity to move between firms (because they might create conflict of interests for the new firm)?

6. Should law firms have an obligation not to act for two clients where the clients have conflicting *commercial* interests ('commercial conflict of interest'), but there are no legal issues between them? For example, a law firm acts for two drug companies in relation to completely separate matters, but the two companies compete with each other for market share? What about where the two clients have conflicting interests in how a legal *issue* should be resolved ('issue conflict of interest') – that is, how a legal doctrine should be interpreted or applied in certain situations – but are not litigating or arguing between themselves in any matter relating to that issue? For example, the one law firm acts for originator drug companies arguing for interpretations of the law that lead to stronger and longer protections for patents in some cases, but acts for generic manufacturers arguing the opposite interpretation in other cases. What do you think would be the consequence on the availability of lawyers as *adversarial advocates* and *moral activists* if lawyers and law firms felt they could not act where there were commercial conflicts of interest and issues conflicts of interest? Are there some clients (or potential clients) in some situations who would be more affected by this than others?[50]

CASE STUDY 8.3 BLAKE DAWSON WALDRON AND THE SHARE BUY-BACK[51]

In this case study another major law firm, Blake Dawson Waldron (Blakes), found itself in a conflict of interest when one partner was retained by one client to attack an arrangement that another partner had been retained to help pull together for another client. Blakes was not even aware of the conflict, until the client on the other side pointed it out.

---

50 On the impact of commercial and issues conflicts on the availability of pro bono legal work, see Elisabeth Wentworth, 'Barriers to Pro Bono: Commercial Conflicts of Interest Reconsidered' in Christopher Arup and Kathy Laster (eds), *For the Public Good: Pro Bono and the Legal Profession in Australia* (The Federation Press, Sydney, 2001) 166. On the impact of commercial conflicts on the availability of lawyers generally, see also Griffiths-Baker, *Serving Two Masters*, 102–3, 113–14.

51 *Village Roadshow Ltd v Blake Dawson Waldron* (2004) Aust Torts Reports ¶81–726.

One Blakes partner was paid by major film distributor Village Roadshow to review a draft trust deed and other documents relating to a proposed share buy-back,[52] and to advise the proposed trustee for the arrangement, Permanent Trustee, about the documents and their obligations under the trust deed. A court later accepted that, although technically Permanent Trustee was Blakes' client, Village Roadshow and Permanent Trustee were working together as a team. The documents had been prepared by Village's main law firm, Minters, and Minters continued to act for Village. Indeed it was Minters, as Village's law firm, that organised Blakes' involvement in the case.

The Blakes partner spent about 30 hours over two weeks in September on this task, and then advised Village on Permanent Trustee's behalf that Permanent Trustee was happy for the deal to go ahead with the documentation. The buy-back process then began. No further work was performed for Permanent Trustee (or Village) by Blakes.

At the end of October of the same year, a different Blakes partner was approached by Boswell, one of Village's shareholders, to help Boswell contest the share buy-back. The second Blakes partner was in the same work team as the first partner, a group of about 20 partners and 50–60 employees all working from the same floor of Blakes' offices. One of Boswell's early objections to the share buy-back, as laid out in a letter on its behalf from Blakes to Minters, was that some aspects of the scheme documentation were misleading and deceptive. Blakes went on to act for Boswell in various court applications seeking to stop the buy-back going ahead.

On 22 November, three weeks after Blakes' first letter to Minters on behalf of Boswell, someone from Minters' client, Village, pointed out to Minters that Blakes had acted for Permanent Trustee and was now acting for Boswell. The Minters partner handling the matter said he had not noticed before, 'due to inadvertence'.[53] In mid-December Minters eventually objected to Blakes acting for Boswell, saying that the work Blakes had previously done for Permanent Trustee and Village represented a conflict.

When Blakes found out that Village was objecting to its representation of Boswell, it contacted Boswell and asked what it wanted them to do. Boswell was happy for Blakes to continue acting, and agreed that it would not expect Blakes

---

52 This is where a company buys back some of its own shares from its shareholders. Because this reduces the total capital available to the company and may reduce the value of other shareholders' shares, company law puts strict conditions on the process by which this can take place, including various requirements for shareholder consultation and votes as well as opportunities for shareholders to object to the proposed buy-back. Share buy-backs can be quite contentious within a company.

53 *Village Roadshow Ltd v Blake Dawson Waldron* (2004) Aust Torts Reports ¶81–726, 65 337.

to disclose any confidential information that had been obtained from Permanent Trustee. Blakes did not, however, contact their former client, Permanent Trustee. Instead Permanent Trustee contacted Blakes and suggested Blakes might cease acting for Boswell. Blakes' response was 'non-committal if not evasive' according to the judge who eventually decided the matter.[54] The decision was made to continue acting for Boswell, but this was not communicated to Permanent Trustee.

In Village's application for an injunction to restrain Blakes from acting for Boswell against it, the court found that Blakes in fact had no confidential information from Permanent Trustee. But Byrne J applied Brooking JA's approach in *Spincode* and granted the injunction according to the test of 'what a fair minded reasonably informed member of the public might think of the administration of justice which permitted this to occur'.[55]

DISCUSSION QUESTIONS

1. The judge in this case simply accepted that Village Roadshow and Permanent Trustee were part of a team with a common goal, in contrast to Boswell (so that Blakes' work for Permanent Trustee meant Blakes would not be allowed to act against Village either on the same matter). But do you see any potential conflicts in relation to Blakes accepting Village's money to advise Permanent Trustee about the scheme?

2. Most law firms have systems for checking for conflicts of interest before taking on a new matter, such as database searches for names related to the new matter to see if the same names are on any files relating to existing matters. What do you think went wrong here? Why do you think neither Blakes nor Minters (who as part of their representation of Village had hired Blakes to act for Permanent Trustee) knew about Blakes' conflict until an officer from Village pointed it out? What would they have had to check to know?

3. Village argued that 'for a firm of solicitors to take money from a client for erecting a legal edifice, it should not then take a fee from some other to dismantle it'.[56] This could be interpreted as a particularly *responsible*

---

54 Ibid.
55 Ibid 65 339, quoting *Sent v John Fairfax Publications Pty Ltd* [2002] VSC 429 (Unreported, Nettle J, 7 October 2002), another decision that followed Justice Brooking's decision in *Spincode*.
56 *Village Roadshow Ltd v Blake Dawson Waldron* (2004) Aust Torts Reports ¶81–726, 65 339.

lawyering concern that a lawyer should not argue that something is legally valid and appropriate one day for one client, and then attack the same thing for another client the next day. Rather they should have a consistent and sincere opinion about what the law requires that is the same every day.[57] It could also be seen as a matter of loyalty to a previous client not to attack a document or arrangement that the lawyer took money to set up for that client. What do you think? Are there reasons why a lawyer or law firm should not ethically argue on behalf of one client that a document it drafted or arrangement it set up for another client is flawed? What are they? (Consider what each of the four ethical approaches would say about this situation.)

4. Would there be a lawyer-client conflict, not just a client-client conflict in such a situation? What if the lawyer or law firm had in fact done a bad job in drafting the documents or setting up the arrangement for the first client? What should their duty to each of the first and second client entail in that situation? (You might find it helpful to think about what each of the four ethical approaches would say in this situation.)

5. Byrne J was not very sympathetic about the difficulties of clients trying to obtain un-conflicted representation from among a very small pool of very large firms:

> To my mind, this is the price which the clients of such firms and the firms themselves must pay. The firms have found it commercially convenient to become large. This is but one disadvantage of this trend. It is certainly no reason for the courts to weaken the traditionally high standard of a practitioner's loyalty to the client which have characterised the practice of law in this State.[58]

Thinking about the facts of both this case and Case Study 8.2, do you think that the concentration of large commercial law firms and their approach to managing conflicts of interest might threaten their ability to live up to the ideal of *adversarial advocacy*, and indeed the other ethical approaches, in relation to handling conflicts? If so, is this a problem? Should the courts' relatively strict approach to conflicts of interest, especially in cases like *Spincode* and *Village Roadshow*, change or should law firm practices change?

---

57 See Robert Eli Rosen, 'Devils, Lawyers and Salvation Lie in the Details: Deontological Legal Ethics, Issue Conflicts of Interest and Civic Education in Law Schools' in Kim Economides (ed), *Ethical Challenges to Legal Education and Conduct* (Hart Publishing, Oxford, 1998) 61, 73–81.

58 *Village Roadshow Ltd v Blake Dawson Waldron* (2004) Aust Torts Reports ¶81–726, 65 339.

CASE STUDY 8.4   A LARGE LAW FIRM WITH MULTIPLE CLIENTS

A large Australian law firm (LLF), was allegedly asked by the directors of a failed company to jointly represent them after the liquidator of the failed company sought to claim a substantial sum from them on behalf of the company's creditors. It is alleged that the liquidator sought to recover the sum from directors A, B and C personally on the basis that they knew that the company was trading while insolvent and did nothing in relation to that knowledge until months later, when creditors' invoices had been allowed to blow out to huge sums. This would be a serious breach of directors' duties that could lead to the directors being subject to civil penalties and banning from future directorships as well as personal liability for the damage caused to creditors.

LLF agreed to represent all three directors jointly and adopted an internal practice of keeping the files of A, B and C separate and private from one another. That is, none of the three directors knew the contents of the files of the other two directors. Relevant LLF staff, however, knew all about each file and LLF did not assert that this strategy amounted to an information barrier.

A subsequently complained to the legal profession regulator about the following ways in which LLF allegedly handled the matter:

- B and C were closer to each other than either was to A, and a relevant LLF partner was a friend of both B and C.

- A was allegedly deceived by B and C as to the fact that B knew that unsustainable amounts were owing to creditors during the time that the company was still trading. LLF learned of this deceit after it commenced to act, but did not tell A that B had that specific knowledge.

- LLF made an effort to settle the liquidator's claim. In doing so, LLF tried to pressure A in a mediation planning session, in the presence of B and C, to contribute to the proposed settlement of the liquidators' claim, even though LLF knew that A did not have any asserted or verifiable knowledge of that insolvent trading during the relevant insolvent trading period. At the mediation planning session, LLF knew from A's ostensibly 'private' file that A was unlikely in any event to have sufficient funds to contribute to the settlement.

- LLF and B agreed privately to a strategy that would expose A to liquidator questioning during a forthcoming mediation session, in an effort to put A under pressure to agree to a subsequent contribution agreement between the three directors. Shortly afterwards, presumably aware of conflicts issues, LLF proposed the contribution agreement which did *not* involve any contribution by A. LLF had received substantial fees at this point and indicated that each director should obtain independent legal advice, but also indicated it could not continue to act for all three unless the agreement was executed in a matter of days.

DISCUSSION QUESTIONS

1. If A had file notes and other memoranda but his complaint to a regulator was rejected on the basis that his serious allegations required documentary support, what sort of evidence would be necessary to prove these sorts of claims?

2. What should LLF have done to avoid these things happening? Even if they didn't happen as A alleges, do you think the law firm did the right thing in acting for all three directors? What could they have done differently?

3. *Spincode* concerned a firm that switched sides in the middle of an active dispute. When different clients are jointly represented and either client asks the firm to mediate or arbitrate between them, how ought the firm respond?

4. If this case were true, would it also involve issues of loyalty? How would a court see the current case if it were litigated?

Conclusion

Understanding and anticipating the ethical challenges raised by conflicting loyalties is arguably one of the most difficult processes for lawyers because 'the facts' do not always present neatly, or may be at first hidden from view. But there usually comes a point at which the competing loyalties do become evident. We cannot say when the LLF in Case Study 8.4 first crossed the ethical line, but the more experience a lawyer acquires, the earlier they should reach that point of recognition in each case. The earlier it is understood that loyalty is being compromised, the more capacity lawyers have to do something about it.

Lawyers can easily become occupationally desensitised to the implications of conflict – the need sometimes to choose between opposed positions. They can come to see the process of living with different competing interests – that is, owing different loyalties to different people and different institutions – as merely one of 'operational management' or 'tweaking' associated with maximising fees. Some firms may choose to compartmentalise concurrent clients' files in a half-baked effort to avoid conflicts and keep up the illusion of separate but intact loyalties for the sake of those fees, but those efforts will eventually be exposed for what they are.

Many successful lawyers might also cultivate the sense among clients with potentially opposed interests that they can in fact juggle their competing loyalties or positions indefinitely, without sacrificing either client: so much so that the art of wearing more than one hat can become, for some of them, a comfortable position, a position from which loyalty is perceived as highly situational. All this continues until one of the parties wakes up or perceives that there is just too much at stake to allow such an ambivalent loyalty to continue, or the firm concerned realises that perception is imminent and tries to do something about it.

A choice of values occurs in all cases of conflicting loyalty, whether we make that choice consciously or not. Sometimes without even realising that we are making a decision, we in fact decide that a problem is 'just too hard' and give up on coming to a principled, ethical resolution to the conflict. Instead we 'go with the gut feeling', without trying to know what is the value behind that feeling. It is often in these situations, where we do not feel we have made an ethical choice at all – we have simply allowed a situation to carry us along – that our actions end up having consequences that we did not expect. We might end up in losing valued clients, having our reputation questioned by colleagues, even facing disciplinary action or ridicule in the media. A conscious choice to know and understand our values base will produce consequences that are, at least, anticipated and, it is to be hoped, defendable and desirable within an ethical and satisfying legal practice.

RECOMMENDED FURTHER READING

G E Dal Pont, *Lawyers' Professional Responsibility* (Lawbook Co, Pyrmont, NSW, 5th edn, 2013) 'Part II: Lawyers' Duty to the Client', especially Chapters 6, 7 and 8.

Adrian Evans, 'A Mutuality of Interest' (2003) 77(7) *Law Institute Journal* 86.

—— 'Concurrent Loyalties' (2004) 78(6) *Law Institute Journal* 82.

Janine Griffiths-Baker, *Serving Two Masters: Conflicts of Interest in the Modern Law Firm* (Hart Publishing, Oxford, 2002).

Law Society of New South Wales in consultation with the Law Institute of Victoria, *Information Barrier Guidelines* (2006) Law Society of New South Wales <www.lawsociety.com.au/page.asp?partID=15645> at 2 June 2006.

Donald Nicolson and Julian Webb, *Professional Legal Ethics: Critical Interrogations* (Oxford University Press, Oxford, 1999) 'Ch 9: Confidentiality' 253–76.

Richard Tur, 'Confidentiality and Accountability' (1992) 1 *Griffith Law Review* 73.

Duncan Webb, 'Autonomy, Paternalism, and Institutional Interest: Why Some Conflicts Can't Be Waived' (2005) 12 *International Journal of the Legal Profession* 261.

LAWYERS' FEES AND COSTS: BILLING AND OVER-CHARGING

Introduction: Legal Fees and Access to Justice

Clients are more likely to complain about their lawyers' fees and costs than any other issue,[1] and even the most conscientious lawyers have trouble controlling costs and explaining them to clients. Typical complaints include that the lawyer has failed to make proper disclosure of likely costs at the commencement of the matter, failed to provide a written bill, failed to provide an itemised bill when requested by the client, or charged for the preparation of an itemised bill (even though clients have a right to request one).[2] Deliberate 'gross' over-charging also features prominently among client complaints, as does the withdrawal of costs from a client's trust account without their permission, or the deduction of fees in the absence of a proper bill. Not surprisingly, clients complain about lawyers who have the temerity to charge costs for litigated matters that amount to more than the amount actually recovered in the litigation. Also featuring prominently among client complaints about lawyers are complaints about excessive hourly billing rates and exploitation of 'no-win, no fee' agreements.[3] Clients routinely complain that they have been promised that they will incur no fees unless they win, but find themselves losing and having to pay the costs of the other side, or disagreeing with their lawyer about whether there has been a 'win'.

One Queensland lawyer was suspended for twelve months for gross over-charging for billing a 'no-win, no fee' client $300 per hour plus a premium of 25% for all work done by any employee of the firm, from partner to paralegal to secretary. The charges included twelve minutes (at $300 an hour) for a secretary wrapping a box of chocolates to be given to a reporting doctor's secretary as thanks for correcting a report, and another twelve minutes discussing the purchase of the chocolates.[4] In

---

1 Adrian Evans, 'Acceptable, But Not Entirely Satisfied: Client Perceptions of Victorian Solicitors' (1995) 20 *Alternative Law Journal* 57; Legal Fees Review Panel, *Report: Legal Costs in New South Wales* (2005) Lawlink New South Wales 7 <www.lawlink.nsw.gov.au/lawlink/legislation policy/lllpd.nsf/pages/lp_publications> at 29 May 2006.

2 These matters would amount to breaches of the *Model Laws* pt 10 ('Costs Disclosure and Review'), specifically cl 1009(1)(c), cl 1029(1), cl 1032(1) and cl 1032(3) respectively. The list of complaints is from Legal Fees Review Panel, *Discussion Paper: Lawyer's Costs and the Time Billing* [sic] (2004) Lawlink New South Wales 7– 8 <www.lawlink.nsw.gov.au/lawlink/olsc/ll olsc.nsf/vwPreviewActivePages/OLSClfrp at> 29 May 2006.

3 For a good example of a lawyer treating unsophisticated clients 'shamefully' in relation to 'no-win, no-fee' agreements see *Baker v Legal Services Commissioner* [2006] QCA 145 (Unreported, McPherson, Jerrod JJA and Douglas J, 5 May 2006).

4 *Council of the Queensland Law Society Inc v Roche* [2004] 2 Qd R 574. See the comment by de Jersey CJ at 584 that he 'hoped' it would be very unusual for a law firm to charge for the time of secretarial staff at the same rate as partners.

another case in New South Wales a solicitor was struck off for charging a client with a personal injuries claim a quarter of her $3.5 million settlement in fees and charges, where the bill contained errors and duplications and charged for work that was not done.[5] This was the result of just one of a series of cases in which clients had complained about similar conduct in relation to the same firm. In another case, the client successfully sued the same lawyer for breach of contract and misleading and deceptive conduct in relation to overcharging throughout a personal injuries case in which 383 items of attendance or work had been billed even though liability had been admitted and the insurance company wanted to settle.[6] Items charged included three-line letters that would take a few seconds to read were billed for 12 minutes of time at a senior litigation lawyer rate of $435 an hour (a charge of $87); another five-line letter was billed at $184 for 'perusal' – that is, a time charge of 24 minutes. There was a charge of 18 minutes at the rate of $460 an hour for sending a four-sentence email to the Motor Accident Authority. Secretaries in the firm were being billed out at partners' rates of $460 an hour, charging for 'perusing and considering' two-line letters.

It is not just because of unethical practices by *individual* lawyers that clients complain about their legal bills. Cultural and structural factors in the *organisation* of litigation and legal practice also often lead to client misunderstanding of, and disillusion about, how they are billed. As we shall see, the predominance of time-based billing as a way of charging clients and managing lawyers' performance within firms can magnify incentives for poor billing practices. Moreover, the ethic of zealous advocacy is itself ambiguous about billing. On the one hand, one might argue that doing all you can as a lawyer to advance the client's interests within the law 'requires lawyers to charge their client as little as possible', but zealous advocacy 'also requires a lawyer to leave no stone unturned in the advancing of their client's case'.[7] This tension is usually resolved in favour of 'no stone unturned', which leads to higher costs.

But it is not a case of 'either-or'. Most rip-offs, when they occur, are the product of both an inadequate system and a practitioner ready to exploit the deficiency. Systemic problems of excessive adversarialism, individual problems of over-charging, and poor lawyer-client communication about costs interact to make access to justice problems worse.

Both lawyers and clients are uncertain about what is reasonable for lawyers to charge, and what methods can fairly be used to calculate legal fees. This creates opportunities for over-charging. But it is not just the level of fees a lawyer

---

5 *Legal Services Commissioner v Keddie* [2012] NSWADT 106.
6 *Liu v Keddies Lawyers*, District Court of New South Wales, Matter 224007 of 2010, 8 November 2011.
7 Richard Moorhead, 'Filthy Lucre: Lawyers' Fees and Lawyers' Ethics – What Is Wrong with Informed Consent?' (2011) 31 *Legal Studies* 345, 352.

charges their *own* client that increases the costs of justice. As we have seen in Chapter 6, the adversarial litigation *system* also creates high, and unpredictable, costs, putting at risk the fundamental values of fair and equal access to justice for all.[8] Large 'defendant firms' (firms that typically act for corporate defendants and insurance companies in personal injury and workers compensation matters) can delay or even completely frustrate the conclusion of litigation by devices such as overburdening plaintiffs with documents in discovery, contesting every step of the pretrial process, and then arguing every point during trial. If the other side decides to play hard and, for example, deliver 700 pages of interrogatories in order to push their opponent to the brink financially (as occurred in the *White Industries Case*, Case Study 6.4 in Chapter 6), costs can blow out quickly. Excessive adversarialism cripples possibilities for access to justice precisely *because* it increases costs in unpredictable ways.

Moreover, the lawyer is often in a position of privilege and power compared with the client, especially the unsophisticated individual client. People may have to use a lawyer for the first time when they are in a vulnerable social, emotional and financial situation and need legal help quickly when they suffer a disputatious relationship breakdown or get arrested and charged for a criminal offence. Indeed, any client who has not previously used a lawyer and had experience with the legal system is at a disadvantage in bargaining with them about what services will be provided and at what cost.

Consider the following two short examples of lawyer misconduct in relation to charging clients. Why do you think so many clients in each of these two cases were willing to do what these lawyers asked? Is there something special about the relationship between lawyer and client that might prevent some clients from complaining about their lawyer or challenging their billing practices earlier on?

- In the late 1980s one suburban Melbourne practitioner devised a scheme to overcharge hundreds of vulnerable clients by first telephoning them and asking to be paid in cash – usually relatively small amounts of several hundred dollars for wills and conveyances – and then, some 12 to 18 months later, sending them a bill for the same amount. Numerous clients could not recall for certain whether they had previously paid or not, since no receipts were ever issued on the first occasion. Many paid a second time before the scam was uncovered and

---

8 Australian Law Reform Commission, *Managing Justice: A Review of the Federal Civil Justice System*, Report No 89 (Australian Government Publishing Service, Canberra, 2000) 'Ch 4: Legal Costs'; Access to Justice Advisory Committee, Legal Fees Review Panel, *Report: Legal Costs in NSW*; Christine Parker, *Just Lawyers: Regulation and Access* (Oxford University Press, Oxford, 1999) 'Ch 3: Access to Justice'; Victorian Law Reform Commission, *Civil Justice Review: Report* (Victorian Law Reform Commission, Melbourne, 2008) 'Ch 11: Reducing the Cost of Litigation'.

terminated. The practitioner was belatedly investigated by the Law Institute of Victoria and eventually agreed to close his practice.[9]

- In *Re Veron: Ex parte Law Society of New South Wales*,[10] a New South Wales court found a practitioner guilty of professional misconduct for charging plaintiffs in simple, uncomplicated personal injuries matters up to $1500 more than the average fee. Prior to settlement, the practitioner would extract from his clients an authority to settle their claims for a set sum, with an added clause that permitted him to also deduct costs of $1000 or more without further reference to his client. The practitioner argued that his clients had consented to the deduction and, by implication, it was no one else's business what those fees were if the client had consented. While it *is* acceptable to withdraw fees from a trust account by prior written arrangement with the client, the combination of the authority and the over-charging here seemed to be designed to prevent client scrutiny until the deduction was a *fait accompli*. Perhaps the practitioner hoped that the difficulty of complaining would discourage his clients, none of whom he expected to represent again. The court showed it was ready to set aside any client consent process where the effect was in fact to deceive the client, and described the arrangements as extortionate and dishonourable in dealing with the client's trust funds.

In the first half of this chapter we analyse where and how ethical issues arise in lawyers' fees and billing practices, including extended examinations of the ethics of time-based billing, and the pressures it puts on individual lawyers to behave unethically, and particular issues with fees in relation to litigation. In the second half, we consider alternative values for lawyers' fees and costs relating first to the way in which lawyers should communicate about costs with their clients and second, to the methods used to calculate legal fees. The chapter concludes with three case studies for discussion.

Ethical Problems with Lawyers' Fees and Billing Practices

The public view that lawyers routinely over-charge stems partly from the fact that lay clients do not understand the worth of their lawyers' work in the way that their lawyers do. Much legal work is invisible to clients because it consists of applying abstract knowledge and conceptual judgement to fact situations that often differ only subtly from prior cases. Precedents from earlier decisions are rarely complete

---

9 From the files of the Springvale Monash Legal Service Inc.
10 [1966] 1 NSWR 511. See also Legal Fees Review Panel, *Discussion Paper*, [3.18].

templates for later disputes, but clients may not understand the significance of minute differences, especially when their own research provides them with what they think is a clear answer to their problem. By contrast, householders can see what their plumber does and can therefore partially relate the (expensive) repairs to their roof to the size of the bill – and their roof no longer leaks. Legal clients see very little happening in their case, and often experience continuing stress in their lawyer-client interactions, yet feel they have achieved only compromised outcomes.

Contact with the legal system is always likely to involve conflict, dispute and difficult choices, and the way clients perceive the worth of their lawyers' work often depends a lot on the quality and amount of information and communication they receive from their lawyer. As we shall see below, this means that good lawyering requires excellent communication between lawyer and client about the work to be done and likely fees. The written costs disclosures required by legislation (see below) are not clear enough for many clients to properly understand. Lawyers should sit down with their prospective clients and 'walk them through' the way they will be charged, checking as they go to see that they have been properly understood. This is also a way of building trust between client and lawyer, and its importance cannot be overemphasised. Clients need to know they can trust their lawyer to handle their case competently and efficiently, because the legal services market is imperfect: the buyers of legal services often do not know where to get quality work done at a fair price and the sellers (lawyers) are commonly unable to predict accurately what their fee will be. An important aspect of client trust in their lawyer is knowing: 'Can I trust my lawyer to tell me the truth in their assessment of the merit of my case and how much it will cost me?' The legal costing system, as it stands, and lack of adequate communication about costs, may entrench dissatisfaction for both lawyer and client.

One reason that clients complain so often about their legal bills is that legal costs are often unpredictable and no one method of calculating legal fees seems to be perfect. Therefore we begin by introducing the two main ways in which lawyers calculate their fees – item remuneration and time-based billing – and the different ethical issues that these two methods of billing raise. As we shall see, both contain significant potential for client disillusion.

The fact that both these costing methods are ethically flawed does not mean that all lawyers abuse them. It does mean that, as with most aspects of the lawyer-client retainer, the vast majority of clients are dependent on their lawyer's sense of integrity. Some clients, such as large organisations or wealthy individuals, have enough purchasing power and experience dealing with lawyers to avoid both these methods of billing and instead require law firms to tender for a package of services, ensuring that the successful tenderer agrees to a lump sum for all work, regardless of the problems that might later occur in providing the contracted services. However, most clients have no alternative but to accept the billing method proposed by their lawyer.

Item Remuneration Billing

Lawyers can charge on an *item remuneration* or *task-completed* basis, which means they apply a predetermined 'scale' or schedule, which specifies the amount of money that may be claimed for each sub-category of legal work, or task, in a larger case or transaction. Item remuneration allows lawyers to be specific about what they have done for their client and to produce a bill itemising the amount charged for each task in the case. Thus, drafting a letter may be charged to the client at, say, $30 per 'folio' (a folio = 100 words). It makes no difference *how long* the lawyer takes to draft the letter of 100 words, the lawyer will still be paid the same amount for the *task*. The actual amount charged per item usually varies upwards according to how much money is being claimed (or defended), to recognise the extra 'skill and responsibility' associated with a larger claim. A typical scale will allow $30 for a letter where the total claim is for, say, $1500, but permit a charge of, say, $45 for exactly the same letter, where the amount claimed is $2500.

Historically, legislation governing the legal profession and legal work allowed the legal profession and the courts to set minimum fee scales for all legal work. These item remuneration scales were considered justified in the past because they were thought to protect unsophisticated clients from being exploited by lawyers in a situation where clients could not judge the quality and appropriate price for legal services. Nor would clients necessarily be in a position to negotiate and bargain effectively with their prospective lawyer to get the best deal. It was considered better to highly regulate lawyers' fees by scales set for the whole profession, on the assumption that the profession would act in the public interest and ensure that all lawyers conformed to the same high quality and that the fees would be fair. These 'scale fees' set by the profession were abolished in the 1990s because they were considered anticompetitive.[11] They effectively allowed the profession to set a minimum floor for their own prices and prevented clients from 'shopping around' for a better price. As one lawyer has commented about the impact of abolition of scales:

> Prior to the mid-80s pretty much everything was done on scale, so you got paid per item, and nobody particularly cared how long it took you as long as you billed enough items. And the conveyancing scales, for example, were so generous that, if you had the clients, you could work maybe 15 hours a week...But all that's changed...Things are getting measured more precisely; the overseers have become crueller.[12]

---

11 See Christine Parker, *Just Lawyers*, 38–41.
12 Lawyer interviewed and quoted by Iain Campbell and Sara Charlesworth, 'Salaried Lawyers and Billable Hours: A New Perspective from the Sociology of Work' (2012) 19 *International Journal of the Legal Profession* 89–122, 98–9.

Despite the abolition of scales as a required method of charging, the courts have continued to publish fee scales for the purposes of assessing disputes about costs in litigation. And since individual lawyers and law firms are free to set their own fees on an item remuneration basis if they wish, many lawyers use these 'court scales' as a basis for their own charging.[13] Item remuneration may well be less dangerous than time-based billing for the unsophisticated client. Clients have the comfort of knowing that, even if the lawyer is a bit slow in completing the task, it is the lawyer not the client who carries the cost of the extra time spent. There are, however, a number of potential ethical disadvantages in item remuneration billing for clients.

Where the scale fee is calculated partly by reference to the amount in dispute (or the value of the property subject to a transaction), clients, understandably, do not understand why they should pay $45 for the same letter that would only cost them $30 if they had less at stake. For most clients, the fact that there is more risk for the lawyer in the larger claim and therefore it is reasonable (or fair) for him or her to charge more, is beside the point. Clients believe that they are entitled to the same proficiency no matter how large the claim, and tend to view fee differences of this nature as simple exploitation.

Moreover, the profession itself has a major influence on how much lawyers can charge for each item in the court scale. The scale amounts are set by committees and, although those committees may be diligent and conscious of their wider responsibilities, they are dominated by lawyers rather than being comprised of a mix of lawyers and consumers.

Finally, court scales of costs generally only specify a *minimum* fee, because the cost committees that set the court scales have always leaned towards lawyers' arguments that fees for individual items under the scales may be increased where the circumstances are peculiar.

Time-Based Billing

Time-based billing is the dominant method of charging legal fees. The lawyer specifies an hourly rate – say $350 – and the client agrees to pay that rate multiplied by however many hours the task takes. Time-based billing cannot operate at all without a valid costs agreement between lawyer and client, since billing other than billing on the basis of scales of costs for litigation cannot occur without a costs agreement (*Model Laws* 3.4.21). This means that cost agreements have become so important to the financial success of legal practice that they are usually lengthy and cover numerous rights and obligations of both lawyers and clients. Firms

---

13 There are also special scales and rules about fees and disputing fees in the family and criminal law jurisdictions.

typically present their preferred form of cost agreement in a long, eye-glazing and standardised format to clients, and are prepared to negotiate on only a few key clauses connected with hourly charging rates.

Time-based billing is attractive to the profession because it normally results in a higher level of fees than item remuneration. It might also reflect lawyers' sense that they are being paid for their professional advice, rather than for a product. It is also a useful way for law firms to keep track of what individual lawyers are doing and how much they are earning for the firm. As Campbell and Charlesworth argue, 'the billable hours system came to prominence as a billing method but its primary function is no longer billing; instead its primary function is as a mechanism of management control, which acts to transmit pressure on salaried solicitors'.[14] But it is not as transparent to the client as the traditional system, because legal work need not be as precisely itemised in any bill. Clients increasingly regard its opacity and unpredictability as both inefficient and unfair, since there is not necessarily any upper limit on the total hours appearing on the time sheet.

Jim Spigelman, former Chief Justice of New South Wales, has gone so far as to say that much of the problem with lawyers' fees centres on time-based billing. He describes it as ethically indefensible, because a mediocre lawyer can charge more time than the efficient lawyer who does the same job in less time, and also unsustainable if access to justice is to be restored and 'external regulation' is to be avoided:

> ...[I]t is difficult to justify a system in which inefficiency is rewarded with higher remuneration...[because] the legal practitioner does not have a financial incentive to do the service as quickly as possible. The control is of course, the practitioner's sense of professional responsibility. For most members of the profession, this restraint is a real one. Only a handful of members of the profession exploit their position by providing services that either do not need to be provided at all, or provide them in a more luxurious manner than is appropriate. The enlightened self-interest of the majority requires some form of professional control of the handful who may abuse the system. Such conduct, even by a minority, affects the reputation of the profession and may determine the nature of external regulation.[15]

Time-based billing will be in a client's interest if the lawyer completes the task quickly, and so charges less than if fees were calculated on an item remuneration

---

14 Campbell and Charlesworth, 'Salaried Lawyers and Billable Hours', 112.

15 J Spigelman, 'Address' (Speech delivered at the Opening of the NSW Law Term Dinner, Sydney, 2 February 2004) <www.cso.nsw.gov.au/lawlink/supreme court/llsc.nsf/pages/SCO speech 020204> at 31 May 2006. See also the extensive critique of time-based billing in Legal Fees Review Panel, *Discussion Paper*.

basis. But it is usually not in a client's best interests, because the final fee is rarely known at the time the client signs the agreement, and the lawyer has no contractual incentive to limit the bill.

Why then would a client sign up to time-based billing? Some lawyers will restrain the number of hours they charge the client if they hope to receive more work from the client. But generally only clients with 'buying power', usually companies and government departments that repeatedly use legal services, can negotiate an upper limit on the amount that can be billed. Other clients will have less negotiating power. Apart from conveyances and probate matters, the set or lump sum fee for service is rarely available to 'consumer' plaintiffs, even though this group is most in need of precise and predictable legal fees.

Irresponsible lawyers may insert an excessively high hourly rate in the cost agreement if they think the client will not notice, understand, or perhaps even care. A high hourly rate in the cost agreement unfortunately strikes the client's eye as just a few hundred dollars and nothing more.[16] Many potential plaintiffs, perhaps one-off litigants anxious to prove a point or recover what they think will be many thousands of dollars in a judgment, do not do the mental arithmetic on the spot and multiply those few hundred dollars by the real killer – total hours anticipated. Too frequently, clients do not think even to ask questions about the number of hours which might be necessary to get to judgment or an offer of compromise, and the likely true cost goes undiscussed.

Unremarkably, all clients care (and many later complain) when they later think about what they have agreed to. This is particularly likely if they begin to get concerned about losing a case which, they believe, their lawyer assured them had 'more than a reasonable prospect of success'. Clients who believe passionately in the correctness of their claim, or are just dazzled by the potential dollars, can find it hard to notice their lawyer's reservations about the strength of the case. But potential over-charging is only one problem with time-based billing.

Time-based billing is not always accurate either because, humans being fallible, all time is not accurately recorded to a file. As one lawyer commented:

> I'd never understood it until I did it, until I had to. I used to think: 'oh what's the big deal about a timesheet'. But until you go, oh you know: 'Remember to start the clock, turn off the clock, start it at this point, turn it off at that point'…Or [you] come to the end of the day and think: 'God, what did I do today and how long did it take me?' I used to try and write things down but it didn't always work – nightmare.[17]

16 See Legal Fees Review Panel, *Discussion Paper*, 29–30.
17 Lawyer interviewed and quoted by Campbell and Charlesworth, 'Salaried Lawyers and Billable Hours', 104.

Time-based billing also encourages its own destructive psychology inside larger firms. Most law firms set targets of numbers of hours to be billed by each lawyer each year. About six and a half hours per day is standard practice in Australia. But eight to eight and a half hours is sometimes required. Billable hours are those that clients can be billed for. Non-billable hours include coffee and meal breaks, toilet breaks, smoking breaks, general training sessions, administration meetings and associated paperwork. Lawyers generally need to work about 10 hours to generate six to eight billable hours. In 2003 the *Australian Financial Review* reported that Workcover (the occupational health and safety regulator) in New South Wales was inquiring into the working hours of young lawyers, and reported that a Victorian young lawyers' survey in 2000 had found that 65% of those surveyed worked longer than 10 hours every day in order to achieve their targeted billable hours.[18] Some United States estimates of associates' (the most junior employee lawyers in a firm) time billing expectations put the number of expected annual billable hours at 2500. This expects nine billable hours every working day of the year, which would take about 3300 hours in the office to achieve.[19] It is no surprise then that larger law firms with high-end billing expectations regularly employ more new graduates than they really need, because they know that up to 30% of them will leave within five years.[20]

In this environment, billing can seem all-important, particularly in the many firms where a practitioner's budget – that is, the number of chargeable (billable) hours per month which they must achieve if they are to retain their job (let alone be promoted) – is the ever-present personal watchdog. It can also make it extremely difficult for lawyers to spend time away from the office fostering their own relationships, interests and community involvements. Consider what some of the lawyers quoted by Campbell and Charlesworth said about this system:

> I remember sitting in a performance review one year where my supervising partner attended with one sheet of paper – a printout of my billings for the year. At the end of a year of long hours and hard work, everything I had given to the firm was reduced to one sheet of numbers – if my time didn't directly result in money made by the firm, it was of no interest to them.[21]
> Law firms are in the position that there are so many law graduates they can cull down to what they think are the best students...I think what law firms

---

18 Marcus Priest, 'Lawyers Caught in Painful Tort', *Australian Financial Review* (Sydney), 10 January 2003, 10.
19 Legal Fees Review Panel, *Discussion Paper*, [3.7].
20 Sara Charlesworth and Iain Campbell, 'Scoping Study for an Attrition Study of Victorian Lawyers', Report to Victoria Law Foundation, 2010, 2 and 9. See <http://vwl.asn.au/cms_files/Publications/Attrition_Scoping_Study_Report.pdf>. The scoping study recommended further investigation and observed that women lawyers appeared to feature more strongly than men among those departing.
21 Campbell and Charlesworth, 'Salaried Lawyers and Billable Hours', 104–5.

are doing, especially the bigger ones, is recruit a hell of a lot of articled clerks, expect half of them to burn out, and then it's sort of like survival of the fittest really. So the people that remain are often those that are willing to put up with those conditions for the rest of their lives.[22]

One legal management consultant has been quoted as saying that billing targets of between six and eight hours a day 'may be fine during a period of high workload but over the long term it is unsustainable. It translates to either huge working hours or fraudulent timesheets'.[23] A survey of more than 2000 solicitors in New South Wales and Victoria focusing on job satisfaction and best practices in law firm management in 1996 found that, according to solicitors, law firms:

...have a preoccupation with billable hours, budgetary targets and fees billed...there is a fixation with quantitative measurement along a single financial dimension of a business – revenue. These findings suggest that in many instances the profitability of a legal services business is understood and pursued primarily in terms of getting more money in by sending out bigger and bigger bills...The prevailing business model of law firms, as constructed from these findings, incorporates its human resources as more or less expendable components of a revenue production machine. Workers are assumed to have uni-dimensional lives, putting job and career first, last and everywhere in between...The character of the process is 'recruit, exploit, and discard'.[24]

In 2011 a billing practices survey in Queensland still found a similar approach, despite attempts to promote and discuss the ethics of billing. As one lawyer commented on the survey:

Here's the thing...you can do all of the surveys of this nature that you want to. The firms can produce pretty policies which say all of the right things. However, while the driving force behind a lawyer's advancement is time recording, you will always have an issue with time sheet padding and 'time theft'. Younger lawyers in a firm, despite all their high ideals, will always fall into line with what the firm wants, and will not be empowered to do anything differently.[25]

It is not difficult to see how these managerial pressures can eat away at possibilities for trust and collegiality between lawyers. Even those lawyers who

22 Ibid, 112.
23 Merritt, 'No Case for Padding'.
24 Mark Herron, Facing the Future: Gender, Employment and Best Practice Issues for Law Firms – Volume 1: The Job Satisfaction Study (Victoria Law Foundation, Melbourne, 1996) 60.
25 Christine Parker and David Ruschena, 'The Pressures of Billable Hours: Lessons from a Survey of Billing Practices Inside Law Firms' (2011) 9 *University of St Thomas Law Journal* 619, 658.

are not padding their bills to make billable hour targets may believe that others must be, leading to a situation where everyone thinks everyone else is probably cheating, and wondering whether they may as well cheat themselves. Parker and Ruschena's analysis of lawyers' experiences of ethics and billing practices in their firms found that lawyers in those firms that did not have clear and explicit ethical billing policies that were monitored and enforced were more likely to believe that their colleagues were engaging in unethical practices such as padding bills.[26]

Rigid requirements about work outputs can also lead to deception of clients about billing. According to the New South Wales Office of the Legal Services Commissioner, the pressure to bill as many hours as humanly possible means that '…lawyers no longer take the time to sit down and communicate with their client about the fees involved or discuss the progress of the matter. The factory environment of the law firm reinforces the ethos that time is money and one cannot waste time on tasks that cannot be billed'.[27] Since there is no 'return' for a lawyer whose own performance is measured by the hour on spending time carefully explaining to a client what likely cost blowouts will occur, it is little wonder that the New South Wales Legal Services Commissioner's office estimates that up to 80% of all complaints received by his office have an element of dissatisfaction about costs.[28] The New South Wales Legal Fees Review Panel's discussion paper on time-based billing goes further:

> It is important to consider whether the entrenching of time billing in the legal
> profession is leading to *systemic breakdown* in the solicitor-client relationship
> by virtue of the fact that the structural assumptions on which time billing is
> based puts it in opposition to principles of good communication.[29]

In other words, the imposition of targets for number of hours billed on individual lawyers and work groups can provide incentives for lawyers and their staff to 'pad' their timesheets, and ultimately the bills sent to clients. Individual lawyers might increase the number of billable hours recorded on their timesheets by doing things like waiting until a time when people are unlikely to be in their office (such

---

26 Christine Parker and David Ruschena, 'The Pressures of Billable Hours: Lessons from a Survey of Billing Practices Inside Law Firms' (2011) 9 *University of St Thomas Law Journal* 619.

27 Ibid [3.20]. See also Susan Saab Fortney, 'The Billable Hours Derby: Empirical Data on the Problems and Pressure Points' (2005) 33 *Fordham Urban Law Journal* 171. Popular culture has not been slow to portray over-charging as closely related to time billing. The 2005 Australian Broadcasting Corporation telemovie *Hell Has Harbour Views* (based on Richard Beasley's novel *Hell Has Harbour Views* (Macmillan, Sydney, 2001)) includes much dark comedy on the effects of some law firm approaches to fee generation, referring in one segment to a grasping associate whose progress was assured because he had billed twenty-five hours in one (twenty-four hour) day.

28 Legal Fees Review Panel, *Discussion Paper*, [2.54].

29 Ibid [2.57]. Emphasis in the original.

as lunchtime) and then making thirty (unanswered) phone calls, recording each one as a separate six-minute task, or by doing tiny tasks on a number of files in one six-minute timeslot so that work done on each file can be recorded as a separate time unit.[30] Time is usually recorded in six-minute units or intervals, 'or part thereof', so a six-second phone call can be billed as a full six minutes. Other notorious practices for increasing billings include: recording time spent thinking about a client matter in the shower or on the bus as billable time; charging one client for time spent doing research on a previous relevant client matter as if it had been done for the first time for the later client; using more senior lawyers (who charge out at a higher rate) than necessary; or charging the client for a whole team of junior lawyers to support a senior lawyer doing work that may not be strictly necessary, and which has to be checked by the senior lawyer anyway. Case Study 9.1 (The Basis for Determining Fees) at the end of this chapter explores in more detail some questionable billing practices, and Case Study 9.3 (The Foreman Case) illustrates in more detail the budgetary pressures that lawyers can feel, and the impact it can have on ethics.

Technology does not necessarily help. There is an almost universal move to some method of automated (computerised) billing in order to achieve accuracy and efficiency in time-based billing, but the benefits of the automation process are overstated. The software companies routinely claim that their products will eliminate under-billing entirely, and reduce over-billing considerably. While under-billing does tend to disappear because, for example, these systems capture the length and purpose of phone calls,[31] permit easily generated interim bills, and allow wireless-linked personal digital assistants to add to billing data while practitioners are on the move, they contain no automatic safeguard against over-charging. In fact, some billing technology appears specifically designed to sell itself by making deliberate overcharging an efficient process. For example, one commercially available time-billing software system enables multiple time clocks for multiple matters to run *simultaneously* in open windows, together on the screen, facilitating the charging of multiple clients for the same time.

Time-Based Billing and Law Firm Values

In the *Australian Lawyers' Values Study* relating to lawyers' attitudes towards overcharging their clients, the following scenario was put to law students and lawyers in each of the three years from 2001–03:

30 See also Lisa Lerman, 'Gross Profits? Questions About Lawyer Billing Practices' (1994) 22 *Hofstra Law Review* 645 for reports of similar practices in the United States.
31 Wilkins, 'Footing the Bill', 17. These systems are particularly useful when there are phone calls that unexpectedly continue for a long time.

> In your first year of work in a law firm, the partner supervising you gives you some files to get ready for 'costing'. She asks you to total the number of hours which you have spent on each file and, from her harried expression, it is pretty clear that she is concerned to charge out a significant amount on each matter. She asks you to 'round up' your hours to the next hundred in each file, saying that, on average, clients are happy because the main thing they demand is quality work. You know that these clients are more or less satisfied with the firm and that your supervisor is not about to debate the issue with you. **Would you round up the hours as requested?**[32]

This scenario specified rounding up *hours* to the next 100, not just *dollars*. Rounding up hours could add many thousands of dollars to a typical bill. Only 40% of respondents in their final year of law school reported that they would *not* round up the hours to the nearest 100 hours. However, this proportion increased to 50% of respondents in year two, and 60% of respondents in year three.[33] In other words, exposure to practice resulted in more lawyers resisting pressure to over-charge their clients, but in the third year of that study, 40% of those surveyed were still ready to over-charge if circumstances required it.

Imagine the type of pressure on a new lawyer that can generate an intention to, in effect, steal from a client. The survey responses indicate that some new lawyers (the majority of respondents in the later years) manage to find the means to identify their values early on and resist over-charging pressure, while others do not. Many identify themselves as 'unhappy' with their working life and may cope with this type of pressure by choosing to leave this type of practice – there is an average 20–40% annual 'churn' rate of personnel across all law firms in Victoria.[34]

Circumstantial, but still anecdotal, evidence exists that such pressure on values is greatest inside the larger legal practices. Consider this reflection by a large law firm partner, who wrote anonymously to a lawyers' trade magazine in 2005:

---

32 Adrian Evans and Josephine Palermo, 'Zero Impact: Are Law Students' Values Affected by Law School?' (2005) 8 *Legal Ethics* 240, 245–6. Note that this study surveyed lawyers in all sorts of practices, not just large law firm practices.

33 Ibid; Josephine Palermo and Adrian Evans, 'Preparing Future Australian Lawyers: An Exposition of Changing Values Over Time in the Context of Teaching About Ethical Dilemmas' (2006) 11 (1) *Deakin Law Review*, 104–30.

34 Law Institute of Victoria, 'Generation Future: Working Towards a More Flexible Workplace' (2006) 80(7) *Law Institute Journal* 18, citing Alicia Patterson, Law Institute of Victoria Marketing Manager. See also Mark Herron, Annie Woodger and George Beaton, *Facing the Future: Gender, Employment and Best Practice Issues for Law Firms* (Victoria Law Foundation, Melbourne, 1996) 22–8 [evidence about the correlation between job satisfaction and intentions to leave the profession]; Andrew Boon, 'From Public Service to Service Industry: The Impact of Socialisation and Work on the Motivation and Values of Lawyers' (2005) 12 *International Journal of the Legal Profession* 229.

The large firms have very little to do with the practice of law as it was normally understood. These workplaces are combinations of several profit centres in one building(s) under centralised management. Partners hardly know each other, or at all. Profit is not a consideration; it is the sole driving force, the only criteria [*sic*] to measure success. Partners are as 'good' as their last quarter. Sometimes, they are no longer partners after one of those quarters…[T]he temptation, or worse than that, the common practice in the large and medium firms is to mask such inhumane pressure by inflating time sheets, undertaking such unnecessary research, exaggerating the need to review everything during discovery, undertaking overzealous due diligence processes, and other practices readers will be familiar with. In other words, we cheat and lie to make ends meet. We act dishonestly as a matter of course. We do it because we have no choice. Everyone else does it to fit within the system. There is no way out…Partners are aware of their colleagues' unhappiness, because they know about their own. However, as long as budgets are met, nobody bothers to inquire (let alone propose an alternative) when a particular partner – as I have recently witnessed – had to replace her rather large entire team twice in a single year. People simply voted with their feet and left quietly en masse.[35]

This anonymous partner was undoubtedly upset. He or she went on to describe life in the large firm as all-encompassing in a way that throws the rest of lawyers' lives out of balance:

…as a result of this, it can hardly be surprising if we feel irascible, abusive, unfit, and stressed. A weak month, or three in a row makes us anxious and insecure. Many tend to fight such feelings by working even harder: arriving at the office before 7 am, never leaving before 9 pm every day. I see them abusing staff, making unreasonable requests, refusing delegation, abdicating responsibility, throwing files, taking many calls at once, getting drunk at office parties, keeping their offices in appalling conditions, all while chained to their routines to preserve a lifestyle they may deplore but feel they must sustain.[36]

This 'slavery' to work appears to be more than just one experience, as was evident in the *Australian Lawyers' Values Study*. In that survey, respondents were also asked to respond to the following scenario:

You are a junior solicitor working for a large city firm. The long working hours are causing a lot of pressure at home with your partner and your young children. This issue has been the topic of many recent conversations at home. The firm's managing practitioner asks you to show commitment on a file.

35 Anonymous, 'Big Firm Partner Breaks Ranks', *Lawyers Weekly* (Sydney), 11 November 2005, 3.
36 Ibid. See also Patrick J Schiltz, 'On Being a Happy, Healthy, and Ethical Member of an Unhappy, Unhealthy, and Unethical Profession' (1999) 52 *Vanderbilt Law Review* 871.

This would involve even longer hours than usual with many late nights for at least the next month. The managing practitioner has intimated that if you perform well in this task it could lead to a promotion. Working longer hours would cause a serious argument at home and be highly detrimental to your relationship with your family. **Would you take on the extra hours?**

Among the minority (26–28% over the three years of the survey) who would take on the extra hours, knowing that their family life would be adversely affected, 'professional ambition' was overwhelmingly the most important value in relation to this decision.[37] The majority, who preferred not to sacrifice their family life for their ambitions, mentioned (perhaps obviously) loyalty to their children and their spouse as their motivating values. Nevertheless, in real life, lawyers might often feel that they have no real choice – their *values* might be loyalty to their family, but their *actions* are likely to reflect professional ambition because they are afraid they will lose their job and therefore the wherewithal to provide for their family if they do not.

Combining the earlier finding about the pressure on lawyers to over-charge together with their preference *not* to work the sort of hours that appear to be associated with over-charging, it may be that only those for whom ambition is more important than their family life will continue to work in large law firms in the future. It is also probable that those who are choosing to leave legal practice are doing so because they see a work–life balance as too difficult to achieve in the prevailing values systems of law firms. If the anonymous partner quoted above is to be believed, those remaining in practice in the larger Australian law firms may also be those for whom over-charging is tacitly acceptable.

Early awareness of these possibilities and especially of the effect that the climate of legal practice can have on lawyers personally may be important for new lawyers' decisions about the type and structure of legal practice they intend to pursue. Such awareness should also lead law students and young lawyers to ask questions (of the firm, and also of colleagues and contacts in the profession more widely) about the values and ethical climate of practice in any law firm they are thinking of joining, *before* they decide whether to take a job there.[38]

Fees and Costs in Litigation

Where the matter involves litigation, both lawyer and client are at the mercy of the tactics chosen by the other side, and the inherent unpredictability of the system,

---

37 Josephine Palermo and Adrian Evans, 'Relationships Between Personal Values and Reported Behaviour on Ethical Scenarios for Law Students' (2006) 24 *Behavioural Sciences & the Law* (forthcoming).

38 Andrew M Perlman, 'A Career Choice Critique of Legal Ethics Theory' (2001) 31 *Seton Hall Law Review* 829.

in working out how much a matter is likely to cost. As former President of the Law Council of Australia, Bret Walker SC has pointed out, 'the poorer litigant has a much greater threat from the unpredictability of litigation than the richer litigant does'. This is not only because the richer litigant has 'relatively deep pockets', but also because the richer litigant has the capacity 'to increase the threat of litigation costs being paid by the other party as a result of complications and elaborations of the dispute and the procedure for deciding it'.[39] This is even more evident when we consider the complicated question of deciding who pays what costs after a litigated matter is concluded.

As part of the final court orders in litigation, the court will usually decide who should pay what legal costs, on the basis of what is fair and equitable between the parties. The cost indemnity rule says that a client who wins a legal action is normally entitled to have their *reasonable and necessary*[40] costs paid by the losing party. These costs are known as *party-party costs*, and they are calculated on an item remuneration basis under the relevant court scale. *Reasonable* costs are all those costs which the lawyer was justified in incurring in running the case and attending to their client's needs for information. *Necessary* costs are more restricted. They cover only those expenses which directly relate to getting the case ready for trial. It may be necessary, for example, to speak to a client in business hours about the evidence they will give the following day, but it is not usually necessary that that conversation occur again at midnight. So while the client might be very anxious and phone their lawyer at midnight to go over their evidence again, charging the client for the second phone call would be reasonable, but not necessary according to the law of costs. A successful party can also recover from the losing party all their reasonable and necessary expenses ('disbursements'), such as court filing fees, medical report fees and barristers' fees.

Party-party costs generally cover only 60–70% of the total costs that the winning party actually owes their lawyer, whether the total costs are calculated on an item or time-based process.[41] These actual costs are called *solicitor-client costs*. The extra 30–40% of solicitor-client costs cannot be recovered from the losing party. In the example above, this would include the midnight phone calls; that is, the actions by their lawyer that the winner did not strictly have to perform in order to run their case but would, nevertheless, be considered reasonable for the party's own lawyer to charge for. These extra costs would have to be paid by the winning party to their own lawyer out of their 'winnings'. In order to understand what legal fees

---

39 Bret Walker, 'Proportionality and Cost-Shifting' (2004) 27 *University of New South Wales Law Journal* 214, 216–7.

40 Some court rules refer to such costs being 'necessary or proper': See, eg, *Supreme Court (General Civil Procedure) Rules 2005* (Vic) r 63.29.

41 Victorian Law Reform Commission, *Civil Justice Review: Report*, 'Ch 11: Reducing the Cost of Litigation' para. 3.2.1, 648.

and costs they might have to pay in relation to litigation, a client therefore needs to understand that even if they win the case, they will also need to personally pay, say, 30% of the costs charged by their lawyer. In order to go ahead with litigation, they would need to be confident that they will win and that paying that 30% of their own costs will not unacceptably reduce their net receipts from the case.

If this is confusing for law students and lawyers, consider how clients feel when they first hear about the types of legal costs and the effect of the system on what they think is their just entitlement? Figure 9.1 describes the relationship between these concepts.

Figure 9.1   Relationship between Solicitor-Client Costs, Party-Party Costs and Total Legal Costs

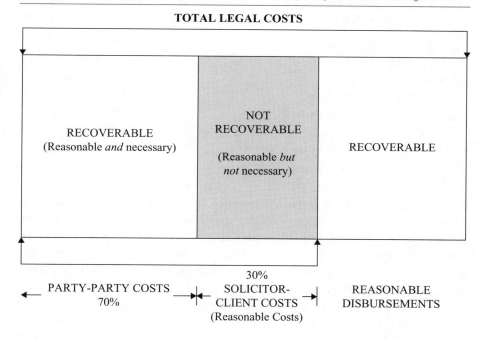

Consider a client who has sued for $10,000 for damage to their boat after it is holed by a jet-ski. Their solicitor-client costs (that is, their actual costs) amount to $3500 and the party-party proportion of those costs totals $2500. They win the case and are entitled to:

Judgment for:	$10,000
Plus party-party costs:	$2500
Sub-total:	$12,500
Less solicitor-client costs:	$3500
Net receipts from action:	$9000

Some clients will be annoyed that they have to, in effect, pay for $1000 of the damage to the boat themselves – particularly if their lawyer has not taken time to explain how costs work in advance.

But it gets worse for the client. Consider a common variation to this calculation. The court finds that the plaintiff has contributed to their own loss through contributory negligence. For example, the plaintiff partially caused the collision by manoeuvring their boat into the path of the jet-ski. A magistrate might decide that the case should be decided 60% in favour of the plaintiff and 40% in favour of the defendant. Costs normally 'follow the event', so the plaintiff would be entitled to only 60% of their party-party costs (60% of $2500 = $1500) and the defendant to 40% of their party-party costs (say, $800). Since the jet-ski was itself severely damaged in the collision and will cost $6000 to repair, the costs calculation for the plaintiff will look like this:

Plaintiff's successful claim:	$6000 (60%)
Plus party-party costs:	<u>$1500</u> (60%)
Sub-total:	$7500
Less 40% of defendant's claim:	$2400
Less 40% of defendant's party-party costs:	$800
Sub-total:	$4300
Less plaintiff's solicitor-client costs (payable to their own lawyer):	$3500
Net receipts from action:	$800

Extreme results like these are not uncommon in lower court litigation. It is not surprising that clients complain that the case they thought was worth $10,000 produces a meagre result. Unless the amount in dispute is substantial, court-based dispute resolution will often be uneconomic for the client and benefit only the lawyers. It is for this reason that lawyers face a considerable obligation to be candid in fully apprising potential clients of the financial risks of their proposed court action. As we have seen in Chapter 6, lawyers who do not communicate effectively on this issue may be criticised for putting their own interests in reaping fees from litigation ahead of their clients' interests.

So long as the proportion of *unrecoverable* costs is not too high, parties to litigation can afford to start a case with some expectation that the extra costs – the 30% mentioned above – can be paid from the judgment amount awarded to them. Recently, however, the proportion of successful parties' costs that is not recoverable from the other side has been approaching 50%, rather than 30%.[42] This is because of relentless annual increases in the amount that the profession can charge for each item of work, and the widening gap between what practitioners are charging under time-based billing, and what costs assessors will approve for recovery from

---

42 Ibid.

the losing party by way of party-party costs.[43] As mentioned in Chapter 6, in some States, especially Victoria, a number of reforms have been introduced to try to contain excessive adversarialism and associated inflation in costs. This includes an 'overarching obligation' to 'use reasonable endeavours to ensure that legal costs and other costs incurred in connection with the civil proceeding are reasonable and proportionate to (a) the complexity or importance of the issues in dispute; and (b) the amount in dispute' (*Civil Procedure Act 2010* (Vic) s 24).

This means that parties to litigation must increasingly ask themselves whether the amount of costs they will have to bear themselves, whether they win or lose, is justified by the amount at stake in the dispute. As a result, even clients who are very likely to succeed in court may feel forced to agree to negotiation or mediation to resolve their disputes, regardless of how suitable their case is for mediation (see Chapter 7). This makes the prospect of equal access to justice in the court system recede further and further, and makes it more likely that matters will be settled unjustly. It is no wonder that some clients fume in frustration because they cannot afford to litigate, and still have to pay their lawyer to be advised of this reality. As mentioned in Chapter 6, successful corporations are not constrained by these concerns because their legal fees are generally tax deductible. But individuals and undercapitalised small businesses often see legal costs and inaccessible justice as interchangeable terms, and this is regardless of whether they might have to deal with any member of the profession who behaves unethically by over-charging.

Conditional and Uplift Fees

One way in which some lawyers attempt to make justice more affordable and accessible for clients who cannot afford litigation is by charging *conditional* and/or *uplift* fees (see descriptions below) that apply only where the client is successful in litigation. Under these arrangements the lawyer will charge no fee, or a reduced fee, if the client is not successful. Conditional and uplift fees are, however, ethically ambiguous. On the one hand these types of fees may help clients access legal and substantive justice in line with *adversarial advocate, moral activist* and *ethics of care* concerns. On the other hand, from a *responsible lawyering* perspective, conditional and uplift fees are seen as dangerous mechanisms that can damage the purity, probity and integrity of the lawyer-client relationship. This is because they have the potential to distort the litigation process by giving lawyers a personal stake or interest in the litigation, which may conflict with their ability to advise clients as to their best interests, or even to obey their duty to the court.

Conditional costs agreements are those in which the lawyer and client agree that the lawyer will only be paid if the client is 'successful'. Conditional agreements

---

43 Tori Strong, 'At What Cost?' (2005) 79(4) *Law Institute Journal* 4.

can include those that merely provide that the lawyer will charge their ordinary base fee if the client succeeds. Most conditional cost agreements, however, allow the lawyer to charge an 'uplift' of their fee (see below) if the litigation succeeds.

Conditional costs agreements have been accepted by the Australian courts as a way of assisting litigants who cannot afford to pay lawyers' fees in advance,[44] and are now explicitly allowed under the *Model Laws* (3.4.25). Professional conduct rules tolerate the conflict of interest of the lawyer effectively having a stake in the client's case because it is thought to be outweighed by the public interest in access to justice.[45] Whether the conflict is in fact justified is open to question. Most disputes about conditional costs agreements arise because lawyers and clients have different understandings of what constitutes a successful outcome, or because some lawyers have taken too much or *all* of their client's 'winnings' – and then some. In one infamous case, after settlement at about $10,000, Queensland law firm Baker Johnson sent a bill for $18,000 and sued the client for the balance of $8000 that the firm could not recover from the settlement amount![46]

Contingent fee arrangements, in contrast to conditional fees, allow a lawyer to take a *percentage* of the actual judgment or settlement sum, if the client is successful. The more a client recovers in a judgment, the more their lawyer is paid. The terminology is confusing, as 'conditional' and 'contingent' are synonyms in normal language. The term 'proportional' fee agreements might better describe contingent arrangements. Contingent or proportional fees do have the advantage of certainty, as the client knows that their lawyer will never take more than a certain percentage of their 'winnings'. But they are *prohibited* in Australia on the basis that they create a more serious conflict of interest than conditional costs agreements (*Model Laws* 3.4.27), although they are common in the United States. The rationale for banning contingent fees is that they create an incentive for the lawyer to seek to maximise the settlement sum while minimising the amount of work he or she does. Accordingly, the lawyer might not advise settlement early on, even though this might be better for the client, in the hope of holding out for a higher fee. Equally the lawyer will not want to go ahead with the actual trial, even though this might give the client a better chance at a higher amount, because the trial creates more work for the lawyer. So contingent fees might create a structure in which lawyers are more likely to pressure their client into a settlement on the steps of the court just before trial. This might also go against a public interest in the prompt settlement of disputes (with reasonable financial recovery), which the

---

44 *Clyne v New South Wales Bar Association* (1960) 104 CLR 186, 203.

45 See, eg, *Legal Profession (Barristers) Rule 2004* (Qld) r 91(d) which states that a barrister must decline a brief if the barrister has a material financial or property interest in the outcome of the case – '*apart* from the prospect of a fee in the case of a brief under a speculative fee agreement' [our emphasis].

46 *Baker Johnson v Jorgensen* [2002] QDC 205 (Unreported, McGill DCJ, 26 July 2002). See also *Legal Services Commissioner v Baker* [2006] QCA 45 (5 May 2006).

community sees as more important than the individual's interest in attempting to maximise a final settlement just before trial, but after lengthy delay.

Instead, the Australian *Model Laws* allow for a modified contingency fee in the form of an *uplift fee*. An uplift fee means that the practitioner charges up to 25% of their normal fee as an addition, or uplift, to their normal fee, if they are successful. This would usually occur where they have a 'no-win, no-fee' costs agreement with their client (*Model Laws* 3.4.26). An uplift fee is not based on the settlement sum, as with the contingency fee, but on the lawyer's ordinary fee for the same work. The argument is that the lawyer should be compensated for the risk of financing a speculative 'no-win, no-fee' case (that is, not charging any professional fees if they lose) with a bonus if they win. This creates an incentive to take on the matter in the first place.

Uplift fees do, however, suffer from an internal ethical contradiction. Lawyers are not permitted to enter into an agreement for an uplift fee under the *Model Laws* (3.4.26(4)) unless they have certified that the case has reasonable prospects of success. Is it consistent to allow an uplift permitting up to an additional 25% of fees as an incentive for taking on a *speculative* case, when the same lawyer must certify to the effect that the case has reasonable prospects of success to start with anyway?[47] Although no litigation is risk free, the 25% uplift may often be used simply as a means of charging higher fees where there is no great risk of an action failing. The NSW Legal Services Commissioner has commented that:

> ...concerns arise when practitioners accept matters on a contingency basis [meaning, no-win, no-fee] where the outcome of the matter is virtually guaranteed. It is the experience of the OLSC that the 25% uplift is applied in these situations, regardless of the lack of risk and without financing of ongoing disbursements by the practitioner.[48]

Additional problems may arise with any form of 'no-win, no-fee' agreement because, apart from the risk of paying the winning defendant's costs in the event of failure, a plaintiff who does not have to put up any money at all at the start of a case might be encouraged to make an unmeritorious ambit claim, notwithstanding the obligation on practitioners to proceed with such cases only if they have merit. When such cases are lost, the defendant faces a plaintiff with no assets and the defendant cannot recover their costs.[49] Plaintiffs who do have assets also often complain that they did not understand (despite the agreement they have signed) that they would have to pay the defendant's costs if they lost, arguing that 'no-win, no-fee' means exactly that.

Ultimately, the effect of both the 'true' contingency fee (that is, the fee which varies directly with the size of the ultimate settlement or judgment) and, to a lesser

---

47 Chris Merritt, 'Lawyers Protest at Ban on Uplift Factor', *Australian Financial Review* (Sydney), 28 January 2005, 46.
48 Legal Fees Review Panel, *Discussion Paper*, 16.
49 Ibid 15–16.

extent, the uplift fee is to give the plaintiff's lawyer a financial interest in the *result* of the litigation. Fee uplifts will be greater if cases proceed closer to trial without settlement, because more work will be done in preparing for trial. Since that lawyer has a fiduciary obligation to dispassionately advise their client as to what to do at each stage of the litigation (that is, to compromise or not), if the size of their fee is a factor in the equation, it becomes more likely that such advice will be unconsciously coloured by their own interest in that result.

Negotiating Fair, Reasonable and Realistic Cost Agreements

So what is the good lawyer to do in relation to billing clients if they want to respect their client and yet not sell themselves short? The standard applied by the courts and legislation is the notion of 'fair and reasonable' charging. This is obviously not a recipe for the exact fee to be charged in every circumstance, like the old scales, but it does signify a value of respect for both the client's right to *fairness* in the *process* of the agreement, and the lawyer's right to be paid what is objectively *reasonable*, having regard to what the case is about.

A Fair Process

The fairness of a legal bill is often reflected in the clarity of its language:

> For the client, a bill provides an itemised summary – or not, as the case may be – of what it has paid for. On reflection, individual items may appear overpriced or of exceptionally good value, essential or largely unnecessary, and clear in description or too vague to be useful. All of these factors are likely to influence the client's assessment of the services provided by the firm.[50]

But the issue of clarity of communication about fees and costs is critical long before a bill is delivered. Confusion often reigns for consumers trying to work out how much they will have to pay their lawyer, and the position is not much better for lawyers themselves. *Model Laws* 3.4.10 addresses this by requiring lawyers to first communicate in writing with their prospective clients about how they will calculate their fees, what rights the client has in relation to negotiating and contesting the costs agreement, and an estimate of the total cost if the fees are expected to exceed $750, before entering into a written costs agreement (*Model Laws* 3.4.21, 3.4.24), and finally to only recover fees after issuing a proper written bill (*Model Laws* 3.4.31). Figure 9.2 summarises the various requirements.

---

50 Francis Wilkins, 'Footing the Bill', *Lawyers Weekly* (Sydney), 30 July 2004, 16.

Figure 9.2   Summary of Disclosure Requirements under *Model Laws* 3.4.10

What must the lawyer disclose to their client?

...the amount of costs	• the basis on which the legal costs will be calculated (including whether a costs determination or scale of costs applies to any of the legal costs); • if the matter is a litigious matter, an estimate of the range of costs that may be recovered if the client is successful in the litigation; and the range of costs the client may be ordered to pay if the client is unsuccessful.
...an estimate of the total legal costs, if practical; or	• if it is not reasonably practicable to estimate the total legal costs, a range of estimates of the total legal costs and an explanation of the major variables that will affect the calculation of those costs; • the client's right to be notified of any substantial changes to the matters disclosed.
...billing	• the client's right to request and receive progress reports; • the client's right to receive a bill; • the client's right to request an itemised bill within 30 days after receipt of a lump sum bill; • details of the intervals (if any) at which the client will be billed; • the rate of interest (if any) that the law practice charges on overdue legal costs; and
...what the client can do if they wish to discuss or dispute costs	• obtain details of the person [in the firm] whom the client may contact to discuss the legal costs • in the event of a dispute in relation to legal costs, a costs review under (*Model Laws* Part 3, Division 7) • the setting aside of a costs agreement if it is not fair and reasonable (*Model Laws* 3.4.30)

Clients also have the right to be told that they can negotiate a costs agreement, to complain about their lawyer's conduct in relation to fees and charging to the relevant complaints handling body in their jurisdiction (*Model Laws* 4.4.2), and to be told about any time limits that apply to the taking of any action referred to.

The *Model Laws* include special protections for clients who enter into conditional costs agreements or costs agreements which contain provision for uplift fees. These must be signed by the client and must define the circumstances which constitute a 'success' sufficient to entitle the uplift (3.4.25(3)). This is intended to address the problem of some practitioners previously leaving the term 'success' undefined or vague in the agreement, but claiming the uplift fee when any settlement, often much less than the client would have considered 'successful', was achieved. To protect both lawyer and client, lawyers must be quite sure that there is both a reasonable chance that the action will succeed, and be able to specify in the agreement what level of success will be acceptable to their client, in order for the fee to be payable. An action may be commenced claiming, say, $100,000, but settled reluctantly by the client for just $45,000. Lawyers will need to find out before the cost agreement is finalised whether the client really understands that they will be paying an uplift fee as well as the normal fees, if they receive just $45,000. Lawyers who are not sure about whether a client understands the implications of the level at which success will be defined or (even worse) that they will be obliged to pay the other side's party-party costs if they lose the action,[51] should re-check with their client, since this might amount to sufficient circumstances to have the costs agreement set aside for being not 'fair, just and reasonable'.

The *Model Laws* provide a good (but not yet ideal) model of how lawyer-client communication about costs should work. The disclosure obligations seek to put clients in a better position to know and understand how their lawyer is charging and to be able to negotiate with the lawyer about fees and charges. That is, they seek to ameliorate the power differential between lawyer and client in relation to fees and costs. But will clients really feel that they can negotiate the terms of the cost agreement with their lawyer just because they are given all this information? Will they even bother if they are stressed and just want to get out of the lawyer's office and get on with whatever is next on their list for the day?

The obligation is therefore on lawyers to communicate carefully about costs. This begins with sensing when their client has other things on their mind, coaxing some discussion about whatever those pressures might be, and helping the client to realise that they need to focus on the here and now. The client needs to be relaxed enough to be able to listen. If that does not happen, the whole point of the interview is lost and the necessary trust relationship will be stifled. Lawyers who want to communicate well with unsophisticated clients and make a fair agreement will go to much greater lengths than those required by the *Model Laws* to explain as much as possible to each and every client about what must be done, the risks of different litigation strategies, and why some aspects of the case, including the final fee, are necessarily unpredictable.

A good lawyer will use language and diagrams that make sense to clients to explain this. For a multicultural clientele, this does mean communicating face-to-face through a trusted interpreter, and not just relying on an unknown telephone interpreter for the all-important initial interview. Unwise lawyers, or those in too

---

51 The so-called 'cost indemnity rule'.

much of a hurry, cut corners and suffer later. They do not receive thanks and prompt payment of their fees, but rather complaints, slackening demand for their services (because clients' word-of-mouth among their acquaintances can be bad, as well as good) and disciplinary investigations.

Fair costs agreements terms – and how they are negotiated with clients – are the linchpin of many successful legal practices, and can be a powerful expression of the *ethics of care*, because they depend on lawyers giving clients information and communicating effectively with them. Few problems will surface at the end of a case if the lawyer engages in the following complaint prevention practices:

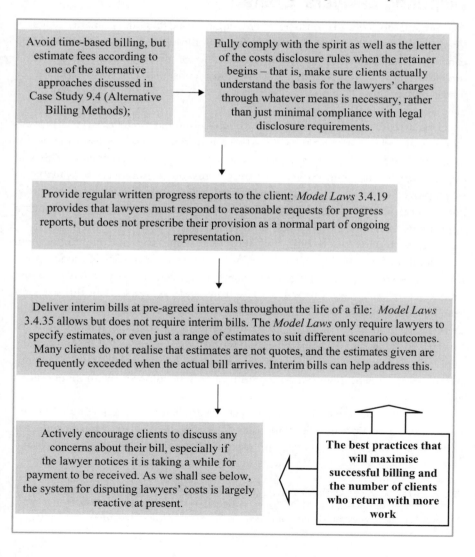

Avoid time-based billing, but estimate fees according to one of the alternative approaches discussed in Case Study 9.4 (Alternative Billing Methods);

Fully comply with the spirit as well as the letter of the costs disclosure rules when the retainer begins – that is, make sure clients actually understand the basis for the lawyers' charges through whatever means is necessary, rather than just minimal compliance with legal disclosure requirements.

Provide regular written progress reports to the client: *Model Laws* 3.4.19 provides that lawyers must respond to reasonable requests for progress reports, but does not prescribe their provision as a normal part of ongoing representation.

Deliver interim bills at pre-agreed intervals throughout the life of a file: *Model Laws* 3.4.35 allows but does not require interim bills. The *Model Laws* only require lawyers to specify estimates, or even just a range of estimates to suit different scenario outcomes. Many clients do not realise that estimates are not quotes, and the estimates given are frequently exceeded when the actual bill arrives. Interim bills can help address this.

Actively encourage clients to discuss any concerns about their bill, especially if the lawyer notices it is taking a while for payment to be received. As we shall see below, the system for disputing lawyers' costs is largely reactive at present.

The best practices that will maximise successful billing and the number of clients who return with more work

If these alternative approaches are followed, an unhappy client will be noticed quite quickly, allowing a check that their understanding of what is happening is realistic, mediation of any disagreement, and probable improvement in communication about the progress of the matter, before they become what is often unfairly categorised as a 'difficult client'. Many lawyers take these 'best practice' precautions already, but there are still too many examples of lawyers failing to follow these precepts for their usage to be described as standard practice.

Disputing Lawyers' Costs

Some regulatory controls exist on over-charging, but they are primarily reactive. Clients can dispute the substance of the bill through costs assessment. They can also complain about overcharging to one of the regulators of the legal profession. The latter would result in either consumer dispute resolution or a disciplinary investigation as discussed in Chapter 3 and in Case Study 9.3 (The Foreman Case).

Costs assessment (or 'review', as it is described in the *Model Laws*) is a process whereby an independent costs assessor (usually a court official) assesses the bill for its fairness and reasonableness when a client or losing party complains. This will depend on 'the size of the solicitor's firm, the resources employed or available to be employed by it, the value which the lawyers place upon their skill and expertise and the urgency of the client's requirements' and 'must be determined following an appropriate analysis of the practice of the particular solicitor'.[52]

Even with time-based bills, the fees that would be payable under item remuneration for a similar matter usually become the unofficial reference point for this assessment: although a client signs an agreement to pay whatever the time adds up to, a decision by both law firms and assessors about the size of a time-based bill needs to be referrable back to some sort of independent baseline in order for the assessment to mean anything. Whether item remuneration or time-based billing is used, therefore, a law firm that is interested in pro-actively avoiding client complaints about its fees should, and often will, check a client's bill to ensure it is no higher than would probably be allowed by an independent assessor.

The costs assessment process corrects over-charging when complaints are made, but complaints usually come only after the client relationship has already been badly damaged. Moreover, the assessment process is itself expensive and

---

52 *Veghelyi v The Law Society of New South Wales* (Unreported, Supreme Court of New South Wales, Court of Appeal, Kirby P, Mahoney and Priestley JJA, 6 October 1995) 6–7, cited in Legal Fees Review Panel, *Discussion Paper*, [3.17]; see also *Model Laws* 3.4.44.

must be paid for.[53] Therefore assessment is often at the cost of reducing the total net revenue available to the client from the matter, further souring the whole experience for lawyer and client.

Costs assessment provides a review of the actual amount of the costs and whether they are fair and reasonable in substance. However, the main focus of the rules in the *Model Laws* is on the fairness of the process of disclosure and negotiation of the costs agreement, not the actual amount of the fees. The *Model Laws* specifically allow a client to apply to set aside a cost agreement that is not 'fair, just and reasonable'. Matters that are relevant in deciding whether a costs agreement is fair, just and reasonable include whether the client was induced to enter into the agreement by the fraud or misrepresentation of the lawyer, whether there was any professional misconduct involved, whether the lawyer failed to make the required disclosures relating to fees, and the time at which the agreement was made (*Model Laws* 3.4.30). No fees may be recovered at all if the agreement attempts to recover a contingency (proportional) fee (3.4.29(5)).[54] Note that the common law suggests that the onus will be upon the lawyer to rebut a presumption of undue influence in executing the agreement.[55] Thus an agreement may be just and reasonable, but not necessarily fair if, for some peculiar reason, the client did not really comprehend what they were doing. This point comes back to the necessity for an early, thorough and face-to-face discussion with the client about costs. Too often, regulators hear allegations (whether justified or not) that clients have been verbally induced to enter cost agreements by unrealistic or merely vague promises as to the likely outcome of litigation – promises which the agreements do not, of course, record. Less satisfactorily, because the *Model Laws* permit a basic (no conditional or uplift fee) agreement to be accepted by conduct and do not necessarily require a client's signature, clients under stress can legally bind themselves without realising that they have done so (3.4.26(3), (4)).

Clients have a specific right to apply to set aside a costs agreement entered into via fraud or misrepresentation (*Model Laws* 3.4.23(2)(a)), providing they complain and apply for a costs review (that is, an assessment) within sixty days of the delivery of the bill *or* payment of the costs (3.4.38(4)). While the application fee for a costs review can be waived on a hardship basis (3.4.40(4)), clients in calamitous circumstances (eg as a result of the financial loss or injury that led to the original

---

53 *Model Laws* cl 1043. Clause 1043(2)(a)(i) provides that the bill complained of must be reduced by at least 15% in a costs review, or the client will have to pay the costs of the review process themselves.

54 Cl 1027(5). See *Equuscorp Pty Ltd v Wilmoth Field Warne (No 4)* [2006] VSC 28 (Unreported, Byrne J, 10 February 2006) for an ingenious but unsuccessful attempt to get around the prohibition on contingency fees.

55 At least in a family law matter: see *Schiliro v Gadens Ridgeway* (1995) 121 FLR 322, 324.

proceedings) are often too preoccupied with more fundamental issues of survival. These clients frequently come to community legal centres and government legal aid offices many months after bills have been delivered, and are incredulous that they have no automatic right to challenge a bill which is older than two months. The *Model Laws* do provide that the cost reviewer must accept a late application for review '...unless...to do so would, in all the circumstances, cause unfair prejudice to the law practice' (3.4.38(5)). But in cases where the law firm thinks that the client is unhappy with the bill and will be unwilling to pay it, the law firm may well have already issued proceedings to recover their costs.[56] However, once an application for a costs review is made, the law practice must not commence any proceedings to recover the legal costs (*Model Laws* 3.4.41(b)).

Although it is inconvenient to practitioners to dispute an old bill, it is not impossible if the file is complete. The client file is the key evidence in any costs review, and the place where all material action on the case should be recorded. The *Model Laws* sixty-day limitation period for complaints about bills is completely out of step with the requirement that client files must be kept for at least seven years after the matter is concluded (*ASCR* 14.2). It seems unlikely, therefore, that there will be unfair prejudice to any legal practice in consenting to a late costs review, if that firm has not seen fit to commence proceedings to recover the fee before the client's application is eventually made.

On the other side of the coin, some complaints about costs are generated by clients who seize upon a minor issue because they do not wish to pay for civil litigation services fairly provided, regardless of the merits. It is very hard to predict which clients will fall into this category, so the best protection for both clients and lawyers is either to avoid time-based billing entirely or to strike a fair costs agreement and, while respecting the client at all times, behave cautiously and act preventively in all client interactions.

Perhaps lawyers should pressure their professional leaders to change a billing system that is dragging down their collective reputation, and the quality of their own work lives. Any reform to the legal fee system that seeks to be just and equitable to all concerned should involve some mechanism that ensures similar legal work will attract a broadly similar fee as a case progresses, not just when a complaint is made after everything is finalised. We have also seen that many of the problems with legal fees and costs stem from lack of early, verbal and comprehensive communication between lawyers and clients about costs, even if

---

56 In practice, even when proceedings are commenced, the defending client will succeed in an interlocutory application to have the bill assessed by an independent costs assessor and the case is adjourned until that assessment is available and both parties can then decide to continue or settle. Most settle, so that the effect of issuing is very similar to the review process. Note that *Model Laws* cl 10463.4.51 also provides that if the client has made a complaint to the legal profession regulator about the bill under Part 11, there cannot be a costs review as well.

such discussions are not easily or fully recoverable in the client's bill. Therefore any reforms should also entrench better communication into the fee structure.

DISCUSSION QUESTIONS

The *Model Laws* specify that a cost agreement must be at least evidenced in writing (*Model Laws* 3.4.24(2)). This means that the client has to be given written disclosure, but the agreement itself does not have to be signed and concluded in writing.

1. Do you think that a standard-form cost agreement should be capable of legally binding a client on the basis of their conduct alone? Would it make a difference to your answer if the agreement was a 'basic' conditional costs agreement or included an uplift clause? What if the client had had an opportunity to discuss the contents of the proposed agreement with an independent adviser?

2. If you were a client who had suffered an injury that left you disoriented and or disabled, would you consider sixty days long enough in which to raise your dissatisfaction with your lawyer's bill? As a lawyer, would you allow a client who wants a costs review to go ahead with the review up until a certain (longer) period is reached, or at any stage, after the bill is received?

CASE STUDY 9.1   THE BASIS FOR DETERMINING FEES: THREE SMALL CASE STUDIES[57]

Read the following three mini case studies and discuss the questions:

A first client, Argus, asks you to prepare a contract. The fee, calculated on a time basis, is $15,000. Later, a second client, Bogus, wants a contract for a similar transaction. As a result of your work for Argus, you now have a precedent which covers most of Bogus' requirements. Only a small percentage of the document needs to be altered. Argus and Bogus do not know each other and are unlikely to have anything to do with each other in future.

---

57 The first scenario is from Legal Fees Review Panel, *Discussion Paper*, [2.59], which in turn drew on Stuart Kay, *Cost, Value and ROI for Knowledge Management in Law Firms* (2003) LLRX.com <www.llrx.com/ features/kmcost.htm> at 31 May 2006. The second two scenarios are from the Queensland Legal Services Commission billing practices survey described in Parker and Ruschena, 'The Pressures of Billable Hours', 647–9.

DISCUSSION QUESTIONS

1. Would you charge Bogus less than Argus, say just $5000, or the same $15,000?

2. What if Argus and Bogus were, by pure chance, to meet and to compare notes? This sort of thing does happen, even in larger cities, because clients with similar legal needs do move in similar networks to one another. What would they think about your charging strategy if you had charged Bogus less than Argus? What if you had charged each the same?

3. How would you explain your fee structure to your two clients? For example, if you decided to charge $15,000 for the second contract, would you attempt to discuss the value of your work to the client's project as a basis for justification of the higher fee? Or would you simply say that you have done the work in the past and that this intellectual property is now reflected in the fee for all subsequent work drawing on your expertise?

Now imagine that Argus retains your firm to draft another contract on the basis that he will be charged an hourly rate. Your partner provides an estimate of work for $10,000. At the conclusion of the matter, the account comes to $5,000 on a time costing basis. Your partner charges the client $9,000 as the work performed by the firm was, in his view, of a high quality and the outcome exceptional.

DISCUSSION QUESTIONS

1. Do you think this is ethically appropriate?

2. Would Argus feel deceived if he found out what had happened?

Now imagine a third scenario: You are taking a two-hour plane trip from Brisbane to Melbourne to conduct an interview in a matter involving client Argus. While on the plane, you review materials for another file you are working on for client Bogus for the following week. Your firm has a billing procedure whereby you normally bill clients for your time spent travelling or waiting on their behalf.

DISCUSSION QUESTIONS

1. Would you bill both client A and client B for two hours? What are the arguments for and against?[58]

2. What would represent true value for each client?

---

[58] *See Bechara v Legal Services Commissioner* [2010] NSWCA 369.

CASE STUDY 9.2 THE COLLAPSE OF HIH AND THE RISE IN LEGAL FEES

In March 2003, HIH Insurance Limited collapsed with $5.3 billion in debt, caused by premiums that were too low, massive under-provision for claims, and losses associated with US and UK businesses. Although the CEO and several other directors were found to have committed criminal offences that added to the consequences of commercial misjudgements,[59] the central losses were of such a magnitude that they caused a ripple effect throughout the entire insurance industry, provoking a period of price-cutting among many insurers that carried on over time into the fee structure of the legal profession. As insurers paid out less on claims, plaintiffs' lawyers' incomes reduced because much of their work was only worthwhile if an insurer stood behind a defendant. These firms were in turn forced to reduce their fees in order to attract a smaller pool of clients whose cases were viable.

Lower legal fees were welcome, but that effect was short-term and not as important as the other consequence – reduced public access to compensation for civil loss. The fallout from the HIH collapse led to insurers withdrawing from some sectors of the market entirely – especially indemnity insurance for the professions, including lawyers – and raising premiums in public liability cover (for 'accidental' injuries) to enormous levels. At one stage, even local scouting organisations, town markets and athletics clubs were reportedly unable to obtain public liability insurance at a reasonable price, and were clamouring for something to be done about the high cost of insurance. The politicians stepped in and, despite the objections of organisations such as the Australian Lawyers' Alliance (an association of predominantly plaintiff lawyers), introduced new rules designed to make insurance more affordable by radically restricting the circumstances in which claims for personal injury could be litigated.[60] The insurers persuaded the public and the various parliaments that insurance would cost less if there were fewer claims being litigated and fewer lawyers involved in the claims process. Insurers' spokesmen were frequently in the media, with the

---

59 David Elias, 'Rocket Rod Crashes To Earth', *The Age* (Melbourne), 17 February 2005, 13.
60 See J J Spigelman, 'Tort Law Reform: An Overview' (2006) 14 *Tort Law Review* 5; Des Butler, 'A Comparison of the Adoption of the Ipp Report Recommendations and Other Personal Injuries Liability Reforms' (2005) 13 *Torts Law Journal* 201; Stella Tarakson, 'Personal Liability' (2005) 51 *Hot Topics: Legal Issues in Plain Language* 1.

support of some politicians, asserting that lawyers' fees were excessive and that the costs of lawyers' involvement in compensation processes made insurance too expensive.

The Australian community seemed willing to agree that lawyers simply cost too much. Few members of the public felt that their own lawyers' fees were reasonable and MPs were prepared to believe that lawyers' collective reputation for over-charging might be one of the causes of the insurance 'crisis'.

At this distance, it is now obvious that insurance affordability is cyclical. The economic cycle is a far more powerful influence on insurance premiums than lawyers, because reduced economic activity usually leads to more corporate collapses, higher insurance claims, bigger payouts, reduced insurer profits and, consequently, higher premiums. Insurance cover, although now readily obtainable, is no cheaper than before the rights of small claimants were removed, despite the fact that insurance companies have regained their profitability.[61]

DISCUSSION QUESTIONS

1. One of the main outcomes of the collapse of HIH and the associated insurance 'crisis' was the loss of people's right to sue for compensation in the courts, and lawyers' loss of a source of income, despite the later recovery in insurer profitability. In the context of the material presented in this chapter, why do you think it was so easy for the insurance companies to convince the public and government that lawyers' greed was to blame for high insurance premiums? Do you think this justified the radical restriction of people's access to the courts to sue for compensation in tort matters that followed?

2. All lawyers are required to have professional indemnity insurance as a condition of holding a practising certificate. Imagine you are in legal practice with many files to handle and the possibility of making mistakes a constant issue. Compulsory insurance against being sued for negligence is very expensive for you and, inevitably, must be paid for by your clients through your fees. Would you think it worthwhile to specify, for the information of each client, the proportion of your fee that is allocated to such insurance? Would it make a difference to your decision if all lawyers had to give this information to clients?

---

61 Marcus Priest, 'Lawyers Slam Insurers Profits', *Australian Financial Review* (Sydney), 3 June 2005, 7.

CASE STUDY 9.3   THE FOREMAN CASE: OVER-CHARGING AND FALSIFYING EVIDENCE UNDER PRESSURE OF LAW FIRM BILLING PRACTICES[62]

In 1994 Carol Foreman, former family law partner at national mega-firm Clayton Utz, was struck off the roll of practising solicitors by the New South Wales Court of Appeal for deception of other practitioners and the court. Her deception occurred in the course of a dispute with a former divorce client, Mrs Avidan, about the firm's bill (based on time-billing) of more than $500,000 for Mrs Avidan's divorce arrangements. Ms Foreman swore that she had given Mrs Avidan a standard costs agreement at their first interview and then again a few months later. However, the costs agreement could not be found and nor was there any record in Ms Foreman's file memos or timesheets relating to the case that the costs agreement had ever been given to the client. The costs dispute was going to a hearing in the Family Court, and without evidence that they had entered into a costs agreement with the client, the firm would not be able to prove any basis for demanding such high fees from the client.

Ms Foreman rewrote her timesheet in her own client file to make it appear that she had recorded the handing over of the costs agreement at the beginning of the relationship with the client. Later, when the matter was about to go to the Family Court, she discovered that another copy of the original (unaltered) time sheet was about to be submitted to the court by her firm. (This copy of the timesheet had been filed in the accounts department as was the normal practice.) Ms Foreman destroyed this copy of the original timesheet and forged a new version to be submitted to the court.

Ultimately the Family Court (hearing the costs dispute) accepted that the costs agreement had been given to the client and signed despite the fact the costs agreement could not be found. The costs dispute between the firm and the client was consequently settled. Nevertheless, Ms Foreman faced disciplinary action in the Legal Profession Disciplinary Tribunal, because she had knowingly misled the court, her colleagues at Clayton Utz and their lawyers in the costs dispute, as well as the lawyers and client on the other side. She was struck off by the New South Wales Court of Appeal.

---

62 Based on *Council of Law Society of New South Wales v Foreman (No2)* (1994) 34 NSWLR 408. Other material for this case study from Ann Daniel, *Scapegoats for a Profession: Uncovering Procedural Injustice* (Chapter 4, 'The Cost of Justice', Gordon and Breach, New York, 1998) 71.

In her disciplinary hearing Ms Foreman accepted that she had acted inappropriately, but argued that she had done so because she was working under great pressure to meet the billing targets for her section of Clayton Utz. Ms Foreman was a very successful family lawyer who had been a partner at another law firm before being headhunted to head up the family law division at Clayton Utz. However, by the time of the Avidan dispute, she had been told that Clayton Utz was going to close down its family law practice because it was not making enough money, and that she and another specialist family law partner would have to work for a more junior partner in another area. She was allowed to run the family law division on a trial basis for six months, at which point its financial performance would be assessed. Her evidence to the court indicated that during that time she was totally cost-driven, working 12.5 hour days in the office and close to breakdown. One of the judges, Kirby P, commented that:

> Astonishingly, the evidence revealed that she and some staff members even slept at the office on occasion after working very late. Many, like [Ms Foreman], were highly stressed by the pressure under which they worked. Part of the stress would appear to have arisen from the obligation to meet budgeted requirements of fee production established by the firm. This was allegedly done by reference to the standards set by the Tobacco Institute, an amply funded client well able to pay its monthly accounts upon presentation.[63]

Originally Ms Foreman had been charged with 'gross over-charging'. However this aspect of the case was dropped, because the Family Court had held that there was in fact a costs agreement. The Disciplinary Tribunal accepted that this meant there could be no basis for a finding of over-charging, and this was not re-opened in the Court of Appeal.

DISCUSSION QUESTIONS

1. Kirby P commented, 'it seems virtually impossible to credit that legal costs in a dispute between a married couple for the most part over their matrimonial property could properly run up legal costs in the figures that are mentioned here [ie half a million dollars]'. Do you think Ms Foreman should have been subject to disciplinary action for over-charging? At that time the principles applied by the court were that

63 *Council of Law Society of New South Wales v Foreman (No2)* (1994) 34 NSWLR 408, 414. See the judgments of Mahoney JA at 433–8 and Giles AJA at 462–3 for descriptions of the firm (the threat to close down the family law section because of its lack of profitability) and budget (the requirement to enter into written costs agreements and to meet monthly preset budgets for billing) pressures that Foreman was under.

the 'deliberate charging of grossly excessive' legal costs or 'deliberate misrepresentations as to costs' could amount to professional misconduct. The test was generally 'whether the lawyer has charged fees grossly in excess of those which would be charged by lawyers of good repute and competency'.[64] Do you think disciplinary action for over-charging would have been successful if it had been continued under that principle?

2. Since then the *Model Laws* (and matching laws in each of the States) has made it a little easier to discipline overcharging by saying that 'the charging of grossly excessive legal costs' can amount to either unsatisfactory professional conduct or professional misconduct. Is it possible that Foreman could have been found to have overcharged under this principle? Remember that the client did in fact agree to the charges and the charges were made in accordance with normal time-based billing rates for a large commercial law firm.

3. Kirby P went on to point out that 'those charges were rendered not by Ms Foreman alone but by her firm' and that Ms Foreman's own 'charging strategy was, to say the least, influenced by a system of time charging and by budget requirements within the firm which were not of her individual making' and that he was 'not satisfied that this matter has been as fully and properly investigated as it should have been'. He suggested that perhaps the law firm itself should have been held responsible for over-charging.[65] To what extent was Clayton Utz as a firm responsible for the fees charged in this case? To what extent was it responsible for Foreman's dishonest conduct? Do you think that Clayton Utz should have been disciplined for over-charging in this case? Why do you think Clayton Utz's charging practices were not more thoroughly investigated and subjected to disciplinary action?

CASE STUDY 9.4 ALTERNATIVE BILLING METHODS

Consider the following three possible alternatives to time-based billing, as methods of getting away from the tyranny – for client *and* lawyer – of the 'six minute interval':

64 G E Dal Pont, *Lawyers' Professional Responsibility* (Lawbook Co, Pyrmont, NSW, 3rd edn, 2006) 565–6.

65 *Council of Law Society of New South Wales v Foreman (No 2)* (1994) 34 NSWLR 408, 422–3.

Event-Based Fees for Litigation

Civil cases are the arena where most disputes about fees occur. Under standard time-based billing, civil cases involve moderate fees being incurred at the beginning with slowly increasing costs as witnesses are interviewed, affidavits prepared and discovery of documents undertaken, rising to very high levels of cost as practitioners prepare briefs for trial, conduct intensive conferences with clients and witnesses, and then spend days in court. The process produces higher fees (on an item remuneration basis) for lawyers only if a case goes to trial, simply because they are paid most for the extensive work done close to the trial date.

An alternative event-based fee structure[66] recognises that more work is done at the end than at the beginning of a case, but allows for more of the value in that work to be charged at the beginning of the matter, compared to the end stages. Under this system an experienced costs committee would set the fee for each 'event' or stage in the proceedings according to their belief as to a reasonable lump-sum return for that event, and revise that fee at regular intervals. Table 9.1 shows the difference in fees charged under the two methods. Figure 9.3 shows how fees increase over time in civil litigation under traditional item-based remuneration billing. Figure 9.4 shows an example of how fees might be charged

Table 9.1:   Amount of Legal Fees Charged at Different Stages of Litigation Under Traditional Item Remuneration Charging Structure and Event-Based Fee Structure[67]

Amount of Legal Fees ($): Traditional Item Remuneration Charging Structure	Progress of Litigation	Amount of Legal Fees ($): Event-Based Fee Structure
500	Letter of demand	500
1000		1000
1500	Issue proceedings	2500
2000	File defence	3500
2500	Discovery	4000
3000	Pretrial direction hearing	4250
3500	Mediation	4500
4000		4750
6000	Brief counsel	4850
7000	Start of trial	5000

66 Philip Williams et al, *Report of the Review of Scales of Legal Professional Fees in Federal Jurisdictions* (Attorney-General's Department, Canberra, 1998); extracted in Australian Law Reform Commission, *Managing Justice*, 285–91.

67 These fee levels are by way of example only and will differ considerably from actual cases.

Figure 9.3   Example of Rate of Increase of Fees in Litigation Under Traditional Item Remuneration Basis

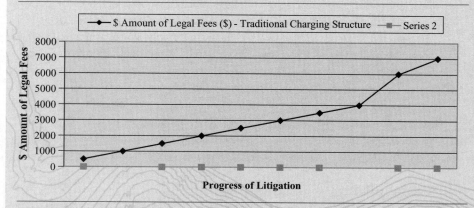

Figure 9.4   Example of Rate of Increase of Fees in Litigation Under Event-Based Fee System

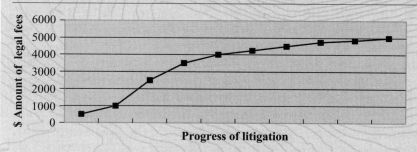

under an events-based system. Time-based billing would not be allowed. This means that the overall costs of litigation would be limited and lawyers would be paid earlier for the same work. Although there are many clients who begin litigation determined to 'have their day in court', this sentiment often changes as the length and stress of the process sinks in.

This system seeks to give the lawyer an incentive to use alternative dispute resolution to maximise the chances of early resolution, when a relatively high proportion of fees has been earned, leading to fewer trials, faster resolution of disputes and greater community satisfaction with the justice system.

Court Control of the Costs Process

Some commentators have suggested that the current costs assessment system for litigation is cumbersome and the outcomes unpredictable because of variation in the training and background of assessors. An alternative would be for the trial judge to control the costs process. This happens in New Zealand where the successful party must make an application to the trial judge for a fixed, lump-sum costs order as a part of the substantive judgment, and the judge makes that decision after receiving evidence from the parties as to their costs.[68] Since the trial judge should understand the issues in the trial better than anyone, there is some prospect that judge-ordered costs would match the fair cost of proceedings more precisely. When married with the now common principles of 'active case management', under which the trial judge decides many procedural issues under strict timelines set by the court rules, judge-ordered costs may also be far more predictable to the parties' lawyers in advance. They might also aid earlier identification of the point in the proceedings at which costs are at a minimum in relation to the likely financial return to the client.

'Value' Billing

The New South Wales Legal Services Commissioner suggests 'flexible, fixed-fee or value billing' as the ideal approach to fair fees and minimal complaints about costs in both court and transaction work. This approach aims to develop a trust relationship between practitioner and client under which they meet early and negotiate as to the value of the 'project' to the client. This might be expressed in the lawyer's initial question 'what do you hope to achieve by this process/ transaction?' Value billing is conceptually similar to event-based billing, because they both focus on defining measurable stages in a case and assigning a particular fee amount to the achievement of that stage. The lawyer would provide a fixed fee (probably based on the relevant court or item remuneration scales) and some estimates of add-ons for extra services that might become necessary if the matter goes in various directions.[69]

Value billing as an alternative approach to billing has now been formally recommended in the report of the New South Wales Legal Fees Review Panel which recommends optional substitution of the cost disclosure rules with a 'budget' plan. Under this proposal, lawyers and clients would agree to draft an initial fees budget for a proposed matter or case, to identify stages at which bills would be issued, and to issue bills only in accordance with the budget. Lawyers

---

68 See Deborah Vine Hall, 'Present Difficulties with the Assessment System' (2004) 27 *University of New South Wales Law Journal* 206.

69 Steve Mark, 'The Cost of Justice or Justice in Costs: The Experience of the OLSC in Handling Costs Complaints' (2004) 27 *University of New South Wales Law Journal* 225. See also Wilkins, 'Footing the Bill', 16, who comments: 'Task or project-based billing systems are now increasingly finding a place within the profession. And some practitioners expect firms' choice of billing system in the future to be increasingly task-based rather than time-based'.

would report on and review compliance with the budget at regular intervals, and modify it only on a strict schedule. If lawyers fail to review and request an update to a budget, any work done after the expiry of the prior stage would be chargeable only at fair and reasonable value, less 20%.[70]

DISCUSSION QUESTIONS

1. To what extent are each of the ethical approaches to lawyering implicit in each of these alternative approaches to billing?

2. Which do you think is best?

3. To what extent do different billing methods suit different contexts: for example, different practice contexts (solo practitioner, large firm, lawyers employed in-house in a corporation or government department), or different types of cases (litigation, preparing and advising on a contract, writing a will)?

4. How would the incentives for ethical and unethical conduct by lawyers offered by each of the event-based fees system (proposed above) and court controlled costs (described above and practised in New Zealand) compare with the incentives offered by conditional costs agreements and contingency fees?

5. The proposal for value-based billing is soundly based on the desirability for straightforward, early communication with clients. This depends not only on the integrity and respect of the lawyer but also on their skill in personal communication. Which clients in which areas of work would benefit from this? What about vulnerable clients?

RECOMMENDED FURTHER READING

Iain Campbell and Sara Charlesworth, 'Salaried Lawyers and Billable Hours: A New Perspective from the Sociology of Work' (2012) 19 *International Journal of the Legal Profession* 89–122.

G E Dal Pont, *Lawyers' Professional Responsibility* (Lawbook Co, Pyrmont, NSW, 5th edn, 2013) 'Part III: Costs'.

70 See Recommendation 27 in Legal Fees Review Panel, *Report*, 66.

Legal Fees Review Panel, *Discussion Paper: Lawyer's Costs and the Time Billing* [sic](2004) Lawlink New South Wales <www.imf.com.au/docs/default-source/site-documents/legalfeesreviewpanel>.

—— *Report: Legal Costs in New South Wales* (2005) Law link New South Wales <www.lpclrd.lawlink.nsw.gov.au/agdbasev7wr/lpclrd/documents/pdf/final_costs_paper_and_recommendations_summary.pdf>.

Lisa Lerman, 'Gross Profits? Questions About Lawyer Billing Practices' (1994) 22 *HofstraLaw Review* 645.

Richard Moorhead, 'Filthy Lucre: Lawyers' Fees and Lawyers' Ethics – What is Wrong with Informed Consent?' (2011) 31 *Legal Studies* 345–71.

Christine Parker, *Just Lawyers: Regulation and Access to Justice* (Oxford University Press, Oxford, 1999) 'Chapter 3: Access to Justice' 30–56.

Christine Parker and David Ruschena, 'The Pressures of Billable Hours: Lessons from a Survey of Billing Practices Inside Law Firms' (2011) 9 *University of St Thomas Law Journal* 619–64.

Various Authors, 'Forum: Stopping the Clock? The Future of the Billable Hour' (2004) 27 *University of New South Wales Law Journal* 198, 198–249.

Victorian Law Reform Commission, *Civil Justice Review: Report* (Victorian Law Reform Commission, Melbourne, 2008) 'Ch 11: Reducing the Cost of Litigation' <www.lawreform.vic.gov.au/projects/civil-justice/civil-justice-review-report> at 12 April 2013.

10

CORPORATE LAWYERS AND CORPORATE MISCONDUCT

Introduction

In 2005, the large national Australian law firm, Allens Arthur Robinson ('Allens') won the *Business Review Weekly* – St George 'Client Choice' awards for being best large law firm, and also best large professional services firm of the year. The managing partner was quoted explaining how the firm had won these accolades:

> We don't run this place as a holiday camp...We expect our people to treat the client as if they were God and to put themselves out for clients. You don't say 'Sorry I can't do it, I'm playing cricket on the weekend'...You don't have a right to any free time.[1]

Lawyers employed in commercial law firms and those employed 'in-house' in a company's legal department often also seem to talk and behave as if they have no right to independent moral judgement. If you are a corporate lawyer, it is not seen as your job to have a moral opinion about your clients' (or employer's) activities. To express one may jeopardise your career.

Traditionally it was thought that the *external* lawyers for a company were automatically more independent and more capable of giving fearless, ethical advice to corporate clients if they thought their client was behaving wrongfully than were *internal or in-house* lawyers employed inside the company whose whole job depended on the company. But nowadays external law firm lawyers can often be almost as financially dependent on, and closely involved in, their corporate clients' businesses as in-house lawyers. And, like in-house legal staff, most external corporate lawyers are themselves also employed in large, profit-oriented organisations, whether it is a law firm, or a consultancy or accounting firm.[2] We therefore use the term 'corporate lawyer' throughout this chapter to refer both to lawyers employed in-house in business corporations, as well as those in law firm practice who are retained as external lawyers to advise or represent corporate clients, since both face many similar ethical pressures and opportunities.

In public opinion, corporate lawyers are morally tainted by their complicity in corporate scandals.[3] In both Chapter 1 and the introduction to Chapter 6 we briefly described *McCabe v British American Tobacco Australia Services Ltd* (BAT)

---

1 Lucinda Schmidt, 'Best Large Law Firm', *Business Review Weekly* (Melbourne), 3 March 2005, 48.

2 At the same time, it is now recognised by many in-house lawyers themselves that they should try to preserve their ethical independence from their clients. See Robert Eli Rosen, 'The Inside Counsel Movement, Professional Judgment and Organizational Representation' (1989) 64 *Indiana Law Journal* 479.

3 Susan Koniak, 'Corporate Fraud: See, Lawyers' (2003) 26 *Harvard Journal of Law & Public Policy* 195; Eli Wald, 'Lawyers and Corporate Scandals' (2004) 7 *Legal Ethics* 54.

as a possible example of excessive adversarialism in litigation.[4] At first instance the Victorian Supreme Court found that Clayton Utz, the solicitors for the defendant BAT, had advised the company on a 'document retention policy' that intentionally resulted in the destruction of thousands of documents, as part of the preparation for an anticipated wave of litigation against the tobacco industry. The Court also found that the defendant and their legal advisers had misled the plaintiff and the Court about the fact and the extent of their document destruction. The trial judge struck out the defendant's defence and ordered judgment for the plaintiff, without a trial, on the basis that the destruction of documents had unfairly prejudiced the plaintiff's chances of success. This sanction was later overturned on appeal,[5] but the precise legal obligations that applied to this situation remain a topic of debate.[6] The firm's conduct was referred to legal profession regulators, to the Victorian Director of Public Prosecutions and to the Australian Crime Commission. At one stage even the Australian Competition and Consumer Commission indicated it was investigating. But no prosecution or disciplinary action was ever forthcoming.[7]

The public and media reaction to the case indicated that ordinary members of the public considered Clayton Utz's advice to be at least unethical, if not illegal. Headlines included: 'Lawyers choking in their own smoke' and 'Call for ethics debate after BAT case',[8] as well as the caustic cartoon reproduced below.

4 *McCabe v British American Tobacco Australia Services Ltd* [2002] VSC 73 (Unreported, Eames J, 22 March 2002).

5 *British American Tobacco Australia Services Ltd v Cowell* (2002) 7 VR 524.

6 Camille Cameron and Jonathon Liberman, 'Destruction of Documents Before Proceedings Commence: What Is a Court to Do?' (2003) 3 *Melbourne University Law Review* 273. The controversy arises only where there is a likelihood of future litigation from any one of a number of potential plaintiffs, but there is no one particular plaintiff or defined cause of action that is in contemplation. If there were a particular plaintiff or cause of action clearly in view, the destruction of relevant documents would clearly be unlawful.

7 If the disclosures to the press about the firm's internal investigations are credible (and they do not appear to have been contradicted), it now seems that Clayton Utz conducted an internal investigation soon after Justice Eames' ruling in 2002 and found significant evidence that at least two of the senior Clayton Utz lawyers handling the McCabe litigation had indeed engaged in serious ethical misconduct, and at least one had intentionally deceived the court. However the firm has used legal action to aggressively defend the confidentiality of the leaked documents and other information. No disciplinary action has been taken at least partly because of the lack of information available to public authorities about exactly what happened within the legal team and in conversations with clients. See William Birnbauer, 'Top Lawyers Face Scrutiny' *The Age* (Melbourne) 19 August 2007 (online edition); William Birnbauer, 'Smoking Gun Aimed at Big Tobacco' *The Sunday Age* (Melbourne) 19 August 2007, 4; Christine Parker, 'Peering Over the Ethical Precipice: Incorporation, Listing, and the Ethical Responsibilities of Law Firms' University of Melbourne Legal Studies Research Paper No 339 at 23. <http://ssrn.com/abstract=1132926>

8 Amanda Keenan and Janet Fife-Yeomans, 'Lawyers Choking in Their Own Smoke', *The Weekend Australian* (Sydney), 13–14 April 2002,1,4; Chris Merritt, 'Call for Ethics Debate After BAT Case', *Australian Financial Review* (Sydney), 2 August 2002, 55; Sarah Crichton and Cynthia Banham, 'Tobacco Lawyers Face Two Inquiries', *The Sydney Morning Herald*, 13 April 2002, 4.

A government report recommended that the law in Victoria, where the case occurred, should make it unambiguously clear that such actions are unlawful.[9] There is now a maximum five-year jail term for wilful document destruction.[10] Yet, as mentioned in Chapter 1, the then Chief Executive Partner of Clayton Utz commented that it would have been wrong for Clayton Utz to take a moral stance on the activities of its tobacco company client. According to this view, it is up to the adversarial system to decide both the legality and the morality of clients' actions, not lawyers. This *adversarial advocate* view of the lawyer's role is particularly apt to rationalise away any need to consider broader ethical concerns.

Source: Jenny Coopes, *Australian Financial Review*, 21 June 2002

9 Peter Sallman, Report on Document Destruction and Civil Litigation in Victoria (Crown Counsel Victoria, Melbourne, 2004).

10 *Crimes (Document Destruction) Act 2006* (Vic) s 3, amending *Crimes Act 1958* (Vic) ss 253–255. See also *Evidence (Document Unavailability) Act 2006* (Vic), amending *Evidence Act 1958* (Vic) and the *Victorian Civil and Administrative Tribunal Act 1998* (Vic). A professional conduct rule to similar effect was also introduced in New South Wales: *Legal Profession Regulation 2005* (NSW) reg 177.

In the next part of this chapter we set out the major ways in which corporate lawyers have been criticised for facilitating and covering up corporate misconduct. We show how the dominant conception of all lawyers as *adversarial advocates* has been particularly useful for corporate lawyers and a powerful tool in the psychological process of rationalisation to deny responsibility for unethical business conduct.[11]

The corollary of the fact that lawyers can enable much economic (and other) activity, including misconduct, is that they can also act as 'gatekeepers' – who can 'disrupt misconduct by withholding their cooperation from a wrongdoer'.[12] Because of their duty to the law and position as officers of the court, regulators and critics of corporate lawyers' ethics now argue that corporate lawyers should undertake these gatekeeper responsibilities more actively. Thus the response to lawyer complicity in corporate scandals has generally been to underscore, reinforce or mandate *responsible lawyering* type obligations on corporate lawyers to remain independent of clients, to help corporate clients comply with the law, not assist in any fraud or other wrongdoing, and even to blow the whistle on individual managers or clients who do engage in wrongdoing.

In the third part of this chapter, we suggest that ethics in corporate law practice might require going beyond *responsible lawyering* values of compliance with the law to include consideration of substantive issues of business ethics. We briefly outline how the law of lawyering already places some *responsible lawyering* obligations on lawyers in relation to the misconduct of corporate (and other) clients. We suggest that corporate lawyers may need to take moral responsibility for their own actions and advice as members of the corporation, a *moral activist* approach, rather than maintain the fiction of independence from it. As in the previous chapters of this book, we use case studies and questions to examine what the key ethical considerations might be in corporate legal practice.

A Line between Corporate Law and Ethics?

Corporate lawyers' ethics may be more important than those of any other sector of the profession. Corporate lawyers play an important part in facilitating almost every economic activity in our society. They negotiate and draft business deals. They often advise what representations can or should be made in advertising campaigns,

---

11 See Kath Hall and Vivien Holmes, 'The power of rationalisation to influence lawyers' decisions to act' (2008) 11 *Legal Ethics* 137–53.

12 Ibid 74; John C Coffee, *Professional Gatekeepers: The Professions and Corporate Governance* (Oxford University Press, Oxford, 2006).

financial statements and disclosure documents for investors. They advise as to how to comply with the host of regulatory laws that apply to business, including environmental, health and safety, competition and fair trading regulation. And, of course, corporate lawyers also advise businesses on a day-to-day basis as to when to litigate and when to settle disputes.

Business corporations are amongst the most powerful actors in our society because of the far-reaching impact that their actions and activities can have on many people and on the natural environment.[13] For example, when Enron Corporation collapsed after the major part of its overwhelming debts were found to have been hidden from shareholders (see Case Study 10.3), more than 4000 employees lost their jobs and thousands of investors lost their life savings as Enron's US$70 billion in market capitalisation vanished.[14] Lawyers might generally be facilitators, more than initiators, of corporate action, but their entwinement in corporate decision-making and activity makes them powerful too.[15] They can facilitate corporate misconduct by explicitly or implicitly giving approval to corporate projects, by not dissuading clients from immoral or illegal courses of action, and by failing to disclose ongoing breaches of the law by their clients to the appropriate authorities once they become aware of them. In some cases, the lawyer can even be the designer of the client's misconduct, for example by designing and selling illegal tax shelters.[16]

Corporate lawyers have been criticised for acting simply as *adversarial advocates* who allow the way their business clients set their own business goals to drive the legal advice and other work they do for their clients in one of three main ways.

(a) Reactive Corporate Lawyering: Narrow Legalism That Ignores Ethical Issues

Corporate lawyers have been criticised for using their legal skills uncritically to enable misleading, illegal or unethical corporate conduct. Lawyers in these situations often claim that they did not know about the problematic nature of

---

13 Joel Bakan, *The Corporation* (The Free Press, New York, 2004).
14 Deborah Rhode and Paul Paton, 'Lawyers, Ethics, and Enron' (2002) 8 *Stanford Journal of Law, Business & Finance* 9, 9–10, citing Greenwood's statement in the hearing on the destruction of Enron-related documents by Andersen personnel before the House of Representatives Committee on Energy and Commerce, Subcommittee on Oversight and Investigations, United States Congress, Washington DC, 24 January 2002, 1 (James C Greenwood, Chairman of the Subcommittee).
15 Robert A Kagan and Robert Eli Rosen, 'On the Social Significance of Large Law Firm Practice' (1985) 37 *Stanford Law Review* 399.
16 Peter Grabosky, 'Professional Advisers and White Collar Illegality: Towards Explaining and Excusing Professional Failure' (1990) 13 *University of New South Wales Law Journal* 73.

the conduct they assisted with. Often they do not 'know' because they have not asked, and they have not asked because they have – intentionally, negligently or subconsciously – closed their eyes, ears and mouths to the discussion of 'non-legal' factors that might raise questions.[17]

- In Case Study 10.3 at the end of this chapter we consider the role of Enron's external law firm, Vinson and Elkins, in allowing misleading and corrupt financial practices at Enron to continue unabated until Enron's collapse. Enron's lawyers have been criticised for their propensity 'to try to preserve plausible deniability, by refraining from asking hard questions that might yield awkwardly unwelcome revelations that might have to be reported to the directors, shareholders, or regulators'.[18]

- In Case Study 10.2, the lawyers for James Hardie gave detailed technical legal advice (over a number of years) about how James Hardie could 'separate itself' from its liabilities to compensate those who had suffered disease or died as a result of exposure to the asbestos that the company had manufactured into various products. At one point during the government-commissioned inquiry into James Hardie's actions, Commissioner David Jackson QC commented in relation to the lawyers' advice, 'Why didn't someone stand back and say "This is just too hot"?'.[19]

It can be in the interests of both lawyers and their corporate clients to keep the scope of the work given to the lawyer very narrow, so as to exclude the possibility that the lawyer might find out about, or need to address their mind to, any unethical or illegal aspects of corporate plans. For example, journalist and observer of the

17 See Robert Eli Rosen, 'Problem-Setting and Serving the Organizational Client: Legal Diagnosis and Professional Independence' (2001) 56 *University of Miami Law Review* 179; William H Simon, 'Wrongs of Ignorance and Ambiguity: Lawyer Responsibility for Collective Misconduct' (2005) 22 *Yale Journal on Regulation* 1.

18 Robert Gordon, 'Portrait of a Profession in Paralysis' (2002) 54 *Stanford Law Review* 1427, 1436.

19 Statement in the hearing before the Special Commission of Inquiry into the Medical Research and Compensation Fund Established by the James Hardie Group, Sydney, 7 July 2004, 2 (David F Jackson QC, Commissioner) <www.lawlink.nsw.gov.au/lawlink/Corporate/ ll corporate.nsf/pages/MRCF transcripts> at 2 June 2006. In his report Jackson eventually concluded that he found it 'disturbing' that none of Hardie's professional advisers and officers, especially its solicitors, 'expressed any view of the merits [or rightness] of the underlying transaction'. But he did not find that Hardie's law firm breached any legal or professional conduct obligation on this issue: D F Jackson, *Report of the Special Commission of Inquiry into the Medical Research and Compensation Fund* (New South Wales, 2004) [29.16] <www.cabinet.nsw.gov.au/publications.html> at 22 May 2006. Eventually the in-house counsel for James Hardie was found to have breached the *Corporations Act* by failing to advise the Board of certain matters: *Shafron v Australian Securities and Investments Commission* [2012] HCA 18 (3 May 2012).

Australian legal profession, Richard Ackland, analysed the James Hardie situation in terms of 'plausible deniability' for both the lawyers and the corporate client:

> Boards of directors and senior directors have schemes that need implementation. Lawyers are hired to get the client over the line. When things go wrong, as they often do, the directors and executives invariably say, 'We acted on advice'. The standard retort of the advisers is; 'We were not given all the information, so the advice was necessarily limited'. This reliable formulation usually saves a lot of bacon.[20]

This type of plausible deniability can be seen as an example of a narrow, reactive approach in which the corporate lawyer avoids consideration of issues that might give rise to ethical obligations:

> Legal departments adopting the narrow view sharply distinguish legal from business advice and confine the lawyer's role to the strictly legal; their advice is reactive, neutral risk analysis, given only when sought, accepting as the 'client' whatever manager at whatever level consults it, and accepting the 'problem' and the corporation's 'interest' as defined by the manager. They don't ask what happens when the 'client' leaves their office – unless required to perform monitoring or auditing functions, in which case they will confine themselves to formal questions and formal responses. Under attack by regulators or civil adversaries, they will see their function as simply minimizing liability in every case…[21]

Ethically unreflective corporate lawyering can sometimes occur not so much because of failures of personal ideals as because of narrow legalistic training and culture that do not equip corporate lawyers to know how to put ethics into action in real-life corporate contexts, or even to recognise ethical issues when they arise. This type of practice will often not be in the interests of the company as a whole. For example, some years ago a major Australian company was subject to a serious complaint of sexual harassment by one of its female employees. They asked their external lawyers (one of the large national law firms) for advice. The lawyers, applying all the technical skills they had learnt in law school, advised fighting the case. There was no possibility of an argument that the harassment had not occurred on the facts. But the lawyers advised that the company may be able to escape liability to compensate the woman because she had let the harassment go on for

---

20 Richard Ackland, 'Irresistible Charms', *Business Review Weekly* (Sydney), 29 September 2004, 50.

21 Robert Gordon and William Simon, 'The Redemption of Professionalism' in Robert Nelson, David Trubek and Robert Solomon (eds), *Lawyers' Ideals / Lawyers' Practices: Transformations in the American Legal Profession* (Cornell University Press, Ithaca, New York, 1992) 230, 252; summarising Rosen, 'The Inside Counsel Movement'.

several years before complaining. In effect, the lawyers advised the company to admit that the harassment had occurred and to argue in defence that the situation within the company had been so bad that the woman should have complained earlier. The case took five years to settle and cost the company much financially (some estimates are half a million dollars), in 'public humiliation' and loss of staff morale. Lawyers who were presumably trying to please a corporate client by telling them how they could escape legal liability on technical legal grounds apparently failed to consider, or to emphasise, how this might affect the company's reputation, let alone the company's ethical obligation to compensate the woman and address its culture of harassment and discrimination.[22]

Perhaps the lawyers in the example above thought that matters of corporate culture, ethics and reputation would be considered by others better equipped to do so in the corporate hierarchy. This is not necessarily so. In-house lawyers may be one of the only members of the corporation who have an opportunity to reflect and advise on ethical matters.

(b) Pro-active Corporate Lawyering: Commercial Savvy That Consciously Uses Law to Achieve Unethical Goals

In recent times, business clients increasingly expect their lawyers to take a more pro-active, 'commercial' approach. They are expected to bring to bear commercial, social and political contexts on the advice they offer and work they do. Lawyers are expected to understand their client's business goals, and advise on how to use law to achieve them. Indeed, in some businesses it is now expected that, rather than being a mere 'cost centre', an in-house legal department should generate profits or 'value-add' through strategies such as aggressive tax planning, intellectual property protections and takeover litigation.[23] More constructively, lawyers might be expected to implement corporate governance systems that improve corporate decision-making processes and corporate social responsibility systems and, in turn, the businesses' credibility with the public and therefore its brand value.

Corporate lawyers have been criticised for legal manipulation and innovation that produces legal devices and techniques that achieve client goals, but without regard to the spirit and ethical substance of the law or the community's ethical

---

22 Example from Christine Parker, 'How to Win Hearts and Minds: Corporate Compliance Policies for Sexual Harassment' (1999) 21 *Law & Policy* 21, 32–3.
23 Robert Eli Rosen, '"We're All Consultants Now": How Change in Client Organizational Strategies Influences Change in the Organization of Corporate Legal Services' (2002) 44 *Arizona Law Review* 637, 650–60, 675–9; G Richard Shell, *Make the Rules or Your Rivals Will* (Crown Business, New York, 2004).

expectations. Unlike the first category of critique of corporate lawyers above, here the lawyers are expected to understand and address the company's broader commercial, political and ethical context, not just their technical legal needs. But they may be expected to come up with strategies for the client to achieve its goals by 'managing' this context. As the following examples illustrate, corporate lawyers can help companies engage in 'creative compliance' by avoiding and evading the imposition of law before it becomes a problem, or by creating legal techniques that make it look like companies are complying with the law and addressing social and governmental expectations of ethical behaviour, while making as little real change as possible. They may also devise legal techniques that abuse the law by achieving corporate goals regardless of the real purpose of the law involved:[24]

- Corporate lawyers sometimes advise their clients to use the 'litigation option' as a tactic to put commercial pressure on their opponents in takeover battles and other corporate disputes.[25] One of Australia's 1980s 'corporate cowboys' used litigation in this way in the *White Industries* case (see Case Study 6.4 in Chapter 6).

- During the 1990s (and continuing today) tax scheme promoters began creating tax shelter products on a massive scale to help wealthy individuals evade tax. These products are commonly backed up with opinion letters from certain barristers stating that the schemes are legal. The promoters then market the schemes by paying commissions to law firms to refer clients to them to participate in the schemes.[26] It is also standard practice for corporate clients to expect advice from their lawyers as to the best way to structure transactions and operations to minimise, or completely avoid, tax. Lawyers sometimes distinguish between tax 'minimisation' or 'planning' (which is legal), as opposed to tax 'avoidance' (which is not), but rarely do lawyers and legal professional regulators comment on the ethics, as opposed to the legality, of these schemes. It is generally left up to the Australian Tax Office to regulate.[27]

---

24 Doreen McBarnet, 'Legal Creativity: Law, Capital and Legal Avoidance' in Maureen Cain and Christine Harrington (eds), *Lawyers in a Postmodern World: Translation and Transgression* (New York University Press, New York, 1994) 73; Michael Powell, 'Professional Innovation: Corporate Lawyers and Private Lawmaking' (1993) 18 *Law & Social Inquiry* 423.

25 Roman Tomasic and Stephen Bottomley, *Directing the Top 500* (Allen & Unwin, St Leonards, NSW, 1993) 3.

26 John Braithwaite, *Markets in Vice: Markets in Virtue* (Federation Press, Leichhardt, NSW, 2005) 6, 37, 43, 48, 110–11.

27 See G E Dal Pont, *Lawyers' Professional Responsibility* (Lawbook Co, Pyrmont, NSW, 5th edn, 2013) 428–33 for a discussion of the professional conduct rules that do apply specifically to the ethics of tax advice.

(c) Abusing Lawyer-Client Confidentiality Protections to Cover up Misconduct and Obstruct Justice

The final and most serious criticism of the ethics of corporate lawyers is that they sometimes aid their clients by helping them obstruct justice where civil litigation or regulatory investigation and prosecution is occurring or likely:

* In the last weeks before Enron's collapse (Case Study 10.3 at the end of this chapter), and when it was already obvious that the regulator would be investigating Enron and multinational accounting firm Arthur Andersen's audits of Enron, an in-house Arthur Andersen lawyer wrote a memo reminding colleagues, who had worked on Enron audits, of what Arthur Andersen's 'document retention policy' was. This policy required the destruction of notes and working papers used to prepare audits. Arthur Andersen's lead partner responsible for Enron then organised the urgent disposal of tons of Enron-related documents.[28] The same lawyer also wrote another email suggesting changes to a draft file record on an Enron matter, to delete any reference to the fact that Arthur Andersen had legal advice that Enron's disclosures in that matter might be misleading. Arthur Andersen was later convicted of the crime of obstruction of justice and then acquitted on appeal.[29] Arthur Andersen, previously one of the 'big five' multinational accounting firms, collapsed as a result of its involvement with the Enron scandal.

One very important way in which business corporations can use lawyers to obstruct justice is where corporate lawyers are able to use their professional responsibilities in relation to confidentiality and client legal privilege to protect corporate activities from scrutiny, and cover up evidence of any wrongdoing.[30] Case Study 4.4 in Chapter 4 discusses the way in which tobacco industry lawyers in the United States devised schemes to try and claim client legal privilege over reports that showed smoking was dangerous. Another example of client legal privilege being invoked to prevent public scrutiny of alleged organisational wrongdoing is the response by AWB, which controls the export sale of all Australian wheat, to an Australian government commission of inquiry into whether it paid 'kickbacks' (a form of

---

28 *Arthur Andersen LLP v United States* 544 U.S. 696 (2005); Gordon, 'Portrait of a Profession', 1436. Loren Schechter, William OPurcell and Cecilia W Kaiser, 'The Effect of the Arthur Andersen Verdict on Inside Counsel' (2002) 3(1) *Journal of Investment Compliance* 27, 27–8.

29 Schechter, Purcell and Kaiser, 'The Effect of the Arthur Andersen Verdict'. The Enron 'engagement partner' pleaded guilty to charges involving the destruction of documents, and stated that he believed he was following the lawyer's memo in doing so: Simon, 'Wrongs of Ignorance', 9.

30 William Simon, 'The Confidentiality Fetish' (2004) 294(5) *The Atlantic Monthly* 113.

bribe) to former Iraqi dictator Saddam Hussein in order to make sure the Iraqi government bought wheat from Australia under the United Nations' Oil-for-Food Programme (that operated while trade sanctions were in place against Iraq) (Case Study 4.5 in Chapter 4; see also Case Study 1.3 in Chapter 1, and Case Study 10.1 below).

What is ethically rotten at the core of the conduct of the lawyers in these case studies is not merely that they committed technical infractions by using confidentiality and privilege inappropriately. Rather the problem is that in cases like *McCabe*, the client companies have used lawyers to shut down the proper operation of the adversary system and therefore legal scrutiny of their conduct. For example, in relation to big tobacco, one can make a very good case that tobacco companies are substantively and systematically immoral and unethical because they sell a product that they know is addictive and lethal to a large proportion of their customers, and often market it in ways that are misleading and designed to appeal to vulnerable people.[31] However the ethical problem in the *McCabe* case, and other tobacco cases, was that the company and its lawyers made sure that the legal system could not even see and determine this substantive and urgent moral and legal issue. They did so by making sure that they themselves could not see the ethical issues as relevant. As we see below, this is not a problem of lack of professional conduct or civil procedure rules, or even of non-compliance with those rules. Rather it is a problem of rationalising away the need to consider broader ethical concerns, and allowing large, powerful organisations to manipulate the law to avoid scrutiny of their conduct.

Commercial Immersion of Corporate Lawyering

Critics argue that the types of uncritical corporate lawyering described above have become more ethically problematic, more widespread, and more deeply entrenched as the market for legal services has become more competitive and fragmented. Big companies (and also government departments) now shop around more for the 'right legal advice at the right price'. They have unbundled their legal services so that no one firm, not even their own in-house legal department, is necessarily guaranteed a steady flow of legal work, or is aware of all legal matters in which the company is involved. Yet, at the same time, there is also more demand for corporate lawyers to be embedded in (employed by, or seconded to) business sub-units within corporate clients so that they can provide commercially realistic advice and anticipate, avoid or resolve legal problems for that unit. While there is demand for a closer relationship between lawyers and business, that relationship is also less secure for the lawyer, as lawyers can easily be sacked if their advice

---

31 See Jonathan Liberman and Jonathan Clough, 'Corporations That Kill: The Criminal Liability of Tobacco Manufacturers' (2002) 26 *Criminal Law Journal* 1.

does not suit. This is one reason that lawyers will come under pressure to please individual managers, executives or work teams (who control the purse strings) rather than consider their obligation to the corporation as a whole, let alone any duty to the law or the public interest.[32]

The ethical dangers posed by businesses' increasingly commercial approach to legal advice are compounded by the fact that law firms themselves are also being managed more and more like large business corporations. Corporate lawyers rarely operate as independent solo practitioners, or work together in equal partnerships. Rather, an increasing number of lawyers today work as employees subject to detailed direction and supervision, especially in large national and international law firms. These firms are vastly more profitable, and more profits-driven, than smaller firms (see for example Case Study 9.3, The Foreman Case, in Chapter 9).[33]

The *McCabe* case provides a good example of the extent of this commercial immersion of corporate lawyers. As the judge described the facts:

> The relationship between the defendant [BAT] and its retained solicitors was so close that solicitors employed by private [law] firms sometimes became employees of Wills [a company in the BAT corporate group] and then continued to work alongside members of their former firm, and employees of one of the legal firms sometimes spent months working on the premises of Wills. Private practitioners and in-house lawyers travelled together to conferences of litigation lawyers, organised by companies in the BAT Group, to discuss litigation tactics... The long standing and very close association between in-house lawyers and private practitioners had the potential for blurring the roles and responsibilities of the lawyers.[34]

Similarly, it seems likely that Vinson and Elkins lawyers felt that they needed to do everything possible for Enron for fear of losing a major source of firm income. According to newspaper reports, Enron and Vinson and Elkins had 'one of the closest lawyer-client relationships in corporate America', with both Enron's general counsel (head in-house lawyer) and deputy general counsel being former partners at the law firm. Another twenty or so Vinson and Elkins lawyers had also taken jobs in Enron's legal department in the previous decade, and Enron was the firm's single

---

32 Rosen, "'We're All Consultants Now'", 672–3.

33 John M Conley and Scott Baker, 'Fall from Grace or Business as Usual? A Retrospective Look at Lawyers on Wall Street and Main Street' (2005) 30 *Law & Social Inquiry* 783, 817. See also Marc Galanter and Thomas Palay, *Tournament of Lawyers: The Transformation of the Big Law Firm* (University of Chicago Press, Chicago and London, 1991); Michael Kirby, 'Billable Hours in a Noble Calling?' (1997) 21 *Alternative Law Journal* 257; Bret Walker, 'Lawyers and Money' (2005) 62 *Living Ethics* 6 – also available via <www.ethics.org.au/things_to_read/articles_to_read/law_and_justice/article_0465.shtm> at 28 July 2006.

34 *McCabe v British American Tobacco Australia Services Ltd* [2002] VSC 73 (Unreported, Eames J, 22 March 2002) [284]–[286].

largest customer, accounting for more than 7% ($31.5 million) of Vinson and Elkins' revenue in 2001. Vinson and Elkins also had several lawyers working virtually full-time on Enron business, with some permanently stationed in the company's offices.[35]

Rationalisation

It would be easy to criticise the role of lawyers in these various cases of corporate misconduct as simply due to unrestrained greed, and individual moral failing. But the loss of ethical discernment is often a subtle and gradual progression, especially in the context of complex corporate decision-making.[36] It is easy to ignore the interests of investors, the public, the courts and the law, without even noticing that is what we are doing, where it is psychologically more comfortable to do so, or the issues have become so complex that we subconsciously screen out uncomfortable facts. In particular, when lawyers become financially dependent on their clients, spend a lot of their time with clients, and try to see things from their client's point of view in order to provide a good service, they will naturally, and often subconsciously, tend to identify with those clients and their purposes.

We all want to believe the best of those we identify with, including clients that we serve. If we were to notice any sign of dishonesty or other conduct that goes against our own personal ethical standards and social values amongst our friends and colleagues, this would cause what psychologists call 'cognitive dissonance' – that is, the uncomfortable feeling of lack of fit between our belief in ourself as an ethical person on the one hand, and our involvement or identification with unethical activity on the other. Psychologists have shown that people often use subconscious strategies to avoid this sort of cognitive dissonance: They either subconsciously strive to 'not notice' unethical activity, or rationalise it as soon as they do notice it. Thus corporate lawyers

> will often unconsciously dismiss or discount evidence of misconduct and its impact on third parties. The risks of such dissonance are exacerbated when lawyers bond socially and professionally with the client's management team. The more that [the lawyer] blends with the culture of corporate insiders, the greater the pressures of cohesiveness. That, in turn, encourages lawyers to underestimate risk and to suppress compromising information in order to preserve internal solidarity.[37]

---

35 Mike France with Wendy Zellner and Christopher Palmeri, 'One Big Client, One Big Hassle', *Business Week Online*, 28 January 2002 <www.businessweek.com/magazine/content/02_04/b3767706.htm> at 2 June 2006.

36 See Rosen, 'Problem-Setting', 182.

37 Rhode and Paton, 'Lawyers, Ethics and Enron', 32. See also Kenneth Mann, *Defending White-Collar Crime: A Portrait of Attorneys at Work* (Yale University Press, New Haven, 1985) for evidence of lawyers purposely remaining ignorant of their clients' guilt so that they can zealously defend them.

Where it is in the client's interest to keep information about unethical conduct from the lawyer, it is even easier for lawyers to choose to remain ignorant of their clients' misconduct.

Rationalisation in a general sense is something we all do – for both good and bad. As Kath Hall and Vivien Holmes explain, on the one hand:

> In the Oxford Dictionary, the general definition of rationalising is: *the act of rendering something comfortable to reason, to explain it on a rational basis.* This definition reflects the common idea that rationalisation is an acceptable process of bringing forth the most logical and compelling reason in support of our actions and beliefs.[38]

We all need to rationalise our life experiences and plans in order to preserve a coherent sense of personal identity and meaning for ourselves. However, as Hall and Holmes go on to explain, there is a second form of rationalisation that we might describe as 'moral rationalisation', because it creates excuses and denies responsibility for behaviour. Hall and Holmes summarise rationalisation in this second negative sense as involving:

- self-serving explanations;
- that assist in making behaviour appear more acceptable to both self and others;
- involve a degree of self-deception;
- often occur outside the realm of the conscious mind;
- can reduce feelings of responsibility and/or anxiety for the negative aspects of behaviour; and
- can neutralise the impact of legal or ethical issues involved in a decision.[39]

It is described in the psychological literature negatively, as 'a self-serving process designed to preserve self-image, legitimate behaviour and facilitate decision making. In this context, the Oxford Dictionary defines rationalisation as: *(psychol) a justification of behaviour to make it appear rational or socially acceptable by (subconsciously) ignoring, concealing or glossing over its real motive'.*[40]

Common rationalisations for illegal and unethical conduct include:[41]

- *Denial of Responsibility – 'It wasn't my fault…I didn't mean it'*: My behaviour was caused by forces outside of me and beyond my control such as a poor

---

38 Kath Hall and Vivien Holmes, 'The Power of Rationalisation to Influence Lawyers' Decisions to Act Unethically' (2008) 11 *Legal Ethics* 137.
39 Ibid 140.
40 Ibid.
41 This list is based on the authors' re-working of Gresham M Sykes and David Matza, 'Techniques of Neutralisation: A Theory of Delinquency' (1957) 22 *American Sociological Review*, 664–70, 667–9.

upbringing and education, bad companions, or a bad situation that I was helpless to change.

- *Denial of Injury – 'I didn't hurt anyone'*: My behaviour may have been wrong but it did not cause any great harm to anyone. If the victim is physically absent, unknown or a vague abstraction then it is easier to deny the injury because there is only a weak awareness of any human victim.

- *Denial of the Victim – 'They had it coming to them'*: My behaviour may have caused injury but the injury is justified as a form of rightful retaliation, punishment or recompense against some individual or group who has done me or society wrong.

- *Condemnation of the Condemners – 'Everybody's picking on me'*: My behaviour may be wrong but the motives and behaviours of those who condemn me are no better or are even worse than mine. My condemners are hypocrites, deviants in disguise, or impelled by personal spite.

- *Appeal to Higher Loyalties – 'I didn't do it for myself'*: I know I did what was wrong according to society but I had to do it for the sake of an individual or group to whom I owe a particular obligation of loyalty such as my family, friendship clique, business partner or client. I found myself in an ethical dilemma and I had to break the law in order to resolve it.

It might be suggested that the adversarial lawyer mindset is particularly attuned to rationalisation. One account of the adversarial advocate's role is to rationalise client conduct through 'creative interpretation of rules and fashioning plausible arguments in support of their interpretations'.[42] Therefore lawyers may be both particularly comfortable and skilled at using their role in the adversary system to rationalise away any need to be aware of, consider and come to a judgement on the broader ethical and social implications of their work – how ordinary people would morally evaluate their work.[43] In Case Study 10.1 below you are asked to consider how these rationalisations might be used by lawyers in a situation of commercial misconduct.

42 Kath Hall, *Mind the Gap: Psychological Jurisprudence and the Professional Regulation of Lawyer Dishonesty*. PhD, Australian National University, 16 June 2011, 63, referring to Milton C Regan, 'Risky business' (2006) 94 *The Georgetown Law Journal* 1957, 1972. See also Doreen McBarnet, 'Legal Creativity: Law, Capital and Legal Avoidance' in Maureen Cain and Christine Harrington (eds), *Lawyers in a Postmodern World: Translation and Transgression* (New York, New York University Press, 1994) 73–84; Maureen Cain, 'The symbol traders' in Maureen Cain and Christine Harrington (eds), *Lawyers in a Postmodern World: Translation and Transgression* (New York, New York University Press, 1994) 15–48.

43 See [Hall n42] pp73 ff Hall. Hall identifies three rationalisations that are part of this account for lawyers: 'This is just the way things are done'; 'If I had not done it, someone else would have'; 'I didn't know what was really going on', at 101. See also Terri L Orbuch 'Peoples's Accounts Count: The Sociology of Accounts' (1997) 23 *Annual Review of Sociology* 455.

Moral rationalisation is an inherently unstable and unsustainable way of dealing with the world. Nevertheless, it is a common way to psychologically deal with stressful and uncertain situations and the cognitive dissonance of being in a situation where a person wants to believe they are an ethical person but it would be easier, and in their interests, to engage in unethical behaviour. People rationalise their own behaviour to make it easier to live with themselves rather than dealing with the problem of the dissonance between ethical principles and behaviour. This can be particularly dangerous in groups and organisations where mutual reinforcement between individual and group behaviour can transform self-serving rationalisations into organisational facts.[44] Since moral rationalisation involves lying to oneself and others, it is psychologically stressful and ultimately can lead to depression.

However, people can learn about their own rationalising and reduce its impact and potential to produce apathy and immoral decisions. Psychological experiments suggest that quite often we do not even notice that we are rationalising. This might be because, at the individual level, our unconscious might cut in and 'save' our conscious mind from troubling thoughts through self-deception. Developing sensitivity to one's own thought processes can help overcome this. This is an important aspect of developing the type of reflection on action and moral judgement that is part of professional competency. Becoming aware of the different types of rationalisation and the cognitive, perceptual and self-deceptive tricks our minds play on us (in our own self-interest) can also be helpful. That is the purpose of this discussion. Indeed it has been suggested that ethics training about the rules is no use if people are not also trained to recognise the mechanisms by which they are likely to rationalise away the rules.

Another reason that we might not notice that we are engaging in rationalisation is because situational factors 'frame' the way we think about our decision-making and behaviours in different contexts. In some contexts, we might be primed to see the situation as involving ethical dimensions, for example when conducting the conflicts of interest check the first time a lawyer sees a new client in a family law practice, or while sitting and writing a legal ethics exam! But there are other situations in which ethical issues have been framed out of the picture. The way our workplaces are set up and even the whole profession – their habits and cultures – can either help us see or blind us to the ethical dimensions of particular situations.

Thus in Case Study 10.1 below we are clearly told that the situation that AWB found itself in involved 'bribing' Saddam Hussein. We are told various factors that might be used to rationalise that bribery, but we are alerted by the mention of bribery (and the fact that the story is told in a legal ethics book) that there is an issue of ethics and quite possibly illegality involved. However, ethical decisions do not always announce themselves as ethical decisions in this way in real life.

---

44 Hall and Holmes, 'Power of Rationalisation', 138.

Compare the version of the story of AWB below with that presented in Case Study 1.3 in Chapter 1. In Chapter 1, more of the story is told about the way the ethical issues became more difficult for the lawyers because the executives in AWB attempted to frame the judgement about what to do as a business decision that had already been made.

CASE STUDY 10.1   RATIONALISATION AND THE LAWYERS FOR AWB

You are an in-house lawyer with AWB and are asked to help draft a contract for selling wheat to Iraq under the UN's Oil-for-Food Programme (while international sanctions are in place against trade with Iraq). This would involve paying a bribe to Saddam Hussein to make sure Australian wheat was chosen. There is a way to do it that will likely keep it secret. If you do not do it, the Australian wheat price will take a dive and Australian wheat growers will suffer – some may be forced off their land – and your own future might also be uncertain. The AWB executive responsible for sales to Iraq has not asked you for your opinion on whether to enter into the contract or not. He has just asked you to draft the contract and inflate the price to be paid for the wheat by the amount of the 'trucking fees' and 'port charges' that will be paid to offload and transport the wheat once it gets to Iraq. He has made it clear implicitly that these amounts will in fact be paid to Saddam Hussein's government.

DISCUSSION QUESTIONS

1. How likely would it be that you would help draft the contract to pay the bribe and keep it secret? On a scale of 0 to 10: Write a number.
2. Is the decision to enter into the contract an ethical decision, a legal decision or a commercial decision? Who should make the call on this decision? (The executive? The lawyer?)
3. If you were inclined to help draft the contract, how might you rationalise your decision?

Now consider again the more detailed version of the AWB scenario in Case Study 1.3, in Chapter 1.

1. Can you identify the different rationalisation strategies mentioned above that the in-house counsel who went ahead and drafted the contracts without protest might have used?

2. Were there any other options available to the in-house counsel other than simply obeying the instructions of your client to draft the contract or refusing to do so?

3. How do you think the lawyers' role as in-house counsel (as opposed to external legal adviser) contributed to what happened in the AWB scenario?

Corporate Lawyers as Corporate Citizens

Adversarial Advocacy and Responsible Lawyering: Hired Gun or Independent Counsellor?

Many of the issues of mutual ethical responsibility between lawyer and corporate client raised by corporate wrongdoing are similar to those raised in Chapter 6, where we discussed the way that the lawyer-client relationship might foster mutual avoidance of responsibility for the ethical dimension of litigation. We showed there that the justification for an *adversarial advocacy* approach in which the lawyer single-mindedly and aggressively pursues client rights may not be justified in the civil litigation context because of the harm it can do to the client, the other side and the legal process. On the other hand, in the civil litigation context there is, at least, always the possibility that the court can choose to rein in excessive adversarialism by lawyers. *Adversarial advocacy* is even less suited to the corporate counselling context. Most of the matters on which a corporate lawyer advises will never be aired in a court, or any other public forum.

Moreover, the power imbalance between the individual criminal defendant and the state means that criminal defence lawyers might be justified in zealous advocacy that protects their clients' autonomy to the limits of the law against the state. But large corporate clients are not necessarily (or generally) the victims of any power imbalance. Indeed, many corporate clients can afford hordes of lawyers to work out ways to interpret the law and to present the company to others (regulators, investors, customers) as legally compliant. Therefore the justification for legal advocacy that goes to the limits of the law and ethics on behalf of corporate clients is correspondingly reduced.

In this type of context, it does not seem justified for lawyers to primarily take the *adversarial advocacy* approach.[45] In most situations where lawyers advise

---

45 Robert Gordon, 'A New Role for Lawyers? The Corporate Counselor After Enron' (2003) 35 *Connecticut Law Review* 1185, 1204–7.

business, they are not just advocating afterwards as to how something the client has done should be interpreted. They are actually helping the client decide whether to comply with the law and if so how. The ideal of *responsible lawyer* as trusted, independent counsellor seems to express this role better than adversarial advocacy:

> In giving advice, [the *responsible lawyer*] refers not only to specific rules of black-letter law, but also to general principles of equity, fair dealing, and public policy in dealing with inchoate or potential legal problems. By advising businesses about the legal risks, constraints and requirements associated with proposed actions, the corporate lawyer plays a crucial role in pushing business toward socially responsible behavior... By telling business executives how to avoid antitrust suits, civil rights suits, and regulatory prosecutions, and by insisting on knowing the truth about financial weaknesses that might affect the accuracy of representations in disclosure statements, license applications, or opinion letters signed by the law firm, the lawyer necessarily forces corporations to be more honest and to establish internal systems for ensuring compliance with the law. The corporate lawyer, from this perspective, is an autonomous agent of social control and enforcement.[46]

In the following section, we explore this alternative ethical approach for corporate lawyering in more detail, and suggest ways in which corporate lawyers will need to go beyond *responsible lawyering* to elements of *moral activism* in order to avoid unethical conduct.

The Corporate Lawyer as Responsible Lawyer

Much that is written or proposed about making corporate lawyers more ethical suggests that corporate lawyers should be required to be more separate and independent from corporate managers and their interests in order to discharge their duties to the law and the corporate entity more reliably, in line with a *responsible lawyering* approach. In particular, much discussion of corporate lawyers' ethics emphasises the need to strengthen their gatekeeping responsibilities by expecting lawyers to act in the interests of the corporation as a whole, including its investors and other stakeholders, to clearly counsel clients against illegal behaviour and behaviour at the margins of legality, and requiring them to report corporate misconduct to appropriate authorities within the organisation or outside it, if they cannot otherwise prevent it occurring.[47]

---

46 Kagan and Rosen, 'On the Social Significance', 409–10. See also Robert Gordon, 'Corporate Law Practice as a Public Calling' (1990) 49 *Maryland Law Review* 255; Gordon, 'A New Role for Lawyers?'; David Luban, *Lawyers and Justice: An Ethical Study* (Princeton University Press, Princeton, New Jersey, 1988) 206–34.

47 See, eg, Coffee, *Professional Gatekeepers*; Gordon, 'A New Role for Lawyers?'.

In fact, in Australia at least, the general principles set out in current professional conduct rules, the law of lawyering, and criminal and regulatory law *already* give corporate lawyers many obligations to act as 'independent counsellors' (*responsible lawyers*). Legal profession regulators in Australia have so far not done much to enforce these obligations in the corporate lawyering context. Nor are these obligations set out very specifically and clearly in the *Australian Solicitors' Conduct Rules*.[48] Nevertheless, corporate lawyers do have legal and professional conduct obligations (a) to the law, and (b) to the corporate entity as a whole, as well as (c) capacities and obligations in relation to whistleblowing (as shown in the three subsections below). However, as we shall see, something more than merely re-stating and reinforcing current obligations in the law of lawyering is likely to be necessary to promote ethical conduct by corporate lawyers.

(a) Duty to the Law

We have seen in Chapter 6 that lawyers owe general obligations to the law and justice, including obligations not to assist in any abuse of process or misleading of the court. Disciplinary action and other sanctions are available if these obligations are breached. These obligations apply equally in lawyers' work for corporate clients as other clients, and mean that lawyers should try to dissuade their clients from illegal or improper courses of action and withdraw from representing them if the client insists on that course of action.[49] For an in-house lawyer, withdrawal from representation may, unfortunately, mean resigning their job.

Similarly, general principles of liability in criminal law and most areas of business regulation prohibit lawyers from helping their clients if this would amount to aiding and abetting illegality, or conspiring to break the law.[50] The Australian Competition and Consumer Commission, Australian Securities and Investment Commission and Australian Taxation Office have all taken action against lawyers on these grounds.[51]

---

48 But see the Australian Corporate Lawyers Association's (ACLA) and Corporate Lawyers Association of New Zealand's booklet, *Ethics for In-House Counsel* (Australian Corporate Lawyers Association, 2nd edn, 2004). In the US the American Bar Association convened a taskforce to look at corporate responsibility issues in relation to lawyers in response to Enron and other scandals, and eventually made some changes to their professional conduct rules as a result: American Bar Association, *Report of the American Bar Association Task Force on Corporate Responsibility* (2003) <www.abanet.org/buslaw/corporate responsibility/home. html> at 22 May 2006.

49 See Dal Pont, *Lawyers' Professional Responsibility*, 423, 427.

50 Russell Lyons and David Handelsmann, 'Corporate Misconduct and Legal Professional Responsibility' (2003) 41(4) *Law Society Journal* 60; see Dal Pont, *Lawyers' Professional Responsibility*, 425–6.

51 Eg *Australian Competition & Consumer Commission v Real Estate Institute of Western Australia Inc* (1999) 161 ALR 79 (solicitor assisted in drafting agreement that amounted to price fixing); *Australian Securities and Investments Commission v Somerville & Ors* [2009] NSWSC 934 (solicitor assisted in 'phoenixing a company so that directors could avoid debts). See also Dal Pont, *Lawyers' Professional Responsibility*, Chapter 19.

However, consistent with the *adversarial advocacy* approach, lawyers (both corporate lawyers and those who act for individual clients) have argued that they are not morally responsible or legally accountable for their clients' misconduct unless they are knowingly and intentionally involved in initiating or assisting the misconduct.[52] But it is often hard to prove that the lawyer had the requisite knowledge and intention to establish this type of liability.[53] As we have seen, lawyers and executives are expert at plausible deniability in many corporate ethical scandals, and the language of the relevant rules themselves often gives them numerous excuses to avoid liability.[54]

Moreover this type of liability will of course only apply to client conduct that is itself illegal. Much of the 'genius' of corporate lawyering is to contrive ways in which unethical conduct can be performed 'legally'. Indeed the law itself is not necessarily tough enough on corporations precisely because lawyers have helped break down the application of law to corporate wrongdoing, and have helped keep corporate misconduct secret through confidentiality and privilege. Lawyers have helped create enough 'wobble' room to make much of the application of law to corporate activities uncertain.[55] Things that would be crimes if individuals did them are only regulatory offences or civil wrongs if corporations do them. For example, why is it that corporate deceit and intentional behaviour in marketing addictive and potentially deadly cigarettes to young people is not legally defined as a crime (see the cartoon referred to earlier)?[56] Or why is it only recently that it has even been contemplated that illegal conspiracies to price-fix by corporations should be a criminal offence (rather than merely a civil offence), while ordinary theft and conspiracy by individuals have always been considered crimes?

Emphasising corporate lawyers' duty to the law is not enough where the law itself has proven to be so easily manipulated, unless the duty to the law encompasses an obligation to consider what ethical and justice concerns the law applying to corporations *should* embrace, and to act accordingly – a more *moral activist* conception of lawyers' ethics.

(b) Duty to the Corporation as a Whole

It is quite clear that lawyers acting for a corporation owe their obligations of care and loyalty to the corporation as a whole, not to individual managers, executives or work teams, since it is the corporation that is the client, not individual officers

---

52 Lyons and Handelsmann, 'Corporate Misconduct'.
53 Simon, 'Wrongs of Ignorance'.
54 William H Simon analyses this in terms of lawyers (wrongfully) being able to avoid liability for corporate misconduct on the grounds of 'ignorance' and 'ambiguity': ibid.
55 Ibid 207.
56 Jonathan Liberman and Jonathan Clough, 'Corporations That Kill: The Criminal Liability of Tobacco Manufacturers' (2002) 26 *Criminal Law Journal* 1.

(see Chapter 8).[57] Much of lawyers' complicity in corporate wrongdoing amounts to conflicts of interest, where lawyers defy their duty to the corporation as a whole to follow the instructions and wishes of individual managers, executives or work teams, at the expense of shareholders and other stakeholders (whether the lawyers are confused about their real clients or not). Moreover it will usually be in the interests of the corporation as a whole to comply with the law (and therefore avoid the legal sanctions and reputational losses that come with breach of the law). Breaches of the obligation to the corporation as a whole could amount to a basis for disciplinary action or actions for breach of duty by the corporation (in negligence or contract). Often where management or the board has breached its duties and a company has collapsed or suffered severe losses as a result, the new management, the shareholders, or the liquidator will sue the previous management and/or board to recover the losses. Lawyers who have contributed to the previous management's wrongful conduct can even be sued.[58]

Corporate lawyers usually deal with individual corporate officers who define the scope of their work, and whose concerns and goals colonise corporate lawyers' consciences. Comprehending and acting on the duty to the corporation as a whole requires lawyers to actively look beyond the instructions they receive from the individuals they are dealing with in order to consider whether the interests of the corporation as a whole are being followed properly. This requires a degree of ethical discernment beyond the law – an element of moral activism.

(c) Taking Active Responsibility

The duty to the corporation as a whole does not mean that corporate lawyers need to substitute their own moral judgement for that of the corporation. What it does mean is that they need to take their share of responsibility for making sure that the broad interests of the company as a whole are pursued (including the corporation's interest in behaving legally and ethically). A persuasive literature in business ethics suggests that corporate decisions can become immoral, illegal or just bad because, although many individuals are involved in making them, none feels personal responsibility for the ultimate outcome – it's a 'corporate' decision, not a personal one.[59] Everybody has their own role within the corporation – whether it is as lawyer, marketer, sales agent or financial controller – but often no one feels that it is their job to understand the whole context, including the ethical context,

---

57 William H Simon, 'Whom (or What) Does the Organization's Lawyer Represent?: An Anatomy of Intraclient Conflict' (2003) 91 *California Law Review* 57.
58 See Milton C Regan, 'Teaching Enron' (2005) 74 *Fordham Law Review* 1139. This is an article based on the Enron liquidator's assessment of what causes of action might be available against Enron's various lawyers.
59 Christine Parker, *The Open Corporation: Effective Self-Regulation and Democracy* (Cambridge University Press, Cambridge, 2002) 31–7.

for decision-making, nor to access all the relevant information for understanding that context. Lawyers, and other corporate advisers and employees, allow their sense of personal responsibility to be subsumed by their role in an organisational bureaucracy. They see themselves as disposable actors hired to play bit parts in bureaucratic games. This analysis holds good even though in-house lawyers very often have the breadth of information and forensic skill needed to be the ethical watchdogs of the corporation. So they take their instructions as they find them, rather than actively taking responsibility for working out whether they have been given all the relevant information to understand a problem or decision in its full context.[60] This is compounded if legal services are 'unbundled' and given to a number of lawyers.

By contrast, *moral activism* would require lawyers to clearly flag potential ethical and legal problems that might otherwise be ignored or overridden, even if they are not directly within the scope of the particular jobs they have been assigned by individual officers. Having flagged these legal and ethical issues, corporate lawyers should then go on to make sure that the corporation as a whole uses proper decision-making processes, and proper substantive principles, to decide what to do about them. This may entail the lawyer disclosing potential misconduct up the corporate hierarchy or even outside the company, as we set out in Chapter 4 in the section on whistleblowing.

It is easy to understand why lawyers might often prefer not to notice, or to rationalise, unethical corporate conduct instead of following this pathway. As we saw in Chapter 4, the content of the current law on confidentiality gives ample room to corporate lawyers to fulfil their ethical duties. But knowing when to breach confidence requires ethical judgement (again an element of *moral activism*), not just legal knowledge, as the circumstances in which the public interest or a client's 'fraud on justice' might justify and, indeed, demand whistleblowing can never be fully specified in the law. The way the legal profession tends to treat confidentiality as an absolute value (see above) may discourage lawyers from this type of ethical judgement, but it need not do so.

Addressing Rationalisation: Legal Ethics and Business Ethics

It would certainly be helpful if the *Model Rules* and professional regulators spelled out more clearly the ethical obligations of corporate lawyers, and actually enforced

---

60 Rosen, 'Problem-Setting'.

them. But when ethical failures in corporate lawyering occur, the problem might be more in the attitude and style of corporate lawyering than in the content of the current rules. As we have seen, the ethical problems for lawyers in many situations of corporate misconduct arise because either: (1) the lawyers or their corporate clients have framed the issue narrowly, approached the solution legalistically, and therefore screened out non-legal factors that would raise ethical alarm bells; or, (2) they have intentionally designed techniques and strategies that will avoid or evade inconvenient applications of the law, while appearing to comply. The dominant conception of the lawyer as *adversarial advocate*, which is legitimate in some areas such as criminal defence and family representation, is less convincing or legitimate in corporate law areas. Adversarial advocacy rationalises this amoral approach to legal advising, and there will usually be other rationalisation available too, such as the importance of the clients' business or government goals.

These are failures of corporate lawyers first to adequately engage in *business* ethics before they are failures of *legal* ethics. Looking to the law alone will never adequately guide lawyers as to how to behave ethically in these types of corporate scandals. For example, as is evident from Case Study 10.2: James Hardie, below, to give legal advice is not enough where a course of action is probably legal, but legal advice is being used by a company's management to urge the Board into action that fails to deal with the real ethical issue – in the James Hardie case, the tragic crisis of thousands and thousands of asbestos related deaths.

Consider this description by Gideon Haigh of the role of the lawyers from James Hardie's external law firm, Allens, during the crucial February 2001 Board meeting at which it was decided to hive off James Hardie's asbestos liabilities into a separate entity, the Medical Research and Compensation Foundation (MRCF) (which was later cut adrift from the Hardie group without adequate funding to compensate all those who would be legally entitled to compensation). Hardie's Chief Executive Officer and chief in-house lawyer urged the Board to make the decision to separate the MRCF, but they also withheld vital claims data from the Board that would have given the Board a more realistic idea of the funding the MRCF was likely to need:

> Through this, too, sat the advisers…the lawyers staved off concern about the data whose absence had made them so anxious that morning. [One of the Allens solicitors present] contemplated raising the subject, but chose not after asking his superior: 'We were available for questions to be asked of us. No questions were asked of us and so we did not say – we did not raise it.'…Yet it may not only be in what they did or did not do that the advisers in this transaction were influential. The impression of having the best advice at one's beck is a reassuring one. The advisers here were by now familiar faces at Hardie, and this was a board culture that placed heavy reliance on them. Recall [the chief in-house counsel's] acid comment on directors in July 2000: 'I don't think we should underestimate the value the Board will place on

outside third party advisers (as insulting as that is to the company's internal advisers – myself included)'. Yet these same advisers were by now so close to the company as to be almost indistinguishable from corporate officers.[61]

Haigh points out that even in saying nothing at all, the external lawyers participated in the management (the CEO and in-house lawyer's) plan to separate off the MRCF, and the Board's acquiescence in that plan. By saying nothing about the missing data, which they were aware of, the external lawyers also played their part in the deception of the Board. The members of the Board, the CEO and the in-house counsel were later all found to have breached the *Corporations Act* in various ways in relation to the misleading announcements made to the market as a result of decisions made at this meeting.[62] The external lawyers, however, were not investigated or prosecuted.

Corporate lawyers cannot 'kiss off', or rationalise away, their moral responsibility by saying 'it's not my job'.[63] It is part of their job whether they like it or not, and whether they actively do anything or not. An *adversarial advocate* might plausibly argue that an individual client always retains some independent capability to make their own decisions regardless of legal advice. But corporate decisions are always made by individuals standing in for the entity as a whole. Business decisions, particularly in corporate contexts, are frequently made collectively, and lawyers and their advice, or lack of it, are an important part of those decisions.[64]

Lawyers advising business need to demonstrate pro-active responsibility for seeing and advising on the broader ethical and legal consequences of what they advise business to do, as should all business people. Corporate lawyers' particular ethical responsibility will relate mainly to their legal expertise and role, but they cannot avoid responsibility for having a substantive ethical view about the situations they are called to advise on and participate in merely because they are lawyers and supposedly independent of the corporate client. This means that corporate lawyers should be business ethicists, and this is likely to require them to use the following three strategies.

---

61 Gideon Haigh, *Asbestos House: The Secret History of James Hardie Industries* (Scribe, Melbourne, 2006) 269–70.

62 *Australian Securities and Investments Commission v Meredith Hellicar and Ors* [2012] HCA 17; *Shafron v Australian Securities and Investments Commission* [2012] HCA 18 (3 May 2012).

63 Rosen, 'Problem-Setting', 181. For this point, Rosen cites William H Simon, 'The Ideology of Advocacy: Procedural Justice and Professional Ethics' (1978) 1978 *Wisconsin Law Review* 29, 74.

64 Richard Painter, 'The Moral Interdependence of Corporate Lawyers and Their Clients' (1994) 67 *Southern California Law Review* 507, 520; see also Rosen, 'The Inside Counsel Movement', 542–5.

Strategy 1: Identifying the Client Correctly

Corporate lawyers regularly participate in, or at least aid, business decisions that affect the wealth and wellbeing of hundreds and thousands of people who hold a 'stake' in that business. Most of the key ethical issues for businesses concern potential conflict between their different stakeholders. Indeed, corporations are basically entities made up of, and exercising power over, different stakeholders.[65] These stakeholders include people who have invested their wealth in the organisation – shareholders, banks, superannuation funds, etc; and those who have invested their time, skill and labour in the business – employees and managers.

When a lawyer acts for a corporation, they are supposed to act for the entity as a whole, not individual managers or work teams. This means that ethical issues are likely to be unavoidable for corporate lawyers. They must constantly keep one eye on whether the managers they take instructions from are adequately taking into account the interests of all the corporation's stakeholders, or whether they are asking their lawyers to help them prefer their own interests over those of, say, the shareholders, or even employees.

Where the lawyer thinks management may not be appropriately pursuing the interests of the entity as a whole, the lawyer, as a participant in corporate decision-making, should be able to initiate discussion and resolution of the issue within the company.[66] This is not the lawyer deciding what is the appropriate thing to do *for* the corporate client; but the lawyer should be in a position to activate a decision-making process within the corporation that will decide properly. As we have seen, debate and controversy over the role of lawyers in corporate misconduct has focused on whether corporate lawyers should (or already do) have a 'whistleblowing' obligation to raise such matters within the organisation and outside it. However, ideally, this role of raising ethical issues should not be seen as extraordinary whistleblowing, but rather as a natural part of their role. This means that in-house lawyers, particularly the chief in-house lawyer in each organisation, need to have a certain degree of power and respect so that, if necessary, they can question corporate activities, goals and commitments, and can ensure that ethical issues are resolved properly at an appropriate place in the corporate decision-making process.

Most commentators on ethics for in-house lawyers acknowledge the fact that in-house lawyers should have a degree of influence and power within the

---

65 C Parker, *The Open Corporation*, 3–7; James E Post, Lee E Preston and Sybille Sachs, *Redefining the Corporation: Stakeholder Management and Organizational Wealth* (Stanford University Press, San Francisco, 2002).

66 See Simon, 'Wrongs of Ignorance'; Rosen, 'The Inside Counsel Movement', 542–5.

organisation by having the possibility of dotted line reporting[67] direct to the Chief Executive Officer and to the Board of Directors itself, and of having the authority to investigate and intervene at any level of a company.[68] The ACLA guidelines on ethics suggest that in-house lawyers 'should preferably report to a senior executive such as the chairman or CEO' and should 'ensure that his/her employment contract specifically recognises that the employee, as counsel, may be obliged to act as a whistleblower and requires that there will not be recriminations in that event'.[69]

Strategy 2: Framing the Problem to Include Ethical Issues

Lawyers advising business need to be aware of the ways in which the business context is likely to shape their own view of the ethics of each situation on which they are asked to advise. Their own judgement is likely to be affected by their relationship to the organisation – what information comes to them, how it comes to them, how the politics of the organisation work, and what influence they themselves have within that organisation. Lawyers ought to take special care and responsibility to make sure that they see the questions and problems brought to them by business in a holistic context that means they can take ethical and legal responsibility for those problems, rather than simply allowing the organisation (with its politics and bureaucratic pathologies) to present problems to them as isolated events or concepts.[70] This requires substantive ethical analysis.

One way of trying to make sure that corporate decisions are always made in an ethical way is for the company (client) to put in place internal controls or management programmes that seek to make sure that the whole organisation meets its legal and ethical responsibilities, and guard against those responsibilities being forgotten or trampled on. These internal controls and management programmes are a way of trying to create a conscience within business organisations.[71] Lawyers might be particularly suited to helping businesses with this.

---

67 'Dotted line' reporting means that in addition to your everyday obligation to report up the line to your direct superior, you also have the capacity to bypass that superior to a higher level. It is a safeguard for where your direct superior may be acting unethically, obstructively or incompetently.

68 Gordon and Simon, 'The Redemption of Professionalism', 253.

69 ACLA, *Ethics for In-House Counsel*, 9 and 6 respectively. For suggestions as to how in-house lawyers should 'interview' their prospective employers in relation to ethical issues and the safeguards available to ensure the lawyer will be able to act ethically, see Adrian Evans, 'Safe Employment for Corporate Counsel' (2003) 77(4) *Law Institute Journal* 84.

70 Rosen, 'Problem-Setting'.

71 See C Parker, *The Open Corporation*.

Consider again the sexual harassment case mentioned above that the company foolishly fought on legalistic grounds in line with legal advice.[72] That company learnt that a broad corporate commitment to preventing sexual harassment and dealing with it fairly within the organisation was much more important than a legalistic focus on how to avoid liability. They then hired both business ethics and equal employment opportunity consultants to start a process of organisational cultural change that culminated in the implementation of a state of the art workplace ethics policy, including a sexual harassment grievance handling process.

Many legal ethicists have suggested that corporate lawyers should take a more pro-active or positive role in making sure adequate internal controls and whistleblowing protections are in place, so that companies can police themselves to make sure they comply with the law and with ethical obligations. Thus the ACLA guidelines suggest under the heading of corporate lawyers' relationship with 'stakeholders generally' that they 'should promote the adoption of compliance and other procedures and policies within their organisations that take account of the legitimate interests of all the organisation's stakeholders and community expectations of proper behaviour'.[73] They also 'should encourage an environment which permits internal whistleblowers to come forward without fear of retribution' and 'should work to help protect the anonymity of whistleblowers and the integrity of their communications'.[74] The *Sarbanes-Oxley Act* requirements in the United States and the Australian Stock Exchange's *Best Practice Principles for Corporate Governance* (also introduced in response to corporate collapses and scandals) both also seek to encourage companies to make sure they have adequate internal controls, codes of conduct, and whistleblowing protections in place to ensure that obligations to the corporation as a whole, including its shareholders and stakeholders, are protected. These institutional safeguards complement rather than replace 'bottom up' cultural change that originates when employees lower down the corporate ladder also push for ethical development.

Strategy 3: Building Ethics into Law Firms

It is even more important that business lawyers engage substantively with business ethics when we consider lawyers' own practice structures. The disciplinary provisions and ethical conduct rules in most jurisdictions are generally directed only at individual practitioners, not at law firms.[75] This reflects the traditional

---

72 See above C Parker, 'How to Win Hearts and Minds', n 20, and accompanying text.
73 ACLA, *Ethics for In-House Counsel*, 9.
74 Ibid 6.
75 See Ted Schneyer, 'Professional Discipline for Law Firms?' (1991) 77 *Cornell Law Review* 1; Elizabeth Chambliss and David B Wilkins, 'Promoting Effective Ethical Infrastructure in Large Law Firms: A Call for Research and Reporting' (2002) 30 *Hofstra Law Review* 691.

assumption that once a person qualifies as a lawyer they will become an independent practitioner who is able and competent to take responsibility for the quality and ethics of their own work. But the majority of lawyers no longer operate as independent professionals. They are employed by law firms, as well as accounting firms and in-house corporate legal departments. One of the biggest challenges for the ethical regulation of lawyering is to see law firms (and other organisational practice contexts) as having their own ethical character and culture, for good or for ill.[76] In some sections of some of these firms, the climate can be almost family-like, with supportive partners, an atmosphere of collegiality, and a shared excitement in pursuing intellectually challenging cases and transactions. But there is also evidence that new lawyers are likely to be under pressure inside larger practices, in particular, to prioritise business values and to discount or ignore entirely traditional professional values.[77]

Since the organisational (law firm) context of legal practice has such an important influence on unethical behaviour, some commentators have suggested that law firms should consciously implement 'ethical infrastructures'. A law firm ethical infrastructure means formal and informal management policies, procedures and controls, work team cultures, and habits of interaction and practice that support and encourage ethical behaviour.[78] It means having a managing partner who lives out the values of integrity and fidelity (rather than just using the language) and provides the ethical leadership which ensures that all other systems are not only in place but practised. It might include the appointment of an ethics partner and/or ethics committee; written policies on ethical conduct in general, and in specific areas such as conflicts of interest, billing, trust accounting, opinion letters, litigation tactics and so on; specified procedures for ensuring ethical policies are not breached and to encourage the raising of ethical problems with colleagues and management; the monitoring of lawyer compliance with policies and procedures; and ethics education, training and discussion within the firm. We have already seen the importance of internal responsibility and management/ethics systems within law firms for explaining fees and communicating about problems with bills and costs (Chapter 9), and avoiding and managing conflicts of interest (Chapter 8).

Large law firms are increasingly using bureaucratic management practices that incorporate commercial pressure into legal practice by, for example, requiring lawyers to meet certain billable hour targets, having client relations partners with the explicit job of ensuring that other lawyers (including other partners) are making

---

76 See Lillian Corbin, 'How "Firm" are Lawyers' Perceptions of Professionalism?' (2005) 8 *Legal Ethics* 265.

77 See Lillian Corbin, 'How "Firm" are Lawyers' Perceptions of Professionalism?' (2005) 8 *Legal Ethics* 265; Bruce A Green, 'Professional Challenges in Large Firm Practices' (2005) 33 *Fordham Urban Law Journal* 7.

78 Schneyer, 'Professional Discipline'; Chambliss and Wilkins, 'Promoting Ethical Infrastructure'.

clients happy, and implementing performance criteria and in-firm professional development all aimed at making sure lawyers meet client needs. If these new bureaucracies are not led by CEOs or managing partners with transparent and moral footprints and do not incorporate controls explicitly aimed at promoting ethical behaviour, they may in fact undermine ethical behaviour by putting pressure on lawyers to cut corners or do 'too much' for clients, and thereby undermine the value of the firm's 'organisational capital'.

Now that most Australian States allow legal practices to incorporate, and the first law firms are listing on the stock exchange, there is potential for even greater pressure on professional ethical responsibilities as incorporated legal practices adopt more commercial business structures, and encourage outside investors and non-lawyer staff to become shareholders in the law practice.[79] For this reason, the legislative provisions that allow law firms to incorporate also require incorporated legal practices to have 'appropriate management systems' in place to deal with ethical issues – in effect, a requirement that incorporated legal practices consciously implement an ethical infrastructure as part of their new business structure.[80] The New South Wales Legal Services Commissioner has developed 'ten commandments' that incorporated legal practices' management systems must follow, and a system for self-assessment and external audit as to how well incorporated legal practices are implementing them.

As law firm management and business structures evolve, 'a crucial question is whether law firms will be able to sustain a distinctive culture' that balances duty to client and duty to court 'rather than becoming purely market-driven organizations'.[81] This concern with the internal management structures within law firms is consistent with an increasing focus on similar structures within business firms to improve corporate ethics, social responsibility and regulatory compliance.[82] The required crucial combination is ethical business structures led by morally responsible

---

79 Steve Mark, 'A Short Paper and Notes on the Issue of Listing of Law Firms in New South Wales', Presentation to the Joint NOBC, APRL and ABA Center for Professional Responsibility entitled 'Brave New World: The Changing Face of Law Firms and the Practice of Law from a Professional Responsibility Perspective' available at <www.lawlink.nsw.gov.au/lawlink/olsc/ll_olsc.nsf/pages/OLSC_speeches> at 21 October 2007. See also Bruce MacEwan, Milton Regan and Larry Ribstein, *Law Firms, Ethics, and Equity Capital: A Conversation* (Georgetown Law, Center for the Study of the Legal Profession, 2007); Christine Parker, 'Law Firms Incorporated: How Incorporation Could and Should Make Firms More Ethically Responsible' *The University of Queensland Law Journal* 23(2), 2004, 347–80.

80 *Model Laws* s 2.7.9. One lawyer, the 'legal practitioner director', has responsibility for the introduction, supervision and monitoring of the practice's ethical systems. *Model Laws* ss 2.7.9, 2.7.10. For MDPs, see *Model Laws* ss 2.7.39, 2.7.40. See also Parker, 'Law Firms Incorporated', 372.

81 Milton C Regan, 'Taking Law Firms Seriously' (2002) 16 *Georgetown Journal of Legal Ethics* 155.

82 See, for example, Parker, *The Open Corporation*, above n 59.

CEOs. Those leaders may be lawyers, but more often they will be advised by company secretaries who are lawyers. Indeed many large commercial law firms in Australia have lawyers who specialise in advising their business clients on how to implement regulatory and ethical compliance systems, and who sell educational and management tools to clients for this purpose.[83] It is logical that large law firms might apply the same principles to themselves, and that regulators,[84] insurers,[85] clients[86] and lawyers should all be interested in understanding and improving the ethical climate of law firms.

In Australia, legal professional associations have been encouraging law firms to voluntarily institute ethics programmes and other internal controls. In the immediate aftermath of the original *McCabe* decision, for example, the President of the Law Institute of Victoria announced an initiative encouraging all law firms to introduce ethics partners to be 'the first contact when someone in the firm has an ethical question or problem'.[87] They might also review internal ethical decisions and rule on internal differences of opinion on ethical matters.

Ethics programmes in law firms and companies can be very helpful if they evidence a real commitment to ethical responsibility; however, they can also be dangerously thin. Research has shown that senior lawyers and junior lawyers in larger law firms have very different views of these ethics programmes. Law firm partners often believe they have very good ethics programmes and an open door for the discussion of ethical issues; while more junior lawyers are not necessarily even aware of the existence of ethics partners and ethics policies within their firms, do not feel empowered to use them openly,[88] and often live in a culture of mutual

---

83 See Tanina Rostain, 'The Emergence of Law Consultants' (2006) 75 *Fordham Law Review* 1397.

84 See the brief discussion of regulatory requirements for incorporated legal practices in Australia above at notes 79 and 80, and accompanying text. See also Steve Mark, 'Harmonization or Homogenization? The Globalization of Law and Legal Ethics – An Australian Viewpoint' (2001) 34 *Vanderbilt Journal of Transnational Law* 1173.

85 In the US and UK some legal insurers, especially the US insurer Attorneys' Liability Assurance Society (ALAS), have promoted in-house ethical compliance efforts within law firms by giving discounts for firms with ethics partners etc: see Elizabeth Chambliss and David B Wilkins, 'The Emerging Role of Ethics Advisors, General Counsel, and Other Compliance Specialists in Large Law Firms' (2002) 44 *Arizona Law Review* 559, 590. In Australia at least one professional liability insurer does provide in-house training with a similar purpose.

86 For example, the Victorian State government has extensive ethical, pro bono and equal employment opportunity requirements on law firms that do work for it: see State of Victoria, *Legal Services to Government Panel Contract* (2002).

87 See, eg, Kim Cull, 'Ethics and Law as an Influence on Business' (2002) 40(9) *Law Society Journal* 50, 50–1; John Cain, 'Good Ethics Requires Constant Vigilance' (2002) 76(8) *Law Institute Journal* 4, 4.

88 Christine Parker and Lyn Aitken, 'The Queensland "Workplace Culture Check": Learning from Reflection on Ethics Inside Law Firms' (2011) 24 *Georgetown Journal of Legal Ethics* 399. But for evidence of the positive impact of ethics audits and international ethics management systems in law firms, see Christine Parker, Tahlia Gordon and Steve Mark, 'Regulating Law

suspicion where everyone believes that everybody *else* is padding their bills, cutting corners and generally gaming the system to meet billable hours requirements and please clients.[89]

DISCUSSION QUESTIONS

1. Think back to the situations described in the introductions to this chapter and Chapter 6 in relation to Clayton Utz's work for British American Tobacco, and also the Foreman case (discussed in Chapter 9): How could Clayton Utz have organised its work differently to avoid the problematic conduct in each of these cases occurring? Are there any policies or structures that might have been put in place that would have prevented these events?

2. Would an ethics partner be an effective tool for improving ethics generally in large law firm practice? Consider again the four ethical approaches introduced in Chapters 1 and 2: What would a whole law firm need to do in order to ensure that its legal practice meets the values of its chosen approach, or combination of approaches?

Conclusion: James Hardie and Enron Case Studies

We conclude this chapter with two case studies. Case Study 10.2 is an extended case study examining in detail James Hardie's attempts to 'separate itself' from its asbestos liabilities, and the role its lawyers played in that series of events. This case study provides a vivid example of the ways in which lawyers can become an important part of corporate decision-making, and the way the law can be used to 'manage' rather than resolve a company's ethical problems. It illustrates well the opportunities that corporate lawyers have to contribute, for good or for ill, to the ethical climate within corporate decision-making and ultimately to the impact of corporate activities on thousands of individuals. Case study 10.3 looks at the activities of the Enron lawyers, who have provided the most compelling reason to look suspiciously at *adversarial advocacy* in a corporate setting.

Unexplored and unchallenged *adversarial advocacy* is dangerous for corporate legal practice because the default corporate culture and character is one of profit

---

Firm Ethical infrastructure: An Empirical Assessment of the Potential for Management-based Regulation of Legal Practices' (2010) 37 *Journal of Law and Society* 466.

89 Christine Parker and David Ruschena, 'The Pressures of Billable Hours: Lessons from a Survey of Billing Practices Inside Law Firms' (2012) 9 *University of St Thomas Law Journal* 619.

not professionalism. The active alternative of ethical infrastructure requires morally engaged, self-aware lawyers. But when the processes of psychological rationalising are allowed to dominate, corporate lawyers can flounder and sink along with their clients. The challenge for corporate lawyers in the face of often unethical infrastructure is therefore to sensitise themselves to the rationalising processes that they and others may use to dull their moral sense. Once exposed, rationalising is less powerful as a controlling tool and it becomes possible to assert alternative models for appropriate corporate lawyering.

CASE STUDY 10.2   JAMES HARDIE'S ATTEMPTS TO SEPARATE ITSELF FROM ITS ASBESTOS LIABILITIES[90]

James Hardie opened its first Australian asbestos factory in 1916. The first known death of a Hardie employee due to asbestos occurred about 1960, and the first asbestos compensation claims were filed against James Hardie and other Australian companies in 1977. Hardie stopped manufacturing asbestos in 1987 and focused on other businesses, including expansion into the US and Europe. However, James Hardie management realised that it would be facing significant asbestos liabilities for years to come. Hardie's asbestos manufacturing business had been enormously successful and Australians were the highest per capita users of asbestos in the world. By 2001 approximately 2000 asbestos compensation claims had been made against James Hardie, but asbestos diseases can have a latency period of up to 40 years before they develop. There are estimates that asbestos-related disease in Australia will not peak until 2020 with about 13,000 cases of mesothelioma (a deadly cancer of the pleural lining of the lungs caused only by asbestos) and 40,000 cases of other asbestos-related lung cancer.[91]

By 2001, James Hardie management were keen to 'resolve' the ongoing liability to compensate asbestos victims, so that management could 'focus entirely on growing the company for the benefit of all shareholders'.[92] Over the period from

90 Case study material based on Jackson, *Special Commission of Inquiry into the MRCF Established by the James Hardie Group*; Haigh, *Asbestos House*; Ackland, 'Irresistible Charms'; Elizabeth Sexton, 'Hardie Writhes in Self-Made Circles of Hell', *Insight, The Age* (Melbourne), 21 August 2004, 8. See also Suzanne Le Mire, 'The Corporation, the Lawyers, Its Schemes and Their Ethics' *Alternative Law Journal* (forthcoming).

91 Peta Spender, 'Blue Asbestos and Golden Eggs: Evaluating Bankruptcy and Class Actions as Just Responses to Mass Tort Liability' (2003) 25 *Sydney Law Review* 223, 235–6.

92 Quoted words are from James Hardie's 16 February 2001 media release upon the establishment of the Medical Research and Compensation Fund (see explanation below):

February 2001 to March 2003, management restructured the James Hardie group of companies with the ultimate result that all the group's asbestos liabilities were vested in the Medical Research and Compensation Foundation (MRCF) together with a set amount of funding for compensation. However, it soon became evident that the money would run out after three years, with a shortfall of between $800 million and $1.5 billion for future liabilities after that time. The MRCF had no legal recourse against the rest of the group for further funds to pay compensation, the parent company moved from Australia to the Netherlands, and there was a public outcry. The New South Wales government set up a Special Commission of Inquiry, under David Jackson QC, into these events.

The facts set out below explain, in summary, the legal manoeuvres through which the James Hardie group tried to separate itself from its asbestos liabilities, and the role played in this process by James Hardie's external law firm, Allens Arthur Robinson. James Hardie and Allens had a relationship going back 100 years, and one of the principal Hardie executives who orchestrated the events (the chief in-house counsel and later Company Financial Officer at James Hardie) was a former Allens partner.[93]

February 2001

Before February 2001, the James Hardie group's main legal responsibilities for asbestos compensation related to claims against two subsidiary companies owned by the parent company, James Hardie Industries Ltd (JHIL). These two companies, Amaba Pty Ltd and Amaca Pty Ltd, had made asbestos products from 1937 until 1987. In February 2001 JHIL transferred ownership of Amaba and Amaca to a new trust, the MRCF. They also gave the MRCF $293 million to meet future compensation claims. At the same time, Amaba and Amaca indemnified JHIL for any further asbestos liabilities.[94] This meant that JHIL would not be liable in the future in relation to asbestos.[95]

James Hardie, 'James Hardie Resolves Its Asbestos Liability Favourably for Claimants and Shareholders' (Press Release, 16 February 2001) available in Annexure R to Jackson, *Special Commission of Inquiry into the MRCF*, 333–4.

93 He later lost his job at James Hardie, as did Chief Executive Officer Peter Macdonald: Ean Higgins, 'Hardie Dumps Asbestos Chiefs', *The Australian*, 16 May 2006, 2.

94 The net assets of Amaca and Amaba were $214 million with JHIL adding the rest: Jackson, *Special Commission of Inquiry into MRCF* [1.6].

95 There is controversy about the exact extent to which JHIL, as the holding company (that is the company that owned Amaca and Amaba at the time asbestos liabilities arose, but was legally a separate entity to them) might be liable in relation to asbestos claims where the asbestos was produced and sold by its subsidiaries (Amaca and Amaba), but JHIL had accepted that it had some responsibility to provide for asbestos compensation claims at least as long as it still owned Amaba and Amaca.

The JHIL's Board's decision to create the MCRF with $293 million was based on an actuarial report on the likely amount of claims that would need to be paid out in relation to asbestos liability (the Trowbridge Report). However this report was based on out-of-date data and other inaccurate methodologies. In fact, $293 million would be nowhere near enough money to pay out all of Amaba and Amaca's asbestos liabilities. JHIL's chief in-house counsel had a more up-to-date 'draft' report and was aware of other problems in the Trowbridge Report, but chose not to make this information available to the Board of JHIL. Allens lawyers were involved in advising on the preparations for the creation of the MRCF, and the Allens lawyers raised concerns about the fact that the report to be given to the Board did not include more up-to-date data, but were assured by Hardie's chief in-house counsel and the CEO that the report was adequate and that the MRCF would be sufficiently funded.[96] The role of the Allens lawyers in relation to this Board meeting was described above.[97]

James Hardie put out a media release and report to the Australian Stock Exchange on 16 February 2001 announcing the creation of the MRCF, and stating that 'The Foundation [MRCF] has sufficient funds to meet all legitimate compensation claims anticipated from people injured by asbestos products that were manufactured in the past by two former subsidiaries of JHIL'. The announcement also stated that all asbestos related costs would be removed from JHIL's future balance sheets and that 'No future provisions are expected to be required'.[98]

Commissioner Jackson later described this announcement as 'seriously misleading'[99] on the provision of funds for asbestos victims, and also stated that, in his view, the CEO and chief in-house counsel had breached their duties as JHIL officers 'by encouraging the Board to act on the Trowbridge Report in forming the view that the Foundation would be fully funded'.[100]

Between February and October 2001

The directors of the MRCF realised that they were facing a shortfall in funds to meet the asbestos liabilities of Amaba and Amaca, and began to insist that JHIL needed to do something about this. It was conceivable that the MRCF might sue JHIL. However JHIL 'was adamant that no further substantial funds would be

96 Haigh, *Asbestos House*, 262–3, 269–71, 281–2; Jackson, *Special Commission of Inquiry into MRCF* [29.14], [24.25]–[24.28].
97 See Haigh, *Asbestos House*, above, n 65 and accompanying text.
98 James Hardie, media release (16 February 2001).
99 Jackson, *Special Commission of Inquiry into MRCF*, [1.15]. See also [1.26].
100 Ibid [24.82].

made available to the Foundation, and that it had taken all proper steps at the establishment of the Foundation'.[101]

Allens advised Hardie that the Foundation would have no compensable legal claim against Hardie. Commissioner Jackson later commented, 'There was no legal obligation for JHIL to provide greater funding to the Foundation, but it was aware – indeed, very aware because it had made extensive efforts to identify and target those who might be "stakeholders", or were regarded as having influence with "stakeholders" – that if it were perceived as not having made adequate provision for the future asbestos liabilities of its former subsidiaries there would be a wave of adverse public opinion which might well result in action being taken by the Commonwealth or State governments (on whom much of the cost of such asbestos victims would be thrown) to legislate to make other companies in the Group liable in addition to Amaca or Amaba'.[102]

October 2001

The Hardie group restructured. The assets of the Australian parent, JHIL, were transferred to a new parent company based in Amsterdam, James Hardie Industries NV (JHINV). JHIL was left as a non-operating 'shell' company with net assets of $20 million. As part of the restructure, JHIL issued partly paid shares to JHINV. The partly paid shares gave JHIL the ability to call on funds up to the value of $1.85 billion from JHINV (the new Dutch parent). Allens continued to act for JHIL. In the lead-up to the restructure Allens and JHIL discussed the possibility that the partly paid shares would be cancelled at some time in the future. Jackson found that while there was no 'fixed intention' to cancel the partly paid shares at this stage, 'it was, in effect, the "operating assumption" on which both management and the Board were proceeding' that it would occur within a year or so of the restructure.

The 2001 restructure had to be approved by the NSW Supreme Court (Justice Kim Santow) in order to ensure that the interests of shareholders and creditors in the company were adequately looked after (as a 'scheme of arrangement'). As part of this process JHIL stated that the $20 million and the funds available from the partly paid shares would be available to the MRCF to meet the asbestos liabilities of JHIL's former subsidiaries, Amaba and Amaca, if necessary.[103] Allens and JHIL did not tell Justice Santow about the concerns about the MRCF's

---

101 Ibid [1.22].
102 Ibid [1.8].
103 Haigh, *Asbestos House*, 286; Jackson, Special Commission of Inquiry into MRCF [25.21], [25.22].

solvency, or the possibility that the partly paid shares would be cancelled. Permission for the restructure was granted.

Jackson later found Allens and JHIL were in breach of their duty of disclosure to the court by not telling the court that cancellation of the partly paid shares was 'almost inevitable', a view that should have been held by 'anyone familiar with JHIL's internal strategic planning' including the JHIL Board, senior management and Allens lawyers.[104] However he found that this failure was not deliberate. He also thought Allens might have breached its duty of care to JHIL in failing to make sure disclosure occurred.[105]

March–July 2002

After October 2001 the MRCF directors became increasingly worried about their lack of funds. MRCF's relationship with JHINV (now standing in the place of JHIL) deteriorated further as MRCF asked for extra funding and JHINV refused. In March 2002 JHINV sought advice from Allens about the possibility of cancelling the partly paid shares. At the meeting where this was discussed, Allens lawyers discussed the possibility that it was 'too soon' to cancel the partly paid shares, because it might look like the company had had the intention to cancel the partly paid shares at the time of having the restructure arrangement approved by the court, and therefore misled the court by not disclosing that intention in the scheme documents at the time.[106] Notes from the meetings also indicated that the lawyers considered that if this were true, there would be nothing that the court could do about it, as the failure to disclose had already occurred. However the Australian Securities and Investment Commission might be able to prosecute for failure to disclose, and there would also be a 'commercial and political risk' in James Hardie being seen to have misled the court.[107]

---

104 Jackson, *Special Commission of Inquiry into MRCF* [25.87]. One of the options that James Hardie had considered before entering into the October 2001 scheme of arrangement was an option in which no partly paid shares would be issued to link JHINV and JHIL. Rather JHIL would be completely separated from the group, possibly even liquidated. That option was explicitly rejected by the JHIL Board in favour of the 'more flexible' option of issuing the partly paid shares that could later be cancelled or called in to bring further funds into JHIL.

105 Ibid [25.91]. They also unintentionally failed to disclose the existence of a put option which would in effect require MRCF to buy all the shares in JHIL, having the same effect as cancelling the partly paid shares.

106 Ibid [26.60]–[26.71], [26.82–26.87]; Haigh, *Asbestos House*, 303–6.

107 One Allens lawyer did attempt to communicate these concerns to JHINV in a letter of advice, but the letter was substantially edited while he was on holidays, and there is no evidence that it received any attention at JHINV anyway: Haigh, *Asbestos House*, 310–12.

15 March 2003

JHIL (now known as ABN 60 and wholly owned and controlled by JHINV) cancelled the partly paid shares, which were all held by JHINV, for no consideration. The cancellation of these shares meant JHINV no longer had any legal liability to give any funds to JHIL (ABN 60), and therefore JHIL had no capacity to fund MRCF, beyond JHIL's own $20 million in assets. The James Hardie group's asbestos liabilities were effectively 'owned' by MRCF, while the group's main assets were owned by JHINV, separate legal entities from one another with no clear legal responsibilities between them. The JHINV Chief Financial Officer, who was also a director of JHIL, was responsible for executing this plan. At the Commission of Inquiry he claimed to rely on advice from Allens that JHIL was not liable to the MRCF for anything.[108]

DISCUSSION QUESTIONS

1. In his findings Commissioner Jackson commented that he was surprised that the lawyers from Allens did not raise the question of the adequacy of the funding for MRCF earlier than just before the fateful Board meeting of February 2001. He also thought that it was 'disturbing' that JHIL's advisers had failed to say that 'separation was unlikely to be successful unless the Foundation was *fully* funded, and that this was required to be rigorously checked'.[109] Why do you think Hardie's lawyers did not provide this advice more forcefully and earlier? Why did they not speak up about this issue and the adequacy of the Trowbridge Report at the Board meeting?

2. Commissioner Jackson described JHIL's chief in-house lawyer as 'a man who seemed determined to control the course of events, and the activities of the participants'.[110] He also commented that 'It may well be, however, that this was a case where the JHIL management were determined so far as possible, to deal with the matter in-house as far as possible [sic] and that outside advice touching the merits of the proposal was unwelcome'.[111] Jackson seems to be suggesting that JHIL

---

108 Jackson, Special Commission of Inquiry into MRCF [27.67].
109 Ibid [29.14], [29.15].
110 Ibid [29.9].
111 Yet later the CEO used Allens' name when journalist Ben Hills raised concerns that the fund may not be adequate – the CEO pointed out that they had received 'in-depth advice from a large number of specialist firms with noted, long-standing experience in relevant areas': Haigh, *Asbestos House*, 276–7, and see also 282–3 (Allens were concerned about their name being used in this way).

management (particularly the CEO and chief in-house lawyer) may have intentionally discouraged the Allens lawyers from looking more broadly at the arrangements for setting up the MRCF in their advice. If you were the external lawyer, how would you feel about this? Should you accept these types of limitations on the way your work is framed? What other options do you have? What would happen if you attempted to bypass the chief in-house lawyer and CEO and go straight to the Board with any concerns? (In answering these questions, think about what the four different ethical approaches would say about how you should respond to this sort of situation.)

3. Jackson found that JHIL and Allens misled the court about JHIL's plans in relation to the cancellation of the partly paid shares (although not intentionally). At the Commission of Inquiry, Allens and JHIL attempted to make a distinction between what was the 'intention' of JHIL at the time and what was in 'contemplation'. (Cancellation was in contemplation but there was no fixed intention to cancel.)[112] Is this type of distinction justified? Could the lawyers have done anything differently to make sure that the court was fully informed of the likely cancellation in the future? (Again, think about how the four different ethical approaches would help you answer these questions.)

4. After the MRCF became aware of its lack of funds and began to demand that JHIL do something about it, Allens provided advice on several occasions that there was little likelihood of JHIL (the parent company) being held legally responsible for the asbestos liabilities of its former subsidiaries, Amaca and Amaba. Yet JHIL, as parent of the group, had previously acted as if it had moral responsibility at least to compensate asbestos sufferers on behalf of the whole group. Moreover, as Jackson commented, regardless of the precise legal situation in relation to JHIL's liability, there was a real possibility that if JHIL failed to adequately provide for the group's asbestos victims, the government would step in and legislate to make them responsible. This is in fact what happened. As a result of the Commission of Inquiry, the New South Wales government threatened to legislate to make the James Hardie group liable unless they were able to negotiate a satisfactory arrangement for compensation of everyone. They suffered much bad publicity before an arrangement was finally negotiated.[113] In hindsight,

---

112 Ibid 303.
113 On 1 December 2005, the company effectively agreed to undo its 2001–02 restructuring and re-establish its liability to compensate victims of asbestos: Marcus Priest, 'Buck Stops with New Local Unit', *Australian Financial Review* (Sydney), 2 December 2005, 5.

should the external lawyers have more strongly advised JHIL about ethical and political considerations? What do you think the duty to the corporation as a whole required? Would you have felt capable of giving this sort of 'hard' advice to JHIL in all the circumstances?

CASE STUDY 10.3 ENRON'S LAWYERS' CONFLICTED LOYALTIES

The two case studies above concerned situations where law firms had separate clients with conflicting interests. This final case study is a situation where the law firm, Vinson and Elkins, clearly owed its obligation of loyalty to one corporate client, Enron, but apparently performed that duty in terms of unconditional loyalty to management no matter how dramatically management's instructions conflicted with legitimate shareholder, employee and public interests, and even when the law firm itself had become so entangled in management's financially corrupt schemes that it could no longer offer the firm independent advice (even if anyone had wanted to hear that).

Enron was a United States energy company that over the course of the 1990s shifted the main focus of its business from buying, transporting and selling oil, gas and electricity to creating and trading in innovative financial products based on rights to buy and sell energy: 'The guiding principle seems to have been that there was more money to be made in buying and selling financial contracts linked to the values of energy assets...than in the actual ownership of physical assets'.[114] It quickly became the major energy trader in the US market. Indeed, with its phenomenal profits and culture of innovation, Enron was a darling of the stockmarket, and one of the highest profile and most successful companies in America. Its apparent success was based on internal systems that aggressively rewarded innovation that would lead to Enron being able to show more profits on its balance sheet. Many of those who did not measure up were sacked under employment contracts that required everyone to re-apply for their jobs periodically (known as the 'Rank and Yank' process). Financial innovation that led to profits on the books was the only criterion for success in the organisation. Those that succeeded at this were seen as correct in everything, and left in charge of their own domains.[115]

114 Deborah Rhode and Paul Paton, 'Lawyers, Ethics and Enron' (2002) 8 *Stanford Journal of Law, Business & Finance* 9, 13; citing Mark Jickling, *The Enron Collapse: An Overview of Financial Issues* (Congressional Research Service, Washington, DC, 2002) 1 <http://fpc.state.gov/documents/organization/9267.pdf> at 13 June 2006.
115 Milton C Regan, 'Teaching Enron' (2005) 74 *Fordham Law Review* 1139, 1146–7; Rhode and Paton, 'Lawyers, Ethics and Enron', 18.

Enron's financial success was, however, a mirage. The company had huge debts, but was able to show a profit to the stockmarket and the public by taking advantage of accounting rules that allowed it to record future profits from its innovative financial products in its balance sheets. In reality, the debt levels of the company were growing and growing, forcing management to create more and more risky financial products and deals to make it look as if the profits were continuing to grow.

Enron's auditors, Arthur Andersen, collapsed soon after Enron's true situation became public knowledge, because of its part in allowing Enron to mislead investors and the public. The evidence suggests that Vinson and Elkins too played a role in assisting Enron to technically comply with accounting standards, while actually deceiving the market about its true position.[116] In particular, Vinson and Elkins assisted Enron to create 'Special Purpose Vehicles' (SPVs) to which Enron was able to transfer its debt so that it did not have to report the debts on its balance sheets. This way Enron's huge debts could be listed as only a footnote to the accounts, rather than appear as a main balance sheet liability. It has also been reported that Vinson and Elkins wrote 'true sale opinion letters' that supported the genuineness of Enron's transactions with the SPVs, for the purposes of getting audit approval, and therefore allowed the SPVs to be used in Enron's public financial reporting to hide their debts. Vinson and Elkins also allegedly provided advice on the legality of many of these transactions, and assisted Enron with preparation of its required public disclosures in relation to these transactions.

In 2001, corporate whistleblower Sherron Watkins wrote an anonymous memo to Kenneth Lay, Enron's Chairman, setting out concerns about the propriety of Enron's disclosures, and its accounting treatment of these transactions, including naturally the fact that they had been approved by Arthur Andersen's audits. She recommended that Lay hire an independent law firm to investigate her concerns. She explicitly stated that Vinson and Elkins should not be hired to do the job, as they faced a conflict of interest from having provided opinion letters supporting the legal propriety of some of the deals that the auditors would have relied on. Nevertheless Lay did ask Vinson and Elkins to conduct the review, which they did. But he specifically asked them not to delve into the accounting treatment of the transactions, and Vinson and Elkins apparently saw no reason to go outside those instructions. Vinson and Elkins concluded that the facts did not 'warrant a

116 See generally Rhode and Paton, 'Lawyers, Ethics and Enron', 15, 17–24; Regan, 'Teaching Enron'; Mike France with Wendy Zellner and Christopher Palmeri, 'One Big Client, One Big Hassle', *Business Week Online*, 28 January 2002 <www.businessweek.com/magazine/content/02 04/b3767706.htm> at 13 June 2006.

further widespread investigation by independent counsel and auditors', but did comment that the 'bad cosmetics' of the deals might lead to 'adverse publicity and litigation'.[117]

A few months later, Enron's true financial position and the nature of the deals became public knowledge, Enron collapsed and thousands of investors lost their money. Enron is now a byword for corporate corruption:

> By October 2002 . . . investigations of Enron-related criminal conduct had resulted in three criminal indictments. In June 2002, a Texas jury convicted Arthur Andersen of federal charges of obstruction of justice. In August 2002, Michael Kopper, an Enron employee working for the company's Chief Financial Officer between 1994 and July 2001, pleaded guilty to conspiracy to commit wire fraud and money laundering. Under the terms of a Co-operation Agreement, Kopper admitted participating in a scheme to secretly use the SPVs to defraud Enron for his own financial benefit. On October 1, 2002, the Justice Department charged Enron's former Chief Financial Officer, Andrew Fastow, with securities fraud, money laundering, mail fraud, wire fraud, bank fraud and conspiracy related to secret deals he allegedly made with the company for his own financial benefit.[118]

In May 2006, Lay and the Chief Executive Officer Jeffrey Skilling were convicted by a Texas jury of fraud and conspiracy arising from the collapse. Lay is now dead.

What might have led Vinson and Elkins to see it as unnecessary to review dubious transactions in which they themselves had been involved, nor to strongly advise Enron senior management and the board about the problems with these transactions, nor to warn anyone else, including the investors who lost their money, the corporate regulator, or stock exchange? It seems that Vinson and Elkins did not even recognise that its overriding obligation of loyalty to the Enron company as a whole might mean that it had to think about the conflicting interests of Enron management (to hide Enron's true financial position) and Enron's shareholders, creditors and employees (to know the true situation and avoid financial loss). Nor did they apparently consider any other obligation to the market or the community. Remember Enron was the United States' largest energy trader and its activities could potentially cut off supply of electricity and gas to millions of people.[119] Enron's 'situational culture' – involving the exercise

---

117 Rhode and Paton, 'Lawyers, Ethics and Enron', 19–21.
118 Ibid 16.
119 In fact there is evidence that Enron energy traders would manipulate the availability of electricity to certain areas if the electricity provider in that area would not agree to pay the right price, in order to force them to come to Enron's price.

of a type of moral power over these 'professionals' – appeared to be irresistible. As Ian Ramsay has observed:

> ...[A]s a lawyer's status and income become increasingly dependent on a single client or on success in a particular proceeding, the pressure to avoid ethical judgments intensifies.[120]

DISCUSSION QUESTIONS

The role of Vinson and Elkins as law firm to Enron illustrates well the way in which lawyers' own ethical values and awareness are likely to be very important in helping them to identify conflicting loyalties and constraints on the duty to clients, and decide how to respond to them. Merely trying to apply the *Model Rules* to this situation might not have helped very much. The questions below are designed to help you consider the different ethical approaches and values that you might apply to difficult situations of conflicting loyalties.

1. If you had been a lawyer in Vinson and Elkins, the law firm which advised Enron on almost everything, would you see yourself as:

    (a) a *zealous advocate*, concerned to get the best deal for management;

    (b) a *responsible lawyer*, working to get the company's debt within the accounting rules and worried about how the disclosure requirements could be met;

    (c) a *moral activist*, about to blow the whistle on the deception; or

    (d) a practitioner of *ethics of care*, weighing up the best way to look after both the shareholders who are about to lose their savings and the Enron employees who were 'just following orders', and other stakeholders?

2. If you see yourself as a *zealous advocate*, where would you be now? If you see yourself as a *responsible lawyer*, who would you be working for now? If you are a *moral activist*, would you be employable now and, if so, in what sort of workplace environment? If you were a practitioner of *ethics of care*, what would be the consequences for you if you had succeeded in caring for both shareholders and low-power employees?

---

120 Ian Ramsay, 'Ethical Perspectives on the Practice of Business Law' (1992) 30(5) *Law Society Journal* 60, 63.

3. Finally, which of the above ethical approaches, or which combination of them, would most influence you if and when you find yourself in a similar position to a Vinson and Elkins partner, working some time in the future for a similarly powerful and valuable client?

RECOMMENDED FURTHER READING

Kenneth E Goodpaster, 'The Concept of Corporate Responsibility' (1983) 2 *Journal of Business Ethics* 1.

Robert Gordon, 'A New Role for Lawyers? The Corporate Counselor After Enron' (2003) 35 *Connecticut Law Review* 1185; also extracted in Milton C Regan and Jeffrey D Bauman (eds), *Legal Ethics and Corporate Practice* (see full reference below) 64.

Kath Hall and Vivien Holmes, 'The Power of Rationalisation to Influence Lawyers' Decisions to Act' (2008) 11 *Legal Ethics* 137–53.

Robert A Kagan and Robert Eli Rosen, 'On the Social Significance of Large Law Firm Practice' (1985) 37 *Stanford Law Review* 399.

Donald C Langevoort, 'The Epistemology of Corporate-Securities Lawyering: Beliefs, Biases and Organizational Behaviour' (1997) 63 *Brooklyn Law Review* 629.

Suzanne LeMire, 'Testing Times: In-House Counsel and Independence' (2011) 14(1) *Legal Ethics* 163.

Suzanne LeMire and Christine Parker 'Keeping It In-House: Ethics in the relationship between large firm lawyers and their corporate clients through the eyes of in-house counsel' (2008) 11 *Legal Ethics* 201.

David Luban, 'Integrity: Its Causes and Cures' (2003) 72 *Fordham Law Review* 279.

Christine Parker, *The Open Corporation: Effective Self-Regulation and Democracy* (Cambridge University Press, Cambridge, 2002).

Christine Parker, Adrian Evans, Linda Haller, Suzanne LeMire, and Reid Mortensen, 'The Ethical Infrastructure of Legal Practice in Larger Law Firms: Values, Policy and Behaviour' (2008) 31 *University of New South Wales Law Journal* 158–87.

Christine Parker and Tanina Rostain, 'Law Firms, Global Capital and the Sociological Imagination' (2012) 80 *Fordham Law Review* 2347–81.

Robert Eli Rosen, 'Problem-Setting and Serving the Organizational Client: Legal Diagnosis and Professional Independence' (2001) 56 *University of Miami Law Review* 179.

William H Simon, 'Wrongs of Ignorance and Ambiguity: Lawyer Responsibility for Collective Misconduct' (2005) 22 *Yale Journal on Regulation* 1.

Jo-Ann Tsang, 'Moral Rationalization and the Integration of Situational Factors and Psychological Processes in Immoral Behavior', *Review of General Psychology* 6(1), 2002, 25–50.

11

CONCLUSION – PERSONAL PROFESSIONALISM: VIRTUE, VALUES AND LEGAL PROFESSIONALISM

Introduction

At the start of this book, four approaches to how we might decide what is ethical behaviour for lawyers were introduced. Zealous, client-focused lawyering was contrasted with lawyering that counterbalances client advocacy with upholding the responsibilities and duties of citizens to society – *responsible lawyering*. A third approach, *moral activism*, sees the ethical duties of lawyering not so much in vigorously asserting clients' rights, or the Rule of Law, as in actively doing one's best in the interests of justice. Finally, the *ethics of care* sees the ethical virtues of all three of the preceding approaches as overrated in comparison with the importance of caring for and respecting the needs and moral aspirations of each client, each witness, even each opponent with whom the lawyer may come in contact, as well as actively cultivating their own virtue as a person and a lawyer.

In practice, of course, lawyers can and do move around between these ideal types. The zealous *adversarial advocate* might still be dominant, but even the determined and fearless criminal barrister can and does change into the quiet and grieving *carer*, standing, if they are so permitted, near their condemned client when the trapdoor drops. Consider for example the case of Nguyen Tuong Van, aged 25, of Melbourne, who was hanged in Singapore on 2 December 2005 for smuggling 496 grams of heroin through Changi airport in 2002. His Australian lawyers, Lex Lasry (then a QC) and Julian McMahon, represented him fearlessly and expertly throughout his trial and subsequent international pleas for mercy. When those pleas were rejected by Singapore, the two lawyers, who had always acted *pro bono*, applied without success simply to be present at the hanging, for no other purpose but to stand alongside their client.

There is probably no virtue in any lawyer rigidly following just one of these four ideals of ethical lawyering all the time. But it seems likely that, just as individuals have preferred or comfortable psychological types,[1] so also ethically aware lawyers will tend to identify more often than not with one ethical type that expresses their values for lawyering and shapes their practice. All lawyers and law students are likely to benefit from identifying their own values, and reflecting about the ethical behaviour that they might derive from those values. In each of the previous chapters we have examined how the values represented by the different approaches would apply to certain specific situations and contexts that commonly arise in legal practice. In this chapter we examine more closely the significance of personal values-awareness for lawyers' ethics. In the third section, underlying

---

1 See, eg, the *Myers-Briggs Type Indicator* (MBTI), a psychological categorisation instrument developed from the work of the Swiss psychologist and psychiatrist Carl Jung (1875–1961): see Isabel Briggs Myers with Peter B Myers, *Gifts Differing: Understanding Personality Type* (Davies-Black Publishing, Palo Alto, California, 2nd edn, 1995).

values are explored in a concrete situation that commonly provokes very personal challenges to lawyers' values: the good character requirement for admission to practice. Finally, the book concludes with a suggested method for using a scale or instrument to help law students and lawyers self-assess their ethical type in a class or law firm discussion setting.

The Significance of Virtue and Personal Values in Legal Professionalism

Underlying all our analysis of the four ethical approaches to lawyering and ethics in legal practice throughout this book are personal value commitments by scholars, as well as by practising lawyers. Consider for example the continuing debate among lawyers and ethicists about lawyers' proper role, if any, in securing justice where law does not do so. The issues of contention between the *responsible lawyer* and the *moral activist* are not merely academic. Rather each participant in this (scholarly and practical) debate conscientiously asserts the moral superiority of their own viewpoint not just because of the values they embody, but because one or more virtues – for example loyalty in the adversarial advocate, resilience in the responsible lawyer, determination in the moral activist or compassion in the carer – are also critical to them. They draw on these and other virtues when preferring one ethical approach or another, and the combination of virtue and value matters enormously to the continued legitimacy of law and legal practice.

On the one hand, for example, ethicists like Stephen Pepper and Bradley Wendel argue that the 'liberal', or neutral, model of legal partisanship, which favours the primacy of legal rules as the major reference point in resolving ethical quandaries, is the proper framework for determining lawyers' ethics.[2] Markovits voices a similar belief when he raises his flag for the essential political function that he hopes law offers to social certainty (as discussed in Chapter 1). Broadly speaking, they ground their powerful advocacy of their positions on the personal conviction that there is no greater guarantee of individual fairness or justice than

2 See, eg, Stephen Pepper, 'Lawyers' Ethics in the Gap Between Law and Justice' (1999) 40 *South Texas Law Review* 181; Stephen Pepper, 'Counseling at the Limits of the Law: An Exercise in the Jurisprudence and Ethics of Lawyering' (1995) 104 *Yale Law Journal* 1545; Stephen Pepper, 'The Lawyer's Amoral Ethical Role: A Defense, A Problem, and Some Possibilities' (1986) 1986 *American Bar Foundation Research Journal* 613; Bradley Wendel, 'Civil Obedience' (2004) 104 *Columbia Law Review* 363. See also Daniel Markovits, 'Legal Ethics from the Lawyer's Point of View' (2003) 15 *Yale Journal of Law & the Humanities* 209.

that provided by the rules, in effect, by the Rule of Law. Their argument is not new, although it is developed by each writer with great care, sophistication and an integrity that demands respect, even if we disagree with it. The essence of the argument is that true security comes from definable rules or, at least, from rules that are capable of flexible interpretation, as circumstances and developing moral dialogues require.[3]

In contrast, ethicists like Donald Nicolson and Julian Webb's equally impassioned injunction is first to look at the justice and fairness of the context facing the lawyer's choice about how to act, regardless of any apparently applicable rules.[4] They suggest that deep-seated social inequality governs the major western economies and that to rely on the Rule of Law (that is, to have blind confidence that the rules are fair and are administered fairly) as an ethical guideline is naive, or worse, complicit in the perpetuation of that inequality. Nicolson and Webb ask about the moral context: Whether the client is, directly or indirectly, behaving oppressively to those more vulnerable than themselves, or being unfairly oppressed.

The important point is not that Pepper, Wendel and Markovits (who might be said to defend *responsible lawyering*) and Nicolson and Webb (who are probably *moral activists*) do not agree – but that they disagree with their virtues of determination and sincerity on display. These ethicists write with energy and conviction because they believe it matters, and think that others need to believe and act as if it matters too. Their actual ethical judgements are almost secondary. Their commitment to the integrity of open discussion of passionate positions is the essential quality that all lawyers, indeed all law students, can seek to identify with, as one way to assist in strengthening their own virtues and working out their own ethical choices.

Inside lawyers' ethics in practice there are many very personal dilemmas. Feelings about what is right and wrong can lurk beneath the surface without being expressed. Law students are still too often told to 'think like a lawyer' and discouraged from linking their values and their feelings to what they are learning.[5] Many go into practice finding it difficult to recognise the importance of their often confused feelings for ethical decision-making, and lawyers can be particularly poor at this skill. We often gloss over the personal dimensions of ethical conflicts by using only rules as our guide, ignoring the fact that rules are often like cryptic crosswords

---

3 Pepper, 'Lawyers' Ethics in the Gap Between Law and Justice'.
4 Donald Nicolson and Julian Webb, *Professional Legal Ethics: Critical Interrogations* (Oxford University Press, Oxford, 1999).
5 Molly O'Brien, Stephen Tang and Kath Hall, 'Changing Our Thinking: Empirical Research on Law Student Wellbeing, Thinking Styles and the Law Curriculum' (2011) 21 *Legal Education Review*; Melanie Poole, 'The Making of Professional Vandals; How Law Schools Degrade the Self' (2011) ANU College of Law Research Paper No 12–13. See <http://ssrn.com/abstract=2029993>.

full of overriding principles, qualifications and provisos, and discounting our 'gut feelings' about what is right.

As we have seen in the previous chapters of this book, all sorts of (possibly unethical) things are possible if bare rules are the start and finish of decision-making about ethical conduct: Whether acting for the tobacco company that is intent on selling its product according to law (but manoeuvring to avoid liability for its past deceit about the fatal effects of tobacco smoke), or over-charging a client because the system of costing makes it possible to do so without being prosecuted for misconduct, or even acting for a new client who has interests that are different to another, long-standing and loyal client.

Rules should be only one part of the complex jigsaw of factors that lawyers consider in taking any ethical decision. The other legitimate jigsaw pieces are far more numerous than just the practice rules, and even the common law and legislation.

More than anything, the jigsaw piece which must be explicitly identified and taken into account in each of these dilemmas is the individual lawyer's virtues and values – the personal, and often quite private, set of characteristics and priorities that are the bedrock for each person's beliefs, attitudes and behaviours. These qualities do not necessarily determine our behaviour, but they are the starting point in understanding that lawyers are as human as the rest of the species, and can and should make choices about what they actually do.[6]

It is not just awareness of values that is important, but also emotions: Hugh Brayne emphasises the importance of feelings in understanding values for everyone, including law students, by citing Daniel Goleman, the author of *Emotional Intelligence*:

> While strong feelings can create havoc in reasoning, the lack of awareness of feeling can also be ruinous, especially in weighing the decisions on which our destiny largely depends: what career to pursue, whether to stay in a secure job or switch to one that is riskier but more interesting, whom to date or marry, where to live, which apartment to rent or house to buy – and on and on through life. Such decisions cannot be made through sheer rationality; they require gut feeling...[7]

An individual lawyer may or may not be fully aware of their values or, more precisely, of the interplay between their ethical reasoning, emotional (feeling)

---

6 Hugh Brayne, 'Learning to Think Like a Lawyer: One Law Teacher's Exploration of the Relevance of Evolutionary Psychology' (2002) 9 *International Journal of the Legal Profession* 283, 301. In contrast to our hopeful view of lawyers' autonomy, consider Markovits' argument that there is a sense in which lawyers can't make those choices – they are forced by their role in helping apply the law to be 'unethical...due to historical forces beyond their control': see Markovits, 'Legal Ethics from the Lawyer's Point of View', 293.

7 Brayne, 'Learning to Think Like a Lawyer', 298; citing Daniel Goleman, *Emotional Intelligence: Why It Can Matter More Than IQ* (Bloomsbury Publishing, London, 1996) 6–13.

processes and professional practice, but personal values awareness is an important aid to ethical practice.[8] The lawyer who is unaware of their own values preferences cannot so easily decide, if they can, for example, live with keeping a possible killer from 'telling what happened', from evading tax by laying a false and confusing trail of bank accounts, which utilise 'commissions' to a succession of foreign merchant banks in exchange for millisecond use of those accounts, from polluting a waterway as a consequence of expanding a client's pine plantation, or from selling shares with their client's inside knowledge, knowing that other smaller shareholders will be trailing along in the ruins of a company that is rapidly going under.

Lawyers may have some inkling of the right thing to do, but if they have not delved into their values very much, if all this ethics and 'psychology' seems a bit too hazy or suspect, and they can find a rule – whether of substantive law or procedure – which just might allow them to not think about it too much, that rule will, all too often, be located and relied upon. For this reason, the emphasis of this book has not been so much on rules of conduct[9] as on exploring the values which underlie the traditional approach to many ethical dilemmas, and then suggesting possible alternatives.

For many new lawyers, knowing what they truly *value* inside these dramas will be the starting point not just for workplace survival, but for longer-term satisfaction in the legal world.

Measuring Awareness of Ethical Preference[10]

The values which can be said to underlie ethical choice may appear well-developed by the time a student is in law school, but the assumption of this book is that an individual law student's ethical preferences in relation to legal professionalism are still in formation and may be open to some change when presented with possible alternatives.[11] If this is correct, then law students' early knowledge of their basic legal ethics preferences, and of the possibilities and challenges of change, may

---

8 Brayne, 'Learning to Think Like a Lawyer', 298. See also Donald Schon, *The Reflective Practitioner: How Professionals Think in Action* (Basic Books, New York, 1983).

9 Although, of course, conduct rules and the law of lawyering form part of the context and values structure for personal decision-making.

10 This section draws on and modifies material originally published in Palermo and Evans, 'Preparing Future Australian Lawyers' and in Evans and Forgasz, 'Framing Lawyers' Choices: Factor Analysis of a Psychological Scale to Self-Assess Lawyers' Ethical Preferences' (2013) 16 (1) *Legal Ethics*, forthcoming.

11 See generally Evans and Palermo, 'Zero Impact'; J D Droddy and C S Peters, 'The Effect of Law School on Political Attitudes: Some Evidence from the Class of 2000' (2003) 53 *Journal of Legal Education* 33.

promote earlier ethical development and more satisfactory working lives. Some might realise sooner that they are not suitable as lawyers. Some will understand that they have a legal vocation, and not just an occupation. Ethics awareness earlier on might also help law students and lawyers make better choices at the beginning of their careers about what area of practice to pursue.[12] Greater clarity about ethical choice could also lead to a better sense of professionalism and contribute to better public regard for those professionals.

Complete transformation is most unlikely, but using an ethics awareness process with students (and lawyers) could assist in strengthening any resolve to behave ethically. In this process, the teacher (discussion leader) should express their own views as well, in the context of respect for divergent views. If this happens, the chances are improved of law students *and* lawyers understanding their own ethics base and their potential choices, before they are under too much pressure to make quick decisions that might not be ethically justified.[13]

One way of uncovering students' and lawyers' legal ethics and challenging them with new perspectives might be the following staged approach to discussing these issues, utilising a purpose-developed scale to measure the strength for an individual student or lawyer of their different ethical preferences:

1. Bring a group of law students or lawyers together and introduce them to the main ethical values-based *approaches* available as decision-making frameworks for lawyers, such as those set out in Chapters 1 and 2 – *adversarial advocacy, responsible lawyering, moral activism* and the *ethics of care*. Ask each student/lawyer to consider the possibility that they have a preferred approach to ethical decision-making (or mixture thereof) which intuitively seems most appropriate for them to apply in their own legal practice (if and when they enter practice).

2. Ask participants to individually and silently complete the Appendix Part 1: 'Self-Assessment of Legal Ethical Preferences' (at the end of the chapter), following the instructions in the appendix, and then Appendix Part 2: 'Scale to Self-Assess Legal Ethical Preferences', strictly in that order. This instrument – technically described as a 'scale' – has been developed in an Australian legal profession setting,[14] but can be used elsewhere with appropriate cautions. Emphasise that the instrument will only be useful if approached conscientiously.

Invite discussion in the group about whether, on reflection, the number they obtained for each ethical preference appears realistic to them. Ask them to

---

12 Perlman, 'A Career Choice Critique'.
13 Adrian Evans, 'Just Following Orders' (2004) 78(5) *Law Institute Journal* 95.
14 Evans and Forgasz, 'Framing Lawyers' Choices'.

comment on whether they were surprised by the result or whether they were merely confirmed in their earlier opinions or guesses. The discussion is important either to validate the process or to discredit it, so far as the particular group is concerned. In either case, class reflection on the exercise is the key ingredient in advancing self-understanding of individual values and ethical preferences.

Ask participants to apply their recently discovered preference(s) to a hypothetical, but realistic, practice scenario to consider whether their preference or preferences ring true or not in the context of the scenario. The case studies in this book and elsewhere[15] are appropriate for this purpose. Begin by asking, 'Has anyone seen anything or heard of anything similar in their work experience or practice environments?'; then go on to ask a series of more specific questions designed to uncover the values each student/lawyer would apply to resolving the scenario. For illustration, we set out below, as Case Study 11.1, one of the scenarios from the *Australian Lawyers' Values Study*.

This approach can be compelling for participants because of its potential to extend their ethical 'horizon', allowing them to observe and reflect upon what they would each do in a similar situation. In many cases, people discuss what they have already done and the discussion builds from there, leading to a further discussion of their preferred (and sometimes newly re-formed) ethical approach. Emphasise that there is rarely a 'correct' answer. The discussion itself tends to raise the various competing values at stake.

3. 'De-brief' participants by informing them about any rules of conduct, legislation and case law that apply to the scenario, and revisit the choice of ethical approach with which they, as individual students/lawyers, feel most comfortable. Take care to highlight any differences between what the ethical rules and law say should be done in the scenario and what the different ethical approaches say should be done, in order to encourage critique of the rules and law.

4. Finally, extend an invitation to participants to consider where they might stand, in the light of these preferences, when the issues in the scenarios come before them in real life.

---

15 Other resources include the scenarios in the *Australian Lawyers' Values Study* in, eg, Evans and Palermo, 'Zero Impact'; Debra Lamb, 'Appendix: Case Studies' in Stephen Parker and Charles Sampford (eds), *Legal Ethics and Legal Practice: Contemporary Issues* (Clarendon Press, Oxford, 1995) 237 (case studies collected from interviews with Australian lawyers about their real experiences); Philip B Heymann and Lance Liebman, *The Social Responsibilities of Lawyers: Case Studies* (Foundation Press, Westbury, New York, 1988). See also Robert Eli Rosen, 'Ethical Soap: LA Law and the Privileging of Character' (1989) 43 *University of Miami Law Review* 1229 (for an excellent discussion of the use of TV shows and popular culture for ethics teaching and the limitations of using only short hypothetical scenarios to explore issues of ethical character).

CASE STUDY 11.1   CONFIDENTIALITY IN THE FACE OF LIKELY CHILD ABUSE

The issue of child abuse has a very high profile in Australia. The injury and death of young children at the hands of family members and institutions regularly feature in metropolitan newspapers. Nevertheless, confidentiality could be described as one of the 'core' values of the Australian legal profession and, despite some policy concerns that now question the utility of confidentiality in achieving just results in the trial process, it remains undeniably crucial as a linchpin of common law systems of representation. Consider the following case study:

You are acting for a mother of three small children in a divorce and intervention order matter. Your client has previously shown you some old photographs of bruises and marks on the children which she, unconvincingly, claims were inflicted not by their father, but by her new boyfriend.

One of the children now has blurred vision. Your client now instructs you to stop all legal proceedings as she intends to return to the children's father with her children. You believe the children will be at risk if this happens but your client tells you, as she leaves, to do nothing. Would you break client confidentiality and inform the relevant welfare department of your fears?[16]

DISCUSSION QUESTIONS

1. Consider your reactions to the scenario. Have you seen anything or heard of anything similar in your work experience environments, or those of your friends?

2. A similar choice may confront you at some point in your career. In reflecting on your decision about what to do here, which of the ethical approaches discussed in this book is most attractive to you? Does this choice 'fit' with the number you have identified for different ethical preferences? If not, why does there appear to be a difference? How would you answer the question posed in this scenario?

3. If you thought that a report to the welfare authorities would result in the Legal Services Commissioner investigating you, would you still proceed and make the report?

---

16 See Adrian Evans and Josephine Palermo, 'Australian Law Students' Perceptions of their Values: Interim Results in the First Year – 2001 – of a Three-Year Empirical Assessment' (2002) 5 *Legal Ethics* 103, 114.

4. Would your answers be different if, upon later, more thorough questioning of your client, you discovered that your client has an old history of drug abuse and was not, in the past, always reliable in what she said?

5. What arguments would you raise if you had reported the matter to the welfare authorities, later discovered your client's history, and your client then complained to the Legal Services Commissioner about your breach of her confidentiality?

6. If you were the Commissioner, what attitude would you have to the complaint if the client complained about a breach of confidentiality?

7. Picture yourself as working in a law firm with peer lawyers and one or more supervisors (all of which is likely). ASCR 9.1 provides that:

'A solicitor must not disclose any information which is confidential to a client and acquired by the solicitor during the client's engagement to any person who is not ... a solicitor who is a partner, principal, director, or employee of the solicitor's law practice ...'

ASCR 9.2 provides that lawyers do not have to maintain confidentiality where the practitioner discloses information in circumstances in which the law would probably compel its disclosure, and for the sole purpose of avoiding the probable commission of a serious criminal offence or for the purpose of preventing *imminent serious physical harm* (our emphasis) (as discussed in Chapter 4).

Does the ASCR exception affect your choice as to what to do in this scenario? Does it change your preferred ethical approach? Do you think the rule, together with its exception, reflects an appropriate ethical approach to this issue?

8. If you decided to report your concerns in relation to this scenario, how would you react if your firm as a whole did not share your sense of ethical preferences and might not agree with your conclusions about what to do in this case? Would you feel able to defend and justify your decision in terms of your identified ethical preferences? Would you be able to assert not just your autonomy in the matter as an individually admitted lawyer, but also a professional *obligation* to reach your own decision? If you were able initially to hold the line and did report your concerns despite the disapproval of your firm, for how long could you continue working in that firm?

9. How might a firm you worked for react if you reported your concerns and your former client made a complaint to the Legal Services Commissioner? Would you be criticised or disciplined by the firm,

either for your actions in relation to this client, or for bringing the firm to the attention of the Commissioner, or both? If you were so criticised internally, would you feel able to defend yourself using the ASCR exceptions to confidentiality? Or would all these difficult consequences of making an initial report of your suspicions (in effect, by becoming an internal witness or whistleblower), deter you from doing anything in the first place?

10. In short, when you are confronted with any case that stirs your ethical conscience, can you be an independently minded practitioner inside a firm which might have different priorities to your own?

11. Thinking through these issues in terms of law firm *ethical infrastructure* (discussed in Chapter 10), is there a case for a similar ethics awareness process for the firm as a whole, so that you know the likely overall position of that firm in advance of likely ethical challenges? How would you modify the statements in the appendices to capture these wider challenges and objectives?

The final case study for this book concerns a decade-long tragedy from South Australia. It raises and in a way summarises all the issues we have discussed concerning lawyers as individuals and as part of a wider profession.

CASE STUDY 11.2   APPROPRIATE SILENCE OR LAWYERS PROTECTING LAWYERS?: EUGENE MCGEE[17]

A well-known criminal defence lawyer, Eugene McGee, attended a leisurely lunch with family members at an Adelaide suburban hotel in late 2003. He drank too much, as the table docket recorded the purchase of three bottles of wine. After leaving the hotel, McGee attempted to drive down Kapunda Road at a reportedly excessive speed, knocking over and killing cyclist Ian Humphrey. McGee left the scene without stopping or rendering assistance.[18] But three minutes after killing the cyclist, McGee made three brief phone calls to his own lawyer, David Edwardson. We do not know what was said despite the establishment of a South

---

17 *Kapunda Road Royal Commission*, Ch 2, 27. This summary of the McGee case is extracted from Adrian Evans, *The Good Lawyer-Revisited* (ACER Press, Camberwell, forthcoming).

18 See Government of South Australia, Report of the *Kapunda Road Royal Commission*, Chapter 2, at <www.sa.gov.au/upload/franchise/Crime,%20justice%20and%20the%20law/KRRC/krrc_report_2.pdf>.

Australian Royal Commission dedicated solely to finding out what happened and why.[19] The problem is that the lawyer who 'did it', McGee, and his lawyer, Edwardson, are not saying what they discussed. And the communication is prima facie privileged.

Significantly, McGee was not interviewed by police until the following day and was not breath-tested. His brother had driven him safely through a police roadblock set up to stop McGee's own car, which he had parked at his mother's place. By the time Edwardson ultimately contacted police, it was over six hours since the actual hit-run had occurred, which was well past the normal three-hour window for an effective breath test. Many years of protracted prosecutions ensued, but the lack of a breath test, of any admissions by McGee or any direct evidence of drunkenness was such that all those efforts could be resisted, if he and his lawyers were able to stay focused. The formal criminal law outcome was a minor conviction for driving without due care and a fine of $3100.

Despite much public agitation and political brawling inside the South Australian government and between the government and opposition,[20] McGee received no significant professional penalty. A prosecution of McGee and his brother for conspiracy to pervert the course of justice failed. The South Australian Legal Practitioners Conduct Board, which was a disciplinary body set up under the exclusive control of the South Australian legal profession, found in November 2011 that he was not guilty of 'infamous' conduct, and could continue practising.[21] Since then, repeated efforts by politicians to reopen the case in some way have come to nothing, because the sort of evidence that would allow more serious action, if such evidence exists, is hidden behind the legal wall of silence known as privilege.

Meanwhile, the South Australian public largely believes there has been a cover-up. The Conduct Board found that McGee '...was suffering from post-traumatic stress disorder when he left the scene of the accident, and it ruled that it could only consider his actions in the first few seconds after the crash and could not consider some of the actions that had happened subsequently, such as the calls to his legal adviser or his actions to avoid police'.[22] The wider political and

19 *Kapunda Road Royal Commission*, Ch 2, 27.

20 Andrew Dowdell, 'New push to have hit-run driver, lawyer Eugene McGee punished', *The Advertiser*, 21 February 2013. See <www.adelaidenow.com.au/news/south-australia/new-push-to-have-hit-run-driver-lawyer-eugene-mcgee-punished/story-e6frea83-1226582712265> Accessed 24 April 2013.

21 See 'Lawyers Act to be reviewed after hit-run', *The Age*, 9 December 2011, <www.theage.com.au/national/lawyers-act-to-be-reviewed-after-hitrun-20111208-1olce.html>

22 Suzanne Le Mire, *The Law Report*, Radio National, 16 April 2013, at <www.abc.net.au/radionational/programs/lawreport/sa-legal-profession-laws/4629776> Accessed 24 April 2013.

public perception is not only that McGee escaped justice, but that the organised community of lawyers in that State is to blame, by Caesar judging Caesar – that is, by lawyers protecting lawyers.[23] McGee continues in legal practice today in Adelaide.

DISCUSSION QUESTIONS

1. *Australian Solicitors' Conduct Rules* 9.2.4 allows a solicitor to disclose '...information for the sole purpose of avoiding the probable commission of a serious criminal offence'. If the McGee case occurred today and you were consulted by a client in the same position, would you seek to rely on the distinction between *commission* and *concealment* in this rule, in order to remain silent in the crucial period after a collision, when it would still be possible to obtain a useful breath test from your client?

2. What is your attitude to the law of privilege, as it is expressed in the case of McGee?

3. Regardless of the conduct rules or client privilege, was it morally appropriate for *McGee's lawyer* to stay quiet in the crucial post-accident period when, on his instructions, a probable serious crime had already been committed?

4. If you were McGee's lawyer, which ethical preference would most strongly appeal to you?

5. Suppose you were the wife, brother or sister of the deceased cyclist: Would your view as to the ethics of the situation be any different from that of the SA Conduct Board?

Conclusion

The legal ethicist Kim Economides has made the point that lawyers need to discover what really motivates them.[24] As we have seen, legal practice serves up a proportion of clients whose objectives, strategies and tactics are morally questionable, even repugnant. New lawyers face pressure to act quickly and with a clear idea as to

---

23 Ibid.
24 Kim Economides, 'Learning the Law of Lawyering' (1999) 52 *Current Legal Problems* 392, 393.

their values and motivation in dealing with these environments. Only with this knowledge is it possible to approach ethical dilemmas with some idea of the way through. The question for the reader here is, therefore: Have you, in reading this book, developed any better ideas as to what might be important to you if you work as a lawyer?

APPENDIX[1]: PART 1 – SELF-ASSESSMENT OF LEGAL ETHICAL PREFERENCES

Instructions

1. Consider each statement carefully and whether or not you agree with it. The reliability of this instrument depends on your candour and willingness to be thorough in your response to each statement.

2. Please indicate your degree of support for each statement by inserting an 'x' in the appropriate column to the right of that statement.

Statement	Strongly Disagree	Disagree	Slightly Disagree	Slightly Agree	Agree	Strongly Agree
If I heard a lie uttered by my client or my witness in Court, I would correct the deception as soon as possible.						
Public interest lawyering is very attractive to me.						

1 This scale was developed for use in an Australian setting and is extracted from Adrian Evans and Helen Forgasz, 'Framing Lawyers' Choices: Factor Analysis of a Psychological Scale to Self-Assess Lawyers' Ethical Preferences' (2013) 16(1) *Legal Ethics* 134.

Statement	Strongly Disagree	Disagree	Slightly Disagree	Slightly Agree	Agree	Strongly Agree
I prefer dialogue, mediation and a careful focus on principled negotiation in resolving disputes for my clients.						
Achieving what my client wants has to be my main priority.						
I might do more than just refuse to act if my client insisted on an illegal course of action.						
The context and circumstances of an individual's suffering are more important than universal legal principles.						
Sometimes it's necessary to think less about your client's personal circumstances and more about what their case could do to improve justice.						

(cont.)

Statement	Strongly Disagree	Disagree	Slightly Disagree	Slightly Agree	Agree	Strongly Agree
I put my client's interests first regardless of who the client is or what area of law is involved.						
I would much rather take a collaborative or restorative approach to problem solving, than a combative stance.						
My aim is to do all for my client that my client would do for themselves, if they had my knowledge and experience.						
I find I can actually do a better job for my clients by helping them navigate beyond 'pure' legal advice into the realm of policy and purpose behind legislation.						

Statement	Strongly Disagree	Disagree	Slightly Disagree	Slightly Agree	Agree	Strongly Agree
My clients' enterprises ultimately depend upon their acceptance of the purpose and not just the letter of the law.						
I prefer to think of law reform and better access to justice as my chief interests.						
Saying 'no' to clients is sometimes necessary in order to preserve the system on which (even though they might not care either way) their own ultimate welfare depends.						
I find it hard to practice within 'the rules' when my clients demand something else.						
Clients need to know that I am not in their pocket.						

(cont.)

Statement	Strongly Disagree	Disagree	Slightly Disagree	Slightly Agree	Agree	Strongly Agree
Social reform and the careful redistribution of wealth through the law are more important than my personal contentment.						
Apology, reconciliation and the acceptance of moral responsibility is more important than the 'just' and rigorous enforcement of legal rights.						
Concerns for justice and service are all very well, but if 'push comes to shove', what my client wants has to come first.						

NOW…

3. Change each 'x' in each column to a number, as follows: Strongly Disagree [1], Disagree [2], Slightly Disagree [3], Slightly Agree [4], Agree [5] and Strongly Agree [6].

4. Transpose each number to the same statement on the accompanying Scale to Self-Assess Legal Ethical Preference on page 386, and total the scores for each ethical type.

5. The higher the score for each type, the more important that ethical preference is to you.

Important: This instrument will be most useful if you discuss your responses and consequential preference, in a collegiate environment, after completion of the scale.

These statements are expressed in an abstract form to assist comparability. Please keep in mind that how we consider abstractions and how we actually act on them are two different things.

It is very unlikely that a single, overwhelming preference will emerge. Rather, an individual's self-understanding of the relative strength of different preferences is useful for their future decision-making.

To maximise the benefit of self-assessment, it is important that participants debrief their results and have a conversation about their reactions, scepticisms and learning, as appropriate. This conversation is the key to any greater insights and hence awareness of preferred ethical approach.

MORAL ACTIVISM	Values
I prefer to think of law reform and better access to justice as my chief interests.	
Sometimes it's necessary to think less about your client's personal circumstances and more about what their case could do to improve justice.	
I find I can actually do a better job for my clients by helping them navigate beyond 'pure' legal advice into the realm of policy and purpose behind legislation.	
Public interest lawyering is very attractive to me.	
Social reform and the careful redistribution of wealth through the law are more important than my personal contentment.	
Total	

ZEALOUS ADVOCACY	Values
Concerns for justice and service are all very well, but if 'push comes to shove', what my client wants has to come first.	
Achieving what my client wants has to be my main priority.	
I find it hard to practice within 'the rules' when my clients demand something else.	
I put my client's interests first regardless of who the client is or what area of law is involved.	
My aim is to do all for my client that my client would do for themselves, if they had my knowledge and experience.	
Total	

RESPONSIBLE LAWYERING	Values
If I heard a lie uttered by my client or my witness in Court, I would correct the deception as soon as possible.	
My clients' enterprises ultimately depend upon their acceptance of the purpose and not just the letter of the law.	
I might do more than just refuse to act if my client insisted on an illegal course of action.	
Clients need to know that I am not in their pocket.	
Saying 'no' to clients is sometimes necessary in order to preserve the system on which (even though they might not care either way) their own ultimate welfare depends.	
Total	

RELATIONSHIP OF CARE[1]	Values
I prefer dialogue, mediation and a careful focus on principled negotiation in resolving disputes for my clients.	

1   As only four items were statistically significant for the *Relationship of Care* (instead of the usual five), please add 25% to your total score for this preference, so that the result is comparable to that recorded for the other preferences.

Apology, reconciliation and the acceptance of moral responsibility is more important than the 'just' and rigorous enforcement of legal rights.	
The context and circumstances of an individual's suffering are more important than universal legal principles.	
I would much rather take a collaborative or restorative approach to problem solving, than a combative stance.	
Total	

INDEX

corporate hierarchies
  reporting unethical conduct,
    124
corporate lawyers
  and active responsibility,
    343–4, 346
  and corporate honesty 340
  and creative compliance,
    330
  and legal manipulation, 329
  and narrow legalism, 326–9
  and negligence, 327
  and obstructing justice, 331
  and plausible deniability,
    328
  as adversarial advocates, 326
  as corporate citizens, 339–44
  as independent counsellors,
    341
  as responsible lawyers,
    340–4
  conduct obligations, 341–4
  duties to corporations,
    342–3
  duties to the law, 341–2
  ethical business strategies,
    349–50
  links to commercial clients,
    332–4
  role of, 325
  See also lawyers
corporations
  law and ethics, 325–38
  misconduct, 326, 345
  scandals, 322
  secrecy, 342
  social responsibility, 176
  wrongdoing, lawyers'
    obligations, 123
corruption-prone economies
  and cloud providers, 105
cost payments, 195
  clients' rights to negotiate,
    302
cost recovery, failure of, 301
cost wastage, 195
costs, disputes over, 306–9
costs assessments, 306
  fairness of, 307
costs orders against lawyers,
  196, 199

Council of Australian
  Governments, 77
court-annexed schemes, 224
court-controlled costs process,
  317–18
Court of Criminal Appeal, 141,
  142
court proceedings, abuses of,
  191, 192
courts
  as public forums, 201
  inherent jurisdiction, 180
Craven, Greg, 190
creative compliance, 330
creative rule interpretation,
  336
criminal advocacy, 155
criminal defence advocacy,
  132
criminal justice, 151–5
  adversarial character, 160
  and adverse political
    agendas, 153
  compliance with
    governments, 151
  fairness in, 152
criminal trials, 133–9
  change pleas, 134
  defence, 139–48
  procedural trends, 134
  public criticism, 133
  reducing costs, 134
Crone, Tom, 103
Cummins J, 255
current affairs media, 149
current client conflicts,
  253–7

Dare, Tim, 26
Deane J, 108
deceit in court, 146, 147
deception of courts, 186
deceptive conduct, 211
declining representation, 147
default corporate cultures,
  353
defence by silence, 143–4
defence in criminal trials, 133,
  139–48
defendant secrecy, 144
defending guilty clients, 135

delaying tactics, 137
deontological ethics, 9
Department of Immigration,
  197
disciplinary action, 79–80
  lawyers' breach of duty, 79
  of lawyers, 179, 243
  States and Territories, 79
disciplinary charges, against
  lawyers, 199
disclosure
  and cloud hacking, 105
  and openness, 98
  and slush funds, 250
  Australian Solicitors'
    Conduct Rules, 111
  client awareness of cloud
    storage, 105
  consent processes, 254
  consequences of, 116
  costs of, 304
  ethical basis, 123
  in the public interest, 113
  of misconduct, 344
  reasons for, 112
  unencrypted cloud storage,
    105
disclosure protection, 117
disclosure trends, 122
dishonesty, by counsel, 135
dishonesty in courts
  lawyers' responsibilities,
    187
dispute mediation, 227
dispute prevention, 222
dispute resolution, 46, 122,
  169
  alternatives, 48
  ethical considerations, 176
  of fees, 306
  processes in, 221–6
  See also alternative dispute
    resolution
dissent, 66
divorce and intervention case,
  45
document destruction,
  penalties for, 324
domestic violence, 233
dominant purpose test, 116,
  117